SPACE TIME PLAY

SPACE TIME PLAY

COMPUTER GAMES, ARCHITECTURE AND URBANISM: THE NEXT LEVEL

Edited by

Friedrich von Borries,
Steffen P. Walz,
Matthias Böttger

In collaboration with

Drew Davidson, Heather Kelley, Julian Kücklich

Birkhäuser
Basel _ Boston _ Berlin

Design: onlab, Nicolas Bourquin
Prepress: Sebastian Schenk
Translation from German into English: Jenna Krumminga, Ian Pepper
Translation from Italian into English: Federico Roascio
Copyediting: Jenna Krumminga, Tobias Kurtz, Ian Pepper
Proofreading: Lucinda Byatt (Edinburgh)
Fonts: Grotesque MT, Walbaum
Printed on acid-free paper produced from chlorine-free pulp. TCF ∞
Printed in Germany

www.spacetimeplay.org

Library of Congress Control Number: 2007933332

Bibliographic information published by the German National Library.
The German National Library lists this publication in the Deutsche
Nationalbibliografie; detailed bibliographic data are available on the
Internet at http://dnb.d-nb.de.

© 2007 Birkhäuser Verlag AG
Basel _ Boston _ Berlin
P.O. Box 133, CH-4010 Basel, Switzerland
Part of Springer Science+Business Media
© 2007 Friedrich von Borries, Steffen P. Walz, Matthias Böttger, authors and individual copyright holders.
© 2007 for images see detailed list in the appendix. Images not otherwise indicated are the property of the named project authors, text
authors and game developers.

ISBN: 978-3-7643-8414-2

Space Time Play would not exist without the help, inspiration and support of many colleagues and friends. Our deepest thanks go out to all
the authors of the book, without whose contributions this compen-
dium could not have come into being. We would also like to thank the
studios and publishers that granted us the right to print pictures of
their games.

We thank Ludger Hovestadt, Hans-Peter Schwarz, Gerhard M. Buurman
and Kees Christiaanse for both their content contributions and their
financial commitment, without which we would not have been able to
produce this book.

We owe the selection of Game Reviews collected in this book, as well
as our connections to many authors, to Drew Davidson, Heather Kelley
and Julian Kücklich. We thank Nicolas Bourquin for the design and the
patience with which he conducted his work. With much dedication,
Jenna Krumminga edited the diverse texts into an easy-to-read whole.

Monika Annen, Tobias Kurtz, Anne Mikoleit, Caroline Pachoud and
Sibylla Spycher supported us in the editorial work with great dedication
and great exertion, for which we would like to thank them sincerely.

We thank our editor Robert Steiger for his faith, without which this
experimental project would not have materialized; we thank Nora
Kempkens for a smooth work flow.

In addition to the many whom we unfortunately cannot name here, we
also thank Ulrich Brinkmann and Katrin Schöbel for their encourage-
ment, guidance and counsel.

This book has been sponsored by:
ETH Zurich, Institute of Building Technology, Chair for Computer
Aided Architectural Design, Switzerland. Zurich University of the
Arts (ZHdK), Switzerland. ZHdK, Department of Design, Interaction
Design & Game Design Study Program, Switzerland. ETH Zurich,
Institute for Urban Design, Chair of Architecture and Urban Design,
Switzerland. KCAP, Rotterdam, The Netherlands. ASTOC, Architects
and Planners, Cologne, Germany.

The editors' work on this book has been partially funded by the
National Competence Center in Research on Mobile Information and
Communication Systems (NCCR-MICS), a center supported by the
Swiss National Science Foundation under grant number 5005-67322
and the German Academic Exchange Service (DAAD).

987654321
www.birkhauser.ch

Table of contents

794.8
SP

Table of contents   Project Descriptions

9

WHY SHOULD AN ARCHITECT CARE ABOUT COMPUTER GAMES?

AND WHAT CAN A GAME DESIGNER TAKE FROM ARCHITECTURE?

Computer games are part and parcel of our present; both their audiovisual language and the interaction processes associated with them have worked their way into our everyday lives. Yet without space, there is no place at which, in which or even based on which a game can take place. Similarly, the specific space of a game is bred from the act of playing, from the gameplay itself. The digital spaces so often frequented by gamers have changed and are changing our notion of space and time, just as film and television did in the 20th century.

But games go even further: with the spread of the Internet, online role-playing games emerged that often have less to do with winning and losing and more to do with the cultivation of social communities and human networks that are actually extended into "real" life. Equipped with wireless technologies and GPS capacities, computer games have abandoned their original location   the stationary computer – and made their way into physical space as mobile and pervasive applications. So-called "Alternate Reality Games" cross-medially blend together the Internet, public phone booths and physical places and conventions in order to create an alternative, ludic reality. The spaces of computer games range from two-dimensional representations of three-dimensional spaces to complex constructions of social communities to new conceptions of, applications for and interactions between existent physical spaces.

In his 1941 book *Space, Time and Architecture: The Growth of a New Tradition*, Siegfried Giedion puts modern architecture and its typologies in their social and chronological context. Today, we again face the development of new typologies of space – spaces that are emerging from the superimposition of the physical and the virtual. The spaces of the digital games that constitute themselves through the convergence of "space," "time" and "play" are only the beginning.

What are the parameters of these new spaces? To what practices and functional specifications do they give rise? What design strategies will come into operation because of them?

In *Space Time Play*, authors with wholly different professional backgrounds try to provide answers to these questions. Practitioners and theorists of architecture and urban planning as well as of game design and game studies have contributed to the collection. The over 180 articles come in various forms; in essays, short statements, interviews, descriptions of innovative projects and critical reviews of commercial games, the synergies between computer games, architecture and urbanism are reflected upon from diverse perspectives.

Space Time Play contains five levels that – played on their own or in sequence – train a variety of skills and address a range of issues:

The first level, THE ARCHITECTURE OF COMPUTER AND VIDEO GAMES, traces a short, spatiotemporal history of the architecture of digital games. Here, architects are interested in the question of what spatial qualities and characteristics arise from computer games and what implications these could have for contemporary architecture. For game designers and researchers, on the other hand, it's about determining what game elements constitute space and which spatial attributes give rise to specific types of interaction. Moreover, it's not just about the gamespaces in the computer, but about the places where the games are actually played; playing on a living-room TV is different from playing in front of a PC, which, in turn, is different from playing in a bar.

Many computer games draw spatial inspiration from physical architecture. Like in a film, certain places and configurations are favored and retroactively shape our perceptions. Computer game players also experience physical space differently and thus use it differently. Newer input possibilities like gesture and substantial physical movement are making this hybridization of virtual and real space available for the mass market, thereby posing new questions to game designers and bringing the disciplines of built and imagined spaces closer together. Computer game design is thus not just about the "Rules of Play" anymore, but also about the "Rules of Place."

In the second level, MAKE BELIEVE URBANISM, the focus of the texts is shifted to the social cohesion of game-generated spaces – that is, to the ludic constructions of digital metropolises – and the question of how such "community spaces" are produced and presented. At the same time, the central topic of this level is the tension between the representation of the city in games and the city as metaphor for the virtual spatialization of social relations. How can sociability across space-time be established, and how will identity be "played out" there? The communities emerging in games, after all, constitute not only parallel cultures and economies, but also previews of the public spaces of the future.

The third level, UBIQUITOUS GAMES, on the other hand, demonstrates how real space – be it a building, city or landscape – changes and expands when it is metamorphosed into a "game board" or "place to play" by means of new technologies and creative game concepts. Here, a new dimension of the notion and use of the city becomes conceivable, one which has the potential to permanently change the composition of future cities. What happens when the spaces and social interactions of computer games are superimposed over physical space? What new forms and control systems of city, architecture and landscape become possible?

The migration of computer games onto the street – that is, the integration of physical spaces into game systems – creates new localities; games intervene in existent spaces. Game designers are thereby made aware of their social responsibility. Ubiquitous games fulfill not only the utopian dreams of the Situationists, but also the early 1990s computer-science vision of a "magicization" of the world. As in simulacra, the borders of the "magic circle" coined by Johan Huizinga blur, and the result is ludic unification.

In the fourth level, SERIOUS FUN, the extent to which games and game elements also have serious uses – namely, as tools for design and planning processes – is examined through examples from architecture and city planning. The articles in this level demonstrate how the ludic conquest of real and imagined gamespace becomes an instrument for the design of space-time. For the playing of cities can affect the lived environment and its occupants just as the building of houses can. In this sense, playing is a serious medium that will increasingly form part of the urban planner's repertory and will open up new prospects for participation. Play cannot replace seriousness, but it can help it along.

The concluding fifth level, FAITES VOS JEUX, critically reflects upon the cultural relevance of games today and in the future. Which gamespaces are desirable and which are not? Which ones should we expect? Life as computer-supported game? War as game? The possibilities range from lived dreams to advertisements in gamespaces to the destruction of cities in games and in today's reality of war and terrorism.

What is the "next level" of architecture and game design? Both these creative worlds could benefit from a mutual exchange: by emulating the complex conceptions of space and design possibilities of the former and by using the expertise, interaction, immersion and spatial fun of the latter.

Game designers and architects can forge the future of ludic space-time as a new form of interactive space, and they can do so in both virtual gamespaces and physical, architectural spaces; this is the "next level" of *Space Time Play*.

THE
ARCHITECTURE OF
COMPUTER
AND VIDEO GAMES

A SHORT SPACE-TIME HISTORY OF INTERACTIVE ENTERTAINMENT

Level

PLACES TO PLAY
What Game Settings Can Tell Us about Games

Increasingly, computer-generated virtual spaces are important elements of everyday life, and computer games are doubtless their most popular manifestations. When these are well designed, users tend to forget that they reside not in an airless void, but are instead surrounded by physical space. The physically existent space is the context for which these games were more or less explicitly created and in which they are played. If this fact is ignored, we fail to do justice to the medium of the computer game and to the concrete playing situation. For players and their bodies are indissolubly connected to the physical plane even if their minds are overwhelmingly oriented during playtime to virtual space. By using selected examples, I attempt here to demonstrate the intimate connection between these two planes of reality and, in the process, to provide a brief historical overview of the development of the computer game as a medium.

Computer games first saw the light of day in the realm of research science at a time when existing computers were as yet incapable of generating virtual spaces. Back then, the spaces constituted by computers were primarily physical and real in nature, a circumstance owing to their considerable bulk and open manner of construction.

Active in these large computers during periods of operation (which were never, as a rule, interrupted) were operators who shuttled ceaselessly between the individual structural members in order to engage in programming, identify errors, replace tubes or control cooling. Only experienced specialists were able, on the basis of a few small lights, to recognize the emerging harbingers of a virtual reality that has today become so complex and painstakingly detailed. And it was precisely such specialists, the architects of the first computers, who recognized and investigated the potential of computer games right from the start: in 1942, on the basis of a chess program, Konrad Zuse demonstrated the strength of his programming language "Plankalkül"; in 1947, Alan Turing developed a chess program, which he processed in his own mind, in order to test its capabilities in matches against opponents; and in 1950, Claude Shannon authored a 12-page article entitled "Programming a Computer for Playing Chess" (Shannon 1950).

In all three above-named cases, it was the space of the research laboratory that was crucial in the construction of the program, for it was not a question of entertainment, but instead of research. In the introduction to his article, for example, Shannon wrote: "Although perhaps of no practical importance, the question [of whether a computer can be taught to play chess] is of theoretical interest, and it is hoped that a satisfactory solution of this problem will act as a wedge in attacking other problems of a similar nature and of greater significance" (ibid.).

16

Interestingly enough, these aspects of greater significance specified by Shannon already constitute the fundamental conditions of possibility for generating virtual worlds as we know them today. Among other things, he mentions "Machines for performing symbolic (nonnumerical) mathematical operations. Machines capable of translating from one language to another. Machines for making strategic decisions in simplified military operations. Machines capable of orchestrating a melody. Machines capable of logical deduction" (ibid.).

We fast forward now to the early 1960s. Computers have become smaller and perform better, but nonetheless remain accessible to only a small number of specialists. We find ourselves in the "Tech Model Railroad Club" at MIT in Cambridge, Massachusetts, where primarily younger scientists are active. The clubrooms are located on the campus of an educational facility, but are clearly marked by an entertainment context. Here, we experience the birth of the first "genuine" computer game, one that still meets today's criteria. A group of young scientists who met through the "Tech Model Railroad Club" have access to a PDP 1 computer manufactured by the D.E.C. firm, one of the first whose monitor is provided with graphic capabilities – and which hence fulfils one of the essential technical preconditions for today's virtual worlds. On the initiative of Steve Russel, they spend their free time, with no special research contract, programming *Spacewar!* (1962), a virtual outer space setting within which two spaceships, each controlled by one player, face off against one another. The game is a big hit right from the beginning, and it spreads like wildfire through the American university landscape to every point where a PDP 1 computer is present. This circumstance, however, can only be really explained by considering the real space surrounding the players. For computers continue to be highly expensive rarities, and hence accessible only to specialists. They are not designed to be played with simply for fun, and this necessarily leads to conflict. This is also the motive for the invention of the first game joysticks: they make it possible for players to avoid damaging keyboards while playing *Spacewar!* (Graetz 1981).

A straight line leads from *Spacewar!* and the MIT "Tech Model Railroad Club" to the real space of the video arcade, the locale where computer games became commercially established. One of the students who had enjoyed playing *Spacewar!* during his MIT years was Nolan Bushnell, later a founder of Atari. His automated version of *Spacewar!*, produced in 1971 by the American video game manufacturer Nutting Associates and dubbed *Computer Space*, was conceived for the video arcade. The fact that the commercial birth of the computer game took place in a public space had exclusively economic reasons. The then only recently developed integrated circuits (ICs) were still too expensive to allow such consoles to be marketed directly to end users. And although *Computer Space* (1971) experienced only sluggish sales, Bushnell's business model met with success just a year later with the Atari *PONG* (1972) machines. In just a few months, video game machines had developed into one of the most lucrative businesses and would remain so right into the 1980s. But the physical space of the video arcade not only made possible the commercialization of the computer game, it also influenced the appearance of the early blockbusters. The high score list, introduced for the first time in 1978 in *Space Invaders*, not only offered players an identity going beyond the actual activity of playing, but also provided them with an incentive to leave behind their visiting cards as players in the real space of the arcade, where they would be noticed by others. Game construction, too, was determined substantially by this context. It was not extended, epic games that guaranteed high revenues, but instead numerous brief matches. Players had to be induced to toss yet another coin into the slot. The game, then, must never be allowed to really come to an end. In one way or another, the narratives games embody are all variations on the Sisyphus motif, with its tendency toward the interminable. An additional motivating factor lay in the social situation of the gaming arcade, where two players would often face off in front of the public.

On another level as well, the video arcade machines had an essential impact on the medium of the computer game. At least in the German Federal Republic, the installation of video games in public spaces was forbidden in 1984 by amendments to the Youth Protection Laws. Along with betting machines, they could only be found from that point onward in locations inaccessible to young people. The new laws doubtless strengthened the existing image of video games as being somehow dangerous to young people.

But in the end, it was not the video arcade, but instead another real space that established itself as the dominant context for games – namely, the private home. This development goes back to the 1960s. In 1968, the inventor Ralph H. Baer registered a patent in the United States for his "Television Gaming and Training Apparatus." In it, he describes the functional principle of the home video game console that was brought onto the market in 1972 by the American firm Magnavox under the name *Odyssey*. [1] In typical advertisements for *Odyssey*, we see a family playing while gathered around the television set in the living room. The living room as a real space of play was almost compulsory, since additional television sets were rarely found in children's bedrooms at that time. Perceptions of the home video game as a toy for children rather than for adults were associated with an additional technical revolution, one that established a new location for playing: the work or hobby room. Beginning in 1977, a mass production of new ICs had progressed so far that an entire computer could fit comfortably onto a writing desk, making it possible to market home computers to private individuals. The triumph of the home computer had begun. Thanks to market competition and the falling prices associated with it, home computers such as the C64 were widely disseminated during the 1980s and were frequently used to play games. These developments were also decisive for the appearance of these games. Since an ongoing game could be stored at any moment and resumed later on, games of epic length emerged whose virtual worlds grew larger and more complex than those found in video arcades or in the home video game consoles that succeeded gaming machines.

Already in preparation at this time was the networking of home computers, which then not only provided the playing field, but could also access virtual realities that were generated somewhere beyond the physical surroundings of the player.

As distinct from home computers, which had generally been reserved for adults, home video games drifted increasingly into children's bedrooms during the 1980s. This development was made possible by the growing prevalence of second and third television sets in private homes, and it experienced powerful reinforcement

1 >
That their price lay under 100 US Dollars was made feasible only by manufacturing these devices using the same traditional analog components found in all television sets.

via the strategies of the at-the-time market leader Nintendo, which marketed its NES console primarily as a game.

For our final real space of play, we now enter another public arena, one that succeeded the video arcade, and one which, unlike the latter, is not fixed in space, not clearly localizable. Already by the mid-1970s (Football 1976), manufacturers had succeeded in establishing a market for mobile pocket video games. Along with their relatively low prices, their in principle unlimited accessibility spoke strongly in their favor. During the past two decades, we have heard a lot about a "Game Boy generation," referring to young people who have grown up with video games. A decisive turn was taken by mobile games when they were successfully networked in recent years. Fusion with GPS-capable mobile telephones in particular created a fundamentally new space of play. With so-called "pervasive games," the real space surrounding the player becomes a component of the virtual playing space. Highly conspicuous in comparison to the examples presented above is the interpenetration of real and virtual spaces.

Games have always followed people wherever they have lived, and it seems as though the act of playing necessarily does so as well. In this respect, computer games are indistinguishable from other games. The fact that they generate complex virtual spaces ought not to distract us from the fact that every player finds him or herself simultaneously in a world of play and in the real world.

◆ *Computer Space* (1971), developed and published by Nutting Associates. ◆ *Football* (1976), developed and published by Mattel ◆ Graetz, J.M. (1981), "The Origins of Spacewar!", *Creative Computing*, August 1981. ◆ *PONG* (1972), developed and published by Atari. ◆ Shannon, C. (1950), "Programming a Computer for Playing Chess," *Philosophical Magazine*, ser.7, vol. 41, no. 314, March 1950. ◆ *Spacewar!* (1962), developed by Massachusetts Institute of Technology.

DANCE DANCE REVOLUTION
Taking Back Arcade Space

Dance Dance Revolution (or *DDR*) is the best known of a series of rhythm games first marketed by Konami in Asia in the late 1990s. Similar titles from other publishers include *Pump It Up* (Andamiro 1999), *In The Groove* (Roxor Games 2004), and *Para Para Paradise* (Konami 2000). In these games, the controller is enlarged to monstrous size, allowing play by "dancing" on a "stage" with inset buttons.

The goal in *DDR* is to step on the correct buttons in time with music, indicated by arrows rising to hit targets at the top of the screen. While the arrows roll over swirling day-glo graphics, dancing anime avatars and music videos, the graphics are little more than a distraction. In dance games, the images on-screen are mere window dressing. Dance games take the space of play out of the machine, returning it to the realm of physical space. Play is writ large on the entire body, not just the avatar and the frantic movement of players' thumbs.

To date, no other post-*PONG* arcade genre has been as revolutionary in terms of space. Before *PONG (Atari 1972)*, arcades often had a number of highly physical games: skeeball, whack-a-mole, shoot hoops to win a teddy bear. And certainly, arcades have long had digital games in which players use nontraditional controllers: "punching" opponents, riding motorcycles or shooting guns. But *DDR* represents a much more dramatic expansion of the physical in digital arcade games. The game frees up the player's head, arms and torso for a nearly full range of movement. The only obligation players have is pressing the buttons in time.

Players take advantage of this freedom in creative ways, incorporating spins, dropping to their knees or even leaping over the safety bar for a grand entrance. Some players leave stage in the middle of the song to flirt or "take a phone call" for comic effect. On the website DDRFreak.com, one commenter recalls a player who left the arcade and ran all the way across the street in the middle of his performance, returning in time for the next step after a break in the music.

The old arcade pastime of cheering local pros on as they pound their way to a high score takes a new shape: now, instead of clustering close to scrutinize the screen, the audience can follow gameplay from across the room. Arcade owners sometimes rearrange their space to accommodate *DDR*'s exuberant overflow, leaving extra room around the machine or moving it to a more visible location to attract business. In Asia, dance games have grown far larger than the arcade: at the peak of the game's popularity, *DDR* competitions were sometimes held in stadiums.

Dance Dance Revolution (US title) was released in Europe under the title *Dancing Stage*.

Project Description	Text	Project	Affiliation
	Florian "Floyd" Müller	Florian "Floyd" Müller, Stefan Agamanolis	Human Connectedness Group, Media Lab Europe, Dublin, IE, MIT Media Lab, Cambridge, US, 2003

BREAKOUT FOR TWO
Connecting Cities via Distributed Physical Activity

Breakout for Two is a cross between soccer and the popular arcade game *Breakout* (**Atari 1976**). Each of two players, who can be miles distant from his/her partner, kicks a ball against a local, physical wall. On each wall is a projection of the remote player, enabling the participants to interact with each other through a life-sized videoconference. Players feel as though they are separated by a glass window that splits the field into two parts. They still hit the ball towards the other player, but it bounces off the wall and is returned. Eight semi-transparent blocks are overlaid on the video stream, and each player has to strike them in order to score. These virtual blocks are connected over the network, which means they are shared between locations. If one player strikes any of them once, it cracks. On the third hit, the block breaks and disappears. Only then does the player receive a point. This scoring theme makes for a challenging game element because it enables each player to watch what the other one is doing, waiting for her/him to hit a block for the second time and then snatching the point by hitting it for the third and final time. The harder the player hits a block, however, the more it cracks, so a player can also choose to crack the blocks more quickly through really hard hits.

Physical games such as soccer are known to be social facilitators and icebreakers. They can support social exchange between players who have never met before and who might otherwise never meet at all, if they are networked to support players in different spaces, allowing them to experience shared gameplay as part of the urban environment. We envision setting games such as *Breakout for Two* in public places with socializing opportunities, allowing inhabitants to engage in social interaction with players from sister cities, in which the game provides something to do and to talk about. We believe the physical sporting game *Breakout for Two* can enrich the link between sister cities by providing inhabitants with a direct personal experience, facilitating a sense of shared space and supporting social connectedness between the remote players.

Thanks to Media Lab Europe and MIT, especially Stefan Agamanolis, Roz Picard and Ted Selker.

Game Review	Text	Developer	Publisher
	Heather Kelley	Nintendo	Nintendo, 2006

Wii SPORTS
Breaking the Fourth Wall

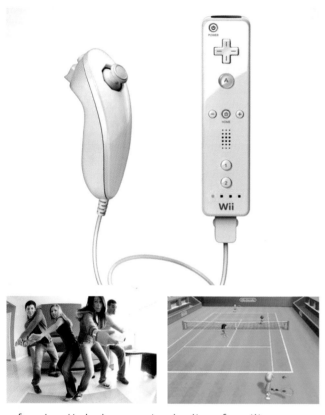

Released in 2006 to both acclaim and speculation, Nintendo's Wii game console attempts to leapfrog its next-gen competitors with its intuitive control device, the wireless "Wii Remote," which resembles a smallish, simplified television remote in shape and size. The Remote is a pointing device that can also detect movement on multiple axes. This innovative controller represents the heart of Nintendo's strategy to reach beyond the known market of "core" gamers and appeal to a wider population of potential players, including families, women and seniors.

Wii Sports is Nintendo's premiere launch title for the Wii; it is shipped in the box along with the Wii hardware. The game offers five popular athletic sports – bowling, tennis, golf, boxing and baseball – all playable using the natural and characteristic gestures required by each sport: swinging a bat, punching a boxing glove and so on. As such, the game could be considered the earliest expression of Nintendo's vision for interactive entertainment: it is approachable, sociable and places a higher value on play accessibility than on graphic resolution.

One of the most innovative spatial aspects of the Wii, evident throughout *Wii Sports*, is the speaker located inside the Wii Remote. As a feedback channel, sound naturally supports our perceptions of what is physical and hence "real." In *Wii Sports*, the effect is subtle but undeniable: players can hear the results of their physical actions at the location of that action. The controller can't offer tactile resistance for physical actions (such as the impact of striking a baseball with a heavy bat), but the audio helps fill these gaps of believability and controllability. When serving the ball in *Wii Tennis*, for instance, players can hear the swishing of their own rackets and time their swings to generate power serves.

While naturalistic gestures such as full-ranged golf swings and bowling ball throws are not absolutely required to play the game, they are supported by the game and constitute a large part of the game's fun – even in the cramped quarters of a typical living space. But the way *Wii Sports* encourages players to use their full range of motion and strength is not without its drawbacks. Perhaps nothing is more indicative of the boundary-crossing "real world feel" of *Wii Sports* than the reports that began appearing on the Internet soon after the launch date, according to which players around the world were accidentally destroying television screens and causing other living room accidents when making enthusiastic physical gestures during play. Within weeks, Nintendo president Satoru Iwata admitted, "Some people are getting a lot more excited than we'd expected. We need to better communicate to people how to deal with Wii as a new form of entertainment." The early days of the Wii will be remembered as those in which the "fourth wall" of video gaming was truly, and sometimes literally, broken.

A SHORT HISTORY OF DIGITAL GAMESPACE

Text-based

To help games appeal to the imagination, a narrative was often employed. A narrative is a story or a tale communicated via word of mouth or written text. One of the very first forms of spatial immersion was text-only space with no pictorial dimension. Text-space as a form of immersion was introduced in the 1970s with early computer games such as *Dungeons and Dragons* (1974). In the latter, the player simply had to read and interpret a text within a character/computer interactive system and to imagine a world while being guided through that text, navigating with the keyboard through imaginary maps. Immersive text-space came in book form as well: many books were based on a kind of "choose your own adventure" theme with varying plot lines. Also popular were game books, which included rules, items, settings and so on and were driven by the user's imagination.

Contained Two-dimensional Space

Following text-based games, graphical games such as *PONG* (1972) and *Space Invaders* (1978) used pixels to draw graphics as representations of objects. In *PONG*, for example, a spot represents a ball and vertical bands of pixels represent paddles. Players control the paddles with a rotating knob. The interaction between the spot and bands obeys the laws of simple physics, allowing the player to relate the play to tennis or ping-pong. From their inception, graphical games deployed symbolism and metaphor; graphics were imbued with a metaphorical value to foster an immersive relationship to play. The associational metaphor enabled the user to suspend disbelief and intuitively relate the gameworld to the real world. Metaphors included gravity, grade, danger, friend, foe, objects, fire, ice and so on. Without the use of real-world metaphors, gameplay would be vague and ambiguous. To encourage immersion in the game, players needed to relate the digital events to real-world experience.

Wraparound Space

The graphical interface of games like *Asteroids* (1979) and *Pac-Man* (1980) warped space by permitting objects to disappear off the edge of the screen only to reappear directly opposite to where they had vanished – that is, on the other side of the screen. This gave the impression that the gamespace was continuous and permitted the subconscious to extrapolate and travel through an invisible space. Such continuity of space was understandable in the game environment, yet impossible in real scenarios – a metaphor formed between the vastness of the cosmos and the endless television "sphere." Newton's fundamental laws of motion were exercised in the flight of the spaceship in *Asteroids*, simulating motion in a zero-gravity environment. The player controlled the spacecraft with a rotating button, a thrust button and a button to fire.

Spaces That Scroll along One Axis

Games such as *Defender* (1980), *Super Mario Bros.* (1985) and *Atari Football* (1978) used scrolling to give the impression of continuous movement through a two-dimensional space. The *Super Mario Bros.* series featured horizontal movement while games such as *Spy Hunter* (1983) privileged vertical movement. Continuous horizontal movement was common in animations such as *The Flintstones* (1960-1966), in which characters stayed within one plane and background repeated behind them as they moved left and right. Movements in games on the popular NES (Nintendo Entertainment System) console were inputted by an eight-button game pad.

Scrolling along Two Axes

Gauntlet (1985) and *SimCity* (1989) permitted scrolling along both the x- and y-axis on a two-dimensional plane; players moved through a puzzle world with free rein over the flat plane of the perpendicularly positioned viewing screen. Later versions of *SimCity*, rather than giving the player a bird's-eye view, evolved to provide an isometric viewing angle. The combination of two axes of movement and a drawn perspective allowed players in side-viewing games such as *Blades of Steel* (1987) and its football equivalents to move from left to right, but also allowed up and down play. The simple eight-button controller sufficed for these games and many of the games to follow. Chiefly, the left hand controlled movement while the right hand controlled the action buttons to shoot, jump, kick, etc.

Adjacent Spaces Displayed in One Room at a Time

Games like *Berzerk* (1980) took place in multiple rooms in which users were able to imagine that their characters were invisible to enemies in other rooms. If a user's character was hidden from the enemy's view, the user would not be seen and therefore not engaged. Thus the user would have to maneuver to stay hidden and/or accomplish desired tasks.

Scrolling with Multiple Background Layers

Double Dragon (1987) used scrolling to simulate a deep and dense background. The depth effect was created by the gradation of movement of the various layers of background images. A slow-scrolling background simulates a distant horizon while a faster-moving backdrop is imagined as being closer. The background of the first level of *Double Dragon* contained an image of a city that imbued the game with a distinct ambience.

Limited Three-dimensional Space: The Use of Perspective in the Scene

The spaces in *Tempest* (1980) and *Night Driver* (1976) were made to simulate a three-dimensional environment. By using vector lines and/or rules of perspective, a simple perspectival scene was implied. One-point perspective can be created with lines that originate from a single point. The rules of perspective state that this single point is at the farthest distance from the viewer. In a game, this can be considered the goal – the point to which the user must travel. *Night Driver*'s white markers on the left and right sides of the road were easy ways to create the illusion of a driving surface stretching out into the distance.

Isometric Three-dimensional Space

Zaxxon (1982), a flying game, introduced a 3D-look-alike isometric perspective to video games. It had brilliant colors, and the graphics made it a hit. Players controlled a ship, avoiding obstacles and oncoming fire from enemies, maneuvering to the end of the scrolling level. Many games, including *Paperboy* (1984), followed suit and used shaded isometric maps to create an interesting playing surface.

A Window to the Outdoors

Duck Hunt (1985), one of Nintendo's first games, used the whole television screen as a plane, or window. The player's input device was a gun, and the challenge was to shoot ducks or clay pigeons with a minimal number of shots. The distance between the clay pigeons and the shooter was simulated by making the pigeons increasingly smaller as they flew further away.

Two Spaces on One Screen or Two Separate Screens

Multiplayer games such as *Spy vs. Spy* (1984) were characterized by having players control their characters while attempting to find the opponent player by searching through a labyrinth of rooms. The location of one's character and the respective environment (as well as those of the enemy) had to be envisioned in the imagination before one could become an effective, intuitive player. The game thus required players to quickly master mental mapping skills.

Video Capture

Mortal Kombat (1992) was one very popular arcade game that utilized video capture technology. Each costumed actor was video recorded punching, kicking and so on. The short, flowing animations were then played back in the game at the speed of the fast-paced action. Rather than controlling bitmapped, drawn characters, players could experience maneuvering a real actor. In a way, the sprite characters had a virtual volume to them. As they moved, jumped and fell, the actors would rotate. This kind of realistic graphical output encroached on the realm of interactive film. While interactive films allowed the audience to make a series of significant choices that influenced the plot, the actors in *Mortal Kombat* were fully controlled by the player. Unfortunately, in this genre, the virtual control of live actors' prerecorded action was limited to fighting.

Games that did not use the first-person perspective also built their maps from polygons. Fighting games like *Tekken* (1994), rather than relying on realism via video-captured actors, used polygons to create their characters. At first, these 3D models contained only a few polygons, but keeping pace with the increasing processing power of graphical output, they soon began to take on a more detailed appearance. With the help of the physics engine, a character's limbs could be made fluid, realistic and life-like, while constraints on the individual parts added a digital "mass." Limbs could interact with the other characters or the environment.

Mapped Space – Prerendered Panoramas

Instead of real-time, on-the-fly rendering, mapped space games such as *Myst* (1993) presented a slower-paced game with prerendered environments. Every animation was pre-recorded, and every viewpoint was precalculated. The computer did not need to run a game engine that would calculate its visuals in real time; it needed only to store the information that was needed for each particular scene. This way, the animation was smoother and more realistic – unfortunately at the price of having to repeal fast-paced (inter)action.

Early 3D Space – One Horizontal Plane

Wolfenstein 3D (1992) was one of the earliest "3D" first-person shooter games. The player was placed in the first-person view mode and had to explore a series of dungeons in an immersive world. In *Wolfenstein 3D*, the ground level was on one level with the corresponding horizon. As a result, aiming could be effective only from left to right; the game could not take into consideration any up/down direction or movement. Drawing on advances in gaming technology, the game *Doom* (1993) presented what is known as a two-and-a-half-dimensional (2.5D) game. The floor level changed heights, and characters were engaged from above or below, yet the aiming gun position remained strictly horizontal.

Full 3D Space – Horizontal/Vertical Movement

Quake (1996), *FarCry* (2004) and most current first-person shooter games (*Doom3* (2004), *Half-Life 2* (2004), etc.) use full, three-dimensional space. In this type of gamespace, players are allowed full freedom of movement. They can walk along the ground plane or look and shoot anywhere that the game allows. They also have the ability to fly or jump in the environment since the plane of movement is no longer limited to the ground and the scene is rendered on the fly. These recent games contain simulations that include technologies that act inside the game, including a particle system simulation and a physics simulation. These will be described later in more detail.

More advanced 3D games could no longer be navigated with the simple controls of the computer keyboard or traditional joystick, but started to rely on the mouse as well. The mouse proved to be the most sensitive input device, with easy, accurate aiming and movement. From ball to current laser mice, these devices continue to be an essential part of contemporary gaming in all genres.

The Spaces of the Future

The three dimensions in gaming have brought about the emergence of further dimensions and phenomena related to them such as time, weather, shifting infrastructure elements, ingame physics engines, the existence of an afterlife, and so on. These helpful game components augment players' experiences and narrate richer stories to them.

As game designer and theorist Katie Salen (2004, p. 32) notes, "meaningful play emerges from the interaction between players and the system of the game, as well as from the context in which the game is played." Today, meaningful play can also emerge from a multiplayer community environment. Using the Internet to connect to a common server, multitudes of players can interact in a detail-rich virtual world (in Massively Multiplayer Online Role Playing Games) the design of which encourages players to challenge and inspire each other, fostering bonds and relationships in the process. With the help of the Internet, the storytelling space has become a social space where the actions of other players can influence the setting.

The assumption that greater realism equals greater immersion still holds true, and many games have and are still advancing in this direction. As processing power improves, a digital game's graphical output will increase, and the result will be an improved simulation of reality in whatever genre the game belongs, be it fantasy, sport, driving simulation or so on. In the future, radical games will represent an interbreeding of various genres and points of view. With the current tools and talent at the game designer's disposal, the only limit to improving game design will inevitably be the irreplaceable imagination of the dreamer.

◆ *Asteroids* (1979), developed and published by Atari. ◆ *Atari Football* (1978), developed and published by Atari. ◆ *Berzerk* (1980), developed and published by Stern Electronics. ◆ *Blades of Steel* (1987), developed and published by Konami. ◆ *Defender* (1980), developed and published by Williams Electronics. ◆ *Doom* (1993), developed and published by id Software. ◆ *Doom3* (2004), developed by id Software, published Activision et al. ◆ *Double Dragon* (1987) developed by Technos, published by Taito. ◆ *Duck Hunt* (1985), developed and published by Nintendo. ◆ *Dungeons and Dragons* (1974), developed by Gary Gygax & Dave Arneson, published by Tactical Studies Rules. ◆ *FarCry* (2004), developed by Crytek, published by Ubisoft. ◆ *The Flintstones* (animated TV series) (1960-1966), produced by Hanna Barbera Productions. ◆ *Gauntlet* (1985), developed and published by Atari. ◆ *Half-Life 2* (2004), developed and published by Valve Corporation. ◆ *Mortal Kombat* (1992), developed and published by Midway. ◆ *Myst* (1993), developed by Cyan, Inc., published by Brøderbund Software, Inc. ◆ *Night Driver* (1976), developed and published by Atari. ◆ *Pac-Man* (1980), developed by Namco, published by Midway. ◆ *Paperboy* (1984), developed and published by Atari. ◆ *PONG* (1972), developed by Magnavox, published by Atari. ◆ *Quake* (1996), developed and published by id Software. ◆ Salen, K. & Zimmerman, E. (2004), *Rules of Play*, MIT Press, Cambridge MA. ◆ *SimCity* (1989), developed by Maxis, published by Maxis et al. ◆ *Space Invaders* (1978), developed by Taito, published by Midway Games. ◆ *Spy Hunter* (1983), developed and published by Bally Midway. ◆ *Spy vs. Spy* (1984), developed and published by First Star Software. ◆ *Super Mario Bros.* (1985), developed and published by Nintendo. ◆ *Tekken* (1994), developed and published by Namco. ◆ *Tempest* (1980), developed and published by Atari. ◆ *Wolfenstein 3D* (1992), developed by id Software, published by Apogee Software. ◆ *Zaxxon* (1982), developed and published by Sega.

Game Review	Text	Developer	Publisher
	Cindy Poremba	Tennis for Two: William A. Higinbotham PONG: Atari	Tennis for Two: unpublished, 1958 PONG: Atari, 1972

TENNIS FOR TWO/PONG
Spatiality in Abstract 2D Environments

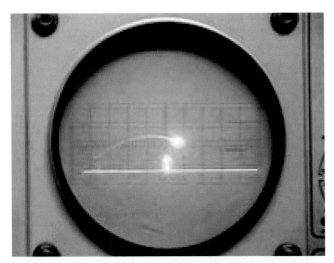

You might not expect games with simple 2D abstract environments like William A. Higinbotham's *Tennis for Two* and its descendant, Atari's *PONG*, to present particularly complex models of spatiality. Each of these two "ball and paddle" games, however, is distinct in the way it represents space.

One obvious difference is the mode of perspective: *Tennis for Two*'s side view versus *PONG*'s top-down perspective. The former necessarily incorporates additional spatial information (such as ball trajectory) that the latter can avoid even without sacrificing behavioral possibilities (and thus object recognition). Both games limit the entirety of the gameworld to the screen itself, with one important exception: the "out" (lose) condition, in which the ball disappears beyond the bounds of the screen space.

PONG's top-down perspective allows for additional deflective surfaces from which to bounce the ball (top and bottom screen) and thus two strategic boundaries that may influence gameplay. In contrast, *Tennis for Two* does not make use of its uppermost boundary, but instead incorporates another spatial obstacle – the game net, which, rather than acting as a neutral deflective surface, causes the ball to deflect unpredictably and lose acceleration. In *PONG*, the "court" itself is entirely passive; the player can only control action at the boundaries of the playing field. As such, it is really the space beyond the screen that is being defended, with the court representing only a place through which the ball passes. In *Tennis for Two*, on the other hand, players must not only defend the left and right boundaries, but also move actively within the court space. The possibility of the ball losing acceleration and going "dead" (by hitting the net) means they must play both within the screen and at its boundaries.

Both games situate players as operators, external to the game-world. While *PONG* visually represents the player's in-world presence in the form of a controllable paddle, *Tennis for Two* completely removes the player from the screen. Instead, the game's invisible striking surface is positioned directly where the ball is when the player presses the button to hit it and can be rotated in any direction using a controller dial. As a result, the player does not, strictly speaking, move within the space of *Tennis for Two*, but rather orients. In *PONG*, on the other hand, paddle movement is restricted to the vertical plane; no orientation, just movement.

Game Review	Text	Developer	Publisher
	Jesper Juul	Atari	Atari, 1979

ASTEROIDS
Forgotten Futurism

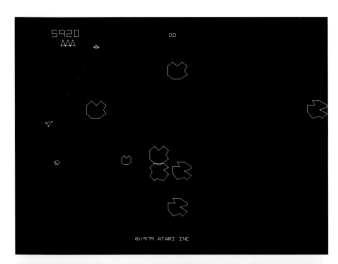

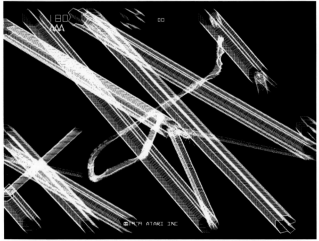

I am in front of an arcade game, and I am a small spaceship on the screen. To move forward, I must think of forward as the direction that my spaceship-me is pointing on the screen. The forward of my spaceship-me is sometimes up, sometimes down, sometimes other directions. When I first played games like this, it was hard to map the presence of the spaceship onto my bodily presence and actions in front of the arcade cabinet. It is an acquired taste.

Asteroids emits an air of forgotten futurism, of roads not taken. The game uses a vector display: not the usual grid of pixels, but a beam that traces the outlines of the game elements. The player's shots burn through the screen, presumably outlined by the beam several times each update. Vector graphics were Atari's signature for a while: *Lunar Lander* (1979), *Battlezone* (1980), *Tempest* (1980), *Space Duel* (1982) and *Star Wars* (1983). Had I been a science fiction writer in the 1950s, these are the games my characters would be playing in the distant future – military, scientific, platonic.

Asteroids is almost a good game. There is a focused core activity – namely, shooting rocks, which makes the rocks break into smaller and faster pieces. This changes the layout of each level, changes the strategy and feel from the beginning to the end of a level and renders the game varied enough to just work. The occasionally appearing UFO is the final ingredient, giving the world just one object with intentions and alleviating the loneliness of the universe. I am not alone with these vacuous rocks after all; there is an opponent that cares about me.

But *Asteroids* fails. There is not enough variation in the tasks I have to perform; the screen is oddly empty. I fly around and shoot, but everything melts into air; I can make no marks on the world. There are only rudimentary strategies for me to devise. The edge of the screen is muddy and unsatisfying. There is no progress. *Asteroids* is a nostalgic game of the future, but the actual future has better games.

BATTLEZONE
The First VR Game

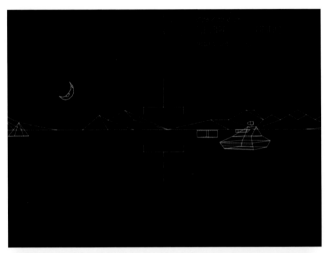

Battlezone is a single-player simulator game created by Atari in 1980. A seminal, 3D wireframe "shoot 'em up" game in which the player views the action from inside a tank, *Battlezone* could be described as the first Virtual Reality (VR) game.

The game is set on a plane surface with a mountainous horizon, active volcanoes, a crescent moon and various objects drawn as vector outlines. These visual features made *Battlezone* the first environmental 3D landscape game. Players feel themselves immersed in a surrealistic landscape, with each level littered with simple geometric objects. These boxes and pyramids were designed as important visual cues to improve interface usability; the horizon does not scale when it is approached, so that only the rotation of the player's tank is conveyed. These elements – which stretch the player's imagination by simulating "buildings" and futuristic "labs" using only a handful of lines – are the game's defining characteristics.

Moving objects are rendered more accurately than static ones. These elements move around freely in the gamespace, restricted only by the static objects and distance culling. When an enemy is hit, the object breaks up into fragments, which are visualized as "eye-candy."

Battlezone is considered to be the first commercial VR game because it used real goggles and a realistic two-joystick steering system combined with the innovative use of first-person 3D graphics to create a convincing VR effect. Comments from players show that the spatial experience the game offered, even in its crude wireframe mode, was its big draw. This is surprising since the level of 3D present in *Battlezone* is limited to vector projections of the objects' wireframes with no hidden-line removal or solid polygon rendering.

E. Rotberg, the principal programmer of *Battlezone*, comments: "Given the technology that we had, the real challenge was how to make the game appear as if we had more technology than we did." Novel circuitry went into the machine – a bit slice processor – to render perspective 3D graphics. Other tricks that created a "tech" look included a simulated two-color display using cellophane and an industry-first set of "periscope" goggles for the player. Overall, about 15,000 units came out of production, making the game a great commercial success with global exposure for the 3D format.

Battlezone had a huge impact on the popular media: a *Battlezone* unit appears in the genre-defining movie *Tron* (Walt Disney 1982), its CRT-green lines identify the beginning of cyberspace in *The Matrix* (Warner Bros. 1999) and the end of it in *The Thirteenth Floor* (Centropolis 1999).

Game Review	Text	Developer	Publisher
	Jesper Juul	Williams Electronics	Williams Electronics, 1980

DEFENDER
Unnecessarily Hard

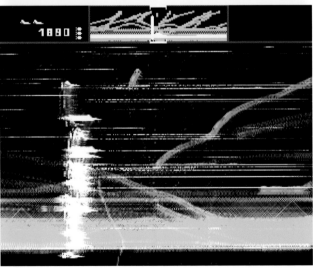

According to Bernard Suits, one of the defining characteristics of games is that their players have to reach game goals using the *less efficient means* available. In a foot race, it would be faster to drive a car; in a high jump, it would be easier to use a ladder. Games are unnecessary work.

Even at the level of its controls, *Defender* reveals its "gameness." The game is unnecessarily hard in a way that exceeds expectations. Conventional wisdom says that the basic controls of a game should be intuitive and satisfying, but *Defender* has a stick for moving up and down and an awkward single button for reversing direction. The designers could have given players more efficient means of moving by way of a four-directional joystick. But they were designing *Defender*, an unnecessarily hard game.

This is also the joy of *Defender*: the pure and personal feeling of overcoming challenges, of improving. Stay alive by evading and shooting enemies. The deeper challenge is to protect the ten humans on the ground. If an alien carries a human to the top of the screen, the human is subsumed and the alien transformed into an aggressive mutant that seeks out the player. Once all humans are lost, the planet explodes, and the player must play in hyperspace where all aliens are mutants. This is the depth of the game: a core activity of staying alive and a second activity of protecting the humans. The player must tend to the latter, or the core activity of staying alive becomes chaotic and extra hard, in consequence of the player's neglect.

Defender is unnecessarily hard, and this makes it a game for the few players who enjoy extreme challenges. *Defender* is an exaggerated version of the early 1980s arcade game in all its virtues: it includes a large number of possible ways to fail, it is extremely unforgiving and it offers no rewards beyond a high score and a few smart bombs. The purest arcade game.

WOLFENSTEIN 3D
Gore Space and the Side Effects of Software

In 1992, id Software took the first steps in introducing the real world onto the computer screen by releasing a video game called *Wolfenstein 3D*. The action game is set during World War II, with the player looking through the eyes of American soldier B.J. Blazkowicz. Armed only with a shotgun, B.J. is trapped in a labyrinth of dungeon-like rooms filled with Nazi soldiers, mean dogs, mutated zombies and Adolf Hitler. He must shoot himself a way out of Castle Wolfenstein and, in several episodes, prevent the Nazis from unleashing a mutant army of undead zombies that could decide the war in their favor.

Wolfenstein 3D introduces an experience of realness into the virtual gaming world in two different ways: through gore and through "do-it-yourself" software. For the first time in gaming history, objects that have been shot down do not dissolve into thin air, but rather change into flying body parts, blood and other gore. This "gore effect" is a cinematographic trick that uses traumatic and excessive images to create a suggestion of real life. Gamers must shoot the dogs and humans as well as the zombies, which need to be shot several times before dying and exploding. Spreading gore by shooting, the players are pulled into the action of the game. Every click draws them deeper into the unreal world.

But innovation does not stop at the visuals. The game also allows reality onto the screen by becoming a social environment. Because in 1992, id Software was a small game producer, it did not have a distributor that could place *Wolfenstein 3D* on store shelves. The company thus came up with the idea of using "shareware" to promote its game. Gamers could download the first episodes of the game for free; if they wanted to finish the rest of the game, they had to order the remaining episodes by normal mail. As a result, the software was divided into simple and transparent folders that could be expanded. This shareware method had an unintended side effect: it allowed players to change the sounds and appearances of the game by themselves. The follow-up of *Wolfenstein 3D*, *Doom* (id Software 1993), had the same structure and distribution. And after *Wolfenstein 3D* gamers were given a powerful tool to create their personal mirror palaces of the real, an avalanche of "do-it-yourself" game titles appeared on the Internet. Powered by the rise of the Internet, these reality games quickly spread and inspired new communities that chose shooting games as a base for their communication.

COUNTER-STRIKE
Lock and Load!

In 1999, computer game developer Minh Le releases a free modification of *Half-Life* (Valve 1998) called *Counter-Strike*. He reworks the *Half-Life* "engine" to create a realistic multiplayer environment where players can play against each other – shooting "real" people instead of bots. Before the battle starts, the player has to choose between acting as part of a terrorist group or as a member of a counter-terrorist team. Depending on the environment (there are multiple ones from which players can choose), the terrorists have to plant a bomb, keep hostages imprisoned or kill a VIP that is defended by the other team. Vice versa, the counter-terrorists have to prevent the other team from planting any bombs, free captured prisoners and defend their VIP.

Counter-Strike has been around for eight years now and still is the most popular action game around. To play one of the three editions of *Counter-Strike*, a gamer first chooses one of more than 150,000 servers, each containing different environments to compete in, teams of various sizes to join and varying rules. Although the first version of *Counter-Strike* was available with only a limited number of three-dimensional environments, soon after its release, gamers started to design and create virtual spaces on their own. As soon as one of these environments – referred to as maps by most gamers – turned out to be a suitable battle space, *Counter-Strike* fanatics started to exchange it.

It is tempting to think that behind the screens of our PCs a treasure of undiscovered architectural wonders is hidden. Playing games would then mean that we could use our keyboards to navigate through new architectural wonders, just as architectural critic Reyner Banham simply learned to drive a car in order to see new designs in Los Angeles in the 1970s. *Counter-Strike* maps, however, serve one purpose only: to provide an arena for the death-matches of gamers. Good maps have different spatial requirements than do good buildings. In fact, the simplest maps – like, for example, "fy poolday," in which players run around a swimming pool to shoot each other – are the most popular. Complex maps with lots of details simply distract players too much from putting up a good fight.

To consider maps of *Counter-Strike* as architectural artifacts would be like describing a ghost town. The very essence of gaming, interaction, would be missing. The architectural invention of *Counter-Strike* works in another way. The game provides the connection that makes it possible for someone to move from one space (ruins, pools, castles) into another. Playing *Counter-Strike* is like moving between spaces that would normally be separated. It offers access to a wide diversity of spaces in which people battle each other. This gets close to the very foundations upon which architecture in our mediated world will have to be based: giving access to environments that are real and virtual at the same time. To do so, architecture will need a theory that combines both architecture's physical and medial aspects.

ALLEGORIES OF SPACE
The Question of Spatiality in Computer Games

The defining element in computer games is spatiality. Computer games are essentially concerned with spatial representation and negotiation, and therefore the classification of a computer game can be based on how it represents or, perhaps, implements space. More than time (which in most games can be stopped), more than actions, events and goals (which are tediously similar from game to game) and unquestionably more than characterization (which is usually nonexistent), games celebrate and explore spatial representation as a central motif and raison d'être. In terms of playability, themes, tasks, subgenres and dramatic structure, nothing much has changed over the last two decades. The innovation takes place in spatial representation, and the genre's more slowly evolving complexity in the other areas (such as physical simulation) can be seen as a result of the increasing complexity of the spatial representation.

But what exactly is "spatial representation" in games, and what is its relation to "real space?"

Space and Spatial Representation

To refer to space as an object is a common trope in media aesthetics: the use of the term "spaces" instead of "places," "rooms," "regions," "zones," etc. is fashionable. But to what does it really refer? What is "a space," and what is its relationship to Space? Philosopher Anita Leirfall takes cyberspace theorists to task for confusing the concept of space with place. Why say spaces when we really mean places? "Cyberspace," she says, should be seen as a system of signs. "In fact the 'sign space' is an example of an operation which reduces or limits the richer and more extensive – or all-embracing – notion of three-dimensional space. A place is always a limitation of, or in, space. Place can never exist independently of its spatial origin. It must stand in a necessary and inevitable relation to space to be considered a space at all. [...] every attempt to give a *definition* of space will face the problem of circularity, while the definition must presuppose space as already given in its definition!" (Leirfall 1997, p. 2).

Leirfall does not accept the notion that cyberspace, virtual spaces and, implicitly, computer games constitute an alternative type of space with autonomous qualities. By being generated, cyberplaces are "regions in space" and cannot exist as parallels of real, three-dimensional space. This is an important point. "Cyberspace" and other such phenomena (e.g. computer games) are constituted of signs and are therefore already too dependent on our bodily experience in and of real space to be "hallucinated" as space. Moreover, the fact that they are not real space but rather objects and places is the only reason we can perceive them at all. If this were not true – that is, if they were not objects but real space (somehow) computer-mediated – then we would not be able to tell them apart from real space unmediated.

This conception of space is, of course, a strict one in light of the word's several common meanings. Other philosophers, in particular Henri Lefebvre, distinguish between natural (physical) space, abstract space, social space etc., and also between representations of space and representational spaces (Lefebvre 1991, p. 33). To Lefebvre, all space is produced, socially constructed by what he calls the "spatial practice" of a society (ibid., p. 38). A representation of space is a logical system of relations, while a representational space is symbolic and "lived," not consistent or rule-based. These two categories are not dyadic, but rather stand in a triadic relationship with spatial practice. While it may be dangerous to map Lefebvre's theory of space onto computer games – they are, after all, a type of spatial representation he did not anticipate – it might provide a useful perspective for our investigation. As spatial practice, computer games are both representations of space (given their formal systems of relations) and representational spaces (given their symbolic imagery with a primarily aesthetic purpose). This conclusion is perhaps too open-ended to be of any real use as is; further refinement and adaptation of Lefebvre's theory than can be pursued here seems to be needed. But the result indicates that spatial representation in computer games is ambivalent and two-sided: it is both conceptual and associative.

But can these two different spatial philosophies be reconciled and united into a useful frame of reference? Both provide helpful perspectives on what exactly we refer to whenever we use the word "space," but they are less directly applicable when it comes to the question of computer games. Should we thus capitulate and adopt the awfully nondescript term "virtual space" to describe gamespace? Even if we disregard all its other problems as an analytical concept, "virtual space" will not help us distinguish between different types of spatial representation in computer games; it merely tells us that space can be simulated. Instead, drawing on both Leirfall and Lefebvre, I will posit spatial representation in computer games as a reductive operation leading to a representation of space that is not in itself spatial, but symbolic and rule-based. The nature of space is not revealed in this operation, and the resulting product, while fabricating a spatial representation, in fact uses the reductions as a means to achieve the object of gameplay, since the difference between the spatial representation and real space is what makes gameplay-by-automatic-rules possible. In real space, there would be no automatic rules, only social rules and physical laws.

A common feature in many, if not most, computer games is the teleporter, a means by which to move instantly from one point in the gameworld to another. In Multi User Dungeons (MUD), for instance, the administrators often take great care in keeping links between rooms "topologically correct" so that what is modeled is a consistent terrain. But even so, the most-used means to move between MUD rooms is teleporting (e.g. in MOOs (MUD object oriented), the players "@join" other players), not progressing through intermediate rooms one by one. This instant relocation is a figurative negation of real space and, as such, a striking contrast to the seemingly naturalistic ideal of the games. But the often central role this device plays begs the question of whether the fetishism of real space is really hypocritical. When it really matters, the discontinuity of digital communication dominates even these illusions of real space.

From *Myst* to *Myth*

Let us briefly examine two different games, both of which seemingly belong to the outdoors category: *Myst* and *Myth*. Both games are about conquering landscapes, but in very different ways. *Myst* (1993) presents a graphical "click 'n go" interface over the classical adventure game structure: explore the paths, solve the puzzles and win the game. The representation seems three-dimensional, but consists of a network of still life pictures filled with "hot spots" that the user clicks on to "move." What seems like a game set in the outdoors is very much an indoor variant: discontinuous, labyrinthine, full of carefully constructed obstacles.

The other game, *Myth* (1997), is a fantasy battle tactics simulator in which the player directs and deploys different types of warriors to destroy the enemy. Featuring lush green parklands, the visual imagery is, superficially, quite similar to *Myst*'s. But while *Myst* is about exploring mystical buildings and other structures, *Myth* takes place in an exclusively outdoors setting. Some houses are visible, but they are only window dressing. Where *Myst* is closed, *Myth* gives the impression of being open, and it allows movement in any direction. Most of the terrain can be reached by simple continuous movement of troops. The player, however, has a second perspective: in the upper right-hand corner of the screen, a map shows his units and the enemy units as color-coded dots. When clicked, this map will be transferred onto the main ("camera") window for closer inspection. Such instant, discontinuous travel would have been invaluable for the field marshals of real wars in the Middle Ages.

Myth can be played in single-player mode as an episodic quest against the machine-controlled "evil forces of the Fallen Lords," or on a network with up to 15 other players, all against all or teams against teams. These two modes represent quite different games, with the same spatial constraints and possibilities, though the network version offers several different gameworld arenas (landscapes) and several different types of play. Users can even create their own landscapes. *Myth* (and other games with multiplayer options) is not, then, a single game, but a type of discursive field, a machine on which to play several related games.

Every game of *Myth* is a fight for position on the landscape. To engage in battle without first securing a strong, ordered position in most cases means to lose the game. The game corresponds well to the standards of classical battle tactics: formation and knowledge of the capabilities and weaknesses of troop types and the opponent's mind are essential to win. The units will go where and do as ordered (with a simple click on the unit and then a click on the position or enemy to be taken), but when the chaos of battle erupts, efficient control is no longer possible, and therefore, much depends on how well the player has taken advantage of formation, landscape variation and knowledge of enemy positions. For all its initial beauty, the landscape in *Myth*, like all computer game landscapes, merely looks like a landscape but is really a three-dimensional scheme carefully designed to offer a balanced challenge to the player. To create a *Myth* landscape, one must have in mind a detailed idea of how one wants the gameplay to commence. Such a landscape is a plan rather than a map. This becomes obvious if one considers the difference between single-player landscapes and multiplayer landscapes. The single-player landscape is asymmetrical and often linear, with one main path leading through it and "evil" troops placed in ambush along the way. Even though it appears to be open for exploration in all directions, obstacles in the landscape – e.g. deep rivers, unclimbable mountainsides or canyons, etc. – effectively linearize the options for movement. The promise of continuous space is negated by what turns out to be a strict topology. This is not too different from the landscape architecture in adventure games such as *Myst*.

Myth's multiplayer landscapes, on the other hand, are symmetrical, open and usually arranged around a central point. Since the opponent is human, the landscape must be "neutral" and equal for all players or else the player with the best starting position would have an unfair advantage. Ultimately, both types of landscapes – single- and multiplayer – are "unrealistic": in real space, landscapes are usually asymmetrical (with the exception of gardens and planned cities), but they are seldom topologically constricted (at least to the degree found in *Myth*). In other words, the topology of even the most "open" computer-generated landscapes makes them quite different from real space, and controlled in ways that are not inherent to the original physical objects they are meant to represent. This makes them allegorical: they are figurative comments on the ultimate impossibility of representing real space.

Even as computer games rely on representational techniques (the simulation of a landscape), they are not exclusively focused on representation since the representation is always serving the primary purpose of gameplay. Gameworld design must defer to gameplay design just as in drama, scenography must defer to dialogue. At the same time, a game without an arena is only a potential, and the artifacts of the gameworld are the player's chief point of entry into ludic comprehension. Computer games are allegories of space: they pretend to portray space in ever more realistic ways but rely on their deviation from reality in order to make the illusion playable.

This is a shortened and edited version of an essay which has been published in M. Eskelinen & R. Koskimaa (eds.), *Cybertext Yearbook*, University of Jyväskylä, Jyväskylä, pp. 152-171.

◆ Leirfall, A. (1997), "Space, place and dimensionality," paper presented to the conference *The digital challenge: New information technology, media and communication*, 11-12, The University of Trondheim, Dept. of Art and Media. ◆ Lefebvre, H. (1991), *The Production of Space*, Blackwell, Oxford. ◆ *Myst* (1995), developed by Cyan, published by Brøderbund Software. ◆ *Myth* (1997), developed and published by Bungie Studios.

MYST
Static Images as Immersive World

Myst was released for the Apple Macintosh in 1993. It is a simple point-and-click adventure game that employs Hypercard software and the then fairly new CD-ROM drive to deliver an immersive experience filled with lush graphics and spatial puzzles. The creators of *Myst* used Hypercard to create intricately detailed static images full of hotspots that players can click to be transported to other images. Navigating through this world is thus somewhat akin to clicking through a multilinear slide show: there is a unique spatial relation between each image of the world. And because all the slides fit together, they create an entire world for the player to discover.

You as the player can, however, subvert this inter-relatedness using the options menu of the game. There you can select lightning travel, which allows you to zoom through the worlds you've already visited. This feature is represented by a lightning cursor, which, when clicked, zips you across several images in a single go, giving you, in other words, the power to leap across space.

Adding even more dynamism to this multilayered world, ambient sounds help give images tone and affect. A good example of this can be found on the initial island where you can descend into a dank, dark basement after being outside in some peaceful woods. Sound and image details help make this transition feel more real. At first, you are out in the woods where the sunlight casts shadows across the forest floor, birds chirp, a light breeze stirs the trees and butterflies flit about. You come upon a brick building that you can enter and in which you find a set of stone stairs. But for the stark light of a single light bulb, the area at the bottom of the stairs is shadowed in deep darkness. The floor is wet, and you hear water dripping and echoing in the tight space. The spatial contrast between the forest and the basement is effectively and affectingly brought about.

As you explore in *Myst*, you find that you are traveling across worlds unique in look and feel, each containing spatial puzzles that must be solved. In order to successfully do so, you must explore the worlds thoroughly and make connections across the spaces. It wouldn't be too far of a stretch, then, to say that the worlds themselves are the puzzles.

Myst also approaches space on a metaphoric level. The fantastic worlds that you explore actually exist in magical books; to enter them, you open a book, click on it and are transported into its world. This gives visual shape to the powerful feeling of reading a story in a book and being imaginatively swept away into its world. In *Myst*, you literally enter the worlds of the books and explore them. The space of imagination is the world of the game.

SUPER MARIO BROS.
One-way Scrolling

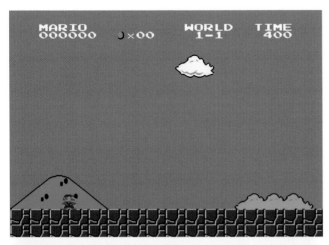

When *Super Mario Bros.* was first released for the NES in 1985, it quickly became a success, driving up the sales of the console with which it was eventually bundled. In the game, the player takes control of Mario or his younger brother Luigi and has him run and jump through the fantastic Mushroom Kingdom on a quest to save its princess.

The gamespace of *Super Mario Bros.* extends far beyond what is visible on one screen. The environment moves past the player, who goes from screen left to screen right, trying to reach the end of the level before he may enter the next. This scrolling is one-way only, which means that the player can advance at his own pace but can never backtrack. This creates a simple-to-understand, yet rigid, tubular space.

The top and bottom edges of the world are static due to the lack of vertical screen movement, but they do not block the avatar. The various ways that a player can leave the visible screen produce different results. When falling out of the screen via the bottom edge, the player loses one life. The upper edge, on the other hand, is harmless, and the player can simply jump up and out of the screen only to reappear a few seconds later. This is the first exception to the purely horizontal alignment of the space.

Another exception is the existence of pipes that can be found within the levels. A few can be used to enter secret underground areas. These not only provide the player with coins, they also double as shortcuts. In some of the later levels, the pipes become obstacles in that they send the player back to an already visited point without first granting him an intermediary bonus area. The player can also jump at blocks in the air to reveal more secrets, such as beanstalks that work in a way similar to the pipes except that they lead up to cloudy heights, not down underground. They give the impression that the gameworld is larger than what can be seen in the regular levels and represent yet another exception to the predominant horizontal spatial alignment. In addition to taking shortcuts within the levels, players can also find hidden Warp Zones, which allow them to skip a large number of levels.

Super Mario Bros. can be considered one of the milestones of video game history. Its bright and colorful environments coupled with its accessible controls made it easy for new players to get into the game. At first glance, the levels seem simple, but thanks in great part to the shortcuts, secret areas and Warp Zones scattered throughout the worlds, the game has a surprising level of depth and spatial complexity. The game also uses its varying environmental background as a narrative device; the last level of each world, for example, culminates in a fiery castle area, which signals the impending final battle.

Game Review	Text	Developer	Publisher
	Katie Salen	Alexey Pajitnov	First published in the US by Spectrum HoloByte, 1985

TETRIS
Puzzling Architecture

The formally simple and logically complex falling puzzle game *Tetris* knows few peers when it comes to addictive gameplay. Random sequences of one-sided tetrominoes – shapes composed of four square blocks each – fall into a grid-based playing field below; players strategically rotate the falling tiles in 90-degree increments and move them horizontally, working to create horizontal lines of tiles without gaps. Doing so allows players to clear lines, earn points and make room for the relentless march of new tiles entering from above. A non-Newtonian gravity known as "naïve gravity" allows blocks to remain floating above any unfilled gap, decreasing the chances of an easy completion of lines. Players refer to the seven different tetrominoes according to their shapes: I, J, L, O, S, T and Z. This method may help players envision the pieces' rotational and combinatory possibilities. The game ends when the player "tops out" – that is, when one or more of the stacks of tiles reach the top of the playing field, leaving no room for new tiles to enter.

Designed by Alexey Pajitnov in 1985 and inspired in part by the mathematical elegance of the pentomino-based puzzle games he loved to play in his native Russia, *Tetris* extends the experiential space of a seemingly small 10x20 square grid into an infinite vertical plane. While players see a limited space of play ordered through strict Euclidian geometry, the gamespace theoretically extends forever beyond the top edge of the screen. Players anxiously anticipate the type of tile to appear next and must reorient each piece in both the gamespace and their own minds as they search for the best alignment. Once a row is complete, traditional versions of the game move the stacks of tiles downward by a distance equal to the height of the cleared rows below them; a tessellation or tiling of the plane is rewarded with the return of a negative space of equal dimension. Thus players claim space only to gain its simultaneous erasure. Sequencing the never-ending supply of interlocking tiles in such a way as to leave no cell empty forces players into a maddening paradox: while the game supports a spatial logic based on positive construction, what remains on-screen is that which players have failed to complete. Rather than the well-ordered grid *Tetris* players desperately seek, they face instead a highly original architecture composed solely of misstep and mistake.

ICO
Holding Hands in a Castle

Ico was released for the PlayStation 2 in 2001. It provides a wonderfully artful gaming experience set almost entirely within an immense old castle. The castle is one huge spatial puzzle from which you, the player, must escape. You do this by climbing, jumping, pulling levers, pushing crates and running around. In a way, the complex design of the castle areas ironically creates a rather linear gameplay experience; you really only progress along the paths that you discover. So while the game is somewhat on rails, it feels organic in that you are simply trying to work your way through the ruins of the castle. This feeling is enhanced by the fact that you not only navigate the player-controlled small boy, but also a mysterious young girl. The girl is not as physically capable as the boy, so you have to spend time figuring out how to get the boy (i.e. yourself) through spaces and then get her through them as well.

The temptation to leave the girl behind is initially inspired by the fact that she is unable to get through spaces as quickly as the boy, but is strengthened by a language barrier: you can't understand what she is saying, and it's apparent that she can't understand you either. But it also becomes obvious that you can't leave her behind. If you do, shade creatures quickly grab her and pull her away into a dark hole, which causes the game to end on an unsuccessful note. Thus in order to continue onward more successfully, you not only have to figure out how to get both the boy and the girl through the ruins, you also have to keep her close to you so that she doesn't get taken away by the creatures.

One particularly charming part of the game is the mechanism by which you save your progress. Save points are denoted by special couches found sporadically throughout the castle. When you sit on a couch and take a nap, you save your progress, and when you resume playing, you wake up. This produces a nice little impression of time passing and of the boy and girl needing to rest as they work their way through the castle.

Having to keep the girl close and having to rest both underline the importance of the boy and girl having to stick together. The best way to keep the girl with you is to hold her hand. This hand-holding is, in fact, a large part of the gameplay and is reinforced by force feedback in the controller so that you, the player, get to feel the act of holding hands. You feel the girl's clasp, you feel it when there is a strain to continue holding hands, and you feel it when the boy and girl lose each others' grips. This creates an intimacy between the two characters lost in the castle; the virtual/physical act of holding hands is the means by which they work together to get through the ruins. Thus while you explore and progress through the game, your relationship with the girl is complemented by the virtually haptic gesture of simply holding her hand.

NARRATIVE SPACES

Spatial Stories and Environmental Storytelling

Game designers don't simply tell stories; they design worlds and sculpt spaces. It is no accident, for example, that game designers have historically been more interested in issues of level design than of plot or character motivation. A prehistory of video and computer games might take us through the evolution of paper mazes or board games, both preoccupied with the design of spaces. *Monopoly* (1935), for example, may tell a narrative about how fortunes are won and lost; its individual Chance cards may provide some story pretext for our gaining or losing a certain number of places. But ultimately, what we remember about the game is the experience of moving around the board and landing on someone's real estate. Performance theorists have described Role-Play Games as a mode of collaborative storytelling, but in the game *Dungeons & Dragons* (1974), for example, the Dungeon Master's activities start with designing the space – the dungeon – where the players' quest will take place. Even many of the early text-based games, such as *Zork* (1980), for example, centered on enabling players to move through narratively compelling spaces. "You are facing the north side of a white house," the game tells you. "There is no door here, and all of the windows are boarded up. To the north a narrow path winds through the trees." The early Nintendo games have simple narrative hooks – rescue Princess Toadstool, for example – but what gamers found astonishing when they first played them were their complex and imaginative graphic realms, which were so much more sophisticated than the simple grids that *PONG* (1972) or *Pac-Man* (1980) had offered a decade earlier. And when gamer magazines describe the experience of gameplay, they are more likely to reproduce maps of a gameworld than to recount a game's narrative.

Don Carson, who worked as a Senior Show Designer for Walt Disney Imagineering, has argued that game designers can learn a great deal by studying techniques of "environmental storytelling," which Disney employs in designing amusement park attractions: "The story element is infused into the physical space a guest walks or rides through. It is the physical space that does much of the work of conveying the story the designers are trying to tell [...]. Armed only with their own knowledge of the world, and those visions collected from movies and books, the audience is ripe to be dropped into your adventure. The trick is to play on those memories and expectations to heighten the thrill of venturing into your created universe" (Carson 2000). Take, for example, the Disney amusement park ride based on the book *The Wind in the Willows* (Grahame 1908). The ride does not so much reproduce the story of the literary work as evoke its atmosphere; the original tale provides "a set of rules that [...]

guide the design and project team to a common goal" and help give structure and meaning to the visitor's experience (Carson 2000). If, for example, the attraction centers on pirates, Carson writes, "every texture you use, every sound you play, every turn in the road should reinforce the concept of pirates" (ibid.). Any contradictory element may shatter the sense of immersion in the narrative universe. The same might be said of a computer game like *Sea Dogs* (2000), whose success, no less than that of *Pirates of the Caribbean* (2003), depends on its ability to map our preexisting pirate fantasies. The most significant difference between designing such theme park rides and designing computer and video games is that amusement park designers count on us visitors keeping our hands and arms in the car at all times, giving the designer greater control in shaping our total experience. Game designers, on the other hand, have to develop worlds in which we can touch, grab and fling things at will.

Nonetheless, environmental storytelling creates the preconditions for an immersive narrative experience in up to four different ways: spatial stories can evoke preexisting narrative associations; they can provide a staging ground on which narrative events are enacted; they may embed narrative information within their mises-en-scène; or they provide resources for emergent narratives.

Evocative Spaces

The most compelling amusement park attractions are based on stories or genre traditions already well known to visitors, allowing them to enter physically into spaces they have visited many times before in their fantasies. These attractions may either remediate a preexisting story (*Back to the Future*) or draw upon a broadly shared genre tradition (Disney's *Haunted Mansion*). Such works do not so much tell self-contained stories as draw upon our previously existing narrative competencies. Their worlds can be painted in fairly broad outlines and the visitors/players can be counted upon to do the rest. Something similar might be said of many games. For example, *American McGee's Alice* (2000) is an original interpretation of Lewis Carroll's *Alice's Adventures in Wonderland* (1865). In it Alice has been driven to madness after years of living with uncertainty about whether her Wonderland experiences were real or hallucinations; now, she's gone back to Wonderland looking for blood. McGee's wonderland is not a whimsical dreamscape, but a dark nightmare realm. McGee can safely assume that players start the game with a pretty well-developed mental map of the spaces, characters and situations associated with Carroll's fictional universe, and that they will read his distorted and often monstrous images against the background of mental images formed from previous encounters with storybook illustrations and Disney movies. McGee rewrites Alice's story in large part by redesigning Alice's spaces.

Games, then, are taking their place within a larger narrative system in which story information is communicated through books, film, television, comics and other media. In such a system, the role and importance of gamers will almost certainly center on their ability to give concrete shape to our memories and imaginings of the story world, creating an immersive environment through which we can wander and with which we can interact.

Enacting Stories

"A good story hangs together the way a good jigsaw puzzle hangs together. When you pick it up, every piece locked tightly in place next to its neighbors" (Adams 1999). Spatial stories are often dismissed as episodic – that is, each episode (or set piece) can become compelling on its own terms without contributing significantly to the plot development and, often, can be reordered without significantly impacting our experience as a whole. There may be broad movements or series of stages within the story, but within each stage, the sequencing of actions may be quite loose (Dunniway 2000). Spatial stories are not badly constructed stories; rather, they are stories that respond to alternative aesthetic principles, privileging spatial exploration over plot development. Spatial stories are held together by broadly defined goals and conflicts and driven by a character's movement across a map. Their resolution often hinges on the players reaching their final destination, though not all travel narratives end successfully or resolve the narrative enigmas that set them into motion (Jenkins & Fuller 1994). Once again, we are back to principles of environmental storytelling: organizing the plot becomes a matter of designing the geography of imaginary worlds so that obstacles thwart and affordances facilitate the protagonist's forward movement towards resolution. Over the past several decades, game designers have become more and more adept at setting and varying the rhythm of gameplay through features of the gamespace.

The player's participation poses a potential threat to the narrative construction, while the "hard rails" of the plotting can overly constrain the "freedom, power, self-expression" associated with interactivity (Adams 1999). The tension between performance (or gameplay) and exposition (or story) is far from unique to games, but game designers have a particularly difficult time with this balancing act. They must try to determine how much plot will create a compelling framework and how much freedom players can enjoy at a local level without totally derailing the larger narrative trajectory. As inexperienced storytellers, they often fall back on rather mechanical exposition through cut scenes, much as early filmmakers were sometimes overly reliant on intertitles because they had not yet mastered the skills of visual storytelling. Yet, as in any other aesthetic tradition, game designers are apt to develop their craft through a process of experimentation and refinement of basic narrative devices, becoming better at shaping narrative experiences without unduly constraining the space for improvisation within their games.

Embedded Narratives

The detective story is the classic example of the principle of embedded narratives. It tells two stories, one more or less chronological (the story of the investigation itself) and the other radically out of sequence (the events motivating and leading up to the murder). Like the creators of detective stories, game designers essentially develop two kinds of narratives: one relatively unstructured, controlled by the player as he explores the gamespace and unlocks its secrets, the other, prestructured but embedded within the *mise en scène* awaiting discovery. The gameworld becomes a kind of information space, a memory palace. *Myst* (1993) is a highly successful example of a game that uses this kind of embedded narrative.

But embedded narrative does not necessarily require an emptying of the space of contemporary narrative activities. Embedded narrative can and often does occur within contested spaces. We may have to battle our way past antagonists, navigate through mazes or figure out how to pick locks in order to move through the narratively impregnated mise-en-scène. Such a mixture of enacted and embedded narrative elements can allow for a balance between the flexibility of interactivity and the coherence of a preauthored narrative. A game like *Majestic* (2001) from game designer Neil Young pushes this notion of embedded narrative to its logical extreme. Here, the embedded narrative is no longer contained within the console, but rather flows across multiple information channels. Our activity as players consists of sorting through documents, deciphering codes or making sense of garbled transmissions, all the while moving step by step towards a fuller understanding of the conspiracy that is the game's primary narrative focus. We follow links between websites and get information through webcasts, faxes, emails and phone calls. Such an embedded narrative doesn't require a branching story structure, but rather depends on scrambling the pieces of a linear story and allowing us to reconstruct the plot through our acts of detection, speculation, exploration and decryption. Not surprisingly, most existing embedded narratives take the form of detective or conspiracy stories since these genres help to motivate the player's active examination of clues and exploration of spaces and provide a rationale for his efforts to reconstruct the narrative of past events.

Emergent Narratives

The Sims (2000) represents yet another model of how narrative possibilities can be mapped onto gamespace. Emergent narratives are not merely prestructured or preprogrammed stories that take shape through the gameplay, yet they are not as unstructured, chaotic and frustrating as life itself. Will Wright, the game's designer, frequently describes *The Sims* as a sandbox or dollhouse game, suggesting that it should be understood as a kind of authoring environment within which players can define their own goals and write their own stories. And yet, the game doesn't open on a blank screen. Most players come away from spending time with *The Sims* with some degree of narrative satisfaction. Wright has created a world ripe with narrative possibilities; each design decision has been made with an eye towards increasing the prospects of interpersonal romance or conflict. The ability to design their "skins" encourages players to create characters who are emotionally significant to them, to rehearse their own relationships with friends, family or coworkers or to map characters from other fictional universes onto *The Sims*. A quick look at the various scrapbooks players have posted on the Web suggests that they have been quick to take advantage of the game's relatively open-ended structure. But let's not underestimate the designers' contributions. I would argue that Wright's choices go deeper than what he accomplishes through procedural authorship, working not simply through the programming, but also through the design of the gamespace. For example, just as a dollhouse offers a streamlined representation that cuts out much of the clutter of an actual domestic space, *The Sims'* houses are stripped down to only a small number of artifacts, each of which performs specific narrative functions.

Newspapers, for example, communicate job information. Characters sleep in beds. Bookcases can improve intelligence. Together, these objects help constitute a highly legible narrative space.

However a game's narrative is expressed, it is always influenced by the way the game creators designed and organized the gamespaces. In the case of evoked narratives, spatial design can either enhance our sense of immersion within a familiar world or communicate a fresh perspective on a well-known story through the altering of established details. In the case of enacted narratives, the story itself may be structured around the character's movement through space, and the features of the environment may retard or accelerate that plot trajectory. In the case of embedded narratives, the gamespace becomes a memory palace whose contents must be deciphered as the player tries to reconstruct the plot. And in the case of emergent narratives, gamespaces are designed to be rich with narrative potential, thereby enabling the story-constructing activity of players. In each case, it makes sense to think of game designers less as storytellers and more as narrative architects.

In his classic 1960 study, *The Image of the City*, urban planner Kevin Lynch made the case that urban designers need to be more sensitive to the narrative potentials of city spaces, describing city planning as "the deliberate manipulation of the world for sensuous ends" (Lynch 1960, p. 116). Urban designers exert even less control than game designers over how people use the spaces they create or what kinds of scenes they stage there. Yet some kinds of spaces lend themselves more readily than others to narratively memorable or emotionally meaningful experiences. Lynch suggested that urban planners should not attempt to totally predetermine the uses and meanings of the spaces they create: "a landscape whose every rock tells a story may make difficult the creation of fresh stories" (ibid., p. 6). As an alternative, he proposes an aesthetic of urban design that endows each space with "poetic and symbolic" potential: "Such a sense of place in itself enhances every human activity that occurs there, and encourages the deposit of a memory trace"(ibid., p. 119). Game designers would do well to study Lynch's book, especially as they move into the production of game platforms that support player-generated narratives.

This is a shortened version of the essay "Game Design as a Narrative Architecture." http://web.mit.edu/cms/People/henry3/games&narrative.html

◆ Adams, E. (1999), "Three Problems for Interactive Storytellers," *Gamasutra.com*. Retrieved March 21, 2007, from http://www.gamasutra.com/features/designers_notebook/19991229.htm ◆ *American McGee's Alice* (2000), developed by Rogue Entertainment, published by Electronic Arts. ◆ Carson, D. (2000), "Environmental Storytelling: Creating Immersive 3D Worlds Using Lessons Learned from the Theme Park Industry," *Gamasutra.com*. Retrieved March 21, 2007, from http://www.gamasutra.com/features/20000301/carson_pfv.htm ◆ *Dungeons & Dragons* (role playing game) (1974), developed by Gary Gygax & Dave Arneson, published by Tactical Studies Rules. ◆ Dunniway, T. (2000), "Using the Hero's Journey in Games," *Gamasutra.com*. Retrieved March 21, 2007, from http://www.gamasutra.com/features/20001127/dunniway_01.htm ◆ Jenkins, H & Fuller, M. (1994), "Nintendo and New World Narrative," in S. Jones (ed.), *Communications in Cyberspace*, Sage, Los Angeles. ◆ Lynch, K. (1960), *The Image of the City*, MIT Press, Cambridge MA. ◆ *Majestic* (2001), developed by Anim-X, published by Electronic Arts. ◆ *Monopoly* (board game) (1935), published by Parker Brothers. ◆ *Myst* (1993), developed by Cyan, published by Brøderbund Software. ◆ *Pac-Man* (1980), developed by Namco, published by Midway. ◆ *Pirates of the Caribbean* (2003), developed by Akella, published by Bethesda Softworks. ◆ *PONG* (1972), developed and published by Atari. ◆ *Sea Dogs* (2000), developed by Akella, published by Bethesda Softworks. ◆ *The Sims* (2000), developed by Maxis, published by Electronic Arts. ◆ *Zork* (1980), developed by Infocom, published by Personal Software.

GAME PHYSICS
The Look & Feel Challenges of Spectacular Worlds

History

In his 1687 treatise *Philosophiae Naturalis Principia Mathematica*, Sir Isaac Newton tried to describe and predict real-world phenomena by means of analytical formulas. Amongst other innovations, he introduced the concept of universal gravitation and the laws of motion, the foundations of our current understanding of physics. Centuries later, Konrad Zuse invented the computer and designed the first high-level programming language, *Plankalkül*. Initially, Zuse invented his technology in order to numerically solve complex differential equations in the field of civil engineering. Believe it or not, Zuse invented the computer to simulate real-world physics, not to replace the typewriter!

A Useful Application of Simulations

My first exposure to simulation was during my university studies in the field of control engineering. Most simulation concepts in science and engineering, whether real-time or non-real-time, aim at accurately describing and predicting real-world phenomena. Science and engineering therefore tend to "virtualize" the real world in order to make it more comprehensible and predictable. When simulating physics in games, we face many problems similar to those faced by scientists and engineers. Take, for example, the problem of diverging worlds in distributed multiplayer games. Such divergence can be caused by – amongst other factors – delayed information arriving from remote players while the simulations on the local player's machine continue to evolve. As in the case of feedback control engineering, the input signals to the simulations have to be the same and arrive at the same time for this situation to be remedied.

Even more problematic, simulations in games tend to have some chaotic components, in the mathematical sense of the term. A virtual rockslide or a building collapse is a good example of a chaotic system. Slight differences in the simulation input may generate entirely different simulation results, although precisely the same physics can be simulated on entirely different computers. In fact, simulations in science and engineering have very much in common with physics simulations in games. But there is one fundamental difference between the simulation concepts applied in science and those applied in games. The scientific approach of "virtualizing" the real world aims at predicting and better understanding real-world phenomena. Physics simulation in games, inversely, aims at making a virtual world feel more realistic, thus "realizing" a virtual world. This leads us to the question of what we define as "realistic" physics for a game.

The Hollywood Effect: Hyperrealism!

Promoting physics simulation to the game developer community can be pretty funny, but also frustrating, especially if you have spent a lot of time improving the accuracy of your physics simulation environment. Try to remember your high school days and that remarkable physics lecture on the law of falling bodies: in a frictionless vacuum, an ultra-light feather will fall at the same speed as a piece of lead! Cut to many years later, when a game developer is seriously telling you that your physics simulation is lousy and unrealistic. According to his extensive simulation experience, a simulated rock of one kilogram should fall much slower than one with the same size but 100 times the density. Needless to say, this anonymous game developer is provided with a "bug fix" for his physics "problem" because the customer is always right!

To make things worse, Hollywood movies do a great job of redefining physics to make it visually more appealing or spectacular. Did you ever wonder why most cars in movies explode in a huge fireball when they are in an accident? Is this realistic or alchemistic? Or did you ever wonder about the destructive power of a laser sword in *Star Wars* (1977)? Such swords must have pretty efficient power supplies in their hilts; I would definitely love to try out such a power supply to replace those lame batteries in my laptop! Game developers have widely adopted the Hollywood look and feel for their games. Who has ever wondered why racing cars rarely flip over in games? The answer is that in such games, a car's center of gravity is often placed below the road level, thereby stabilizing it like the keel of a ship. Game physics simulation has to meet expectations set by Hollywood movie special effects ranging from zero gravity to spectacular explosions, while at the same time providing the game with a realistic, consistent and stable world.

But special effects are just one of several features that make a movie or a game excel. Despite the massive use of technology, it is ultimately the plot that makes the difference. After all, the entire purpose of physics simulation is theoretically to improve the quality of gaming. Or is it more the quality of playing that is supposed to improve?

Gaming versus Playing

My personal definition of gaming is a more or less structured activity performed according to a set of rules or even laws. In contrast to gaming, playing is fantasy-driven and less limited by fixed rules, although the definition of rules can be an integral part of playing. For me, a typical game is chess or *Monopoly*, but also a lottery, while a typical form of play is building with Lego or a role-play such as "Barbie fights the dark knight of the castle." In observing my children, I very often get the impression that playing becomes more attractive the more that rules are violated in a structured way. Complete anarchy in a game, however, like in a "fully destructible environment," in my opinion definitely destroys gameplay. Considering my two definitions of gaming and playing, one could ask whether or not physics simulation as used in most of today's physics-enabled games really helps to improve the quality of gaming.

Conclusions and Outlook

Game physics definitely has a bright future; the technology behind it is just beginning to be widely used in games. Nevertheless, there are many more challenges that a physics engine and computer peripherals must master before gamers can make full use of the simulation concept. From a usability point of view, there should be a set of shared rules for physics interaction. Even advanced human-machine interface devices such as force feedback joysticks and inertia-driven game controllers lack the ability to accurately interface the player with the three-dimensional worlds of game physics. From a programmer's point of view, the API (Application Programming Interface) of a physics engine should be standardized pretty much the same way as today's graphics APIs are. Without going into the technical details, I will say that physics simulation is extremely computationally demanding. Graphics chips manufacturers such as NVIDIA and ATI/AMD are in a fierce battle with Intel and also Ageia to meet these demands and to provide additional computational power for physics simulations. It is difficult to predict the outcome of this battle, but it is certain that physics simulation technology will greatly advance in such a competitive environment.

◆ Newton, I. (1687), *Philosophiae Naturalis Principia Mathematica,* London. ◆ *Star Wars* (Movies) (1977-2005), produced and distributed by Lucasfilm and 20th Century Fox.

ZORK
Text-based Spatiality

```
ZORK I: The Great Underground Empire
Copyright (c) 1981, 1982, 1983 Infocom, Inc. All rights reserved.
ZORK is a registered trademark of Infocom, Inc.
Revision 88 / Serial number 840726

West of House
You are standing in an open field west of a white house, with a boarded front
door.
There is a small mailbox here.

>open mailbox
Opening the small mailbox reveals a leaflet.

>read leaflet
(Taken)
"WELCOME TO ZORK!

ZORK is a game of adventure, danger, and low cunning. In it you will explore
some of the most amazing territory ever seen by mortals. No computer should be
without one!"
```

Areas within the Great Underground Empire – West of House, Flood Control Dam #3, Aragain Falls – are vivid, but have an unusual appearance compared to the spaces in many other video games. They are presented entirely textually, within a type of game called a *text adventure*, in which the player types short natural-language commands and reads the text that the computer outputs in reply. The *Empire* was originally carved out by four authors/programmers at the Massachusetts Institute of Technology (Zork 1977-1979). The personal-computer trilogy that followed (Zork I 1980, Zork II 1981 and Zork III 1982: Infocom) helped set the standard for interactive fiction and inspired other games, both textual and graphical.

Zork draws on *Adventure* (Crowther & Woods 1975), which was the first text adventure and was based on a real cave. Both of these games include an above-ground forest that opens to an underground space, a treasure hunt, magic, fantastical opponents and the same interactive framework. *Zork* adds to this the simulation of containers and vehicles, the ability to understand more complex sentences and richer actors. One of these actors is the thief, who, like the gamer/adventurer, travels through the *Zork* world stealing loot. The fictional landscape of *Zork* incorporates both technological and fantasy elements, and tends to mock the bureaucracy and comment on the culture of the university where it was developed (Montfort 2003, *Twisty Little Passages*). The *Zork* creators also carved out

64

absurd spaces – a giant underground reservoir and dam, for example – quite unlike those that exist in *Adventure*.

     Zork's architecture mimics *Adventure's* in that it uses the caver's concept of discrete "rooms" that are connected by passages. Typing "go south," "south" or simply "s" moves the adventurer to a new room; while magic provides some shortcuts, it takes time and typing to traverse the *Empire*. Movement feels more like "walking" through a directory structure than like steering an avatar in a first-person shooter or Massively Multiplayer Online Game (MMOG). Drawing a map on paper is a standard technique for playing interactive fiction; it is helpful in many cases and essential for dealing with mazes. And indeed, a player can mentally map *Zork's* world. But the problems posed in *Zork* require conceptual thinking and experimentation, not the careful positioning required in platformers and some graphical adventure games. Space does matter, however: because the ability to engage characters in deep conversations does not exist, the surroundings particularly enrich the game and give context to the puzzles and figures encountered, providing backstory and helping to defamiliarize the everyday.

Game Review	Text	Developer	Publisher
	Martin Nerurkar	DMA Design	Psygnosis, 1991

LEMMINGS
Navigation through Obstacles in the Landscape

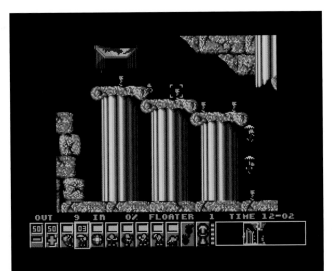

In *Lemmings*, first released for the Amiga in 1991, the player has to safely herd small creatures from their entry point in a level to that level's exit. The game shows the world from a side view, giving the player control over a cursor with which to guide his scores of lemmings.

The entire environment – as is common in many video games – is an obstacle to the player on his way to success. It is filled with, for example, blocked paths that have to be cleared or chasms that need to be bridged so that the small creatures don't fall to their deaths. Unlike most video game worlds, however, it does not remain a passive obstacle, but becomes a puzzle that the player must actively deal with, figuring out ways to change it in order to succeed.

A level is completed once a set number of lemmings have reached the exit. To get them there unharmed, the player has a limited supply of different actions he can have his creatures execute. He can make those in front stop and block those behind them, forcing the whole lot to turn around. He can let them explode to create holes in the surrounding area. He can even have them dig in various directions or build bridges. The existence of these different possible behaviors means that many levels in *Lemmings* can be solved in multiple ways.

However, all of the actions the lemmings take are indirect; that is, the player can select an action and click on a lemming to force it to behave accordingly, but he has no way of manipulating the environment directly. Herein lies the main conflict of the game: the player has to figure out a path through the world and literally create it by having the lemmings change that world. Even though he is free to move his cursor anywhere on the screen, he cannot interact where there are no creatures.

When interaction does occur, it operates on a very fine scale. Most games that allow the player to change the environment employ a grid of sorts. This helps quantify changes in the environment that are caused by the player. *Lemmings* has no visible grid and instead reduces the smallest unit down to individual pixels. This produces a finely-grained world that makes precise timing even more important. It also helps display more of the world on-screen at any given moment.

Lemmings benefits from the simplicity of its two-dimensional space: as the game relies on accurate control over the mass of beings, a third dimension would add an immeasurable amount of complexity.

Game Review	Text	Developer	Publisher
	Clara Fernández-Vara	Team 17	Team 17, Ocean Software, 1994

WORMS
Battling On- and Off-Screen

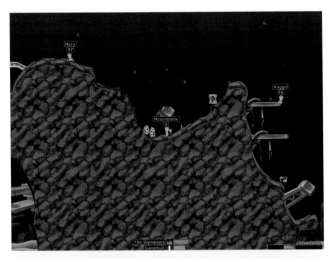

Worms is a classic turn-based strategy game in which the player controls a squadron of four worms who have to destroy the opponents' worms, be they human- or computer-controlled. At the beginning of the game, the terrain is generated, and the player gets a general view of the playfield. The player can then accept to play in that terrain or ask the computer to generate a different one; if the player has its code number, she can also choose to play in a specific terrain.

Once the game starts, the point of view zooms into the playfield, which can be explored by dragging the mouse to survey the whole area. The worms can crawl and jump slowly from their original positions within the limited time of the turn, though obstacles can very much constrict their movement. Players thus not so much navigate the worms freely through space as position them to aim better or take refuge from future attacks. Depending on the type of terrain – from

http://worms.team17.com

beaches to mountains, from Mars to Hell – either a few or many obstacles will hamper the already limited movement of the worms. All terrains include, for example, some sort of liquid-filled chasm (e.g. water-filled or lava-filled) into which worms may fall and drown. The player can use ropes to climb to ledges, girders to go over chasms and a couple of turns to teleport a worm from one point to another. Spending too much time moving troops, however, may waste precious turns to blast the enemy.

The generated terrain transforms during gameplay; the explosions of most attacks, for example, leave craters in the ground. These can either expose a worm by making its position vulnerable or create a tunnel that can be used as shelter or to reach the enemy's position from below ground. Craters can also serve as obstacles to delay other worms from reaching one's position or as a means by which to isolate the enemy from the mainland.

The spatial challenge of the game is that it is a 2D space that usually cannot be contained in one single screen during gameplay, so that the player must pan from side to side to learn the locations of all the worms. Often, enemies may be within the range of fire, but not within the range of the screen, forcing the player to picture the whole space in her mind in order to plan an attack. Though the gameworld is not very extensive – usually no more than two or three screens wide – its constant reshaping keeps the challenges of the game fresh and engaging.

MAX PAYNE
The Dream of Control over Time

Max Payne is a third-person shooter set in a noir New York full of gangsters, drugs, prostitutes and corrupted politicians. The main character, for whom the game is named, is a policeman looking for revenge against the people who killed his family. In a presentation to the press before the official release of the game in July 2001, a trailer was shown featuring the brand new "bullet time," the technical and ludic improvement that differentiates *Max Payne* from all previous third-person shooters. The idea for "bullet time" came directly from *The Matrix* series (War-ner Bros. et al. 1999): by pressing a button on the keyboard, the player can slow down time and move in slow motion just like characters in the movies. Thanks to this feature, the player can handle multiple enemies at once, avoiding their shoots and firing with extreme precision. At the same time, however, Max Payne is extremely vulnerable, and the villains are very often stronger than normal people thanks to their intake of super-drugs.

www.rockstargames.com/maxpayne

"Bullet time" is a magnified satisfaction of a yearning that lies behind much computer game playing: the dream of control over time. Games are very often concerned with control, and in order to give it to their players, they need to make a very clear distinction between what is allowed and what is not. Space is defined as a place where the player can move or cannot move, and the breaching of its rules is usually defined as a "bug" in the game, an error not foreseen by its programmers. Time is another defined entity. The rules that govern it dictate that it can be stopped; it's possible to pause games or rewind them by saving and reloading. *Max Payne* also includes these genre-defining features of third-person shooters – i.e. the possibility to save and a strict control over the places that can and cannot be visited. In the game, the player has to follow a very clear path and challenge all the enemies room by room.

"Bullet time" is just an add-on, something more for the player's ludic and aesthetic pleasure. It transforms fights into quasi-ballets in which the meaning of a position – its importance – is defined as a function of the position of other objects and human characters on screen. As in a dance, every step of the fight determines and is determined by the steps of the other "dancers." This happens in a slow motion that shows every single movement of the arms, the shoulders, the pelvis and the legs of Max Payne.

Take away this purely aesthetic pleasure, and *Max Payne* does little to revolutionize the genre. Its only innovation, maybe, is a clear consciousness of the conception of time and space in third-person shooters. After all, to play with the flow of time is a way of playing with the rules of the genre.

Project Description	Text	Project	Affiliation
	Michael Nitsche	Michael Nitsche, Calvin Ashmore, Jason Alderman, Mike Biggs, Kate Compton, Rob Fitzpatrick, Will Hankinson, Matthias Shapiro	Experimental Game Lab, Georgia Tech University, Atlanta, US, supported by Turner Broadcasting, Atlanta, US, 2005

CHARBITAT
Procedural Player-driven Gamespaces

Charbitat is an experimental game project. The setting is a virtual world inspired by Asian motifs that features a young princess as the main player-controlled character. The princess has been poisoned, and the poison has destroyed the internal balance of elements necessary for the well-being of body and mind. Now she is in a coma, trapped in a potentially infinite dreamscape in which these elements run amok. Players navigate the heroine through this world in search of a cure.

Although computers are procedural engines, video games rarely utilize these procedural powers for the generation of their gameworlds. If they do, it often remains on the level of random level generators. In contrast, *Charbitat* connects procedurally generated gameworlds to the interaction of the player. Depending on how the game is played, new sections of an infinite and consistent 3D world materialize. The players consciously generate the world while playing in it. They not only fight monsters and overcome obstacles, but simultaneously have to balance the generation of this world.

Charbitat is a full modification of the Unreal Engine with a Java program running in parallel to support world generation. The 3D world consists of separate tiles that seamlessly attach to each other and gradually form the gameworld. Whenever the player reaches the end of one tile and steps into the space beyond, a new tile is generated based on the player's performance. The system creates specific terrain, including rivers, roads, forests and cliffs, which it populates with objects, lights, sounds and entities. We use Taoism's elemental system of wood, fire, earth, metal and water as the main variables to drive this world creation. Each object and entity has certain elemental values attached to it. There are, for example, five enemy classes, one for each element. Defeating a fire enemy will raise the player's fire value, which in turn implies a stronger fire theme for the next generated tile. In this way, the player directly affects the growth of the world. We also use this feature to direct interaction and structure quests through the world via procedurally generated patterns that organize thresholds and keys as well as visual aids for orientation and navigation.

http://egl.gatech.edu/charbitat

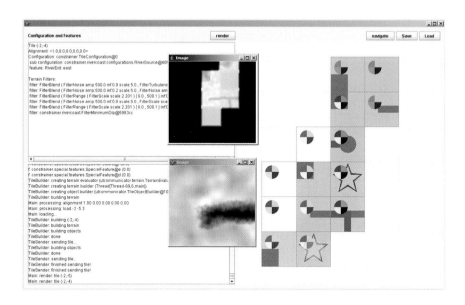

Clara Fernández-Vara

LABYRINTH AND MAZE
Video Game Navigation Challenges

Since Plutarch wrote about the myth of the Minotaur, labyrinths and mazes have been visual motifs, both as architectural spaces and as metaphors. Physically, labyrinths and mazes are bounded spaces to be traversed; their main purpose is to delay the walker as he goes from point A to point B. This delay can be achieved by extending the distance between those two points, tracing meandering paths or branching those paths and forcing the walker to guess the correct one. Confusion and disorientation are also ways to obstruct the path to the exit. Metaphorically, literary labyrinths and mazes thrive on just such confusion as well as on the impossibility of their representation – think, for example, of Borges' short tale "La Biblioteca de Babel" (The Library of Babel) (1995). The video game, as a digital medium whose basic properties include spatiality (Murray 1997, p. 79), has also taken up the maze as a common motif and added new properties to it. Most significantly, instead of just recreating physical spaces, some games represent impossible spaces that until recently were only conceivable in literature.

In the gaming context, the general term for any intricate structure is "labyrinth"; this term refers to all labyrinthine structures, including mazes. The terms "labyrinth" and "maze" tend to be used interchangeably, even though Umberto Eco (1984, pp. 80-81) and Hermann Kern (2000, p. 23) have (separately) made a very useful distinction between the two. The classic labyrinth is unicursal – that is, it consists of one single winding path that folds within itself; the labyrinth in Chartres Cathedral is the classic example of this type. Though walkers cannot get lost traversing such a labyrinth, they are disorientated and delayed in the seemingly simple process of going from one point to another. Labyrinths do not present a test to their visitors; rather, they are a way to stretch the distance from one point to another. The absence of a difficult task along with the existence of a unique path, make labyrinths an unproductive structure in video games. If there is only a single path the game feels as though it is "on rails" like a theme park ride: the user cannot choose where to go. Unicursal structures are thus scarce in video games. Even games that go "on rails," such as *House of the Dead* (1997), offer branching paths (though the player cannot really get lost because all branches eventually lead to the same place).

The maze is a special type of labyrinth that was born as a literary construct and later became a visual space (Kern 2000, p. 23). Mazes are more complex than classical labyrinths; they are multicursal, meaning that there are many ways in which they can be traversed. They are characterized by branching paths and dead ends so that the walker is forced to choose her direction. Video games favor maze structures since navigating them already constitutes a challenge, which can be further

The classic labyrinth.

amplified by obstacles along the path, such as enemies, chasms or projectiles. They represent a consistent architectural location, imitating a space that is in accordance with our perception of the physical world. Games such as *Wolfenstein 3D* (1992) or *Castlevania: Symphony of the Night* (1997) present spaces that can be mapped and traced as if they were real. These spaces are stable and unchangeable.

When dealing with mazes and labyrinths, one must also bear in mind the fact that having a complete view of the circuit is very different from being inside the circuit. Solving a maze from a top-down view, as in *Maze Craze* (1980), is relatively easier than solving it while walking inside it, as in *3D Monster Maze* (1982). Looking in on the maze from above, the walker knows where she starts and where she is supposed to go and can preview the route she wants to take. From a first-person point of view, on the other hand, the walker is forced to navigate in order to learn what the structure of the space is and to make a mental map of it.

The quintessential top-down maze game is *Pac-Man* (1980), which presents a multicursal structure, but one in which the player cannot get lost because she has a complete view of the playfield. The meandering paths are meant to delay and hinder the movement from one spot on the screen to another. Conversely, in *Pac-Man Vs.* (2003), up to four players control the ghosts simultaneously chasing Pac-Man in a 3D maze, but they have a limited view of the space around them and do not have a map. In this case, the playfield is more disorienting and feels more like the maze that it is.

The paths in video game labyrinths can also be dynamic. They can include, for example, walls that open and close so that timing becomes an important factor in their navigation. *Lock 'n' Chase* (1981), for instance, is an interesting variation on the *Pac-Man* model: the player character is the famous thief Lupin, who must pick up the treasures in a maze without getting caught. The doors play an important strategic role, as the player can open and close them (for a limited time) in order to stall the policemen chasing him. Other interesting examples of dynamic mazes (though they are not usually referred to as such) are the popular *Snake*-type games, such as *Nibbles* (1990). In *Nibbles*, the player must move a snake around the screen, picking up food and thereby elongating the snake's body. The player must avoid hitting walls – either those surrounding the playfield or those of the obstacles that appear in the middle of it – as well as the snake's own body, which becomes yet another wall and one in constant motion, at that. Because the snake can only move forward, not pull back, the player must be careful not to end up in a cul-de-sac as a result of the snake's meandering, since that would mean that the game is over. Video games can challenge traditional concepts of mazes by creating liminal spaces that seem to reproduce physical spaces but in fact incorporate ever-changing, unmappable features. This topic has already been addressed by some philosophers, though not in the context of video games. In addition to classical labyrinths and multicursal mazes, Eco proposed a third type of labyrinthine space: the rhizome. Based on a concept first proposed by Gilles Deleuze and Felix Guattari, Eco describes the rhizome as a structure in which every point is interconnected with every other point. Eco equates encyclopedias with labyrinths, which makes it all the more appropriate that the structure of the Internet is often considered to be a rhizome. The encyclopedic properties of video games as digital media (Murray 1997, p. 83) also make it possible to integrate some of the qualities of the rhizome into the creation of digital spaces that are unstable, untraceable and volatile. This variability increases the challenges of navigation, since the inherent confusion caused by navigating the maze is combined with the confusion caused by encountering digital elements that have no real-world equivalents.

At times, the complication can arise simply from a segmented representation of the whole space. This is the case, for instance, in the original *Prince of Persia* (1990), in which finding the way out of the dungeon in the first level is made more complex by having to traverse the space screen by screen. This fragmentation can also be exploited to create unmappable spaces, which constitute mazes in and of themselves. The signpost maze in *The Legend of Zelda: The Minish Cap* (2005) is one such maze, generated through the segmented representation of the space. The player must choose the correct exit to the next screen according to a given clue. For example, the player goes left in the first screen, then right, which does not take her back to the previous screen, but is actually the next step in the maze. If the player chooses the wrong exit, the player character, Link, will end up back in the first screen of the maze.

The challenge can also be increased by the possibility of creating spaces procedurally, so that a map is created on the fly. This is, for example, the case in *Rogue* (1983), in which the graphics are constructed with ASCII characters, and the player discloses the space as she navigates. The dungeon map is generated anew whenever a game starts, increasing the replay value by offering potentially infinite dungeon configurations.

Labyrinths as ways of directing and delaying navigation and mazes as challenges to traverse are not only good assets for video game worlds. The properties of digital media make them even more challenging by making the spaces they occupy dynamic, unstable and ever-changing or by proposing new spatial configurations that players are not familiar with in the real world.

The author wishes to thank Professor Manuel Aguirre, who introduced her to the study of labyrinths and other fictional spaces and encouraged her to pursue the study of video games.

◆ Borges, J. L. (1995), *Ficciones*, Alianza Editorial, Madrid. ◆ Eco, U. (1984), *Semiotics and the Philosophy of Language*, Indiana University Press, Bloomington. ◆ Kern, H. (2000), *Through the Labyrinth: Designs and Meanings over 5000 Years*, Prestel, Munich. ◆ Murray, J. H. (1997), *Hamlet On The Holodeck: The Future Of Narrative In Cyberspace*, The MIT Press, Cambridge MA. ◆ *3D Monster Maze* (Sinclair ZX81) (1982), developed by Malcolm Evans, published by J.K. Greye Software. ◆ *Castlevania: Symphony of the Night* (Sony PlayStation) (1997), developed and published by Konami, Japan Release. ◆ *House of the Dead* (Arcade) (1997), developed and published by Sega, US Release. ◆ *The Legend of Zelda: The Minish Cap* (Gameboy Advance) (2005), developed by Flagship Co. Ltd., published by Nintendo of America, US Release. ◆ *Lock 'n' Chase* (Arcade) (1981), developed by Data East, published by Taito. ◆ *Maze Craze: A Game of Cops 'n Robbers* (Atari 2600) (1980), developed and published by Atari, US Release. ◆ *Nibbles* (DOS) (1990), developed and published by Microsoft Game Studios. ◆ *Pac-Man* (Arcade) (1980), developed by Namco, Published by Midway, US Release. ◆ *Pac-Man Vs.* (GameCube) (2003), developed by Nintendo, published by Namco, US Release. ◆ *Prince of Persia* (DOS) (1990), developed and published by Brøderbund Software. ◆ *Rogue* (DOS) (1983), developed and published by Artificial Intelligence Design. ◆ *Wolfenstein 3D* (DOS) (1992), developed by id Software, published by Apogee Software.

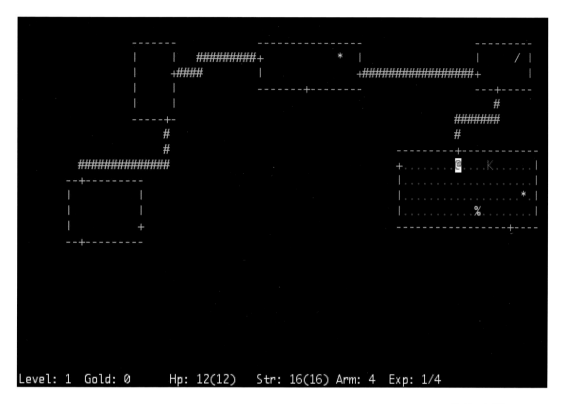

First level of *Rogue*,
procedurally generated.

PAC-MAN
A Maze with Multiple Meanings

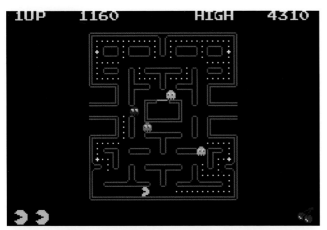

Pac-Man was the most popular arcade game in the world: over 100,000 machines were sold in the United States alone. The dream of Toru Iwatani, Pac-Man's designer, to create a nonviolent game that everyone could enjoy came true. Using the kanji word "taberu" – to eat – as a jumping off-point, Iwatani and his team devised a game in which Pac-Man, a little monster with a giant mouth, eats his way through a maze while outwitting his pursuers. Pac-Man was named after the Japanese colloquialism that describes a mouth opening and closing: "paku paku," and Pac-Man's shape is a rounded version of the kanji symbol for "mouth" (kuchi).

When playing Pac-Man, the player must balance three easily understandable and interrelated activities: eating pellets, avoiding ghosts and capturing ghosts. Clear and satisfying feedback explains what is going on and how far the player has to go. An overview of the player's progress towards the goal of clearing the maze is always apparent because every remaining pellet is visible. Key events such as the start of the game, getting caught and capturing a ghost are announced with theatrical flourishes that include dramatic sound effects, visual feedback and slowdowns in the flow of time.

Pac-Man is fascinating because of its dramatic rhythm and pacing. The movements of the ghosts, in Iwatani's own words, form "the heart of the game" and help generate a carefully calibrated rising and falling tension that climaxes as each level approaches its end. In this respect, *Pac-Man* prefigures *Metal Gear* (Konami 1987), *The Sims* (Maxis 2000) and *Façade* (Procedural Arts 2005), games in which drama and entertainment value hinge upon the behavior of virtual characters. Besides unleashing the feeling of revenge, the topsy-turvy reversals of power between Pac-Man and the ghosts, brought on by the consumption of the power pellets in the corners of the maze, nurture the game's dramatic pacing.

Spatially speaking, *Pac-Man*'s maze helps to structure the game's dynamics and drama. Power pellets are tucked away in the corners, making them hard-to-reach treats. As an arena, the maze forces the ghosts, Pac-Man and the pellets into constant contact, releasing a focused and continuous drama. The maze is also a recognizable puzzle form, which motivates the player to move through it. Tactically, the *Pac-Man* maze has multiple meanings: it is both an obstacle to acquiring food and escaping ghosts and a means to trap and outwit those ghosts. Each maze also functions as a level to complete, breaking the game up into discrete dramatic units. The escalating difficulty of each level helps to match player skill against difficulty and also serves as a metric for player accomplishment.

Game Review	Text	Developer	Publisher
	Stephen Jacobs	Blizzard North	Blizzard Entertainment, 1997

DIABLO
Randomness within Structure

Diablo is a real-time combat, point-and-click role-playing game (RPG) with single-player mode and networked (up to four) multiplayer modes. It was originally developed by the independent company Condor, which was purchased by Blizzard Entertainment in 1996 and renamed Blizzard North. *Diablo* was released by this Blizzard division in January of 1997. The game feature that I will focus on is the random regeneration of "dungeon" levels and quests, which gives *Diablo* an extremely high replay value.

Diablo is "set" in the town of Tristam in the Kingdom of Khandaras, which has been overtaken by an unknown evil. Tristam is a small rustic village populated by private and public dwellings, a well, some streams and creeks, a cathedral and a graveyard. The town is populated by seven nonplayable characters and functions primarily as a place to collect information about quests, to buy and sell items and to be healed.

Most of the action of *Diablo* takes place in the 16 levels below the town cathedral. In a "game" of *Diablo,* players must embark upon six to eight quests semi-randomly selected out of a pool of 30. The game provides them with a ¾-overhead isometric view of the ensuing action. The graphics are displayed 640x480 in 256 colors and include 3D modeled characters and real-time lighting effects in the dark dungeon levels. Quests, dungeon levels, monsters and loot are randomly generated with

www.blizzard.com/diablo

each new game. A convenient automap feature helps players remember where they've been and provides a limited view of where they haven't.

The look and feel of the subterranean world changes every four levels – that is, at levels 1 (the formal dungeons), 5 (catacombs of the older monastery ruins upon which the cathedral was built), 9 (lava-strewn caverns) and 13 (Hell itself, with much lava and few flames). In the first two types of level settings (i.e. dungeons and catacombs), dank, gray stone walls and stone patterns accentuate the dim environment navigated by the player character. The following eight levels are partially illuminated by lava. Real-time lighting effects brighten the area around the player with a circle of light whose radius can be enhanced by magical items. In these deeper-down levels, pools and streams of lava define a great deal of the terrain to be navigated, much as the formal stone walls do in the upper ones. Each of these levels also has portals with direct links to locations just outside of Tristam, meaning that the player is spared a lot of stair climbing. Travel from dungeon level to town can also be accomplished by the use of a "Scroll of Town Portal" anywhere, at any time.

Garnering nine out of ten points or better in reviews when it first appeared, *Diablo* revitalized interest in RPGs and represented another triumph for its publisher and its early, often-emulated network, battlezone.net, the system behind the networked play.

SILENT HILL 2
Space as Maze

Labyrinthine structures belong to the functional network core of the new computer game medium. To understand this analytically, one must distinguish, like philosopher Umberto Eco, between three types of labyrinths: the meander, the maze and the rhizome. *Silent Hill 2* belongs to the set of complex games that interweave the three labyrinthine architectures and are enhanced by their various effects. The game makes use, for example, of the contemplative impact of the meander through a long, (almost) uneventful path that one's avatar must walk in order to reach the entrance sequence to the small town Silent Hill. But the focusing of one's mind in preparation for the ensuing game is then radically disturbed by the audible presence of a hostile entity. The architecture of the safe, salvation path to the godly "center" from the diabolical periphery becomes a dynamic space on the road towards certain calamity. And, in the course of solving the game's plot puzzle, the dead nook in which the monster lurks is changed into a metaphor: it is no longer an architectural entity, but rather the blind spot of self-surveillance.

In form as in content, *Silent Hill 2* can be described as a maze. The player must follow a multiply branched story that, in the end, leads her to the "center" – a (if not *the*) solution. This narrative tree structure is mapped in the form of paths through the labyrinthine cityscape of Silent Hill. The progress the player makes in the story parallels the development of the urban space, which is displayed visually in the map function that can be called up. But *Silent Hill 2* uses this provision of (apparent) overview as a narrative snare; throughout the course of the game, the discursive ordinal schemata (left/right, in/out, good/bad) are increasingly dissolved. And in the end, the main character must (like Oedipus) recognize his own guilt, while the game's player must recognize the fact that she has – through many perils – identified herself with a murderer.

The spatial organization of the prison visit shown in the game's introductory sequence is prototypical of the game's staged disintegration of binary structures: a close look reveals that it is unclear on which side of the prison bars the player (and the hero) is located. In true avant-garde fashion, the game thereby simultaneously circumvents not only the border between in and out, good and bad, but also between game and life, art and reality. For the first time, a computer game has made possible a rhizomatic openness that can instigate an infinite process – the metaphysical shuddering that accompanies the search for one's own identity.

SPLINTER CELL
On the Dark Side of Gameplay

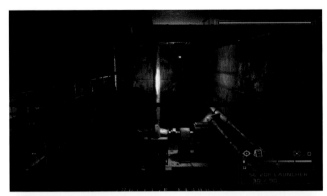

Splinter Cell was born out of a desire to manipulate light and shadow – a concept that has spanned four episodes to date. The franchise is rooted in realism – of environments, physical abilities and stories. The tension between light and shadow not only defined the gameplay but also had a tremendous impact on how we created the environments and the way we thought of those spaces. Our initial intention was to create very realistic settings: not small "boxes" linked by corridors, but real architectural spaces in which realism and gameplay necessities were to be mixed.

In creating the first *Splinter Cell*, we focused on providing original and unique spaces. We pushed realism to levels of detail rarely approached in those days, detailing plumbing, HVAC systems and electrical components. Those elements, born from a wish to re-create reality, were then used in the gameplay; that is, players were required to interact with some of them (e.g. climbing on a pipe). Producing the realistic environments and designing interesting gameplay proved to be two sides of the same coin; both are omnipresent, and each enhances the other. And the provision of a free-cam and access to usually inaccessible areas offered the player a new perception of the spaces created.

The core gameplay was based on the "shadowpath," defined as the strict opposition between light and shadow. Shadow spaces were the territory of the player – the place where he could hide. Lit spaces were the territory of the system. The amount of light vs. shadow formed gameplay complexity. We were defining "non-spaces" within our environments: using the realism of our initial architectural intentions, we created volumes that were outside the system. Within his own shadow territory, the player was in a private space, nonexistent for the system (unless because of some player error). Transgression and tension, the results of going from the private space to the public space, were necessary to moving forward; the shadowpath was intentionally broken to get this result.

While shadows and darkness are traditionally used to either mask a problem or solve a technical limitation (such as memory), our intensive use of shadowed areas forced us to be detailed and precise in order to offer a visually appealing experience.

Introduction of new shader technology turned *SC1*'s very "mechanical" use of light and shadow into a more artistic exploration in *Splinter Cell: Chaos Theory* (Ubisoft 2005), the game's second episode. From "non-space" in a realistic environment to an artistic expression of realism, we made shadows the highlight of the *Splinter Cell* franchise. For the first time, the opposition of light and shadow became the space-defining element of a game and the means by which complex hierarchies of space were created.

Game Review	Text	Developer	Publisher
	Julian Kücklich	LucasArts	LucasArts, 1993

SAM & MAX HIT THE ROAD
Unrealistic Freedom

When *Sam & Max Hit the Road* was published in 1993, the era of point-and-click adventure games was already coming to an end. Early first-person shooters such as *Wolfenstein 3D* (id Software 1992) promised unlimited freedom of movement, while the adventure game genre still relied on 2D graphics and a limited number of paths a player could take. If the space of *Doom* (id Software 1993) and its ilk was cinematic, adventure game space was theatrical. The individual screens of games like *Maniac Mansion* (LucasArts 1987) or *Space Quest* (Serria On-Line 1986) were like backdrops on a stage, and characters would typically enter the screen on one side, similar to actors in a play.

But *Sam & Max* stretched these generic conventions to their breaking point. While earlier LucasArts games had already begun to experiment with the rules of the genre, the makers of *Sam & Max* went even further in trying to break the mold. The cinematic trailer sets the mood for the game, evoking memories of *Day of the Tentacle* (LucasArts 1993) and catapulting the player into a similar world of distorted perspectives and cartoonish proportions.

Yet at the same time, the game has a distinct film noir feel to it, which is only heightened by the option to play the game in black and white.

One of the earliest locations the player explores in the game is a carnival that boasts dubious attractions like the aptly named Cone of Tragedy. A Hall of Oddities exhibits bizarre freaks of nature such as the three-legged Insect Lad, a tap-headed Human Enigma and a grotesquely overweight man in a giant test tube under a sign that reads, "Man or Chicken Dumpling?" This Barthian fun house is a metaphorical microcosm of the caricatured image of America depicted in *Sam & Max*.

As a guide to this utopian place, the player is given a postcard that shows an obscenely bloated continent that bulges rather than stretches from sea to shining sea. Superimposed on this image are the words "Greetings from the USA." The landscape is dotted with peculiar sights such as the World's Largest Ball of Twine, the Mystery Vortex and the Celebrity Vegetable Museum. Even stranger than these odd landmarks, however, is the overwhelming emptiness of this place, whose monotony is broken only by the occasional roadside fast food joint.

The places scattered in this immense empty space, on the other hand, are lavishly decked out with the brightest eye candy, achieving an effect of visual overabundance. This baroque splendor makes the sparsely decorated interiors of first-person shooters look quite impoverished by comparison. If the vast American landscape is a nod towards the new breed of games, its locations are a jubilant celebration of the possibilities of two dimensions unencumbered by geometry, physics or probability. Thus *Sam & Max* brilliantly displayed the strengths of a genre that was soon to be surpassed by more realistic games and reveled in the freedom that came from being blatantly and gloriously unrealistic.

STEERING THROUGH THE MICROWORLD
A Short History and Terminology of Video Game Controllers

The first game console that reached the mass market came with analog and digital controllers. Atari's paddles on the left and archetypical 1-button joysticks on the right (1977).

Electronic Game Basics: A "Closed-loop System"

Computer and video game systems combine three main elements: computer, display and controller, the latter being the computer's interface with the human user. While the computer processes data, renders graphics, takes the user's input, etc., the display shows the game and the controller allows human to interact with the game.

An early, simplified definition of such systems came from Walter H. Buchsbaum: "The player watches the game display and acts on it by manipulating the controls" (Buchsbaum 1979, p.5). This manipulation, in turn, changes the flow of the game running on the computer. As Buchsbaum stated, the player and the three elements form a closed-loop system in which all "must be able to interface with each other correctly" (ibid., p.6).

This hasn't changed since the invention of electronic games. In this essay, I will show how game mechanics and level architectures influenced the evolution and diversification of controlling devices.

Digital and Analog Game Controllers

Manipulated by a human user, the game controller enables the avatar's movement within the computer-generated gameworld.[1] Technically, the basic elements of most controllers are the digital switch (which may have two positions: on or off) and the analog potentiometer. The switch is the prototype of all digital elements of a controller, most notably "fire buttons," but also "choice devices" (Foley et al. 1995, p. 352) like Start and Select buttons. The modern joypad's steering cross ("d-pad") uses four or eight switches, one for each direction of movement.

< 1

In this text, I use the term "avatar" for a game's main object, vehicle or hero, which is always moved via the controller.

In contrast, the potentiometer, which came in the shape of a dial ("game paddle") in early games, creates analog movement: tracked and translated into on-screen movement is not only the direction in which it is pushed, but also the intensity of the player's manipulation – that is, how hard, fast or far the controller is moved. Analog devices don't give on or off signals, but rather a more accurate continuous signal, which brings acceleration into the game.

Potentiometers make very precise and smooth movement possible. American sociologist David Sudnow describes the feeling of analog game control in his 1983 book, *Pilgrim in the Microworld*: "That's how knob [the game paddle] and paddle [avatar] are geared, a natural correspondence of scale between the body's motion, the equipment, and the environs preserved in the interface. There's that world space over there, this one over there, and we traverse the wired gap with motions that make us nonetheless feel in a balanced extending touch with things." (Sudnow 1983)

Sudnow goes on to describe the early Atari game *Breakout* (1976): "Held by the fingertips and rotated... the little paddle steering wheel afforded rapid enough horizontal movement... to handle the pace of action ... Ideally geared for travel through the terrains and tempos of a microwold." (Sudnow 1983)

Almost 20 years later, Chris Kohler experienced a similar feeling: "Arcade joysticks ...were digital ... the signal was only 'on' or 'off', regardless how hard you pressed. But the analog joystick measured how far you pushed it." (Kohler 2005, p.75)

To differentiate between analog devices and digital controllers, computer scientists called the latter "joyswitch" (Foley et al. 1995). But generally, the term "joystick" is common for all kinds of stick-shaped controllers.

Controller Types and Complexity

The evolution of controlling devices is inextricably linked with the evolution of game content and game environment.

Early gamespaces were not 3D spaces, but "flat" ones shown from the side or from above. The movement of the avatar was limited to one axis and thus two directions: the paddles of *PONG* (1972) moved up and down (y-axis), and the cannon of *Space Invaders* (1978) moved left and right (x-axis). Early controllers followed a very simple layout: bi-directional movement on one axis can be achieved through either two buttons, one joystick or one dial (i.e. one potentiometer).

Soon devices for four-way steering were created; movement on both x-axis and y-axis could be achieved using either four buttons, one joystick or one trackball (i.e. two potentiometers).[2]

Most action games were controlled by a joystick, but there were exceptions. The spacecraft of *Defender* (1980), for example, was controlled by buttons only, which made the game appropriate only for experienced (or bold) players. Later, some home computers stuck to the button-only control scheme until the end of the 90s. Many PC games were controlled by the four cursor buttons or by many buttons on the keyboard.

< 2

Flight and other vehicle simulators created a niche for themselves as the only games that rendered real-time vector and polygon graphics at a time when all other games moved flat and hand-drawn pictures. For movement within a 3D environment, special "flight sticks" were used. Some of them had a third degree of freedom – the stick could be twisted clockwise and counterclockwise on the so-called "z-axis." Other variants came with a "coolie hat" on top, a small, thumb-operated digital joystick. While simulator software and special controllers were too complicated and expensive for the average user in their early days, their 360-degree maneuverability hinted at things to come for mainstream gamers.

Early Game Movement, Early Game Architecture

In early games, the avatar moved through empty space; there was no architecture. Also, movement was on one axis only. Both the lack of architecture and the limited movement were the result of technical limitations that were soon overcome. A third attribute that some games had in common is particularly interesting from a game designer's point of view: movement was often the only way of interaction between the player/avatar and the game/gameworld. In *PONG* or *Pac-Man* (1980), for example, all the player was allowed to do was move.

Pac-Man was one of the first games with a distinctive level architecture. Nintendo's *Donkey Kong* (1981) tilted the maze mechanics from an overhead view to a side view, showing the hero's descent on a scaffold. Again, a joystick was used for the movement. In *Super Mario Bros.* (1985), an additional button enhanced Mario's mobility: while the jump was a means of defense in the debut game (in which Mario leaps over barrels), it became a fundamental kind of movement in later Super Mario games. The button-triggered jump expanded the gamespace and made possible more complex architecture. It coined level design and gave a prominent game genre its name: "Jump 'n Run."

The exploration of gamespace was the striking element of the games designed by Shigeru Miyamoto. While *Super Mario Bros.* had a horizontal scrolling world, remained linear and confined the player's exploration to the x-axis, *The Legend of Zelda* (1986) opened a new dimension. Kohler remembers: "Rather than being on the forced, straight line path of a Super Mario game, the player was able to move around the world of Hyrule at will, going form place to place in any of the four compass directions." (Kohler 2005, p.77)

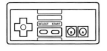

Joypads forced trackball, paddle and other controller types into niches. The classic joystick turned into the bigger and more robust "fight stick" for 2D action games. There were steering wheels and pedals for racing games, as well as a "light gun" that was pointed at the screen. Another pointing device that sneaked from the labs of Stanford and the Palo Alto Research Center into the game

The controller of choice for both Mario and Zelda games was Nintendo's "joypad."

Getting Complex, Then Getting Simple: Controllers During the 80s

The joysticks of the 1980s were usually equipped with one or two fire buttons, but became increasingly glutted with additional elements by later manufacturers. At the climax of their evolution, even small keyboards ("keypads") were integrated into the devices. Controllers used by the Intellivision and ColecoVision video game systems were so complex that they outdistanced contemporary game content and mechanics: the devices offered too much functionality and couldn't yet be used to their utmost potential by software designers or players.

Over-complicated joysticks were not the only reason that the video game market crashed in 1984, but a simplified controller scheme did play a major role in the renaissance of game consoles. This comeback was triggered by Nintendo in Japan, while Atari failed in the US. Nintendo rethought controls and gave its NES game system small joypads: the manufacturer shrank the stick down to a small cross that could be manipulated with one finger. To the right of this d-pad were two fire buttons. All other companies embraced (i.e. copied) this simple concept, and the joypad became the dominant game controller. Its basic layout wasn't changed for almost a decade, apart from the addition of action buttons: Sega's joypad (1989) sported three fire buttons, while the Super NES controller (1990) sported four, as well as two "shoulder buttons," digital switches placed on the joypad's back for manipulation with the index fingers.[3]

scene was the mouse, which was conceived as an easy-to-use device to accompany or replace the multi-function keyboard. It triggered many new games: *SimCity* (1989), *Lemmings* (1990) and *Populous* (1990) are some famous examples of mouse-controlled games in which not creatures or vehicles, but windows, icons and other graphical elements are manipulated.

< 3

Getting Complex Again: The 3D Controller of the 90s

When gameworlds became 3D in the mid-90s, Nintendo took the analog joystick from the world of simulation and brought it as an innovation to the mainstream. In the process, it was downsized to fit between the d-pad and fire buttons. With stick, d-pad, eight buttons and an analog "z-trigger," the N64's joypad (1996) was the most complex to date. Kohler remembers the sensation of using it: "[It] featured something revolutionary for a console game system: an analog joystick. Pushing the joystick a tiny bit would make Mario tiptoe, pushing it halfway would make him walk at normal speed, and all the way would make him run at full speed." (Kohler 2005, p.75)[4]

Rivals Sega and Sony likewise upgraded their joypads. Two analog "thumbsticks" became standard with the release of Sony's DualShock pad for PlayStation 2 (2000). In most cases, the second stick handled the 3D camera.

Today's game controllers freely mix digital and analog elements: on the joypads of modern consoles, even shoulder and fire buttons work as analog devices – throttle and brake for sensitive fingers.

< 4

More controller functionality was also needed because the 360-degree gamespace created new ways of movement. For example, there are different ways to go in one direction in 3D games: the avatar can go right by turning right, but also by sidestepping ("strafing") right, whereby it moves in the desired direction without changing its line of sight.

Modern Controllers

The 21st century's joypads provide the player with vast possibilities for movement and interaction and thereby satisfy the needs of experienced players. On the other hand, video game newcomers, casual gamers and light users, all of whom are major target groups for the industry, can be discouraged by the complex joypads of the PlayStation age. The control device is thus not the key to gaming pleasure, but rather an obstacle for potential players.

Donald A. Norman, former director of the Institute of Cognitive Science at the University of California, San Diego, noticed a similar problem a decade earlier when he analyzed the universal input device for personal computers: the keyboard. He compared Apple's product design to that of Nintendo and applauded the latter: "Nintendo takes advantage of specialized input devices. Computer users tend to use the keyboard for everything, but as usual, specialization is superior" (Norman 1990, p. 212). He clearly saw the strength of simplicity and the problems of multi-function devices.

Complexity haunted game software too: the move to 3D turned simple fun into real-time simulation, with complicated features and increasingly demanding mechanics. Many games offered too much, and newcomers were frustrated, not entertained. In reaction, new game mechanics emerged that stood in sharp contrast to 3D adventure, shooting and strategy games. Konami's *Beatmania* (1997), for example, was not controlled by a joystick, but by five rectangular black and white keys arranged to resemble the layout of a piano. While the left hand played music, the

Movement is the game, and the game is movement in *Katamari Damacy* (2004): the New Wave of Japanese game design picks up early mechanics of *Pac-Man*.

second control element – an imitation of a turntable – was manipulated by the right hand to simulate "scratching." While *Beatmania* was targeted at male and female youth, the nine huge and brightly colored action buttons of its derivation, *Pop'n Music* (1998), were geared toward children. Another example of a game with intuitive not intellectual controls is *Dance Dance Revolution* (1998), which is completely played with the feet.

Children, girls and other people who tend to shun traditional "hardcore" games, are attracted to such simplified control schemes because they don't come with the strain of having to memorize complicated layouts and assignments. In 2002, Sony successfully reached out to this target group with a camera that tracked body movement; the EyeToy made switches and potentiometers obsolete, just as did the microphone of Sony's karaoke video game, *Singstar* (2004). Voice-controlled games became reality.

To pay tribute to the wish for simplified controls, the hardware manufacturers integrated motion tracking into their current joypads: Sony's six-axis controller for PlayStation 3 (2006) senses orientation and acceleration, with the integrated gyroscope giving the player six degrees of freedom. Nintendo uses accelerometers for the controllers that come with its Wii console. Both concepts combine traditional elements (d-pad and analog sticks) with the ability to track the natural movement of the human body or hand.

92

Closing the Loop

Will mind-controlled games be the next, maybe last, step of the evolution? In fact, games are already played without any body movement, as biomedical researcher Tony Fitzpatrick reports: "The use of a grid atop the brain to record brain surface signals is a brain-machine interface technique that uses electrocorticographic (ECoG) activity-data" (Fitzpatrick 2004). He cites Daniel Moran of Washington University: "The patients could play [a] game by using signals that come off the surface of the brain." Indeed in 2006, Moran and his team were able to report on the first mind-controlled game of *Space Invaders*, during which a 14-year-old suffering from epilepsy "cleared out the whole level basically on brain control" (Fitzpatrick 2006).

"We closed the loop" (ibid.): Moran's statement is a nice phrase with which to end this chapter, though his research may not be as relevant to video games as it is to medicine. The mind interacting directly with things outside the body – this is a dream of humanity, of course. On the other hand, there might be a reason why God gave us fingers.

◆ *Beatmania* (1997), developed by Koji Okamoto and team, published by Konami. ◆ *Breakout* (1976), developed and published by Atari. ◆ Buchsbaum, W.H. (1979), *Electronic Games*, McGraw-Hill, New York NY. ◆ *Dance Dance Revolution* (1998), developed and published by Konami. ◆ *Defender* (1980), developed and published by Williams Electronics. ◆ *Donkey Kong* (1981), developed and published by Nintendo. ◆ *EyeToy* (2003), developed by SCEE Studio London, published by Sony Computer Entertainment Europe. ◆ Fitzpatrick, T. (2004), "Human subjects play mind games, "*Washington University in St. Louis News & Information*. Retrieved June 9, 2004, from http://news-info.wustl.edu/tips/page/normal/911.html ◆ Fitzpatrick, T. (2006), "Teenager moves video icons just by imagination, "*Washington University in St. Louis News & Information*. Retrieved October 9, 2006, from http://news-info.wustl.edu/news/page/normal/7800.html ◆ Foley J.D., van Dam, A., Feiner, S.K. & Hughes, J.F. (1995), *Computer Graphics – Principles and Practice*, 2nd edition in C, Addison-Wesley, New York NY. ◆ Forster, W. (2003), *Joysticks*, Gameplan, Utting Germany. ◆ Forster, W. (2005), *The Encyclopedia of Game Machines*, Gameplan, Utting Germany. ◆ *Katamari Damacy* (2004), developed and published by Namco. ◆ Kohler, C. (2005), *Power Up*, BradyGames/Pearson, Indianapolis IN. ◆ *The Legend of Zelda* (1986), developed and published by Nintendo. ◆ Norman, D.A. (1990), "Why Interfaces Don't Work," in B. Laurel (ed.), *The Art of Human Computer Interface Design*, Addison-Wesley, New York NY, pp. 209-218. ◆ *Pac-Man* (1980), developed by Namco, published by Midway. ◆ *PONG* (1972), developed and published by Atari. ◆ *Pop'n Music* (1998), developed and published by Konami. ◆ *Singstar* (2004), developed by SCEE Studio London, published by Sony Computer Entertainment Europe. ◆ *Space Invaders* (1978), developed by Taito, published by Midway. ◆ Sudnow, D. (1983), *Pilgrim in the Microworld*, Warner Books, New York NY. ◆ *Super Mario Bros.* (1985), developed and published by Nintendo.

KIRBY: CANVAS CURSE
A New Interface Covers New Space

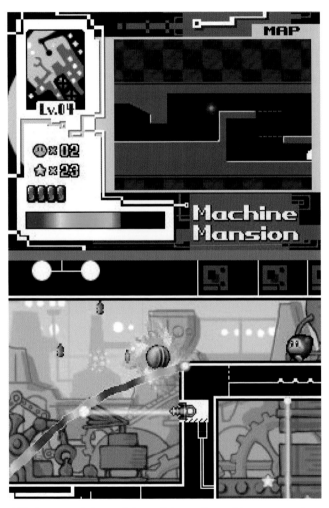

Kirby: Canvas Curse appeared in 2005, in the early days of the Nintendo DS when solid titles demonstrating the platform's uniqueness were most needed. As such, it received much critical acclaim not only for its innovative gameplay, but especially because it was much more than a short-lived gimmick pasted onto existing formulas.

Self in relation to space: Players interact with the game through a combination of direct and indirect stylus controls on the touchscreen. The mixture takes some getting used to because the player's mind has to shift gears constantly between drawing around Kirby and touching him directly, even to produce a similar result (i.e. movement). The nature of this scheme accentuates the existence of the interface and the separation between you, the player and the world with which you interact because the only common element in all your actions, the stylus, doesn't exist in the world's fiction. As the game's television spot highlighted, you are not Kirby, you are rather a protective force in the shape of an oversized finger, pushing or guiding the lemming-like ball of pinkness.

Mastering new space: What sets *Canvas Curse* apart from earlier similar attempts at having players draw lines to indirectly interact with a character (namely, *Yoshi Touch & Go* (Nintendo 2005)) is its intensive combination of complete spatial freedom with skill-based limits. You are free to explore the totality of a level in almost any direction, at any pace, so long as you do not run out of ink to draw lines. Drawn lines fade progressively after a few moments, replenishing your meter so that you are able to draw additional lines. This encourages a conservationist gameplay mindset in which the player seeks to gain maximum effect with minimal input, thereby reinforcing the guardian identity over the protagonist identity. As the player progresses to more advanced levels, his abilities evolve in response to the growing complexity of the challenges that face him: managing surface versus air space, necessary momentum versus side-scroller framing and the chaos of hostile enemies versus Kirby's adaptive arsenal. This conscious mastery of the spatial grammar, fueled by flexible exploration skill, ensures an intense gameplay experience, which is the key to why *Kirby: Canvas Curse* remains a platform reference even a few years after its release.

Game Review	Text	Developer	Publisher
	Julian Kücklich	Namco	Namco, 2004

KATAMARI DAMACY
Rolling up the World

Fried Rice

Falling Rock

The most amazing thing about *Katamari Damacy* is the staggering sense of scale it conveys to the player. Playing as the minuscule son of the King of All Cosmos – a truly imposing father figure – a player starts to roll up tiny objects such as pushpins, erasers and pieces of candy. This is what the game is all about: rolling things up with the prince's katamari ball, described on the game's back cover as a "rolling, sticking, never-stopping, ever-swelling clump of stuff."

In other words, everything touched by the katamari clings to it with a supernatural adhesive strength. Thus the ball keeps getting larger and larger, picking up larger and larger objects as it rolls along. Soon, the ball is large enough for the prince to venture outside and roll up the flowers, tools and toys in the garden. Of course, the katamari not only picks up inanimate objects, but people and animals as well. And we're not just talking about cats and dogs, but also cows, bears, giraffes, whales and even dinosaurs.

Every time the katamari's growing diameter passes a certain threshold, the player gains a better overview of the surroundings, as the gameworld and the objects within it become smaller in relation to the katamari. As the game progresses, the player's view of the world approaches a bird's-eye view. No longer confined by garden fences, roadblocks or even solid walls – all of which are integrated into the katamari – the prince soon begins to roll up cars, trees and roads.

There is an immense satisfaction in reaching the point at which you can roll up the house in which you started, complete with the dinner table on which you rolled up your very first object. You could even imagine a tiny katamari still rolling around inside the house, maybe pushed by one of the princes many cousins. In fact, every object in the gameworld could be a microcosm of tiny objects, each of which contains even smaller objects and so on, ad infinitum.

For all its primary-colored cheerfulness, *Katamari Damacy* is a profoundly philosophical game, as it invites the player to imagine worlds infinitesimally smaller and infinitely larger than our own. The result of this playful *mise en abyme* is an ontological vertigo rarely felt when playing video games. As surreal and incongruous as it may seem, *Katamari Damacy* is one of the few games that can make us view the world with fresh eyes.

Game Review	Text	Developer	Publisher
	Heather Kelley	SCEE Studio London	Sony Computer Entertainment Europe, 2003

EYETOY PLAY
Playing the Player's Image

Released in 2003 as the first game to work with Sony Computer Entertainment's camera add-on the EyeToy, *EyeToy: Play* is a minigame suite highlighting the physical play made possible by a video feed as gameplay input. In 12 minigames, players can watch their images on the TV screen and wave their arms, bend their knees and extend their hands to interact with other on-screen characters and objects. Most of the time, the players see themselves in reflection, with their left arms visible on the left side of the screen and so on.

One might presume that such a physical input would give a more three-dimensional, natural interaction experience. However, it quickly becomes apparent that the single-lens camera creates only a 2D surface. The game software is able to see boundary edges (such as the outline of the player's hand) and detect motion (such as when the player's hand is waved rapidly). The game thus uses physical gestures, but only understands and reacts to these physical gestures within a flat plane. As a result, the player's body space works as a 2D image generator, mapping to the game's equally flat play space.

Within this context, the player-game interface is intuitive. The minigame *Soccer Craze* asks the player to mimic the head-butting action of a soccer player to keep a virtual ball in the air. The game *Slap*

Stream is a 2D "whack-a-mole" that detects when the player makes a slapping hand gesture toward the screen. A number of the games, as well as the game's menu interface, require a "waving" gesture. The wave movement adds an element of time to the game input – it's necessary to continue waving in one place over the course of a few seconds.

One minigame of special note is *Mirror Time*. Like *Slap Stream*, it asks the player to hit certain characters on the screen and avoid hitting others. This gameplay is straightforward, but after a few rounds of normal play, one enemy character reorients the screen image, rotating or flipping it relative to the normal mode and thus relative to the player's normal actions. For instance, the player may need to raise her arm in order to reach an enemy appearing at the bottom of the screen or move her hands to the left to hit an enemy on the right. More difficult modes divide the screen into two or four independent quadrants so that, for instance, the two arms on screen may need to be controlled by moving in completely different directions. This reorientation changes with every round of play and requires the player to discover each time how the sections of the screen have been altered. The fun of *Mirror Time*, more than any other minigame in *EyeToy: Play*, is that it challenges the presumed natural relationship between the player's body and her reflected image on a 2D screen.

VARIATION OVER TIME
The Transformation of Space in Single-screen Action Games

The question is this: How can a game provide variation to keep the player interested?

The question implies a few assumptions; I assume that players generally prefer games with some element of difficulty, but that the level of difficulty should change during the playing of the game. Players generally respond very negatively to games they find too easy or too hard, and players respond very negatively towards games they perceive as repetitive. All games run the risk of exhaustion, of the player reaching a point where he or she experiences the game as not presenting anything new.

Difficulty forces players to reconsider their strategies. We can conveniently distinguish between quantitative and qualitative variations in difficulty. For example, in a hypothetical game in which the player must collect boxes within a specific time period, the difficulty of the game can be modified in two ways: *quantitative difficulty change* (e.g. require the player to collect more objects during the allotted time period or make the time period shorter) or *qualitative difficulty change* (e.g. modify the layout of the playing field or provide the player with new obstacles or tools).

A player will then have several ways of improving his or her *performance*: quantitatively (by, for example, making decisions faster and turning around corners more quickly) or by qualitatively modifying playing strategies (by finding a shorter route through the playing field, for instance).

A quantitative difficulty increase may be overcome by improving playing strategies quantitatively *or* qualitatively, but a qualitative increase in difficulty *requires* the player to make a qualitative change in strategy – to look at the game in a new way.

Process over Data

My interest here is in a specific way of providing variation, the qualitative change of difficulty that is created by modifying the playing field during a game level. This is a type of design in which obstacles are gradually removed and the playing field becomes more open as a result. We can see this design in a number of board games (e.g. backgammon, chess, checkers), and it was a popular design in the non-scrolling action game, most prominently in the 1980s. But for reasons I will discuss later, this design is unusual in contemporary video games.

Consider *Space Invaders* (1978) as a first example. In *Space Invaders*, shooting the opponents speeds up the game and changes the playfield. Shooting columns of opponents to the side of the field buys the player time, as it slows the opponents' advance towards the player. Shooting rows of opponents at the bottom (generally considered the inferior strategy) also buys the player time. Each level begins with an almost-full screen of slow-moving opponents and ends with an almost-empty screen of fast-moving opponents.

In a fundamental way, this is what makes *Space Invaders* an interesting game: the player must adapt to a constantly changing playing field and modify it by shooting, thereby influencing the strategies that will be needed during the rest of the level.

Using this game as a jumping off point, we can for a moment consider a video game *poetics* that celebrates games with a minimal number of elements working together to create variation and depth. According to game designer Chris Crawford, video games *should* focus on calculation over data, on *process intensity* over the storage of data.

The role of information storage in a computer is often misunderstood. A computer is not primarily an information storage device; it is instead an information processing device. Thus a game that sports huge quantities of static data is not making best use of the strengths of the machine. Rather, a game that emphasizes information processing and treats information dynamically is more in tune with the machine. Another argument in favor of this precept arises from more fundamental considerations about the nature of gameplay. Interactiveness is a central element of game enjoyment. As mentioned earlier, the computer's plasticity makes it an intrinsically interactive device. Yet the potential inherent in the computer can easily go unrealized if a game is programmed poorly. A program emphasizing static data is not very dynamic. It is not plastic, hence not responsive, hence not interactive. A process-intensive program, by contrast, is dynamic, plastic, responsive and interactive. Therefore, store less and process more (Crawford 1982, p. 96).

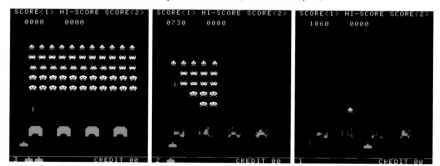

Space Invaders (1978)

In Crawford's view, then, *Space Invaders* could constitute a landmark work, perhaps a pinnacle of video game design. The basic economy of the game is a maximal amount of variation from a minimal amount of data. It is worth noting that the speeding up of opponents in *Space Invaders* is quite "in tune with the machine" in that it is born out of technological necessity: the machine only moves one opponent at a time, so fewer opponents on the screen means that each opponent is updated more frequently and consequently moves faster.

Changing Spaces

Space Invaders exemplifies the process-over-storage game design and its corresponding playing experience. I will now touch briefly on three additional games similarly characterized by level layouts that change during levels.

Pac-Man (1980) and *Ms. Pac-Man* (1981) are games in which the playing field changes not by way of obstacles being removed, but by the removal of *targets* that the player seeks out: the dots and power pills. The player must plan ahead so that the later stages of a level do not leave him or her completely vulnerable, as they do when, for example he or she eats all the power pills too soon.

Ms. Pac-Man (1981)

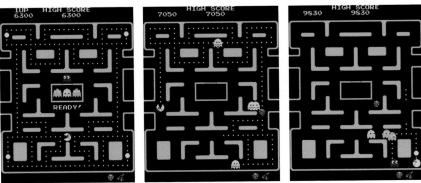

Pengo (1982) begins with a labyrinthine level layout, which the player can modify by destroying its constituent tiles or which the monsters may destroy in search of the player. Unlike in *Pac-Man*, the paths of the playing field change during a level. A special bonus is awarded for aligning three diamonds. Aligning the diamonds is easier when the level is more open, but at that point, the player is also less protected by walls, creating an interesting trade-off for the player who wants to reach a high score.

Pengo (1982)

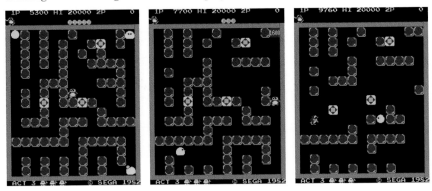

Super Bomberman (1993) is quite similar to *Pengo* in having a labyrinth that gradually becomes an open landscape, in this case playable as a multiplayer game. In it, players must blow up obstacles (at the risk of mistakenly blowing themselves up). *Super Bomberman* is special in that it has two distinct phases, a beginning during which players are isolated and cannot reach each other and an endgame during which players can directly attack each other. The opening of the level space thus entails meeting other players, and this yields a structured and tellable gameplay centered on personal mistakes, allowing for taunts during the buildup towards and preparation for the actual showdown.

Data over Process

Game variation by means of a playing field that opens up during each level is the signature of a specific moment in video game history. In Chris Crawford's argument, video games *should* be like this: possessing the beauty of having the same basic setup and rules and generating variation using these means only. Ironically, it is straightforward to turn this argument on its head: the introduction of the high-capacity game cartridges and CD-ROMs as distribution formats made game machines into good *storage* devices. The history of game design is not simply a result of technological developments, but increases in data storage capacity certainly *allowed* the scrolling game to replace the non-scrolling game: suddenly, new playing experiences came from games that were *data-intensive*, and the processual economy of the changing level layout became irrelevant.

Learning to play any game is a process of creating strategies for playing that game, but changing the level layout forces the player to constantly reconsider his or her strategies. In the history of video games, this way of creating variation was superseded by data storage, by new games with vast expanses for the player to explore.

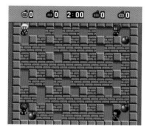 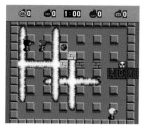 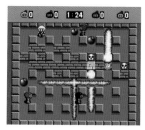

Super Bomberman (1993)

◆ Crawford, C. (1982), *The Art of Computer Game Design*. Retrieved January 2, 2007, from http://www.mindsim.com/MindSim/Corporate/artCGD.pdf ◆ *Ms. Pac-Man* (Arcade) (1981), developed and published by Midway. ◆ *Pac-Man* (Arcade) (1980), developed by Namco, published by Midway. ◆ *Pengo* (Arcade) (1982), developed and published by Sega. ◆ *Space Invaders* (Arcade) (1978), developed by Taito, published by Midway. ◆ *Super Bomberman* (SNES) (1993), developed and published by Hudson Soft.

Game Review	Text	Developer	Publisher
	Ed Byrne	David Braben, Ian Bell	Acornsoft, Firebird, 1984

ELITE
Living Space

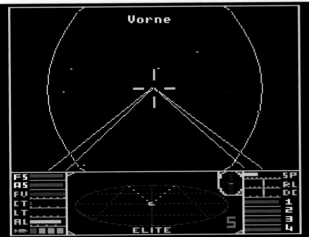

Elite was a landmark "space trading" computer game. Inside its humble 22K footprint lay the foundation for a modern video game mainstay: a dynamic 3D universe responsive to the player's actions with player-driven goals. It transcended the "arcade" mentality and microcosms of its contemporaries and paved the way for modern epics such as *Eve Online* (CCP Games 2003), *Elder Scrolls: Oblivion* (Bethesda Softworks 2006) and even *Grand Theft Auto* (Rockstar North et al. 1997-2006). From the start, there were no tutorials, no obvious path and no helpful assistant; the player was delivered into an unforgiving universe and allowed to reach the ultimate goal of being ranked "Elite" through whatever means – moral and physical – he deemed appropriate.

The use of space and time in *Elite* was groundbreaking. When first released in 1984, its realistic representation of space as a 3D world rendered as wire-frame models set it clearly apart from its contemporaries.

It was arguably the first game to deliver truly immersive spaceflight; instead of basic directional controls (up, down, left and right), the pilot had to get used to rolling his ship while pitching up or down at the same time. To gamers accustomed to text or 2D views of the cosmos, the frictionless movement, immense distances and overall sense of space in *Elite* were magical.

In fact, the sheer scale of the gameworld was staggering for the time. Its universe contained thousands of planetary systems spread out amongst eight galaxies. Each system had variables – such as a market economy and relative safety – that led to a wide variety of potential encounters or events. Even the timescale for success was unusual: a player would need weeks, sometimes years, of play to reach "Elite" status.

Ultimately, *Elite* was most impressive in that it didn't restrict access to the gameworld based on the user's progress. There was little progress-metered content, and the impact of *Elite*'s immense, dangerous universe on the novice was incredibly intimidating. As a fledgling pilot, every hyperspace jump was a tense transition into the void. Early encounters were often deadly, forcing the player to stick to familiar planets and avoid undue exploration. However, as the player's skills and resources strengthened, the wide-open spaces of the universe changed from a malevolent fabric into a wealth of opportunities and lucrative encounters. The systems that at first had been avoided so thoroughly became favored haunts – space became tame. And as the player transformed, so did his environment. While this sort of depth is present, even expected, in modern titles, it was *Elite*'s creators Ian Bell and David Braben who first delivered it to the common gamer.

Game Review	Text	Developer	Publisher
	Drew Davidson	Ubisoft Montreal Studios	Ubisoft, 2003

PRINCE OF PERSIA
Time as Gameplay

Prince of Persia: The Sands of Time was released on multiple consoles (PS2, GameCube and XBox) in 2003. Spatially speaking, it is a linear game that uses architecture to constrain the player and control the flow of the game. *The Sands of Time* takes place in a palace under attack by hordes of zombies that were released along with the sands of time when the hourglass holding them was broken. Players have to move forward through the palace in a balance of gameplay, with moments of platforming through the space interspersed with moments of combat within the space.

Interaction with space is thus the defining characteristic of how you as the player make your way through the game. The effects of the overarching battle often alter the spaces to create more daunting platforming challenges. And peppered throughout the game, little detours – sometimes hidden behind suspicious-looking walls – often present a choice between two routes. If you take these detours, you find yourself running through sheer curtains into a black darkness and then reappearing near an ethereal set of suspended bridges bathed in shimmering blue light. Crossing these bridges brings you to a fountain of sparkling water, which, when drunk, induces a trance and extends your health bar. This magical space is never directly connected to any of the other spaces, and upon returning to the palace, you find that the detour has vanished.

www.princeotpersiagame.com/sandsoftime/us

You also spend much of the game working to help a princess flee the pal-ace. She is not as physically dexterous as you the prince, and you often have to figure out how to help her get through spaces. Thus space becomes something you have to consider twice.

Furthermore, the game is driven by a spatial goal. You have to get to the top of the tallest tower in order to return the sands of time to the hourglass. You see this tower throughout the game and are thereby con-stantly reminded of your end goal of getting to the top of it.

In addition to space, this game incorporates the element of time, which you must manipulate to your advantage throughout the course of play. You gain control over time by sucking up the spilled sands of time when you find them in piles, or by dispatching the sand zombies. Pos-sessing sand gives you the ability to rewind time, stop time, speed up time, etc. With this power in hand, you can, for example, miss a jump while platforming and quickly rewind to try it again. And during combat, you can freeze zombies or speed yourself up so that you can kill sever-al of them in a flash.

The game ends with a time-shifting twist (spoilers ahead): to successfully complete it, you actually return to its beginning, so that the catastrophe – i.e. the hourglass breaking – never happened. In ef-fect, the whole game you just played has no longer occurred. The game ends where it begins.

SUPER MARIO 64
Hyperdimensional Space

Published for Nintendo 64 in 1996, *Super Mario 64* was a follow-up to the hugely successful *Super Mario Bros.*, which had been released for Nintendo Entertainment System (NES) in 1985. *Super Mario 64* transformed the flat world of Mario and his signature platform mechanics into three dimensions. No longer bound by the limits of the screen, Mario was now free to run, jump, swim, crawl and tiptoe in any direction. Shigeru Miyamoto, the game's designer, had created a new kind of experience, a game that transcended genres and, effectively, a textbook for intuitive level design.

The environment itself was constructed as a platform game only in the sense that its conceptual focus is the intersection of space and time; *Super Mario 64* is a game about being in the right place at the right time. The game *is* the environment – exploring, understanding and mastering its rules, negotiating its obstacles and avoiding its dangers.

From the opening moments of the game, as the camera swirls down from the clouds and flies over Princess Peach's Castle, there is a distinct sense of the tactility of the environment. The innovative uses of third-person perspective, an analog controller, the water and particle effects – all lend to the realism of Mario's world and the suspension of disbelief. But it is the simple act of moving Mario around the castle grounds, bounding him about with a hearty "Wahoo!," which actualizes the innately satisfying sense of interacting with material objects in a tangible environment.

The gamespace is simultaneously a sprawling, open-ended world and a quiet, closed and intimate space. Never before its 1996 release had a game felt so physical, expressive, tactile and real. Playing *Super Mario 64* is almost like playing with a physical toy. Modern games seek to enhance the sense of immersion using the illusion of infinite depth, whereas *Mario 64* seduces the user with the intimacy of its construction.

The castle's paintings act as portals to each of the game's levels, creating a magical, hyperdimensional space. The entire gameworld is thus connected through the central hub of the castle. Each environment operates according to its own microcosm of rules and mechanics. Miyamoto describes this design aesthetic as a "miniature garden" composed of a multiplicity of environments that form an integral, necessary whole.

The physical logic of each space acts as a rhetorical device, instructing and directing the user. The levels are constructed to allude to future moments – one of Miyamoto's trademarks. Players are introduced to the level's layout, learn its basic rules, explore its limits and complete the goal. Placed tantalizingly out of reach, inaccessible goodies compel the player to return recursively to gain a new ability or sudden insight. The effect of this design is to provide players with spaces that they uncover slowly, as though peeling back the layers of an onion.

LISTEN TO THE BULK OF THE ICEBERG
On the Impact of Sound in Digital Games

Sound established itself as a defining element of computer and video games right from the first attempts and experiments that eventually led to the complex and diverse games we face today. Although the first version of *Spacewar!* (1962) had no means of generating sound, audio capabilities were developed and added shortly after its first release. It could even be argued that the experience of sound in the first generation of video and tele-games sparked the subsequent development of sonifying GUIs (Graphical User Interface) if one considers that, for example, Steve Wozniak ported *Breakout* for the Apple II in 1977 and specifically added a speaker with 1 bit of sound. At present, it would be hard not to agree that video and computer games have to be regarded as audiovisual media systems par excellence.

In this context, it is puzzling that the impact of sound has been at best considered very briefly and at worst entirely disregarded in the discourse surrounding digital games. For the purpose of this essay, I am not interested in the details of sound technology, which already have been widely described and discussed, but rather in what sound truly means for the medium and how it affects the spatiotemporal nature of games. Whereas I have previously attempted to develop a model that addresses the very specific roles and functions of different types of sounds within the game universe (Stockburger 2003), I want to maintain a slightly more withdrawn approach here. Before detail can become fruitful, it is necessary to return to certain very basic issues that lead straight to the core of what could be regarded as the unconscious realm of digital games. In order to do this, we will have to leave the visual tip of the iceberg on the surface and attempt to dive a bit deeper.

Animated Life

When Sergej Eisenstein was considering the potential of adding sound to film in 1929, he was deeply affected by Disney's early cartoon films, such as the famous *Steamboat Willy* (1928). Douglas Kahn writes about this period of change: "[w]hereas Eisenstein sought to find an auditive equivalent to his visually derived montage, Disney extended the elements of silent cinema into sound under the actuality (not metaphoricity) of music in such a way that the music and sound performed the visual elements of the film – its characters, objects and actions" (Kahn 2001, p. 149). The sounds "performing" the elastic transformations of the cartoon bodies can be regarded as a kind of glue or gum that averts the disintegration of the visual elements and provides the necessary coherence for the actions on screen. "Voices, sounds, and music," Kahn writes, "were spread over the bodies of both characters

110

and objects in a new form of homologous puppetry, whether a squeaking elbow joint, fly footsteps, flesh ripped off to play a rib-cage xylophone, or a piece of clothing mentioned in the title or verse of a familiar song"(ibid.). In other words, the tight linkage and synchronization between specific sounds and noises and their visual counterparts literally brought the phantasmatic cartoon world to life.

The sonic sphere in games has exactly the same function – namely, that of providing the spark of life for a complex universe of visual characters, objects and actions. One of the major differences between video game sound and cartoon film sound, however, is that in the former, the link between objects, actions, places and sounds is usually maintained throughout the whole period of gameplay. Thus sound effects transcend their normally ephemeral quality and instead become permanently associated with certain game actions, locations and characters, essentially helping to create a "living" audiovisual world that becomes familiar and believable to the player. This was a highly significant function at the time when games were visually very reduced and abstract, but it has never lost its importance even in the present day. What, then, are the spatiotemporal characteristics of this "life" in the game universe?

Auditory Space

Marshall McLuhan describes the particularities of auditory experience as follows: "[t]he universe is the potential map of auditory space. We are not Argus-eyed but we are Argus-eared. We hear instantly anything from any direction and at any distance within very wide limits. Whereas the eyes are bounded, directed, and limited to considerably less than half the visible world at any given moment, the ears are all-encompassing, constantly alert to any sound originating in their boundless sphere" (McLuhan 1960, p. 69). It is precisely this sensory disposition that constitutes the basics of the role of sound in the simulation of the 3D environments that have become standard in contemporary digital games. While at any given moment the player is engaging with a small visual fraction of the gamespace, the auditory sphere remains always open and activates the remaining space. Whether sounds signal certain states in the gameplay, warn of enemy characters approaching from outside the visual field or generate the foundation for a spatial atmosphere does not matter. The crucial point is to realize that although much more has been written about 3D visualization techniques, it is truly sound that holds the key to fully accessing 3D representational spaces simply because the human perceptional system presupposes this. Thus scholars and commentators must recognize the integral and even primary role that sound can play in establishing gamespace. Sound in games enables the extension of spatial representation beyond the visual sphere and synchronizes the kinesthetic link between player and game through instant feedback. Or, in the words of Brenda Laurel, "[t]ight linkage between visual, kinesthetic, and auditory modalities is the key to the sense of immersion that is created by many computer games, simulations, and virtual-reality systems" (Laurel 1991, p. 161). From an auditory perspective, this "tight linkage" extends itself into the temporal aspects of gameplay and presents itself as a kind of rhythm.

System Rhythm

In this context, Claus Pias presents a crucial observation about the prototypical game *PONG* (1972) when he writes: "[t]he 'pong'-sound of the collision detection seems like the reward given by a responsible game for finding the right answer; its rhythmic recurrence enables the functioning of the game and makes audible the coupling between human and game in a shared system tact" (Pias 2002, p. 133). Here it becomes evident that apart from breathing life into visual characters and objects, it is crucial that sounds also mediate and demarcate the rhythm of the feedback system that emerges between player and game. The temporal structure of a game thus becomes audible in the form of a rhythm.

In his final published work, Henri Lefebvre sought to synthesize his earlier efforts concerning the nature of space with a new investigation into the structures of time in the form of a project dedicated to the analysis of rhythms. He envisages the discipline "Rhythmanalysis," which will generate "[...] a new field of knowledge (savoir): the analysis of rhythms; with consequences" (Lefebvre 2004, p. 3). Lefebvre positions the human body at the heart of this discipline when he writes "[t]he theory of rhythms is founded on the experience and knowledge (connaissance) of the body; the concepts derive from this consciousness and this knowledge; simultaneously banal and full of surprises – of the unknown and the misunderstood" (ibid., p. 67). But he expands the concept of rhythm to incorporate not only the "polyrhythmia" of the body but rather the entire sensual world when he states that "[e]verywhere where there is interaction between a place, a time and an expenditure of energy, there is a rhythm. Therefore: a) repetition (of movements, gestures, actions, situations, differences); b) interferences of linear processes and cyclical processes; c) birth, growth, peak, the decline and the end" (ibid., p. 15). All of the elements Lefebvre posits as inherent to rhythm are decisive factors in computer and video games. Firstly, repetitive structures are ubiquitous: consider the repetitive animation cycles, textures and movements, the inherently iterative nature of computer programming, the constant repetition of actions during gameplay (e.g. pressing a button), the repetition of parts of the game during gameplay and the repetition of spaces and places that are revisited throughout play. Secondly, interferences between the linear process of a teleological narrative space (i.e. find this object, kill this monster) and the cyclical processes that lead to closure are an integral feature of computer and video games.

However, in addition to this opposition between linear and cyclical structures, there exists a much more fundamental relationship between the two. Lefebvre writes, "[t]ime and space, the cyclical and the linear, exert a reciprocal action; they measure themselves against one another; each one makes itself and is made measuring-measure; everything is cyclical repetition through linear repetitions" (ibid., p. 8). This reciprocal relationship is geared towards a dialectic process whereby the synthesis unfurls itself as mediated and mediator: rhythm. In this context, game sound is clearly not the sole provider of the different rhythms originating from gameplay, but it aurally traces and defines the outer borders of the gameplay process and thus links the player's body to the machine. Lefebvre writes that "[i]n order to analyze a rhythm, one must get outside of it. Externality is necessary; and yet in order to grasp rhythm one must have been grasped by it, have given or abandoned oneself 'inwardly' to the time that is rhythmed" (ibid., p. 88). Interestingly, this shift between being grasped and remaining external resonates strongly with the problems facing anybody who attempts to analyze games since a perspective that remains "outside" is doomed to overlook the most valuable phenomena. In this sense, one has to hope that those who analyze the sonic worlds presented by digital games as well as those who create them start to listen much more closely to the bulk of the submerged iceberg that is game audio.

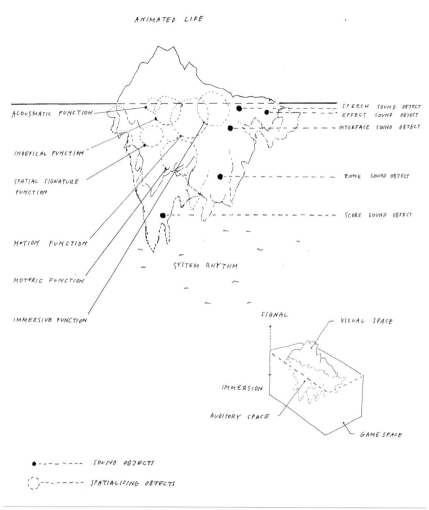

◆ *Breakout* (Apple II) (1977), developed by Steve Wozniak. ◆ Kahn, D. (2001), *Noise, Water, Meat: A History of Sound in the Arts*, MIT Press, Cambridge MA. ◆ Laurel, B. (1991), *Computers as Theatre*, Addison Wesley, Menlo Park CA. ◆ Lefebvre, H. (2004), *Rhythmanalysis: Space, Time And Everyday Life*, Continuum, London, New York. ◆ McLuhan, M. & Parker, H. (1968), *Through The Vanishing Point: Space in Poetry and Painting*, Harper & Row, New York. ◆ Pias, C. (2002), *Computer Spiel Welten*, Sequenzia Publishing, Munich. ◆ *PONG* (1972), developed and published by Atari. ◆ *Spacewar!* (1962), developed by Massachusetts Institute of Technology. ◆ Stockburger, A. (2003), "The Game Environment from an Auditive Perspective," paper given at: *LEVEL UP, Digital Games research Conference*, Utrecht, NL. Retrieved September 5, 2006, from: www.stockburger.co.uk/research/pdf/AUDIO-stockburger.pdf

Game Review	Text	Developer	Publisher
	Julian Kücklich	United Game Artists	SEGA, BigBen Interactive, Sony Computer Entertainment, 2001

REZ
Merging Sound and Space

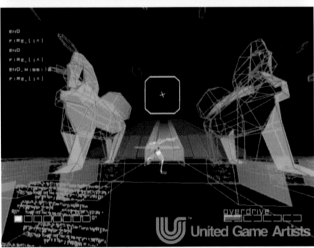

At first glance, *Rez* is reminiscent of early vector graphics, 3D computer games like *Battlezone* (Atari 1980). When the game begins, the screen is largely black, save for a small humanoid figure in its lower half, pulsating to the rhythm of a thumping heartbeat. Slowly, glowing objects emerge from the darkness, and as the player targets them, they are briefly connected in a pattern until the trigger is released and they dissolve in flashes of bright color. Simultaneously, layers upon layers are added to the soundtrack, and the heartbeat slowly segues into a hypnotic electronic music track.

The beauty of *Rez* lies in the way it goes from simplicity to complexity, from the sparseness of individual lines on a black screen to the richness of highly layered compositions, which nevertheless remain largely abstract. While the objects on the screen may resemble dragonflies, serpents, jellyfish or nautili, they never remain on screen long enough to disambiguate their abstract multivalence, like shapes glimpsed out of the corner of the eye. Some of them are even entirely abstract, like the iridescent cubes that mark the beginning of a new level segment.

In terms of gameplay, *Rez* might as well be a 2D vertical scrolling shooter because the third dimension is largely representational. But it is used to great effect, as the converging lines, hypnotic soundtrack and rhythmic pulsing of the DualShock controller lull the player into a mild trance. Synesthesia seems to be the entire point of the game, which is dedicated to the Russian painter Wassily Kandinsky. Kandinsky, well known for his synesthetic vision, may as well have been describing *Rez* when he said: "Color is the keyboard, the eyes are the hammers, the soul is the piano with many strings."

Indeed, the perception of space and the perception of sound in *Rez* seem to become indistinguishable from each other as the player progresses, enabling her to explore the individual layers of tracks, add sound effects and watch it all blend effortlessly into a seamless whole. In playing *Rez*, the difference between time and space becomes meaningless since the game creates a dream-like state in which everything flows and nothing remains constant. The game thus inverts Goethe's dictum that architecture is frozen music: in *Rez*, music is fluid architecture.

DESCENT
The Freedom of Movement in Space

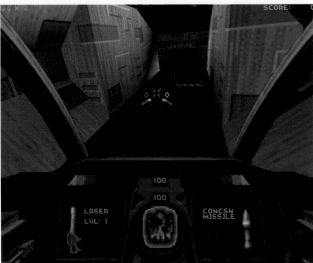

Descent uses 3D environments, zero gravity and a control scheme that allows motion through them in three axes at once. Released in 1995 – more than a year before its counterpart *Quake* (id Software 1996) – *Descent*'s unique blend of claustrophobia and disorienting navigation is an experience that few games have attempted since.

Descent takes place in a series of asteroid and planetary mines that grow in complexity with each new level. Laid out in a wire frame, the tunnels resemble overlapping, interconnected tubes, much like a hamster maze. They are complex, but can be traced by a careful eye. Where *Descent* makes its mark, however, is in the six degrees of freedom it offers players.

Other first-person games place the player in the role of a character with feet and a mostly terrestrial sense of gravity. "Down" is clearly marked, and orientation is a matter of compass points. *Descent* tosses Newtonian gravity out the window and allows the players to move their ships in any direction or combination of directions, provided they can master the controls. Simultaneously moving upwards and sideways and rotating to face a target is a necessary skill at higher difficulty levels or when playing experienced online opponents.

To the inexperienced player, this kind of motion immediately multiplies the complexity of the already winding environment several times over. It's not uncommon to see new players lose their orientation just trying to get from point A to point B, then spending a minute trying to reorient. Confusing at the best of times, this becomes deadly when the player is under attack.

Further complicating matters, each level ends with a timed rush for an exit. Without a solid mental map of the escape route and the corresponding piloting skills, the pressure of this sudden restriction dooms many players.

It's indicative of just how difficult – and nausea-inducing – most players found the game that despite its impressive 3D graphics and unique gameplay, it only ever reached cult status, never becoming truly mainstream the way *Doom* (id Software 1993) and later *Quake* did. To this day, however, no other game has matched the combination of claustrophobic tunnels and complete freedom of movement offered by *Descent* and its sequels.

Julian Kücklich

WALLHACKS AND AIMBOTS
How Cheating Changes the Perception of Gamespace

Learning how to play a computer game always involves learning how to negotiate gamespace. In simple games with a fixed perspective such as *Tetris* (1989), this is a trivial matter of associating buttons with movements on screen. In more complex games – especially 3D games such as *Half-Life* (1998), in which game space is experienced from a first-person or third-person perspective – this involves a process of inhabiting the body of one's on-screen representation and understanding this virtual body's relationship with gamespace. Generic conventions such as using the W, A, S and D keys on the computer keyboard for movement in first-person shooters simplify this process of inhabitation similarly to the way that learning the conventions of film enables the viewer to "suture" the gap between self and screen (Miller 1978).

However, gamespace is much more open to manipulation than real space or film space. The fact that gamespace is not bound by the laws of physics means that space does not have to be continuous; it's not an accident that teleportation is a recurrent motif in computer games. But even if there are no teleportation devices, the discontinuity of gamespace can be exploited. One especially interesting way of increasing the spatial possibilities of computer games is the practice of cheating. Cheats allow players to instantly teleport their avatars from one level to the next, to make them lighter than air to gain a bird's-eye view of the gameworld and to enable them to walk through walls. In other words: cheats offer numerous ways of changing players' perceptions of gamespace.

In game culture as well as in games research, cheating is often frowned upon, both in single-player and multiplayer settings. However, in order to appreciate the aesthetic qualities of cheating, one must understand that cheating encompasses a wide variety of practices and is, in many cases, a misnomer. Quite often, all cheat codes do alter certain representational elements of the gameworld, for example, by changing the weather in *Grand Theft Auto III* (2001). But even if cheats change the gameplay more profoundly, it is possible to regard them from an aesthetic perspective as gameplay techniques that exploit the malleability of gamespace. Thus cheats highlight the "topological constraints" (Aarseth 1997, p. 78) of gamespace and the way the player negotiates them.

This also draws attention to the fact that narrative and space are often deeply intertwined in games and that taking a shortcut through gamespace may entail speeding up narrative progression, a phenomenon that Roland Barthes (1975) described as "tmesis," or skipping, in regard to literary texts. But skipping is not the only way in which cheats can alter, distort or augment the perception of gamespace in 3D games.

118

Next to the "god mode" cheats, which make player characters invincible, the "fly mode" and "noclip mode" cheats are among the most common for first-person shooters. While the former does not need much explanation, the latter requires an understanding of how gamespace is constructed in 3D computer games. In computer games, clipping refers to a technology that determines whether or not an object is "solid" or "permeable." Turning clipping off thus enables the player character to pass through walls, floors and ceilings, often creating "broken" images of the gameworld and allowing access to otherwise inaccessible areas.

The disorienting hall-of-mirrors effect that results from tampering with the way the ingame camera renders images has also been used as an aesthetic purpose by artists such as Brody Condon and JODI, who have used first-person shooter technology to create original artworks in which the representational layer is ripped off a game to reveal the code that lies beneath. Cheating can thus be regarded as a means of laying bare the technological foundations of gamespace and of denaturalizing its representational aspects.

In this regard, cheating is quite similar to the phenomenon of "emergent gameplay," a term that refers to play strategies that have not been foreseen by the designers. One of the most famous examples of emergent gameplay is the possibility of using mines to climb walls in *Deus Ex* (2000), a practice which became known as "proximity mine climbing." Allowing the player character to scale sheer walls, proximity mine climbing brings with it a realization of the arbitrariness of the game's topological constraints and an understanding of the discontinuity of gamespace.

In multiplayer games such as *Counter-Strike* (1999) or *Battlefield 1942* (2002), this cheats-induced change in the perception of space is even more pronounced. Through the use of special plug-ins developed by the player community, cheaters can see through walls ("wallhacks"), shoot other player characters without taking aim ("aimbots") and embed topological information such as the distance between themselves and other players into the interface of the game. In massively multiplayer online games such as *EverQuest* (2003), programs like ShowEQ serve a similar function by displaying otherwise hidden information to the player who uses them. Therefore, cheats in online games can be seen as techniques of spatiotemporal manipulation that have a profound impact on how gamespace is perceived and negotiated not only by the player who uses them but by her opponents and teammates as well.

In multiplayer first-person shooter games, cheating is actively discouraged by players and server providers. Nevertheless, cheating is a widespread practice in all kinds of multiplayer settings, from amateur death matches to professional e-sports tournaments. "Aimbots" are probably one of the most widespread cheating devices and have been used at least since the publication of *Quake* (1996). When using an "aimbot," all the player usually has to do is establish line of sight with an opponent and pull the trigger – the "aimbot" will automatically aim to kill the other player's character. The change in the perception of space is rather slight, but considering that the complex topology of gamespace is one of the means of inspiring a sense of paranoia and threat in the player, these cheats can help the player to feel more in control of space and thus of the game.

"Wallhacks" alter the perception of gamespace much more obviously. Implementing these cheats allows players to see and sometimes even shoot through walls, thus enabling them to kill opponents from a position where they themselves cannot be seen. Similar to the "noclip mode" cheat of single-player games, some "wallhacks" also enable the player character to pass through walls. However, the use of "wallhacks" can be very disorienting for the player. If all the walls in a level are partially transparent, it becomes very hard to judge one's own position in gamespace. More sophisticated "wallhacks" remedy this problem by causing the game engine to draw characters and other game entities such as guns and ammunition on top of the level's architecture.

Due to the way that they can change players' perceptions of space, many cheats are referred to as ESP (extra-sensory perception) cheats. This evocative term seems especially appropriate for multi-cheats that combine several cheat features in one package. These might include a "distance ESP" that displays distances between player characters, a "weapon ESP," that identifies how opponents are armed and a "player ESP" that replaces the textures of the opponents' character models with a bright color, thus making them much easier to identify against visually complex backgrounds.

The combination of several cheat features can change a player's perception of gamespace quite radically. Combined with manipulations considered legitimate by most players – such as turning off the details in the game client in order to reduce potential distractions – cheats can cause the interfaces of hardcore gamers to differ substantially from the game's standard interface. Importantly, this spatial aesthetic is highly functional despite the fact that it might look quite confusing to an outside observer. Cheating is not only a way of stripping gamespace of its representational qualities, but also a way of revealing its functional architecture. From this perspective, cheating can be regarded as a way of deconstructing gamespace that allows players and academics to gain insight into the way space is constructed in computer games.

◆ Aarseth, E. (1997), *Cybertext - Perspectives on Ergodic Literature*, Johns Hopkins University Press, Baltimore MD. ◆ Barthes, R. (1975), *The Pleasure of the Text*, (R. Miller, trans.), Noonday, New York. ◆ *Battlefield 1942* (PC) (2002), developed by Digital Illusions, published by Electronic Arts, US Release. ◆ *Deus Ex* (PC) (2000), developed by Ion Storm, published by Eidos, US Release. ◆ *EverQuest* (PC) (2003), developed by Verant Interactive, published by Sony Online Entertainment, US Release. ◆ *Grand Theft Auto III* (Sony PlayStation 2) (2001), developed by DMA Design, published by Rockstar Games, UK Release. ◆ *Half-Life: Counter-Strike* (PC) (1999), modification of *Half-Life* (PC) (1998), developed by Valve Software, published by Sierra, UK Release. ◆ *Half-Life: Game of The Year Edition* (PC) (1998), developed by Valve Software, published by Sierra, UK Release. ◆ Miller, J.-A. (1978), "Suture: Elements of the Logic of the Signifier," *Screen*, vol. 18, no. 4, pp. 24-34. ◆ *Quake* (PC) (1996), developed and published by id Software, US Release. ◆ *Tetris* (Nintendo Game Boy) (1989), developed by Bulletproof Software, published by Nintendo of America, US Release.

Game Review	Text	Developer	Publisher
	Troels Degn Johansson	Amusement Vision	SEGA, 2001

SUPER MONKEY BALL
Mastering the Vertical Dimension

Super Monkey Ball (SMB) distinguishes itself amongst video games by its emphasis on the vertical dimension; it invites you to meditate on the role of vertigo and verticality – on falling and failing – in the construction of space and gameplay in computer games. As a video game, *SMB* is thus what scholars of literature would call a *mise en abyme*, a "staging of an abyss" (i.e. André Gide's pun on the French expression *mise en scène* (Gide 1948, *Journal 1889-1938*)). In *SMB*, the vertical dimension should be mastered (you must land on tiny islands with the ball glider) or avoided (you must not fall off golf courses, race tracks or fight arenas elevated almost astronomically above the ground). On the other hand, the game provides the (albeit dangerous) downslide acceleration and shortcuts that will give your baby monkey ball a lead in the race (e.g. by descending tilting planes or falling from one level to another while staying on the course). But most notably, verticality is emphasized by falling and failing. Slipping off the race track or shooting yourself off the golf course by mistake always means dropping into a spectacular free fall, losing the poor baby monkey in dark swamps, sparkling oceans or void desert-like spaces.

In *SMB*, your little monkey is trapped in a ball and can move only by trying to make the ball roll. In the fixed third-person perspective, rolling your monkey around is like tilting the planes of a world that passes by the ball rather than actually navigating the ball through a world; it's reminiscent of a particular kid's toy where you have to get a steel ball through a wooden labyrinth filled with holes by tilting the labyrinth's plane on two separate axes with your right and left hands, respectively. The resemblance to the tilting labyrinth is emphasized by the use of dramatically descending planes in certain levels of *SMB* and by the giant lianas, rock pillars and spiral castle-like constructions that extend and vanish into both vertical directions. And when your monkey ball falls off the track, it disappears into an abysmal environment of clouds and darkness; it is as though one were virtually falling kilometers without ever hitting the ground – before being re-spawned on the track at the location where one fell off.

The vertical theme of *SMB* is emphasized further by the game's visual design. In *Monkey Race*, for example – one of *SMB*'s party games – the monkey ball rolls rapidly through ditch-like courses. The extreme wide-angle perspective and the visual patterns of the course make you feel like the ball is actually rolling down a slope. Your ability as a player to estimate distances thus become distorted – it is as if the world just kept coming toward you at a tremendous pace. This optical impression is further underlined by the sparkles that radiate in all directions from a fixed center behind the ball as it rolls through a course; combined with all the other effects, these sparkles help create an almost abysmal perspective.

TONY HAWK'S AMERICAN WASTELAND
New Functions of Architecture

Grab your board and hit the streets of L.A.: in *Tony Hawk's American Wasteland,* the player experiences the story of a young man who goes out to Los Angeles to become a famous skater. He quickly becomes part of the L.A. skater community, which has its own language, dress code, music and way of making use of the built environment. The first video game of the *Tony Hawk's* series – *Tony Hawk's Pro Skater* – was released in 1999. Since then, at least one new installment has been released every year, though the game principle remains largely unchanged. In short tutorials, the player learns the basics of skating: reverts, manuals and the ollie – that is, sliding round when coming out of a trick, lifting two wheels off the ground and jumping with the board. Then, on his own, he practices grinding rails and managing grab, flip and lip tricks.

At first glance, the design of the buildings mainly contributes to the atmosphere of the game. The façades appear to the player only as scenery. Later in the game, the player gains experience in using railings, balustrades and ramps to access the roofs of the city. The whole built environment becomes his playground. Architecture becomes the challenge of the game: to grind a rail requires balance and perfect timing when jumping from rail to rail. Topography becomes the opponent, a spatial challenge the player must overcome.

But the more intensely the player has trained and increased his skills, the more the role of the architecture changes into that of an ally. To master more and more spectacular tricks and jumps, the player must look for the built environments in which to execute them. The new challenge is to find the combination of tricks that will receive the highest score. The architecture is thus of the utmost importance to the player, and the charm of the game lies in the conquest of the whole city space. All secret gaps and hidden paths are tracked down; the player investigates every corner of the city from the street level up to the roofs to find the perfect rail for the perfect score. He identifies with the places he discovers, "adopting" the architecture by spraying graffiti tags on its walls.

Architecture has an additional (though less integral) function in the game. In the story mode, the player helps a friend change a barren piece of land into the most exciting skater park in L.A. To build the park, he must collect architectural components and structures like pieces of rooftops or fire escapes.

In *Tony Hawk's American Wasteland*, architecture receives a new function: the challenge of the game is to find the best way to interact with it.

LEGACY OF KAIN: SOUL REAVER
Shifting Back and Forth between Dimensions

In *Legacy of Kain: Soul Reaver,* you play as Raziel, a fallen vampire who walks the land of Nosgoth in search of bloody vengeance on the ruler who betrayed him. Raziel's demonic ability to consume the souls of the dead grants him the power to shift between Nosgoth's two dimensions: the material and the spectral. These two realms are different versions of a single environment, with the spectral realm tending to be a darker, twisted version of the physical world. When Raziel shifts between dimensions, whether by choice or because his life force has been depleted, the world around him morphs in real time. For instance, a series of straight pillars will change height, twist and turn to become a series of "platforms" that Raziel can use to reach higher ground, only to then shift back as he continues his quest.

Life is hard for vampires in Nosgoth; simply occupying the material plane eats away at Raziel's life force, the depletion of which requires his return to the spirit world. Conversely, existing in the spectral realm in spirit form slowly fills up the life force gauge, allowing Raziel to return to material reality after a period of time. The game constantly forces the player to shift back and forth between the two dimensions. New powers acquired throughout the quest change the dynamics of this mechanic. One power, for example, enables Raziel to walk through gates and fences in the spirit world as if they didn't exist.

Nosgoth's architecture and landscapes are used as puzzles throughout the game, forcing the player to familiarize himself with both versions of the same place. Certain bodies of water don't exist in the spectral realm, making for interesting "water puzzles" when the player shifts back into the physical world to find himself submerged under water. The player becomes aware of both "layers" of a single environment, shifting back and forth to use a twisted steam pipe in the spirit world in order to reach a different place that only exists in the material realm. This game mechanic often creates a strange feeling of being in two places at the same time.

RESCUE ON FRACTALUS
First Steps into Fractal 3D World

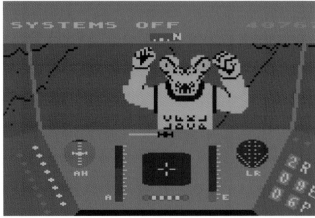

In December of 1983, I interviewed with the Games Division of Lucasfilm Ltd. At that point, only a few months after the release of *Return of the Jedi* (Lucasfilm 1983), it seemed that everyone in the world knew about George Lucas and Lucasfilm – but not about the existence of that latter's Games Division, much less what it was doing. So it was with great excitement that I saw a demonstration of its first, unfinished game, called at that time *Behind Jaggi Lines,* but later retitled *Rescue on Fractalus.*

The game was the first for the home PC to even attempt the depiction of flight through a solid-filled polygonal 3D space, and it was stunning in how it managed to do so on the 1-megahertz 8-bit processor of the Atari 800 computer. The game itself was designed and programmed primarily by David Fox, but he had struck up a friendship with Loren Carpenter, a computer scientist working in the graphics group of Lucasfilm's Computer Division (which years later became the core of Pixar). Loren was one of the foremost researchers in fractal mathematics at the time. He took it as a challenge to translate the sophisticated algorithms he had written for the multimillion dollar special effects sequences of the day into the 6502 assembly language of the Atari. The mathematical and programming ingenuity behind the resultant fractal graphics was amazing – they tricked the eye in numerous ways, seemingly depicting a fully detailed world that scaled, tilted and panned accurately, while actually storing only a tiny handful of 3D coordinates.

In the game, you as the player flew a spaceship down to a fog-shrouded planet to rescue stranded space pilots. On the peaks of some hilltops were enemy gun emplacements that fired at you, and in the valleys lay the beacons of other pilots. Land close to one of these, and you would see the pilot leave his stranded ship and come to yours. The graphics convincingly depicted a colorful real-time 3D world that scaled realistically, and the sense of stepping into a *Star Wars* experience was strong and compelling.

The best-remembered aspect of the game was one suggested in part by George Lucas himself. At higher levels of the game, some of the approaching pilots would turn out to be alien "Jaggi Monsters," who would pop up in front of your screen and break your windshield, killing you – unless you activated your shields in time. The sense of being in a real 3D space was enhanced by great sound effects: you heard the footsteps of the approaching pilot followed by a short pause, after which you would either hear a human pilot knocking on the rear door or a startlingly discordant blast of sound announcing the attack of the Jaggi. The sound reportedly caused many people to drop their game controllers in fright. There were even letters from people who swore they had let the Jaggi into their ship and seen him reach around from behind them, even though these graphics were never coded into the game.

The game seems primitive by modern standards, but my life was forever changed by the thrill of entering that 3D world for the first time.

QUAKE
The Turning Point of 3D Games

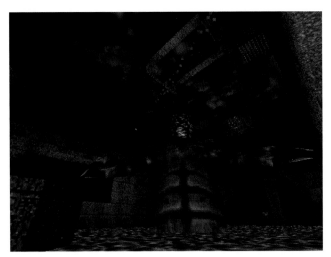

Quake, developed and published in 1996 by id Software, represented a critical turning point in the world of first-person shooters, leaving behind the likes of *Doom* (id Software 1993), *Marathon* (Bungie Software 1994) and *Duke Nukem 3D* (3D Realms 1996), and paving the way for *Half-Life* (Valve Software 1998), *Unreal* (Epic Games & Digital Extremes 1998) and *Halo* (Bungie Studios 2001). *Quake*'s technical achievements are numerous, but most important is its ability to let the player explore a truly 3D virtual world. Previous generations of first-person shooters featured worlds that looked and acted 3D, but *Quake* was the first to deliver such architectural features as multistoried buildings, spiral staircases and bridges that could be traveled both over and under.

Quake's gameplay formula remains largely unchanged from id's previous games, *Doom* and *Doom II* (id Software 1994). The player is transported to a strange realm of dark magic and must proceed through a series of gloomy, labyrinthine environments, defeating monsters, avoiding traps and solving puzzles. One important change from the *Doom* series is that *Quake* begins with a central "hub-level" where the player is given the choice of which of the four "episodes" of levels he wishes to play. After completing an episode, the player is returned back to this hub. In most games, this process is handled via a series of menus, but *Quake* sets it in a spatial environment, giving the player a completely safe area in which to explore the game's controls while admiring the new features of its architecture.

And *Quake*'s architecture is certainly worth admiration. Previous first-person shooters consisted of mostly abstract environments, but *Quake*'s technology allowed its designers to construct recognizable edifices. The world consists of dark, gothic structures: castles, temples, graveyards, dungeons and mines. As the player moves through the world, he is frequently presented with memorable landmarks such as a castle carved out of a cliff, a stone ziggurat surrounded by a lava moat or a murky swamp from which zombies emerge. Since *Quake* doesn't attempt to feature real-world locales like office buildings or shopping malls, it is free to feature elaborate traps, like paintings that spit nails at the player or a pit of lava that can only be crossed by jumping onto small moving platforms.

While the world of *Quake* would be considered simplistic by today's standards, it does what all truly great gameworlds do: it presents a set of consistent rules and builds a solid case for its reality. And although *Quake*'s novelty has worn off in the ten years since its release, today one can better appreciate its innovation and recognize the role it had in inspiring an entire generation of truly 3D games.

Olivier Azémar (OA)
in conversation with the Editors of Space Time Play (STP)

FORM FOLLOWS FUN
Working as a Space Gameplay Architect

STP   **Why are you, as an architect, working for a software company?**

OA   At the beginning of 2000, I moved to Holland and worked in several
       offices in which the production of architecture was closely linked to
       other disciplines like marketing and communications. My experiences
       there confirmed my earlier feelings as a student that the contemporary
       practice of architecture should go far beyond the boundaries of physical
       construction. Soon after graduating, I started to work at the game devel-
       opment firm Ubisoft as an architect/level designer for the video game
       Splinter Cell. On the Ubisoft production team, I am basically a "space
       gameplay" architect. My main task is to create realistic urban environ-
       ments and architectural forms that provide gameplay fun. Unlike most
       offline games in which a player crosses an area only once, a multiplayer
       game has to produce environments that will be visited thousand of times
       by numerous players. The maps have to be easy to understand, rich in
       game possibilities and, above all, fun.

STP   **What architectural expertise do you bring to the artistic and gameplay devel-
       opment of a video game production?**

OA   My role on the Ubisoft team is twofold: I am a level designer and an ex-
       pert on architecture. As a level designer, I have to build maps of the game
       and create game situations. As an architect, I have to bring my spatial
       and design expertise to the production team. This dual position affords
       me the possibility to both create a realistic environment in which play-
       ers can have fun and to provide architectural solutions to display-related
       spatial problems. A large part of my work at the beginning of the project
       consisted of giving architectural theory presentations to the team in or-
       der to communicate the basics of spatial composition: space distribution
       in a building, horizontal and vertical circulations, scale and dimension
       of architecture and similar topics. In doing so, I provided the team with
       a wide array of architectural examples that could help them produce
       realistic environments. In addition to this instruction, I also produced
       urban analyses of existing city areas to provide the team with exploitable
       gameplay-oriented data.

How does the spatial concept in a video game differ from those used in physical space?

My work entails some exciting graphic and technical optimization challenges. CPU and GPU performance limits along with computer memory constraints force me to use realistic items intelligently and creatively. What, for example, will constitute the main identity items of a specific situation I'm trying to create? It's important to realize that a process of translation has to be in operation to adapt pure architecture theory to the video game display, where perception of scale and time is quite different. For example, the law of gravity does not rule the virtual space, but on screen, it has to look like it would. Convincing immersion can only be sustained by those realistic elements that are not naturally displayed by the virtual space creation tools.

My work also involves investigating the optimization of realism's elements to minimize the display constraints: those familiar with FPS games know that unrealistic space display can undermine the realistic features of a game. So-called Z–corridors, for example, are used to separate the graphical display of two rooms or large spaces only because computational limits require it. It's my job to find realistic architectural means by which to reduce the impact of such display constraints.

STP **How can architectural and urban design influence a game's success?**

OA
Level design is a complex field of creation, especially for *Splinter Cell* multiplayer, in which each volume and each surface is meant to be experienced thousands of times by the players. The environment in this game is no longer a decoration, but itself a game tool that defines the overall spatial experience while simultaneously providing excitement and fun. I'm truly convinced that architectural expertise has strongly influenced and will continue to influence the creation of this spatial experience, not only in the field of realistic representation, but, above all, in the reinvention of video game spatial qualities and codes.

LOAD AND SUPPORT
Architectural Realism in Video Games

Real architecture and the virtual spaces often produced in video games are increasingly considered as having a close relationship to and compared with one another. Why, given that at first, the congruence is not apparent? Classical architecture is concerned with the built world, made up of technical, cultural or functional spaces. In contrast, the relatively young genre of video games converts computing machines into instruments for entertainment, adding computer-aided games to the existing culture of storytelling and narration. These are two clearly distinct disciplines – but apparently, they are becoming ever more convergent and mutually influencing. Is the convergence real? And if so, what consequences does it have for video gaming?

So long as the world of video games was limited to *PONG* (1972), *Space Invaders* (1978) and *Tetris* (1985), there was no similarity to speak of between the two disciplines. A nominal relationship was discussed in comics and film (*Tron* (1982), for example), but stronger links were first established by the avant-garde of technical and conceptual games in the beginning of the 1990s (*Wolfenstein 3D* (1992), for example), when the plot and spatial context of games were first connected. Since the end of purely graphic narration in games, plots of video games have been propelled by almost filmic presentations. Games now offer interactive paths through three-dimensional narrative spaces, a development comparable to the architectonic concept of buildings that explain themselves through exploration of the paths traveled in them. Three-dimensional movement has become an integral part of games. It establishes a narrative space and opens new possibilities for reception, action and interaction. For it is not only visualization, but also the game concept that is expanded into this third dimension, thereby requiring players to understand and be able to navigate the three-dimensional space. Games and architecture converge at the point of this visual presentation and experience of spatial constructs.

As both game designers and architects experience similar problems in the construction of space, it is not surprising that they use similar working methods in their planning and development phases. In few other artistic spheres are there so many congruent tools used as in architecture and game design. Typical 3D-modeling software is one fundamental interface between the two disciplines that allows mutual exchange between them. But data and models are not the only resources exchanged between the disciplines: personnel are too. The knowledge of software and working methods are so similar in the two fields that often the development backgrounds of architects and game designers overlap. This convergence in development methods and aesthetic appreciation translates into similarity in artistic results. Architectural designs, for example, avail themselves of the styles and spa-tial solutions of today's games. Conversely, video games copy architecture in finely nuanced photorealistic detail. The mutual proclivity for similar software, optimized for realistic presentation, strongly impacts the products of both branches. Tools, after all, lend themselves to a specific manner of use. With the increasing degree of filtration and abstraction of the design process, artistic disciplines become more and more similar; this is also a direct consequence of the often nonintuitive han-dling of contemporary 3D software.

The aesthetic principles guiding contemporary mainstream game design tend to imitate or parody real space. This is as true of the visualization of games as of their physical attributes. The game developer understands himself as the creator of "virtual worlds"; more than discovering game spaces and rules, he acts as an architect and designer of these worlds. With the extraordinary artistic freedom allowed by virtual space, illustrators, 3D-modelers and programmers exert them-selves everyday in game studios to painstakingly and convincingly reproduce brake marks, paint scratches, blades of grass blowing in the wind and changes in weather. As absurd as these activities may appear, they seem to be extremely important for marketing: when the rustling of leaves in a new game is elaborately recreated to ap-pear almost "like in real life," the perceived quality of the game is extremely high.

The reasons for this bias towards naturalistic simulation are open to specula-tion. Does the possibility of comparing real and gameworlds strengthen the essence of a game? Video games are particularly successful when they combine a break with particular limitations of reality in some areas with a retention of reality in others, inviting both comparison with real life and with the spectacular. The achievements of a player are then meaningful not only in the virtual play world, but also in the real world.

Can the triumphal march of realistic representation be explained by relative facility in development? A game that reproduces real motifs is easy to develop. The moving perspective projection defines a film-like, interactive, space- and time-based narration, which enables the combination of commonly used reality-based design attributes and plot structures. This type of narration may be easy to coor-dinate, but it limits itself in the type of story it allows to be presented and told and excludes alternative narrative types (e.g. surreal plots). In this structure, if the trusted is abandoned in favor of the unknown, then narration has to depend on the presentation of shocking and extreme situations.

Do the technological and artistic signals that promote realistic storytelling come from the software industry? Representative realism is widespread in the USA, where most game design software is produced today as most photorealistic art was in the 1960s. Perhaps the cultural preferences of the USA are reflected in the game industry. Or could it be that the mainstream public is already so condi-tioned by the repetitive visual experience of realism that narration that takes any other form generates no interest? The time allowed for a new game to reach its turnover targets is very short. The market therefore has great significance for and impact on what is made available, and experimental concepts must face stiff proof of their marketability.

Logic dictates that the consequence of the one-to-one correlation of game architecture to real architecture is the source of a multitude of artistic errors. Architecturally schooled observers readily identify measurement and material mistakes in games. Architectural detail in the real world is heavily dependent on its capacity for construction and translation by building engineers – a particular circumstance not well-appreciated by the game designers who copy architecture for the virtual world in an often dilatory fashion. That which in the conceptual phase of architectural design may be drafted, as a naturalistic model can become a critical, even resource-draining problem in production, setting all persons involved under pressure. The architectural concept of "load and support" assumes, from this perspective, a different – ironic – meaning in game design.

It takes a lot of effort for game designers to follow a chosen, realistic production through to its end. Would this effort not be better invested in the conceptual phase, in the development of free creative work or in the optimization of the mechanics of play? The way things currently function gives the inescapable impression that realistic, true-to-nature developments in games design are questionable, if not altogether mistaken. Mimicking reality (e.g. architecture) brings artistic problems starkly to the fore, and these handicap rather than support the desired outcome – i.e. the production of well thought-through games.

A critical perspective would illustrate to the game industry that current productions depend heavily on the possibilities of visualization and the resulting storylines. This fixation works against the game concept and is punished by the resultant "triviality of the visible," in which the quality of a given scene is judged on the basis of how "real" or "unreal" it appears. The deficiencies are all the more obvious when one sees which storytelling techniques must be excluded: it is impossible simply to hint at a plot and to deliberately create situations that are opaque, abstract or secretive and so to generate complex associations with other topics.

The preference for realistic appearance has significant consequences for the content of a game itself. It has become so pervasive that games are no longer about using the freedom of virtual creative space to make the impossible possible, but instead about making it possible to experience that which in real life is improbable. In realistic-appearing game developments, the limitations of real benefits must be intricately reproduced in order to achieve convincing results even though the absence of form-giving benefits and constraints in the game design environment is the decisive difference between the gameworld and the world of real design. The model in the design phase of a video game need never be tested against its possibilities in the real world; it can be worked and reworked into a product within the model world itself, in stark contrast to an architectural model. And so arises the paradox that game designers copy the limits under which real architects operate even though these have no significance for virtual space. Curiously enough, game designers purposely develop their products in this manner, which represents a direct conceptual contrast to architects' behavior. What architects experience as undesirable limits are welcomed by game designers because they confer authenticity on the desired end-product.

Could this development be reversed or reworked? Competition is stiff between the international game production houses to release ever more complex, ever more convincing visual replications of real life. This emphasis opens up opportunities for creative concepts and aesthetics outside the mainstream. Smaller developers have no chance against the global game concerns in the competition to market realistic productions. It is thus their choice of aesthetic that impacts directly on their capacity for success. Their handicap in direct competition could be an opportunity to relocate game ideas and visualization styles to a new market for different and differently produced ideas. Such a development would benefit games themselves: contemporary video game designers badly need to concentrate on the game idea itself in order to shift the emphasis away from realistic visualization and back to the core topic of the game.

◆ *PONG* (1972), developed and published by Atari. ◆ *Space Invaders* (1978), developed by Taito, published by Midway Games. ◆ *Tetris* (1985), developed by Alexey Pajitnov, various publishers. ◆ *Tron* (Movie) (1982), produced and distributed by Buena Vista/Walt Disney Pictures. ◆ *Wolfenstein 3D* (1992), developed by id Software, published by Apogee Software.

MAKE BELIEVE URBANISM

THE LUDIC CONSTRUCTION OF THE DIGITAL METROPOLIS

Game Review	Text	Director	Production
	Rolf F. Nohr	Steven Lisberger	Walt Disney Pictures, 1982

TRON
A Battle for Cyberspace

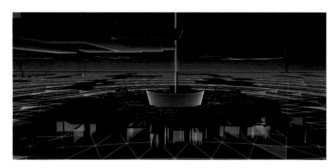

When we compare computer games with films, a number of striking common aspects emerge. Not only do both media operate primarily in narrative terms, both also function by evoking spatial structures, and both are wholly dependent for their effectiveness upon immersive phenomena. The most impressive trick of these media is their capacity to conceal their manufactured character and to appear immediate to the spectator – in short, to seem entirely natural. It is mainly the manipulation of spatial representations that facilitates the seeming naturalness of artificially generated texts and narratives. But are cinematic spaces of action and narration really so different from those of games? Our working argument here is that the spaces of cinema are similar to those of computer games. Hence the decision to discuss the film *Tron* as though it were actually a game.

The first cutscenes of *Tron* make clear that this game is something special: it is concerned with gameplay, and with the relationship of game to world. Before the first level even begins, the opening sequence showing the nocturnal architecture of the city is amalgamated with the voxel latticework of cyberspace. A long traveling shot through blinking, pulsating fields of light, light quadrants and light streams leads us into an arcaded hall. Without extensive digressions, we leap directly into the first level. The "Light Cycle Duel" (a high-speed game on a two-dimensional wire mesh) is the concentrated highpoint of the game. The essence of this level is the battle for space, which the enemy attempts to block off (to wall up, so to speak). The ensuing quests, too, are devoted

140

to this concept. We pursue the avatar (here representing the proverbial interface between the interior world of the game and the outer one of real life) as well as perpetually novel challenges involving the mastering of space. Whether we defend ourselves against the control program or the now out-of-control MCP (Master Control Program), go on a hacker run with a tank or play a LightDisc martial arts game, it is always a question of mastering space. *Tron* is an action-adventure with a pronounced role-playing touch as well as borrowings from Jump 'n Run and high-speed games. *Tron* is a geopolitical "battle for (information) space."

But what kind of space is it that must be traversed, conquered, defended and appropriated? It is the space of the processing architecture itself. The game engine becomes visible, the actual setting for the game's enactment. And the architecture has a look, an aesthetic and a coding that would become typical in subsequent media history. The look of *Tron* would become stereotypical. The impression of reduced vector graphics in neon Pop Art style, the cubist element and the continuous visual fusion of urban space and computing architecture: these elements would give rise to a distinct style.

The graphic engine developed by the firm Triple I is generated by a Super Foonly F-1 processor (a custom version of PDP-10). The designer and comic artist Moebius (John Difool, among others) designed the main level and costumes, while designer Syd Mead created the automotive shades. Both made the cyberspace aesthetic and the processing architecture in *Tron* pacesetting. This aesthetic is found in the accompanying game *Tron 2.0* (Monolith Productions 2003) as well as in many other visualizations based on the film, whether in the areas of film, gaming, design or art. Remaining in the memory are not individual details or the aesthetic itself, but instead the overall look and feeling of this game-film: the sense that we now know what cyberspace really looks like, and the awareness that this sense plays a significant role in generating the immersive power of the narrative.

NEUROMANCER

Playing inside the Earth's Computer Matrix

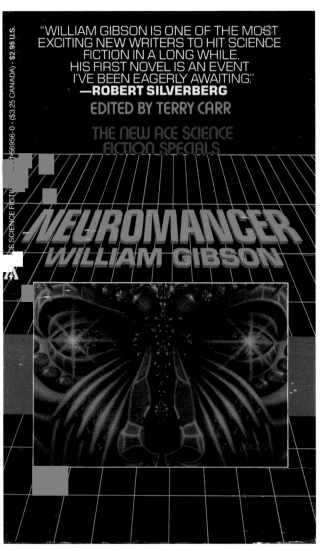

In a brilliant and famous passage from his 1984 novel *Neuromancer*, the science fiction writer William Gibson analyzes the still (e)merging elements of computer culture, ironically describing the digitalization of games, graphics, warfare, work, education, global communication, cityscapes and the cyborg integration of nerves and electronics through the voice of a narrator in a children's TV documentary: "The matrix has its roots in primitive arcade games," says the voice-over. "In early graphics programs and military experimentation with cranial jacks." On the Sony, a two-dimensional space war faded behind a forest of mathematically generated ferns, demonstrating the spatial possibilities of logarithmic spirals; cold military footage burned through – lab animals wired into test systems, helmets feeding into fire control circuits of tanks and war planes. "Cyberspace.

A consensual hallucination experienced daily by billions of legitimate operators, in every nation, by children being taught mathematical concepts.
A graphic representation of data abstracted from the banks of every computer in the human system. Unthinkable complexity. Lines of light ranged
in the nonspace of the mind, clusters and constellations of data. Like city
lights, receding..."

The keyword here is space: "space war," "spatial possibilities,"
"cyberspace," "nonspace." In the early eighties, Gibson observed young
players in video game parlors and extrapolated a future of communication and control through game-like, globally linked graphical computer
systems. His "space" is "consensually hallucinated": not real (a "non-
space of the mind"), but effective and dominant. Before the digital culture theorists, Gibson has seen the digital future and identifies the computer game as one of its main roots. His vision is bleak and ironic (unlike
that of the cyberspace theorists and technologists that he unintention-
ally inspired and who failed to perceive his irony), but his diagnosis of
the importance of the computer game culture is highly perceptive.

SNOW CRASH
Discovering the Metaverse

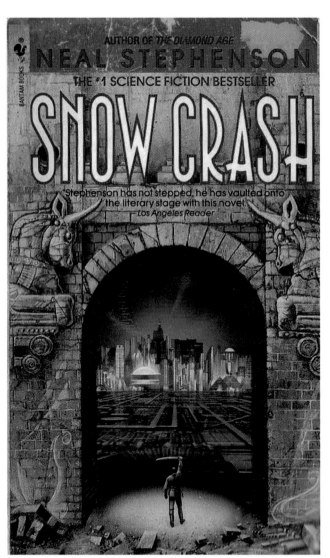

The "Metaverse" as imagined by Neal Stephenson in his 1992 postcyberpunk science fiction book *Snow Crash* has been an inspiration to video game design, refining the idea of an Internet-turned-virtual reality a decade after William Gibson first presented it in *Neuromancer* (1984). The Metaverse has many similarities to traditional gamespaces, but is primarily an isolated environment that does not have real-world implications; in the Metaverse, death is just an inconvenience – a stark contrast to what it is in the real world. However, the most important contrast between the Metaverse and a traditional gamespace is that the former bends to the whims and desires of the user within a given set of rules, whereas the latter is tailored and controlled by the designer to convey a specific experience to the player.

Snow Crash came onto the market at a crucial time in the Internet's development, when broadband was becoming more the norm than the exception, and overall growth was exponential. The early virtual reality projects all borrowed something from *Snow Crash*'s ideals: *Active Worlds* (Active Worlds 1995) and *Blaxxun* (Blaxxun Technologies 1995), for example, were conceived as huge and seamless worlds with densely populated main streets and expansive, lawless fringes. Games like *Second Life* (Linden Lab 2003) followed in their footsteps. The developers of these games strived to capture that which made the Metaverse imagery so powerful: a universe of near-infinite possibilities set in an understandable and intuitive framework loosely based on the reality shared by us all.

So why do we sit behind keyboards staring at monitors instead of cutting swaths through a digital landscape that can at times be more real than this one? Limitations of technology and Internet infrastructure have resulted in a far more gradual evolution, so we hadn't yet been presented with such a shocking a vision of things to come. Even with the past decade's leaps and bounds in graphic technology, hyper-real graphics on a large scale are still a long way away, and even now that broadband is finally widely available, the bandwidth is nothing like what would be needed to make the Metaverse happen.

Will we ever get there? Probably not, if a comparison is made in the strictest of senses. But if you broaden your vision, you will see that in many ways, we already have our Metaverse: the Internet has allowed the global economy to blossom, major websites often act as "streets" that allow users to navigate what is literally a flow of information and our lives are increasingly tied to the Internet as something that persists and is necessary.

USE YOUR ILLUSION
Immersion in Parallel Worlds

Immersion is not merely a buzzword, but also a state of mind. Immersion means to be completely absorbed in a make-believe world. Most people love to be immersed in fiction. This fondness is born in childhood play, when very little is needed in order to enter a parallel universe. A stick makes one a knight, a hat makes one a cowboy. Children can totally immerse themselves in a fantasy world with a minimum of props.

As we age, however, reality intervenes. We require more and stronger external stimuli to create a world in which we can immerse ourselves. Therefore, we turn to books, movies or games; almost any form of "grown-up" entertainment requires a degree of voluntary immersion. We seek play in many forms to counteract everyday toil. The quest for ludic indulgence is formative for our (western) society.

Because there are numerous ways to achieve this goal of immersing ourselves in another world, it is necessary to examine the precise meaning of the term "immersion." Any immersive action can be divided into two parts: the contribution of the human being and the tool of immersion – the reader and the book, for example. There is a specific relationship between the two that depends on the amount of effort the person has to expend and the degree of freedom he has in expending it. As we all know, a good book can be very immersive, and it supports our imagination. But while reading it, we have to strictly follow a linear plot. A small child's fantasy world, on the other hand, has no boundaries. The "tool" part of the relevant immersion equation may be negligible, but the human contribution is therefore large – namely, a strong imagination. Watching TV, in contrast, does not require any imagination at all; our options are reduced to switching between channels. But it can still be immersive enough to make people gaze at the screen all day long. The following observations will concentrate on the immersive power of computer games – especially of the so-called Massively Multiplayer Online Role-Playing Games, abbreviated MMORPGs.

Due to the overwhelming technical progress in the entertainment industry, it seems that every new medium we humans have innovated has made it easier to dive into parallel worlds. But at the same time, each has also narrowed our freedom and imagination. The invention of video games, though, represents a new twist on this development. Computer games have reintroduced the freedom of influence to our fictional worlds and therewith amplified the degree of our immersion in them in a way that cannot be overestimated.

Although the first digital games were reduced to merely graphical symbols as abstract representations of ongoing action, they were highly immersive. The first

Multi User Dungeons (MUDs) worked perfectly with text only. The early gamers were attached to the ingame worlds because they allowed them to gain mastery over well-defined systems while simultaneously indulging in their very own fantasies. Influence and imagination easily compensated for the lack of photorealism. But it is only recently that the majority of the public has begun to take video games seriously. It has taken nearly 30 years for the medium to become a mass phenomenon.

The idea of immersion in virtual worlds became popular and newsworthy in the early 1990s. Besides the influence of *Star Trek*, this was mostly triggered by science fiction novels such as *Neuromancer* (Gibson 1984) and *Snow Crash* (Stephenson 1992). Additionally, the first pictures of Virtual Reality (VR) helmets and cyber gloves were shown to the public at around the same time, and they nourished a feeling of standing at the advent of a completely new, immersive medium. Everybody expected the scientists to come up with the holodeck-like hardware that would be able to trick not only its users' intellects, but also their physical senses, to come up with, in other words, a tool for passive immersion that needed no contribution from its human user.

As it turned out, the game designers were on the vanguard of development, not the scientists. They concentrated on enhancing the much cheaper, software-induced immersion. And since most households already had a personal computer, by expanding the possibilities of desktop VR, they allowed users to avoid buying expensive extra hardware equipment. But much more important was the fact that game designers relied on the players' "willing suspension of disbelief" (Samuel Taylor Coleridge). Surprisingly, it was not necessary to outwit the player's mind and senses – both just had to be stimulated. The big challenge now is to develop a user interface that mediates between reality and fiction without affecting the experience of immersion.

Video games involve the player on many different levels, depending on the preferences of the user and the genre of the game. Richard A. Bartle, game researcher and developer of the first MUD, distinguishes between four types of player: the achiever, the explorer, the socializer and the killer. They all immerse – even in the same game – but in different ways. The software can weave the user into a synthetic world by means of good gameplay, aesthetics, narration or degree of simulation. Games demand involvement on the human side in the form of imagination and physical, social and intellectual engagement. Obviously, the video game medium is capable of including and combining all previous tools of immersion and even adding completely new ones to the mix. Given that, the restraints of classic media make them appear almost ridiculous in retrospect.

It is their participatory nature that makes video games so attractive. According to game designer Sid Meier (Civilization 1991), a game is a series of interesting choices. The player knows that every action he takes has an influence on the outcome of the game and is therefore emotionally attached to it. Only when given the freedom to choose between good and evil can we experience strong emotions such as pride, regret, power or responsibility, all of which stem from a feeling that our actions are meaningful. Freedom – the liberty to risk failure – is essential to all games.

By playing good games, we can easily get into an exhilarating state of flow (Csikszentmi-halyi 1990), becoming completely occupied with a task that perfectly matches our skills. It must be challenging – but not too hard – with clear goals and instant feedback. We experience progression and success while being concentrated and relaxed at the same time. Immersion is about being in the moment. Thanks to role-playing and a consistent physics engine, we can achieve a relieving loss of self-consciousness and transformation of time in a believable artificial environment. And the latest break-through in computer gaming is just now making itself felt: widespread broadband Internet connections are enabling a never-before-seen extension of immersion, re-creating and reshaping our contemporary notions about virtual worlds.

But what is it that makes MMORPGs feel so real?

According to the classic definition of play/games as Johan Huizinga proclaimed it in 1950, MMORPGs are not even games, since they are limited to neither a specific time nor specific space. They are not clearly delineated from the outside world; quite to the contrary, the boundaries of the "magical circle" have been progressively blurred. An MMORPG is played in a space without place, but with permanence of objects and time (*Echtzeit*). Virtual worlds have no final state; they cannot be won. In them, every moment is unique and therefore cannot be "saved" or repeated. The saga continues – with or without you, the player.

MMORPGs are progressional illusions of persistence and solidity. They convey to you the strong feeling of actually being in them, not sitting in front of your com-puter. The use of an avatar as the virtual representation of your body affords you a sense of presence – not physical, but emotional (telepresence). You experience your avatar as an extension of your ego.

But most important for the success of MMORPGs and truly unique to them is the feeling of shared space they provide. This is not only about mingling with people from all over the world in a three-dimensional chatroom; it's about others witness-ing your actions and therefore making them real. Surviving heroic adventures only by cooperating with one another, gamers experience intense friendship, camara-derie and feelings of togetherness. The shared struggle for a good reputation and the feeling of responsibility towards a guild, for example, really attach gamers to their virtual world. The social realism, in other words, is more appealing than the perceptual realism. Artificial Intelligence (AI) is still no substitute for a human op-ponent. Over the years, lonely cyberspace has morphed into social metaverse.

Unfortunately, computer games can become a dangerous threat to their users. They are often very addictive and can even lead to so-called toxic immersion – that is to say, losing oneself in obsessive playing. Some hardcore gamers actually prefer to live their lives in synthetic worlds, in make-believe computer programs, neglect-ing all their duties in the meatspace; a contemporary form of escapism.

Those unfamiliar with the workings of virtual worlds are often tempted to regard them merely as collective hallucinations. But their inhabitants' fictional actions have real consequences; some players, for example, have converted high virtual game scores into high real-world profits ... and sometimes losses.

The volume of business conducted in relation to virtual worlds is tremendous – both ingame and external. Only time will tell if the growing importance of ingame currencies will harm immersion. Shady practices – e.g. "gold-farming" – can easily cause the illusion of the world to totter.

Where is the line between the world of the gamer and the world of the game? The proprietors of virtual worlds will have to find an answer to the question of how thick the membrane should be that separates game from reality.

Finally, what is the function of these immersive parallel worlds? They all share a commonality in how surprising they can be to both game designers and gamers. As game designer Will Wright's latest masterpiece, *Spore* (in development), demonstrates, this is a result of the coding of possibilities. Virtual worlds provide us with versatile tools for recreation, education and entertainment. With its new console Wii, Nintendo allows gamers to engage in real physical action, thereby shifting their focus from look to feel. Games like *World of Warcraft* (2004) enable completely new forms of nonlinear, collective narration that have yet to be fathomed. And a virtual sandbox like *Second Life* (2003) probably gets closest of any virtual world to that magic state of childlike creativity – except that now the castles are made of silicon instead of sand. What counts in the end is what we can take back from immersion into our real lives. Virtual worlds must not be a replacement for reality, but a contribution to it. Ultimately, play affects our reality, and the real world informs our play.

◆ Csikszentmihalyi, M. (1990), *Flow: The Psychology of Optimal Experience*, Harper & Row, New York NY. ◆ Gibson, W. (1984), *Neuromancer*, Ace Books, New York NY. ◆ Johan Huizinga (1949), *Homo ludens: A Study of the Play-Element in Culture*, Routledge & Kegan Paul, London UK. ◆ *Second Life* (2003), developed and published by Linden Lab. ◆ *Spore* (in development), developed by Maxis, to be published by Electronic Arts. ◆ Stephenson, N. (1992), *Snow Crash*, Bantam Books, New York NY. ◆ *World of Warcraft* (2004), developed by Blizzard Entertainment, published by Vivendi.

Game Review	Text	Developer	Publisher
	Mary Flanagan	Maxis Software	Electronic Arts, 2000

THE SIMS
Suburban Utopia

Since the release of Activision's *Little Computer People* (1985), the "action" of domestic space has been an alternative to other forms of action in computer games. *The Sims* games allow players to create a neighborhood of simulated people (Sims) and manage their lives. Called a "virtual dollhouse," *The Sims* quickly became a universal gaming and cultural phenomenon. With expansion packs used to create parties, magic shows and vacations, *The Sims* games are perennial best-sellers, translated into 17 different languages. Part of the reason for their popularity is that they attract a large number of female and nontraditional players.

In the games, players maintain a consumer-driven suburban household, focusing on everyday activities such as sleeping and eating. In this way, the games avoid stereotypical, often violent game models. Players manage a virtual budget to purchase appliances, furniture, lamps and books. Characters seem happier when they have expensive commodities and larger homes; once players learn this, they direct characters to look for an income. When Sims are unhappy, the virtual world quite literally descends into chaos: characters stop using the lavatory, filth accumulates and joy decreases.

The Sims is a human simulator, a creative toy, a game and a design tool. Players can create their own personal objects for "importation"

http://thesims.ea.com

into the game. The original game was noted for its affordances in design and decorating; indeed, many players used the game as a tool for exploration and experimentation. A 3D game allows multiple views of interiors and exteriors; its virtual houses are designed from the foundation up, offering choices such as masonry or wood siding, dormers and stairways, and the roof design tool is far more sophisticated than any DIY home improvement center's software.

Sims space follows the real estate development logic of American suburbia: to build their own houses, players can choose to bulldoze existing homes or purchase open lots of land. In this way, the "clean slate" of US frontier thinking and urban sprawl is reinforced. If a typical American player's physical home is a romanticized "castle," then the player's *Sims* house and the suburbs surrounding it are easily a utopia. Suburbs offer not only particular kinds of architectural spaces and controlled access to them, but represent a way of life – a set of values, beliefs and expectations. The space of *The Sims* provides a site of negotiation between the real and the virtual domestic experience, wholeheartedly embracing suburban-style consumption and domesticity.

THERE
Been There, Done That

There is a virtual world released in 2003 by the American software company Makena Technologies. It has very low system requirements compared to other 3D environments on the Web, and the basic membership is free, though for a premium account, a user must pay 9.95 US Dollars. The biggest advantage of a subscription is the possibility to use voice chat as a method of conversation. As far as money is concerned, the ingame currency is called Therebucks and is exchangeable into real cash – 1 US Dollar equals 1,800 Tbuxs, which can be spent on fashion as well as on property and houses.

There offers several services like, for example, the possibility to join or create groups. All options are controlled over a user interface in a pop-up window, which is not very immersive. *There* is more of a 3D chatroom than a game: its only aim is to provide a forum for socializing. This purpose is well-served by the availability of voice chat, which is a great advantage over some other virtual environments like, for example, *Second Life* (Linden Lab 2003). Another perk of the world is that *Thereians* have advanced facial expressions. Role-playing, however, seems to be a secondary focus in *There*. The clothing is rather casual, and once the user has chosen its gender, it is fixed. And though Makena Technologies supports the production of machinimas and offers users some possibilities to create their own objects, these are very limited compared

www.there.com

to those in games like *Second Life*. This explains why MTV used Linden Lab's building tools – not Makena Technologies' – to create a dummy for a show that was later realized in *There*.

There, which has a PG-13 rating, is especially designed for teens: nudity and violence are explicitly banned, swearwords are censored and the overall picture is strikingly clean and tidy. The user can be sure of not finding any obscene or ugly content. Quite to the contrary, *There* has the atmosphere of a holiday resort hotel with beautiful beaches and palm trees. The impression of being on vacation is further enhanced by the look and fashion of *There*'s avatars: *Thereians* seem to be very happy and relaxed. But they also look very much the same – namely, like adolescents on spring break. These avatars can engage in various activities on the different islands of *There*. Scooter driving is an option, as are playing soccer, listening to music, dancing and, of course, shopping. The world also offers nice vehicles that can be used by up to four people to explore the virtual paradise. A user can even have a virtual pet.

But Makena Technologies' virtual world is bare of any surprises or challenges. It feels more like a teenage beach club where visitors engage in harmless – almost prude – activities. Overall, *There* is exactly what it promises to be: an everyday hangout where users can have fun with their friends as well as meet new ones.

Game Review	Text	Developer	Publisher
	Florian Schmidt	MindArk PE AB	MindArk PE AB, 2003

ENTROPIA UNIVERSE
Money Makes the World Go 'Round

Entropia Universe, formerly known as *Project Entropia,* is a synthetic world developed by the Swedish company MindArk. It was released in 2003, and there are currently about half a million inhabitants on its planet Calypso. The universe can be entered without subscription fees.

The environment of the virtual planet is vast and beautifully crafted. It contains a large variety of different landscapes with hostile fauna and obscure flora. A science fiction story serves as its framework and is converted into an elaborate design with many details. Players assume the role of pioneers or first colonists who have to explore the dangerous wilderness of the planet at the frontier of civilization. They can gain skills in different professions like hunting, craftsmanship or trading. There are a few protected cities that function as marketplaces, but the largest part of the planet is untamed, and there, the colonists are on their own. Chances of survival in the wilderness are slim, if not impossible, without investing in weapons. Not only is a newbie constantly subject to danger, he also has to wear a distinctive orange overall (as do political prisoners). Every other player is thereby made immediately aware of his inexperience and status as an underdog. Adding insult to injury, the employment opportunities for poor players are limited to humiliating jobs such as gathering sweat and dung from wild creatures. It's not surprising, then, that players are more than willing to invest to speed up their virtual careers.

This can be an expensive undertaking. To play the game, one needs a good deal of money, and the ingame currency is directly linked to the US Dollar. The Real Cash Economy is MindArk's strongest advertising argument. "Finally gamers get paid for killing monsters," the company proclaims. In order to truly have fun in *Entropia Universe*, one has to spend real cash – approximately one US Dollar per hour on weapons, armor and tools. It takes quite a while before a player sees any returns on his investment in the form of loot or minerals; nevertheless, some players can make a real-world living by hunting and trading on Calypso. A special credit card enables them to book expenses in the real economy directly from their ingame accounts (ten Project Entropia Dollars (PED) = one US Dollar (USD)). In fact, *Entropia Universe* has gained fame beyond the gaming community for the huge amounts of money users have spent on virtual property. In 2005, a virtual asteroid was sold to an entrepreneur for 100,000 US Dollars. MindArk's world even made it into "Guinness World Records" as the place where the highest prices ever spent on virtual goods were paid.

SECOND LIFE
Lego on Acid

In 2003, the Californian software company Linden Lab opened its virtual world to the public. *Second Life (SL)* is based on a unique concept that goes much further than all other MMORPGs (Massively Multiplayer Online Role-Playing Games) in that the entire content of this synthetic environment is user-generated. In addition to the option of buying and selling land, Linden Lab's service includes complex 3D modeling tools, a powerful scripting language and the possibility to use streaming audio and video. *Second Life* runs on Windows machines as well as on Macintosh and Linux, and its client was just released as open source. The basic account is free, but in order to own land, a premium membership with a monthly fee is required. Furthermore, landowners must pay taxes.

After logging in, a user explores the gigantic world with a fully editable avatar whose gender and appearance may be changed at any time and who has the ability to fly. As far as the physical environment goes, the architecture is very eclectic and surreal. And the residents, as Linden Lab's customers refer to themselves, pursue a wide range of interests from role-playing to shopping, the ultimate goal being simply creativity. It is not surprising, then, that *SL* has become the home of many obscure subcultures; there seems to be no limit to the number of shared interests and activities of users. Residents spend their time creating all kinds of material objects such as clothing, houses, vehicles, animations and even games. In doing so, they have created from scratch an amazingly versatile cosmos. They acquire intellectual property rights for their creations, for example, and can thus sell them to other users. The ingame currency, the Linden Dollar, is convertible into US Dollars at any time. The population of *Second Life* is growing exponentially, as is its economy. A woman from Germany already made one million US Dollars in revenues as a real estate agent in the virtual world. As a result, real-world companies like American Apparel and Nissan are trying to get a foot in the growing market. And with media networks like MTV, BBC and Reuters operating in *Second Life*, the boundary between the virtual world and reality is really beginning to blur.

But the freedom Linden Lab offers does have its downsides. Due to urban sprawl, for example, navigation is a challenge. And the presence in *SL* of mature content like prostitution and gambling might offend some users. More seriously, there have been many problems with criminal activities and hacker attacks. The user interface is complex and requires some effort to master; for newbies, *Second Life* can be a very frustrating and boring experience. Thus because the learning curve is so high, *SL* is often more attractive to sophisticated users. Furthermore, its environment looks quite weird, like a crossover of a digital suburbia and Las Vegas, and it is still full of bugs. But despite all this, it is definitely one of the most interesting places on the Web. It is a beta version of the Web 3D – ugly and inconvenient, perhaps, but a milestone in virtual gaming history nonetheless.

MAKING PLACES

The online computer games known as virtual worlds or MMORPGs (Massively Multi-player Online Role-Playing Games) attract millions of players across the globe, each investing many hours a week in his hobby for months if not years. Few other forms of entertainment are this compelling, and yet MMORPGs remain little understood. There are theories as to *why* people play them with such dedication, but little discussion of what they *are*. In the past, they've been described as games, simulations, services and media. But fundamentally, they are none of these; virtual worlds are *places*.

As places, virtual worlds have a number of place-like features: they exist at all times, you can visit them and you can do things while you're visiting them. The main difference between virtual worlds and other places is that the former are not real – they're maintained entirely by computers and exist only in the human imagination. Formally, a virtual world is an automated, shared, persistent environment with and through which people can interact in real time by means of a virtual self; informally, it's an imaginary place able (through the magic of computers) to masquerade as real, such that you and other people can go there whenever you want and do things both in it and to it.

In real life, place is a natural consequence of space, which in turn is a given. In virtual worlds, this is not the case; rather space has to be *represented*. To date, there have been three main representations employed corresponding to three prevailing display formats: nodes for textual worlds, grids for isometric graphical worlds and polygons for 3D graphical worlds.

Text and Nodes

The first virtual worlds were text-based. Everything in them was described in words: the world, its inhabitants, the objects, the players, the events that occurred, the actions that the players undertook – everything! Almost all today's virtual worlds are directly descended from a single, textual primogenitor, *MUD* ("Multi User Dungeon"), which was written in 1978 (Bartle & Trubshaw 1978). *MUD* begat many imitators, one of which, *AberMUD* (Cox 1987), was released to the nascent Internet and soon afterwards became responsible for three new branches of virtual worlds: *TinyMUD* (Aspnes 1989), which eschewed game-like aspects and concentrated instead on the social side of things as well as world-building, *DikuMUD* (Nyboe et al. 1990), which emphasized strong, combat-oriented gameplay, and *LPMUD* (Pensjö 1989), which was very customizable and fell somewhere in between the other two. *TinyMUD* led to *LambdaMOO* (Curtis 1990), the textual precursor to today's *Second Life* (2003), *DikuMUD* led to the majority of today's game-style worlds, such as *World of Warcraft* (2004).

158

Textual worlds represent space as a set of interlinked nodes. Each node embodies an atomic location (commonly called a *room*), which generally conceptualizes the smallest meaningful space into which a player's character can fit. This does *not* mean that a virtual world's rooms are all the same geographical size, nor that they are indoors: a mountain and a cupboard can both be valid as single rooms.

A room's description will usually place that room within a context, noting other rooms that are to be regarded as adjacent. These adjacent rooms can then be reached from the original room using primitive, directional movement commands. Typing a direction will move the player's character from the current room to the one pointed at by the appropriate exit link. A map for a textual world therefore consists of a network of rooms connected by a set of arrows that correspond to movement commands. Such an approach implies a fairly coarse granularity, but it is not one that unduly offends players' sense of locale.

This modeling of the virtual world as a network of nodes has some interesting properties, all of which are at times useful to designers:

> The arrows on the map need not be bi-directional – north from room A may lead to room B, but south from room B could lead to room C.

> Arrows need not connect different rooms. North from room A could lead back to room A.

> Because rooms are just another kind of object, they can be picked up, carried around and placed inside one another – or, indeed, inside themselves.

> Arrows can be changed dynamically to point at different rooms.

To implement a set of rooms networked in this fashion involves many data records connected by many more pointers. It is far easier to arrange rooms as a simple, two-dimensional array of squares; a grid 100 by 100 rooms large would deliver 10,000 rooms immediately. Although some of the early textual worlds did experiment with this kind of setup (MirrorWorld 1986), on the whole, it did not find favor: the resulting rooms were boring and too similar compared to those of the linked-node system. Ease-of-implementation issues were outweighed by the loss of flexibility in design that they implied. What, then, could possibly be gained by switching to a grid format?

The answer is: swift access to a *visual* representation of the world.

Graphics and Grids

The main reason for having textual worlds was that computers in those days had only limited display devices. Although some primitive graphical games were developed at around the same time as *MUD* and were independent of it (most notably *Avatar* (Maggs et al. 1979) on the PLATO system), they never broke free of their hardware and had negligible influence on the future evolution of the virtual world genre.

A more enduring line of graphical virtual worlds began with *Islands of Kesmai*, which was written in 1981 (Islands of Kesmai 1981). Its world was a square grid rendered in ASCII graphics. Character combinations represented different features of the environment, with "[]" meaning a wall, "~~" water, "{}" a tree and so on. In the early 1990s, a number of *IOK*-inspired virtual worlds were written that replaced the ASCII squares with bitmaps; the view presented to the player was from an angle directly overhead, usually with north fixed at the top of the screen. This "flat graphics" approach met with only limited success, however, and the line died out.

The first graphical worlds to overtake their textual forebearers in popularity came from the *MUD* tree. They rendered views in 2.5D – i.e. their worlds were still represented internally in 2D but were displayed as if they were 3D. They adopted an isometric viewpoint, a trend being established by *Ultima Online* (1997), *Nexus: The Kingdom of the Winds* (1996) and *Lineage* (1997). Nevertheless, their internal representation was not all that different from *IOK*'s.

The reasons for the switch from nodes to tiles were entirely based on visual impact. Players could still feel that their characters were in "rooms," but those rooms were now made up of several squares. The granularity had become finer.

To virtual world designers, this tessellated representation presented new challenges:

> The constant scale meant that distance could no longer be finessed. Twenty rooms of textual wilderness meant 200 squares of isometric wilderness.

> Because distance changed, so did velocity. Some means of fast transportation was needed so that the time required to travel between distant points was acceptable to players (teleporting, ships, portals, etc.).

> The world was 2D. Buildings were restricted to a single story, and caves and bridges were impossible to include.

The latter was particularly problematic. The practical solution was to introduce a degree of nodality back into the system. Parts of the location-definition array were given over to self-contained areas that could not be reached by regular means. Access was gained through particular squares flagged as being *coincident*. If on the main map you entered a square containing a staircase leading upwards, it would teleport you to a submap of the floor "above"; if, on that sub-map, you entered a square containing a staircase leading downwards, you'd be taken back to the main map.

Although the granularity became finer than what was commonly available in a node-based world, it was far from ideal. In particular, anything large and curved was a problem (paths, rivers and circular buildings showed their right angles), and the world *felt* as if it conformed to the squares. When you moved, you moved from the center of one square to the center of another. Walls, roads and coastlines followed the boundaries of squares. Trees, furniture and rocks neatly occupied squares and were arranged in tidy, equidistant patterns. People, animals and monsters followed right-angled lines of movement. You *knew* you were in a world made of squares, which was a little disappointing as that is not quite how the real world is ...

What if the world were not made of squares, but of polygons instead?

Graphics and Polygons

Fully 3D[1] worlds arrived with *EverQuest* (1999), and this is where we are today. Almost all of the several hundred commercial virtual worlds currently in development display their content as a 3D scene. In this method, the one-to-one mapping between

There was a 2.5D world, *Meridian 69*, which presented its players with a first-person point of view and therefore looked 3D.

1 >

the structure of the virtual space and the software data structure that models it no longer exists. It has been replaced by a relationship in which sets of polygons represent *surfaces*, whether those surfaces are of the ground, of buildings, of denizens or of objects. Space is that apparent volume that does not have a surface in it. Thus rather than creating a set of nodes or squares and saying that each node/square corresponds to a particular location, game designers instead define a location as a mere point in a 3D coordinate system. Most of the world is empty so does not need to be represented explicitly in a data structure; lists of objects within visual range are maintained instead and rendered in terms of the polygons that make up their surfaces.

This approach uses surfaces because that's all that a video card needs to know in order to display an object's image. Objects are, in fact, hollow inside. Indeed, sometimes glitches in the world model or incomplete collision-detection by the camera can mean you get to see what's inside a creature or below a planet's surface.

Although 3D overcomes the main problem of 2.5D in that it allows for things like multistory buildings, its principal advantage is that it looks less blocky; its greater persuasiveness, not its associated representational capabilities, is the main reason why developers prefer it. This isn't to say that modern virtual worlds are full of smooth surfaces and wavy lines – they're not. On close inspection, wheels might be octagonal, for example. Nevertheless, the current virtual worlds are far superior to those that were tile-based and thus locked into having square-edged terrain features no matter what.

Shards and Zones

The three representations of virtual worlds follow a path of increasing detail: from room to space to point. In a 3D world, you are located by a point, but feel you occupy a space, which is bordered by planes to give the impression of a room.

There is also a path of decreasing detail, with groups of related rooms themselves forming conceptual *areas*. Beyond these, there are two even greater abstractions, both of which emerged from implementation issues: shards and zones.

Virtual worlds, much as the real world, can only hold so many people. Their limiting factor is *content* – that which, if players are thought of as consumers, is consumed. Content is a hard concept for non-gamers to grasp, but it's the stuff from which players fashion the events that they find fun. A virtual world with many things that the players want to do has much content; one bereft of desirable activities lacks content. The problem is that a virtual world may have sufficient content for only a certain number of players before those players start treading on each other's toes. As an analogy, consider Disneyland: the park is full of many fun activities, but if it didn't shut its doors when it got full, then few visitors would get to experience them.

Virtual worlds have an advantage over Disneyland in that they can easily be cloned. If there is only enough content for 5,000 people, a copy of the virtual world can be set up so that the overflow has somewhere to go. This is a long-established practice; even *MUD* was able to crank up a new incarnation of itself if it filled up with players. Most commercial virtual worlds today[2] will open with multiple instantiations running on separate sets of computers. Thus even though it's common to refer to the cities and continents of virtual worlds as if they were unique, it should

The main exceptions are *EVE Online* and *Second Life*, which each run only one instantiation that can be scaled up as new players arrive.

< 2

be remembered that actually there may be dozens of them. Saying, "I've been to the top of the Tower of Althalaxx" is not the same as saying, "I've been to the top of the Eiffel Tower"; actually, you've only been to the top of *a* Tower of Althalaxx.

These instantiations are commonly termed *servers*, but the term *shard*[3] is also prevalent and is the more correct because it refers to the virtual world itself rather than the hardware upon which it runs. A shard is a single instance of a virtual world.

Zones are different geographical regions of a virtual world that have the same look throughout – a tundra zone looks different than a jungle zone, for example. In textual and 2.5D worlds, this is no big deal, but in 3D worlds, the textures for each zone have to be preloaded into memory by the client software so that they can be displayed as soon as they are needed.

Shards do not interconnect geographically: you can't go east from one shard and find yourself in another. Zones do interconnect and can thus be drawn as a network of nodes (as can areas and, of course, rooms). Although graphical worlds may eschew nodes as a data format, they nevertheless continue to use them as a conceptualizing framework – sometimes for rooms, often for areas and always for zones. These *are* just conceptual nodes, though; the underlying geography of modern virtual worlds still denies designers the flexibility that was possible in textual worlds.

3 >

The term is *Ultima Online*'s. As fictional cover for why there were multiple canonical copies of the Ultima universe, its designers used the wonderful metaphor of a mirror breaking into a myriad of shards, each one able to reflect what the whole reflected.

Instances

In graphical worlds, handling crowds is a problem. A textual world can hold arbitrary numbers of players in a single location, but a graphical world has to grapple with certain occupancy problems. What happens when two characters try to stand in the same place? If characters can block each other, a crowd becomes an impassable object. Because of this, the trend is to disable collision-detection for characters in 3D virtual worlds: you can move your avatar completely through the space occupied by another character. This is somewhat fiction-busting, but players have come to accept it as a fact of (virtual) life.

Such a solution has a side effect, though. If multiple people can occupy the same physical space, then they can also simultaneously access the content associated with that space. Textual worlds could fairly easily include alternative content nearby, but this is not possible in graphical worlds as the constraints of visually simulating reality mean there simply isn't room for it. The problem is exacerbated by the higher number of players that circulate graphical worlds compared to textual ones. Basically, 50 people may want to access an area in which there's only content enough for five.

The modern solution is to switch to an *instance*. This takes the coincident squares idea of 2.5D worlds and converts it to that of coincident *planes*. You step through such a plane, and you're transported to a self-contained mini-world beyond it. The idea is extended, however, by allowing multiple copies of the mini-world to exist. One group of players will go to its own, private instantiation of the place – an instantiation that will disappear when it is abandoned, but that can never be accessed by other players. The next group of players will be taken to *its* own replica of the place instead. Thus, instances can be regarded as sharded zones of a virtual world.

In the case of instances, the links between zones again become concrete rather than conceptual. You can enter an instance by going north from a point, but upon immediately going south from within the instance reappear at a different point. Other long-lost designer tricks such as rooms-within-rooms are also made possible by the instance mechanism.

Future Worlds

The way that space is represented in a virtual world is strongly related to how that space is displayed: the closer to reality its appearance, the more constrained its representation. Over time, virtual world designers have developed techniques to address some of these constraints, leading to solutions that are now considered to be part and parcel of the virtual world paradigm.

These solutions reprise the older, flexible and representational structures that were present in textual virtual worlds: a world of nodes (text) has become a world of polygons (3D) arranged as a network of nodes (zones and instances). We're almost back to where we started.

Almost. Actually, we've gained something new: if we can shard instances, we can *also shard zones*. From a designer's point of view, this opens up exciting new possibilities!

Although textual worlds *could* have sharded their nodes, they didn't – their designers didn't give it any thought. Instances, which were introduced to solve a problem that textual worlds didn't have, now make sharding a node fairly routine. Yet nodes don't have to be instances; they could be zones. Suddenly, overlapping, coincident worlds become possible in which players who make one decision are taken to one version of a zone, but players who make a different decision are taken to a different version. From the point of view of the individual player, the world is consistent; from a god's-eye view, it's anything but – a multidimensional layering of differently phased zones, each one personal to every player, but at heart fundamentally the same. In this scenario, actions *could* have global consequences, but only for those involved. Your group might cause a volcano to explode, exposing a strange netherworld of troglodytes and their demonic slaves, but to the players who haven't unleashed the necessary magic, the same volcano is still just a mountain. This is a startling opportunity for designers to do something really *new* with virtual worlds.

What began as a partial solution to the representational problems posed by the higher look-and-feel expectations of players has thus led to an improvement of the original representation itself.

◆ J. Aspnes (1989), *TinyMUD*, Carnegie Mellon University. ◆ R.A. Bartle & R. Trubshaw (1978), *MUD*, University of Essex. ◆ A. Cox (1987), *AberMUD*, University of Wales, Aberystwyth. ◆ P. Curtis (1990), *LambdaMOO*. ◆ *EverQuest* (1999), developed by Verant Interactive, published by Sony Online Entertainment. ◆ *Islands of Kesmai* (1981), developed by K. Flinn & J. Taylor, University of Virginia. ◆ *Lineage* (1997), developed and published by NCSoft. ◆ *Avatar* (1979), B. Maggs, A. Shapira, D. Sides et al., University of Illinois. ◆ *MirrorWorld* Input/Output World of Adventure (1986), developed by T. Rogers, L. Wood, N. Billington run by P. Cordrey ◆ *Nexus: The Kingdom of the Winds* (1996), developed by Nexon Inc., published by KRU Interactive. ◆ K. Nyboe, T. Madsen, H. Staerfeldt, M. Seifert & S. Hammer (1990), *DikuMUD*, Datalogisk Institutved Københavns Universitet, Denmark. ◆ L. Pensjö, (1989), *LPMUD*, University of Gothenburg, Sweden. ◆ *Second Life* (2003), developed and published by Linden Lab. ◆ *Ultima Online* (1997), developed by Origin Systems, published by Electronic Arts. ◆ *World of Warcraft* (2004), developed by Blizzard Entertainment, published by Vivendi.

ACTIVITY FLOW ARCHITECTURE
Environment Design in Active Worlds and EverQuest

We all acknowledge the importance of carefully planning urban environments to make them functional for the people living and working in them. Everything from the creation of a working infrastructure to considerations of sociocultural character has to be taken into account. When virtual worlds reach high enough levels of complexity, these issues become relevant for them as well. In this essay, I will contrast two systems in an attempt to illuminate the connection between structural and procedural aspects of virtual worlds.

Active Worlds

Active Worlds started out as a single world – *Alphaworld* – which went live in June 1995. It is a system of three-dimensional graphical environments in which participants can move around and interact with each other. Each world is a continuous space. A player's environment is downloaded and rendered based on what is within his view. The participants navigate using the arrow keys and can teleport to any place in the world by typing in the coordinates of the destination.

Alphaworld is now one of over 1,000 different worlds in the *Active Worlds* universe. With an area greater than the state of California's, it is the largest world in the system. In *Alphaworld*, anyone can build creations out of a library of over 3,000 different objects and textures. There are over a 100 million objects in *Alphaworld*.

Teleportation Architecture

In the physical world, the architecture surrounding a road exclusively for cars is typically very different from that surrounding one near which people walk. The former is sometimes referred to as 50 km/h architecture, a contrast to the 5 km/h architecture of the latter. The difference arises from the fact that it is impossible for people to take in as much visual information when passing by an area in a car as when walking. While a storeowner by a freeway puts up a big billboard with limited but easily perceivable information, an inner-city merchant fills his store window with an abundance of items and offers.

This difference in architecture is hard to see in *Alphaworld*. The fixed speed of avatar movement seems to be a key feature to consider, but an even more significant fact to take into account is that the avatars in this world are not using their feet that much; *Alphaworld* inhabitants are instead more likely to teleport to their destinations. This has given rise to what could be called a "teleportation architecture."

In a world where teleportation is possible, it does not matter so much how far away a place is as how easy its coordinates are to remember. Since one number is easier to memorize than two, it has become popular to build along the x- and y-axis, where one of the coordinates is zero, and along the diagonals, where both coordinates are the same. This emergent behavior was not discovered until a tool was constructed that could produce bird's-eye maps of the world. The star pattern is particularly noticeable in the picture on the left, taken in 1996. In the picture on the right, taken five years later, we see that the building activities have sprawled out to most parts of the center area of the world.

In a system in which the center of the world serves as the point of entry for all avatars, we can expect the colonization of space to follow the template of *Alpha-*

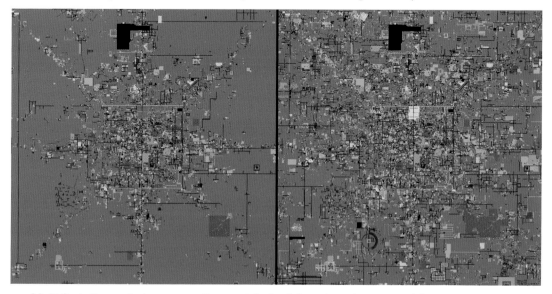

world. At first, the central areas are the most desired, but since the core activity of these worlds is building, not dwelling, people will be drawn to the rim of the developed areas in order to find free space to claim for their own creations. This development – and the sprawling city landscapes and suburbanization it produces – in some ways resembles that of many big cities in the physical world.

Alphaworld seen from above. The pictures were taken in 1996 and 2001.

The very center of *Alphaworld* is not open for free building and is instead maintained by the owners of the system. This area is very well structured and lively, reminiscent of Times Square or Piccadilly Circus, but it is surrounded by an inner-city area that has transformed into a ghost town. This problem parallels that of the deterioration of many real-world inner cities that have been deemed inappropriate for dwelling for various socioeconomic reasons. Just as efforts are made to rejuvenate inner-city areas in physical cities, it has been suggested that old developments should be deleted in *Alphaworld*. But who should decide what to tear down and what to leave? Some argue that all buildings are equally valuable and should be kept in order to preserve the history of the place. In relation to this debate, it has been suggested that it would be good if virtual buildings deteriorated the way physical buildings do so that one could see which are cared for and maintained and get rid of those that are not. The persistence of the digital building material turns out to be a mixed blessing when virtual urbanization is concerned.

EverQuest

When *EverQuest* went live in March 1999, it set a new standard for the scale and complexity of virtual-world-based games. It is a game in which players battle a variety of creatures in the virtual world of Norrath. The game is built on a system similar to *Active Worlds*', but with a closed graphics library. The participants wander over a vast terrain covering a number of continents divided into a large number of zones. The objective of the game is to advance one's character by increasing its experience and skill levels, which is achieved by killing beasts and completing quests.

Designers of digital games have always had to deal with how to limit the freedom of movement of the players. The classic example is the use of islands, which allow the designer to use the sea surrounding the island as a natural limitation for the exploration-minded player. In *EverQuest*, it is monsters that are used to restrict the freedom of movement. Low-level creatures surround the cities where an avatar begins to play, and the further out a player goes, the more dangerous the wildlife gets. In this way, the players are contained in a fairly limited area while they learn the basics and thus run less risk of becoming overwhelmed by the complexity of the game.

EverQuest is both a game and a virtual world. As a game, it needs to drive forward the process of playing. The most important driving force in the game is the desire to increase the abilities and experience level of one's character, which in turn allows one to see new zones and encounter new monsters. The pursuit of so-called experience points can be seen in terms of a number of possible paths traversing the geographical space. This means that the players must map the game landscape in two different ways. The first is as a traditional geographical map that shows which zones are adjacent to each other and how to get from one place to another. The second is as multiple process-oriented descriptions related to game goals.

Map of the moon
Luclin in *EverQuest*.

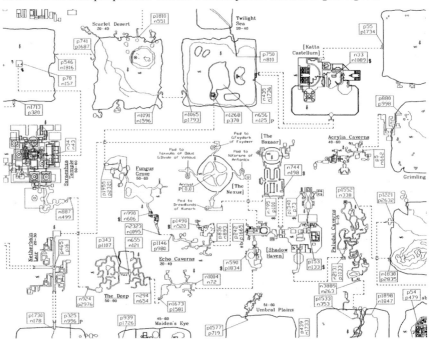

The process-oriented progression through the game becomes even clearer in the more advanced zones. In the figure below, the high-end zones are ordered in a flow-chart that describes how to progress through them to get to the Plane of Time, the most rewarding zone in the game at the time this illustration was made. The flow-chart also tells us that the *EverQuest* world can be understood as a flow of people through an environment, working their way towards achieving their goals.

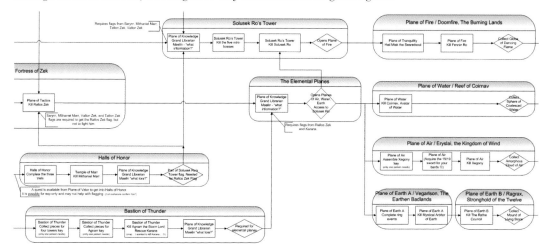

Activity Flow Architecture

In the case of *EverQuest*, the process that the world supports – or provides a pleasur-able resistance against – is the development of the player's character. The process-oriented nature of this task is not unique for gameworlds. In *Alphaworld*, it is the activity of building that drives the world and defines its structure. Virtual worlds need an activity of some kind to keep them going, and the architecture of the worlds should provide for the flow of this activity. Understanding this helps explain the success of Massively Multiplayer Online Games (MMOGs) and tells us something about how to create successful virtual worlds for other purposes as well.

A flowchart show-ing how to get to the Plane of Time.

◆ *Active Worlds* (1995), developed and published by Active Worlds. ◆ *EverQuest* (1999), developed and published by Sony Online Entertainment.

LINEAGE
Expansion of Space

On a normal day of 1999, some lines on a newspaper caught my eye. It was a story about two teenagers arrested on suspicion of theft. After a month of sitting in a PC-Baang (a Korean-style Internet cafe) playing the online game *Lineage* for ten hours a day, they had managed to steal armor and swords from other players and to move them into their own game accounts. The police traced the hiding place of the stolen items with the help of a game service company and arrested the thieves. A few months later, I saw another news story about the sudden death of a thirtysomething who had engaged in an online game all day and night for weeks on end and finally died from physical exhaustion. A few months after that, I heard about a game-addicted middle school student who killed his own brother because he could not discriminate the real from the game.

Cities in the past evolved around piazzas and marketplaces, where most social and economic activities took place. Unlike these meeting places of the past, the spaces of online gameworlds, which host from dozens to millions of citizens, do not require physical urban facilities. *Lineage* is full of interesting and dynamic rules, social activities and interactions between various agents. One can purchase a seemingly endless variety of items that might be needed in the gameworld, ranging from a tiny garment to almost everything imaginable. The number of items available increases continuously, and limited edition goods

168

are also available. Free trade is guaranteed for these items, and their value is as valid offline as online. A player can make conversation with other people in the game or even buy a house. All these things are graphically displayed in the *Lineage* world, whose overall spatial graphics concept evokes a fantasy world full of forgotten myths and wandering souls.

The territory in *Lineage* is constantly expanding. In addition, frequent "updates" change the features of the existing space either to accommodate increasing numbers of participants and their gaming demands or to control the balance of the game. In the case of *Lineage*, a characteristic update method is to expand the activity realm by "episode." Some users may think that their territory is expanded by their bloody ingame action. But though the physical space seems to grow larger, in actuality, it remains the same; in point of fact, it is the gamers themselves who change. Gamers are not always online, so they get access to the different zones of the gamespace at different times. They can thus meet anyone, at any time and any place, but it will almost always be a new experience with new people; it rarely occurs that someone meets the same gamer again in the same space. So the terrain of the gamespace keeps changing and expanding although the physical features remain the same. This environment is attractive to gamers because it provides them with endless new areas of exploration and goal-driven activity. They need to level up and earn money all the time to buy equipment and items and fight with stronger monsters. In *Lineage*, they can always explore more (newly created) areas of the world where adventure will always await them. Thus the space – both physical and emotional – keeps expanding as a result of the continual blurring of the border between online and offline worlds.

Game Review	Text	Developer	Publisher
	Troy Whitlock	Square Enix, The Walt Disney Company	Sony Computer Entertainment Europe, 2002

KINGDOM HEARTS
The Amusement Park as Metaverse

Kingdom Hearts is a popular action Role-Playing Game (RPG) for PlayStation 2, developed collaboratively by Square Enyx, known for its stylistic series *Final Fantasy* (1987-2006), and Disney, known around the world for its animated movies and characters. The world of *Kingdom Hearts* is a metaverse: a multidimensional reality through which an infinite number of fantastical worlds are interconnected. This multilayer approach is not only convenient, but also represents likely the only viable premise that can accommodate the diversity of Disney's characters and worlds. In the game, a growing darkness threatens to consume these worlds, and it is the player's task to journey from world to world, sealing each one off and thereby saving it from the approaching danger.

While the game itself is fairly linear, with gameplay serving as a narrative vehicle between rendered cut scenes, there are a number of interesting side missions and a diversity of architectural styles and environments that players encounter during their quests.

The 100 Acre Wood, home of Winnie the Pooh, is one of the most intimate locations players can visit in the game. The world exists inside a book, which players must assemble by collecting the torn and missing pages scattered in various levels of the game. Each page players add to the book opens a new minigame they can visit in the Wood.

The most interesting level of the game, The End of the World, reassembles the architectures of various worlds that have been consumed by the darkness. The ambiance and eerie sense of displacement there are as unsettling as the classic Disney short from Fantasia, "Night on Bald Mountain."

The most elaborate side mission in the game incorporates a unique "real-time" mechanic. Inside the Clock Tower of the Neverland level, players can find a series of stat upgrades and other power items hidden behind 12 doors. After each hour of gametime has elapsed, one of the doors opens for a few moments. To collect all of the items, players must diligently return to the Clock Tower every hour, on the hour.

Many aspects of the game evoke a nostalgic response from those with childhood memories of Disney movies or amusement parks. At times, the levels themselves feel as though they were constructed as location-based attractions. In particular, the Neverland level evokes the same sense of effortless flight captured by the ride Disney Imagineers created for Peter Pan's Flight in 1955.

Game Review	Text	Developer	Publisher
	Diane Carr	Blizzard Entertainment	Vivendi, 2004

WORLD OF WARCRAFT
Travel and Experience

World of Warcraft is a game, a place, a journey, a fiction and a stage shared by millions of subscribers. Playing this Massively Multiplayer Online Role-Playing Game (MMOR-PG) involves constructing a character and then "leveling up" in experience while adventuring across deserts and seas, exploring monster-infested forests, trading and socializing in cities and journeying deep into haunted dungeons.

New characters will arrive in the particular home territory determined by their "species" – elf, troll or human, for instance – and their politics (Alliance or Horde). They will make their way between villages and cities on foot, guided by signposts, or risk perilous cross-country detours. Players undertake quests alone or in groups, and the first challenge of most missions is arriving at the correct location. Characters journey across the game's varied and sometimes contested territories and into different dimensions ("instances" and "battlefields," for example). New modes of travel are discovered (giant bats, quadrupeds, zeppelins, portals) as a player's mileage and competence increase.

www.worldofwarcraft.com
www.wow-europe.com

Expertise is assessed by the game in battles lost or points scored. Expertise is marked by a character's level, gear and combat skills. A player's skills are demonstrated by effective team play, an ability to multitask with finesse and a fluency in *World of Warcraft* jargon, conventions and etiquette.

As a player, my perceptions of the game's offer, and of my fellow players' behavior will be shaped in part by my expectations, and these will alter according to the experiences I gain, seek out or stumble upon, the relationships that I form and the preferences that I acquire. For many, the social aspects of the game remain paramount. Full or in-character role-players exploit the dramatic potentials of *World of Warcraft*. Archivists delve deep into lore and history. Others, meanwhile, might choose to focus on player-versus-player ambush or specialist gear acquisition. During beginner and intermediate level gameplay, there is room for variability and experimentation. In high-level encounters, team management and precision are critical. Players might flit between all these possibilities, and clashes between different interpretations or realizations of the game are one source of tension between participants.

World of Warcraft is graphically rendered and persistent; players log on and off, but the game goes on. This colorful and inhabited world floats on a sea of user-generated content. Guild websites and player forums play host to heated debate, foster a sense of community and mentor new players. The fictional world of the game attains its varied meanings in part through this "off world" phenomena.

Essay   Text

Edward Castronova,
James J. Cummings,
Will Emigh, Michael
Fatten, Nathan Mishler,
Travis Ross, Will Ryan

WHAT IS A SYNTHETIC WORLD?

Synthetic worlds, or virtual worlds (we will use the terms interchangeably), are persistent online 3D spaces that replicate many of the features of the real world. One negotiates them using a virtual body much like a video game character, and many thousands of people can be in the world at the same time, making the environments much like a real place, socially speaking. The worlds have a sort of fantastical yet logical reality to them, such that people can fly, but only if they have wings or a flying spell or happen to be birds to begin with. The economies of synthetic worlds also have this fantastic-yet-logical flavor to them, enabling their creators to design not only buildings and roads but also geographies, markets, politics and communications. Our goal in this paper is to demonstrate the architectural procedure for building an economy.

Previous research into synthetic economies (and synthetic societies more generally) has focused exclusively on what they look like from the *outside* – that is, how we might understand them as *users*. Here, we report on our experience as *builders*. We represent an element of the design team for *Arden: The World of William Shakespeare*, which has been conceived as a massive gameworld that will serve Indiana University's dual missions of teaching and research. *Arden*'s teaching function is served by immersing its users in the language, plots and historical contexts of Shakespeare's plays. The research function is served by conducting controlled experiments on the genuine human social structures that will emerge within the world.

One structure that will certainly emerge is the market, and thus we will be in a position to conduct experiments on market dynamics. Yet the market can emerge in various ways. If we simply put items into the world and allow people to trade them, there will be economic activity: people will trade things they don't want for things they do want. Trade will happen at a more intense level to the extent that we create specialization, that is, to the extent that we endow different people with different goods and services. As an example: we could make a world where people can ride horses, and everyone also is a rancher, saddler and blacksmith. In that world, everyone would use his or her own ranch to raise a horse, own saddling skills to make a saddle and own smithing skills to shoe the horse. Alternatively, we could make a world where everyone must choose one of these occupations and "skill up" in it – that is, devote time to improving his or her character's ability to produce quality items. In this alternative world, there would be ranchers with many horses but no saddles and no shoes; saddlers with many saddles but no horses and no shoes; and smiths with many shoes but no horses and no saddles. To get all of these people on horses and riding, trade must occur. And the point is that there would be far more trade in the latter world than in the former. It is something that we can design into the game or not, depending on our objectives. If our objective involves research on market dynamics – and it does – we would want a thriving economy to exist in our world.

This paper lays out our approach to building a thriving economy. It also discusses some experiments we expect to be able to conduct with the economy we have built.

What Drives an MMOG Economy?

In video games in general and in MMOGs (Massively Multiplayer Online Games) in particular, players start the game with only a fraction of the play options and abilities that they will have at the end of the game. A newly created player character starts with the most rudimentary abilities and will later gain additional advancements through exploring the world and accomplishing various tasks. One type of character advancement is the acquiring of "innate" abilities – abilities that allow the character to attack in a certain way, heal other characters or accomplish any number of actions in the world. These innate abilities cannot be transferred from character to character. The second type of advancement is the acquiring of items more "external" to the player character: armor, weapons and tools that enhance a character's innate abilities. These items can be transferred from character to character and constitute a MMOG's source of market demand.

Within a given virtual gameworld there is a demand for "finished" items such as weapons that allow characters to hit harder, armor that enables them to withstand more blows from a weapon, or potions that give them temporary benefits. Players usually demand these better weapons and equipment because they assist in their survival while venturing into new areas of the world; innate abilities are not always enough to ensure safe passage. Further, new equipment also tends to bestow a new appearance on the wearer and functions as a status symbol. Anyone who sees a character with a particular piece of equipment knows that its player spent the time and energy to go through the necessary steps to obtain it.

Finished items can usually be obtained in two ways. The first is for a character to venture out in the world and discover an item, either through completing a specific task or defeating an enemy. The second method is similar to the first, but instead of obtaining finished items, characters obtain item components, which then must be taken to a character that is skilled in item creation. This crafting character can turn the components into a finished, useable item. The components themselves have no innate use: they do nothing but take up space until a crafter turns them into something useful.

This leads us to the demand for components. Not all items can be directly obtained through killing monsters and completing quests. Often, the best items (those that allow for the greatest character advancements) can only be made by player crafters. However, crafters cannot create items out of thin air; they require components that are gathered in dangerous areas or obtained through defeating monsters.

There is an obvious link of supply and demand between crafters and people who venture out into the world to kill monsters. Monster-killing adventurers need items, and crafters need raw materials to create items. Additionally, crafters are often bound to each other through supply and demand: most finished materials require items made by crafters of various different specialties. For example, a blacksmith might need a leather strap produced by another crafter in order to create the hilt for a sword.

What Makes These Items Scarce and Valuable?

There are three main reasons why items are valuable: some items, such as arrows or food, are constantly being used up and need to be replaced; other items are made valuable by the extent to which they increase a character's abilities; and other items are valuable simply because they are hard to obtain, and anyone who acquires them gains social prestige.

Most MMOGs attempt to enforce value through rarity. Less-powerful finished items and raw materials are allowed into the world on a frequent basis, but the truly powerful and valuable finished items and raw materials are much more difficult to collect. For instance, a valuable raw material might only appear one out of every 100 times a character collects raw materials from the ground. Likewise, the monster that drops the "Sword of Magic" might only drop the sword once every 100 times he is defeated or may only appear once a day, or the route to the monster might require the cooperation of multiple characters in order to gain passage.

Arden will make use of a system based on the broad ideas outlined above. It will have a constant turnover of items that need to be replaced, but players will retain more exceptional abilities and mementos that show the rest of the player base what they have achieved. Abilities and titles will fulfill the role of rare items, and the common items will be used as enablers to allow characters to use the abilities that they have obtained.

Possible Experiments

The economy of *Arden* has been designed to be rich, deep, persistent, complex, nuanced and rigorous. It is not an exact analog of a contemporary economy; indeed, it is not an exact analog of the economies on which it is based, namely, those of medieval England. Yet a wooden maze is not an exact analog of any real puzzle that humans face on a day-to-day basis, and a rat's mind is not an exact analog of a human's. Yet we can learn something about how humans act by examining the behavior of rats in wooden mazes. Our claim is that we can learn something about how societies of humans act by examining the behavior of human societies in synthetic worlds. Any experimental environment can be relevant to questions about the real world if the questions are posed at the proper level of abstraction. The questions we would like to pose to the economy of *Arden* involve very general issues of market dynamics at the macroeconomic level.

One general question, for example, involves the relationship of the money supply to the price level. It is believed that increases in money, unless accompanied by increases in trade, will lead to increases in the price level – that is, inflation. Questions posed at that level of abstraction can indeed be studied within *Arden* because *Arden* contains genuine, real instances of all the items being queried: it has money, it has trade, it has a price level and it has inflation.

Thus one can imagine the following sort of experiment. Set up two versions of *Arden*, exactly alike. Allocate players to the two versions randomly. In one, set the money supply at an arbitrary level, say £1,000. In the other, set the money supply at £2,000. We would predict that the price level ought to be higher in the latter world. If not, we would have to examine the environment and see whether the result is replicable. If robust, such a finding would serve as an empirical challenge to some fairly fundamental notions in macroeconomics.

This strategy of random assignment to controlled environments satisfies the "all else equal" requirement often stated in economic theories (and many other social theories as well). Indeed, this requirement is exceedingly difficult to meet under any of the contemporary methodologies now available. A great deal of processor power and econometric theorizing is spilled attempting to control for the various influences that get in the way of the independent variable's effect on the dependent variable. As the unit of observation becomes a larger and larger aggregate (families, towns, provinces, nations), it becomes harder to adequately model the structure of influences. Causation is difficult to establish with any confidence at all. Yet with this simple macro-level random-assignment experimental method, causation is established beyond a reasonable doubt. In a synthetic world experiment, all else is, indeed, held constant.

SID MEIER'S CIVILIZATION
Iterative Development

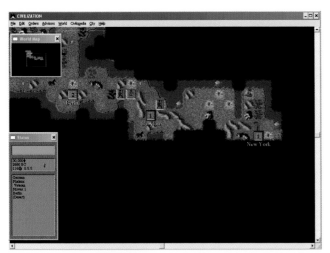

Civilization is an empire-building PC game developed by MicroProse and released in 1991. Play begins ca. 3000 BC, when the player selects his tribe, sets up his first city and sets out to advance his civilization from these beginnings. A clever mix of about 45 city improvements (e.g. city wall, courthouse, market place, palace), 65 civilization advances (e.g. alphabet, map making, mathematics, religion, trade) and 30 military units (e.g. catapult, cavalry, phalanx, trireme) allows the player to pursue his individual goal, whatever it may be – building the biggest city, conquering the world or attaining the ultimate "civilization score."

During the first hours of play, the interface is troublesome. Relevant options are not shown to the player at all times, and some are only accessible via menus (shortcuts are available, however). Even after these first hours, unintended system reactions will occur from time to time. A third and potentially most irritating weakness of the game – especially for players who like to delve into military conflict – lies in the enemy AI. Enemy units hanging around foolishly close to potential targets and bad unit balancing (e.g. weak units easily winning against a battleship) are two of the more annoying virtuality–reality discrepancies.

On the pro side, game goals are communicated clearly, players are rewarded constantly and full feedback is given at all times. Player motivation is encouraged by a shrewd combination of long-term goals (civilization score) with short- or mid-term objectives (winning the next battle, improving a city ranking, toggling the next civilization or making a military advance). Due to the tech tree concept introduced for the first time by *Civilization*, the player is always confronted with new challenges and gameplay options, but never flooded with too many.

Civilization borrows some of the most basic concepts from games like *Empire* (Northwest Software 1987), *Railroad Tycoon* (MicroProse 1990) and *SimCity* (Maxis 1989). But still, it must be considered a game industry milestone for two reasons. First, because thanks to its tremendous market success, many design teams have adopted the "iterative game development" methodology used by Sid Meier. The fruits of this technique encourage players to create a running version of the game every day. Play it! Improve it! The approach has had a significant influence on the way leading game development studios create their games nowadays. Second, because *Civilization* is still a benchmark title of excellent gameplay. Constant feedback and rewards, new challenges, fair treatment of players and the opportunity for ongoing exploration together create pure and enduring flow for both the casual and the hardcore audience.

What more can you expect from a game?

ANIMAL CROSSING
A Game in Time

In *Animal Crossing*, released by Nintendo for Game-Cube and later the Nintendo DS, the player moves into a town populated by cute, anthropomorphic animals. To succeed, the player must navigate the social and commercial world of his new town by acquiring a larger house, a group of loyal friends, fruitful employment, community awards and so forth. The primary activity of the game is acquiring and exchanging objects, either as gifts or by using money earned from running errands, fishing, hunting insects, gardening, recycling, and digging for fossils for the local museum.

Animal Crossing is one of the most thoroughly developed experiments in real-time-aware game design. The gameworld is synched to the console calendar and clock so that events in the game occur simultaneously with events in the real world, including major holidays, weather, seasons and the transition between night and day. The game design intentionally draws on the passage of time to create both emotional resonance and economic value in the gameworld.

The temporal nature of *Animal Crossing* not only encourages, but almost requires regular visits to the gameworld in order to reap full advantage from the game's numerous timed events. Certain fish, for instance, can only be caught at night or in winter. Some vendors only appear once a week – for example K.K. Slider, a musician who appears every Saturday night at the cafe and is the player's sole means of acquiring new songs to play on his ingame radio. On certain days of the year, there are contests in which the player can compete with ingame characters for the most beautifully grown garden, or swap meet days, on which players can bargain to buy and sell items they see in the houses of other residents. Many money-making opportunities reward real-world patience or attention: fruit growing on trees can be picked and sold to the local shopkeeper, but they take a certain number of days to ripen. Certain special vegetables like the Red Turnip become more and more valuable the longer the player leaves them planted, but they must be watered every day or they will die immediately. Some valuable bugs appear only in summertime.

Social relationships, too, are affected by time. Visit Brewster the Pigeon frequently, and he will offer you more friendly service and superior brews of coffee. Neglect to visit your friends and neighbors, and they'll move out of town. Miss the weekly tent sales of Crazy Redd, and you won't be able to fill the art gallery of the local museum. On the player's real-world birthday (which the game learns during character creation), all the citizens of the town wish the player a happy birthday and present him with a special birthday cake item accessible only on that day.

COMPETING IN METAGAME GAMESPACE
eSports as the First Professionalized Computer Metagames

Recent research on fandom spaces from Henry Jenkins (2006) highlights the emergence of media-oriented communities of practice, or "affinity groups" (Gee 2004). They form within the virtual spaces enabled by new media and communication technologies and create so-called "new third places" through the emergent behavior of their participants (Steinkuehler & Williams 2006). One example of such an affinity group is the eSports community.

What Is eSports?

There has been a long debate over whether we should think of competitive computer gameplay as a sport or not. Regardless of our view on this particular issue, it has to be expected that the activities society accepts as sport disciplines will change over time as underlying value systems change. In recent years, we have seen a rapid development and cultural integration of information and communication technology. The mastery of multimodal communication by means of synchronous and asynchronous voice and text messaging has become one of the most fundamental capabilities necessary to acquire high status within a group, particularly in youth culture. It is therefore expected that anybody who is part of such a group will feel the need to demonstrate such mastery by succeeding in competition.

"Sports" is a cultural field of activity in which people voluntarily engage with others with the conscious intention of developing and training abilities of cultural importance as well as of comparing themselves with the other people in these abilities according to generally accepted rules and without deliberately harming anybody. "eSports" is an area of sports activities in which people develop and train mental or physical abilities in the use of information and communication technologies.

The emergence of eSports can thus be interpreted as a logical and irreversible consequence of the transition from an industrial society to an information- and communication-based society. Beneath the *Counter-Strike* image, competitive computer gamers are training and comparing player competencies in networked and multimodal communication strategies or, more generally, competencies in the use of information and communication technology, something one might refer to as "cyberfitness."

History, Part 1: Children of *Doom*

The terms electronic Sports and eSports date back to the late nineties. One of the earliest reliable sources that uses the term eSports is a 1999 press release for the

launch of the Online Gamers Association (OGA) in which then Eurogamer evange-
list Mat Bettington compared eSports to traditional sports (The OGA 1999). Around the
same time, the discussion over eSports was fuelled by the failed 1999 attempt of the
organization of the UK Professional Computer Gaming Championship (UKPCGC)
to have the English Sports Council recognize competitive gaming as an official
sport (Knox 1999).

In the United States and Europe, the history of competitive gaming is usually
associated with the release of networked first-person shooting games, in particular,
Doom, released by id software in 1993, and the 1996 follow-up title, *Quake* (Kushner 2004).

Around the same time, teams of online players – also called "Clans" – started to
compete in online tournaments. By 1997, several professional and semi-professional
online gaming leagues had formed, most noticeably the still influential "Cyberath-
lete Professional League" (CPL), whose business concept was modeled on that of
the major professional sports leagues in the United States (Welch 2002). Among the first
CPL tournament events held in front of live audiences was "The Foremost Roundup
of Advanced Gamers," otherwise known as "The Frag," in 1997 (The Frag Diary 1997). According to the philosophy of the CPL, professional computer gaming was an emerging spectator sport. In 2000, game development company Valve released the game
Counter-Strike, a modification of its first-person shooter, *Half-Life* (1998). The game
quickly replaced *Quake* as the most popular title in competitive gaming and has
since then remained the central element in western eSports events.

Mousesports Profession-
al Gaming Clan. Source:
Deutscher eSport
Verband/Frank Sliwka.

History, Part 2: Children of *WarCraft*

Eastern eSports culture has its origin in Korea (Kim 2005). In the mid-nineties, Korean policy makers deregulated advanced telecom applications, causing a rapid growth of the Korean broadband infrastructure. This infrastructure needed to be filled with content, which was mainly provided by digital television and online gaming. In contrast to Americans and Europeans, however, Koreans preferred Real-Time Strategy Games and Massively Multiplayer Online Role-Playing Games (MMORPGs) such as *Lineage*, released in 1998 by the Korean game development company NCsoft, over first-person shooting games.

Since the late nineties, the Korean gaming market has been dominated by the multiuser real-time strategy game *StarCraft*, released in 1998 by Californian Company Blizzard Entertainment as a successor to the 1994 title *WarCraft*. The game is particularly well-suited to competitive gameplay. Furthermore, the vast broadband infrastructure in Korea favored the creation of television stations that were able to focus on broadcasting computer gaming events. The combination of these elements has resulted in a gaming culture in which individual *StarCraft* players are able to gain a cult-like status similar to that of professional athletes competing in major sports leagues.

Even though there is an increasing number of global eSports events – such as, for example, the World Cyber Games – that try to bring western and eastern eSports cultures together, the two systems remain largely separated and seem to develop almost independently.

Towards a Theory of Metagame Creation

In some sense, an eSport is a game played at the metalevel within the affinity group of a computer game. Competitors do not play the game, they play *with* the game; they play a metagame. In his book, *What Video Games Have to Teach Us About Learning and Literacy*, James Gee (2004) provides the theoretical background that allows us to explain how and why such metagames develop. According to Gee, a player immersed in a game utilizes the interactions between three separate identities to succeed at that game. First, there is the real identity of the player representing his or her real-world self. When playing a game, this real identity takes on a virtual representation in a virtual world, creating a virtual identity that lives inside the game. Any game interactions are defined by the rules of the game and are therefore restricted to the virtual identities of individual players. Gee continues by arguing that game immersion requires that these two identities be connected through a projection of the real identity onto the virtual identity. He calls this the "projected identity" of the player. If there is no such projection, the player will not be able to experience meaning in the game and will thus not enjoy playing the game.

At this point, however, we are not yet able to explain how meaning is transferred from within the game to the outside world. Generalizing Gee's argument, we propose that there has to be a back-projection from the virtual identity onto the real identity for such a transfer to occur. In other words, activities in the game-world must have meaning in the real world. As soon as such a transfer of meaning takes place, the rules that govern the interactions between virtual identities within the game will create metarules that govern real-world interactions between the real identities of the players. The result will be an affinity group acting within a metagame gamespace according to metarules – hence, a metagame.

Only the Beginning

It has to be noted that not all game activities can be transferred to the metalevel. In fact, designing scenarios that ensure such a transfer is the key issue in the theory of digital game-based learning. One of the game elements most easily transferred from the gameworld to the metagame world, however, is the element of competition. It is therefore not surprising that eSports is one of the first computer metagames to fully professionalize. It only represents the beginning, though. New institutionalized metagames such as machinima or virtual economies are already around the corner, and many more will follow.

◆ *Half-Life: Counter-Strike* (2000), modification for *Half-Life* (1998), developed by Valve Corporation, published by Sierra On-Line. ◆ *Doom* (1993), developed and published by id Software. ◆ Gee, J. (2004), *What Video Games Have to Teach Us About Learning and Literacy*, Palgrave Macmillan, New York NY. ◆ *Half-Life* (1998), developed by Valve Corporation, published by Sierra On-Line. ◆ Jenkins, H. (2006), *Convergence Culture: Where Old and New Media Collide*, NYU Press, New York NY. ◆ Kim, M. (2005), *Spiele-Boom in Korea*. Retrieved December 11, 2006, from http://www.game-face.de/article.php3?id_article=162 ◆ Knox, M. (1999), *The Sport of Computer Gaming*. Retrieved December 11, 2006, from http://www.3dactionplanet.com/features/editorials/sport/ ◆ Kushner, D. (2004), *Masters of Doom: How Two Guys Created an Empire and Transformed Pop Culture*, Random House Trade Paperbacks, New York NY. ◆ *Lineage* (1998), developed and published by NCsoft. ◆ *Quake* (1996), developed and published by id Software. ◆ *StarCraft* (1998), developed and published by Blizzard Entertainment. ◆ Steinkuehler, C. & Williams, D. (2006), "Where everybody knows your (screen) name: Online games as third places," *Journal of Computer-Mediated Communication*, vol. 11, no. 4. Retrieved December 11, 2006, from http://jcmc.indiana.edu/vol11/issue4/steinkuehler.html ◆ *The Frag Diary* (1997). Retrieved December 11, 2006, from http://bluesnews.com/articles/thefrag.html ◆ *The OGA* (1999). Retrieved December 11, 2006, from http://www.eurogamer.net/article.php?article_id=105 ◆ *WarCraft* (1994), developed and published by Blizzard Entertainment. ◆ Welch, T. (2002), *The History of the CPL*. Retrieved December 11, 2006, from http://www.thecpl.com/league/?p=history

PLAYING WITH FRIENDS AND FAMILIES
Current Scene of Reality-based Games in Beijing

A Trend of Playing in Reality

"Players are getting tired of screen-based games," says Nintendo game designer Shigeru Miyamoto. "It is important to offer something perceptible." (Lin 2007)

This statement was intended to advertise Nintendo's new product, Wii, but indirectly, it also illustrates the current trend of playing games based in reality and the close combination of games and physical environments. In Beijing, for one, reality-based games are getting quite popular. Three cases will be introduced in the following pages to illustrate the idea behind these reality-based games. The first, *Seek Bou Journey*, is a series of treasure hunts similar to riddle-solving tasks like those in *The Da Vinci Code* (2006). The second, *Killer Game*, is a social game based on Dimitry Davidoff's *Mafia*. And the third is *Majoy*, which turns screen combats into reality and has become the industrial catalyst for the development of Beijing's Capital Recreational District (CRD). The three games, all played in a real, physical environment, have characteristics and purposes that go beyond those of traditional screen-based games.

Discovering Beijing through *Seek Bou Journey*

"ZizhuYuan Park used to be a reservoir in the west of Beijing Zoo. In the Ming dynasty, people built the Zizhu temple on the north bank of the reservoir. That's why the park is called 'ZizhuYuan'. Standing on the west side of it, you will find a place named 'Bamboo' with dangling metallic plates. Find the first plate in the south. The first password should be the third character counting from the end." [1]

1 >
From "Password in Bamboo Grove," a treasure hunt in *Seek Bou Journey.* http://event.mosh. cn/jx/index_5292.html

Seek Bou Journey, first introduced in summer 2006, is the general term for a series of riddle-solving treasure hunts played within downtown Beijing. It is a game with two simple purposes: hunting treasures and getting acquainted with history. Because Beijing features geographically diversified cultures, potential playgrounds are pretty easy to find. Thanks to such diversities, the *Seek Bou Journey* series offers different kinds of tasks in each new installment, which, taken together, constitute a tour through Beijing enriched with various cultures. To date, there are already 18 *Seek Bou Journeys*. The very succession of these theme-based hunts proves that interest in the game is not temporary. To the contrary, it experiences monthly growth of hundreds of participants. Sixty percent of the participants are within the age range of 25 to 30, and most of them say that they enjoy such "learning while playing." Given this vast support base, the game's founder, Changxun, has released more hunts, now

186

focusing not only on educating players, but also on commercializing *Seek Bou Journey*. Although some tasks in *Seek Bou Journey* bear similarity to the popular treasure hunting game "geocaching" (begun in 2000),[2] most of them are designed based on regional cultural elements. For instance, in the 13th *Seek Bou Journey*, "The Art of Food," one task was to find clues in a chain restaurant that belongs to the well-known Huatian Group. The players had to follow instructions and order specific dishes in order to complete the task. The restaurant was thereby promoted in an innovative way. Because they are linked with specific businesses, the tasks in the hunt represent great opportunities for direct-marketing events as well as customized commercial activities. It is also likely that the future *Seek Bou Journeys* will become tourist packages. According to Changxun, travel agencies have already been contracted to develop packages, and various routes are in development. The tours will be announced in the first quarter of 2007.

< 2
Geocaching, released in 2000, is a game that consists of GPS-based treasure hunts. For more information, go to www.geocaching.com

Playing a Role in *Killer Game*

"Although I have lived in Beijing for 12 years, playing *Killer Game* for two months has been surprisingly helpful in better understanding Beijing people." (Rex, *Killer Game* player)

Killer Game, derived from the game *Mafia* invented by Dimitry Davidoff in 1986, is a role-playing and mind-reading game that is fun and enlightening. The game involves players sitting around a table arguing over who amongst them is the "killer," with each individual trying to prove his innocence. Situated either indoors or outdoors, *Killer Game* has an educational nature that helps players develop their ability to reason, express themselves and work in teams. Some Chinese corporations have even introduced *Killer Game* into their HR training programs to improve teamwork and self-expression skills (Yung 2006). Making its first appearance in Shanghai in 1999, *Killer Game* has quickly gotten quite popular among PR practitioners, journalists and IT professionals.[3] Thus far, those who play the game have not come exclusively from any one social group; quite to the contrary, the new web-based *Killer Game* provides a virtual alternative that has helped broaden the range of participants.[4] Moreover, the game has evolved gradually from a leisure activity into a paid entertainment in Beijing. A novel phenomenon named "Killer Bar" has quickly become a popular form of indoor entertainment along the lines of the video arcade, KTV, comic house and net café.

www.xclub.com. cn/Forums/games/ TopGame1.htm
< 3

< 4
http://www.killbar.com

The bar provides a set of standardized tools that facilitate fair gaming and comfortable environments. For instance, Xclub, founded in 2004, is the first specialized bar for *Killer Game*. Thanks in part to its fairly low service charge, Xclub has more than 1.5 million members. It is now the most authoritative commercialized model of a Killer Bar and has more than 20 chains nationwide. The Xclub incorporates an integrated gaming console that includes judging, player ID and charting functions, as well as a PA system. The console inspires further software and hardware development and encourages the making of game by-products like toys, masks and magazines. So far, there are about ten console manufacturers. And because the console is portable, *Killer Game* can be played in other commercial settings such as KTVs, net cafés, comic houses, restaurants or dating clubs.

Experiencing Reality *Counter-Strike* with *Majoy*

The name *Majoy* refers to a series of digitalized task-based reality games. Similar to *Counter-Strike* (1999), it is a war game with battle tasks like flag-catching and hostage-rescuing. As in classic Role-Playing Games (RPGs), players assume different roles and play in different playgrounds situated in "Majoy City," located at Shijingshan Sculpture Park in a western suburb of Beijing. In the semi-closed park, players need to complete tasks using varied digital equipment provided by the game operator, including, amongst other things, a PDA, a force feedback rifle and an outfit to which sensors are attached. The battle gear used in *Majoy* is more sophisticated, realistic and even more practical than that used in *Counter-Strike*. In a typical catch-the-flag task, the players must constantly run between distant information posts, all the while wearing their heavy equipment. The game forces them to achieve a high level of physical fitness as well as practice teamwork for the simple reason that it is impossible for a single player to manage survival without his fellow teammates.

Currently still in operational testing, a WAN-enabled "Majoy engine" adaptable to various tasks will soon be released. This will allow the game to extend beyond existing venues and enable players to continue playing at either physical or virtual playgrounds via various network devices. With such flexibility, more immersive *Majoy* experiences will be possible.

Majoy is not just a game; it also represents a Chinese entrepreneurial dream. At present, the game is situated at Shijingshan, Beijing's designated CRD. According to a 2005 news report, the regional government has already invested RMB 30,000,000,000 (close to four billion US Dollars) for the infrastructures that will facilitate recreational projects located there (Liang 2005). These projects – some completed, some still in the planning stages – include Majoy City, Dotman Cyber Recreation District, China Electronic Sports Development Center, Shijingshan Theme Park and Capital Steel Park. *Majoy*, for its part, is now played on both the municipal and national level and, thanks to this growth, has already attracted a large number of investors (Ministry of Science and Technology 2006). It is thus really not a surprise that *Majoy* has become the showcase for all other similar domestic projects.

The Advantages of Implementing Reality Games in Beijing

Beijing is currently attracting both global attention and international gold rushers who are investing heavily in new recreational facilities. The city has inherent advantages both social and spatial for playing host to reality-based games. The social advantage derives from Beijing being a megacity with a large population that can accommodate various types of players whose support of new games improves their profitability. Moreover, it is a city whose citizens usually welcome new ideas and have even come to expect more innovative and crazier ideas infused into additional games. As for the spatial advantage, it lies in Beijing's amazingly high density of diversified spaces used for entertainment purposes. A space like Shijingshan not only hosts Majoy City, but also many other entertainment venues such as Dotman Cyber Recreation District, Shijingshan Theme Park, Pleasure Land and Trans Global Festival, amongst others. A single commercial building accommodates a variety of commercial spaces such as a service club, a tea house, an Internet cafe, a comic house, a karaoke bar and a Killer Bar. And an average household contains a myriad of entertainment systems such as Karaoke, home theatre, TV game console and integrated media center.

As part of an effort to make Beijing China's digital entertainment center, major municipal policies launched last year greatly benefit game industries. These policies include the building up of platforms for business operations, digital property ownership, digital real estate transactions and game engines (Beijing Municipal Science and Technology Commission 2002). Preparation for the 2008 Olympics include providing all public areas in Beijing with 3G and Wi-Fi coverage; will this open the door for Beijing citizens to experience an even more pervasive existence of games in their city?

◆ Beijing Municipal Science and Technology Commission (2002), *The three policies of Beijing help the development of software industry*. Retrieved January 31, 2007, from http://www.most.gov.cn/dfkjg-znew/200610/t20061025_36947.htm ◆ *Counter-Strike* (2004), developed by Valve Software, published by Vivendi. ◆ Fen, Yung (2006), "Killer, A Wealth Game," *Beijing Business Daily*, 14 April. Retrieved January 13, 2007, from http://www.bjbusiness.com.cn/20060414/xiaofei2508.htm ◆ *Is Killer Game for crookers?* (2006). XIZI.NET discussion list, 28 February. Retrieved January 13, 2007, from http://www.xici.net/Cul/b385037/d35120961.htm ◆ Liang, Jen Pong (2005), "Shijingshan Facilitates the Capital Recreational District," *First Finance Daily*, 15 August. Retrieved January 8, 2007, from http://game.strongly.cn/shownews.asp?tables=s_center3&id=29 ◆ Lin, Jia Shu (2007), "Revolution of Nintendo," *Economy Observer*, 15 January, p. 9. ◆ Ministry of Science and Technology (2006), *A Study on Shi-jingshan's regional economic and social change through the economic and industrial reconstruction*. Retrieved December 20, 2006, from http://www.bjsjs.gov.cn ◆ Yung, Yu Mo (2006), "Killing Becomes An Industry," Manager, vol.9, pp. 32-33.

Game Review	Text	Developer	Publisher
	Dean Chan	Level-5	Sony Computer Entertainment , 2003

DARK CHRONICLE
A Game on Spatializing Social Relations

Dark Chronicle is a unique combination of role-playing game and town-building simulator that highlights the social consequences of spatial planning.

Players must rebuild a destroyed world by reconstructing each town in piecemeal fashion. Archival blueprints and construction materials for each site have to be tracked down. Prospective occupants must be sourced from elsewhere, and their individual needs also met prior to relocation. These multiple preconditions determine the spatial design of each town, but there is considerable latitude for player customization and manipulation of the core elements.

Town reconstruction requires players to alternate between object placement (accomplished in a bird's-eye isometric view) and subject negotiation (which involves interacting with the townspeople in a standard ground-level view). Hence, macro and micro perspectives are rendered equally important. This creates a spatial context within the game for engaging with both the personal and the social and experiencing how the two are inextricably entangled.

The contemporaneity of urbanized space is presented in the game as a complex interweaving of historical and present-day social relations. These relations are not only physically located in space, they are also produced by and positioned in-time.

Time travel in *Dark Chronicle* enables players to see how present-day actions bear tangible consequences for the future. For example, the reconstructed seaside town is the basis, or "origin point," as it is known in the game, for a huge science laboratory in the future. Yet this is not a case of abstract architectural development. Interaction with the scientific community reveals its connections to the historical townsfolk. A reflexive appreciation of spatiotemporal social linkages is thereby continually effected in the game.

All of the towns are socially connected. The movement of characters from one town to another allegorizes the voluntary migratory and multicultural dispersal of modern populations. Such spatiality is underpinned in the game as a dialogic and necessarily consultative process. Mutual respect is therefore crucial in forging intercultural bonds across these intricately networked social ecologies.

THE GETAWAY
Blending Video Game, Cinema and the City

In *The Getaway* (2002) and its sequel *Getaway Black Monday* (2004), the player navigates a character through the urban environments of London. *The Getaway* is unique amongst video games thanks to its accurate replication of the spaces and landmarks of contemporary London, including architectural features such as the London Eye, the Tate Modern and The Gherkin. In traversing the city spaces of *The Getaway*, players with some knowledge of real-world London enjoy an advantage, since London, albeit as a simulation, has been re-mapped onto the space of the video game.

The Getaway blends together the city, the video game and the cinema. Players (re)experience the city by playing the central characters of the video game narrative from a third-person perspective. These characters are placed on either side of the law – there's the ex-criminal and the policeman – and inhabit the gritty spaces of the criminal underworld: nightclubs, container docks, boxing halls and warehouses. As a player, you witness the unfolding of the story through filmic cut scenes. By driving at speed through the city, you reach relevant mission targets, and by undertaking missions, you achieve the game objectives through shooting and stealth.

The Getaway is designed for the adult gaming audience and has the cinematic look and feel of a London gangster film. To reinforce this cinematic appearance and to make the video game seem more immersive, all heads-up graphics (e.g. a health bar or map) are removed from the screen. Player health, or more to the point, lack of health, is indicated solely by the sound of heavy breathing, blood-stained clothing and the reduction of a character's gait to a stagger. The omission of heads-up display information reinforces the designer's cinematic ideals and allows players a greater sense of controlling characters within an urban environment.

To reinforce the reality of the city beyond replicating London's architecture, the generic socioeconomic conditions characterizing each individual district of London has its own distinct matching of pedestrian appearance and car types. Moreover, all cars in these environments are branded types drawn from the real world. With the advent of high-definition video games, London will return with even higher resolution imagery in the scheduled new edition of this game, The Getaway 3 for PlayStation 3. The Getaway series is an excellent example of how a real-world city can be reexperienced through the spatiotemporal media of the video game.

GRAND THEFT AUTO: SAN ANDREAS
An Immersive Real-Time 3D Urban Environment

In *Grand Theft Auto: San Andreas*, the player can drive, run and fly above and around an urban landscape. The way in which significant urban landmarks from the real world have been recreated within the space of this video game is bound to impress architects and urban designers. Here, the cities of Los Angeles, San Francisco and Las Vegas have been mimicked to form a new landscape called San Andreas. Replicas of the Golden Gate Bridge, the Hollywood sign and Santa Monica Pier, for example, are all present in San Andreas, yet located in a new geography. Rather than resembling the West Coast of the USA, the geography of San Andreas viewed from above reveals a series of islands, interconnected by a network of bridges.

In this video game, the player controls the character Carl Johnson, an ex-criminal returning home to find any plans for rehabilitation ruined by an onset of gang violence, corrupt law enforcement and a profitable black-market economy. In the video game, a series of non-linear storylines unfold during gameplay, and the completion of specific tasks, generally requiring a combination of driving and shooting, allows the player to progress and unlock more areas (islands) of the gamespace. Los Santos (Los Angeles) is experienced first, followed by San Fierro (San Francisco) and then Las Venturas (Las Vegas). Aside from the designated storyline, players will be well entertained by the game's simulation features. Players can induce characters to improve themselves via exercise, become fat by over-indulging in pizza, take driving lessons or get haircuts and new outfits. *Grand Theft Auto: San Andreas* is set in 1992, and the best indicator of this is the songs played on the various radio stations accessible while driving vehicles. Sonically, the video game also simulates the noise of an active city, including traffic sounds, of course, but also unsolicited comments from pedestrians and background environmental sounds produced by industry, docks and airports.

Grand Theft Auto: San Andreas is one of the *Grand Theft Auto (GTA)* video game series. Since its inception in 1998, the *GTA* series has continually utilized simulations of urban environments for interactive gameplay, and to do so has turned to real-world models of London, Miami, New York, Los Angeles, Las Vegas and San Francisco. *Grand Theft Auto III* (Rockstar North 2001) was the first in the series to create an immersive real-time 3D urban environment. *Grand Theft Auto: San Andreas* furthers the 3D representation of space by focusing on the role of simulation. As a video game, it offers the player the enjoyment of an unfolding storyline and the equally enjoyable experience of driving around a series of urban spaces and their surrounding landscapes.

Game Review	Text	Developer	Publisher
	Julian Kücklich	LucasArts	LucasArts, 1998

GRIM FANDANGO
Space as a Surreal Collage

Most computer games are over when you lose your life, but *Grim Fandango* isn't like most games. Here, death is only the beginning. The game is set in the Land of the Dead, where the protagonist, Manny Calavera, works as a travel agent. And no profession could be more apt for the central character of a game that takes the player on a fantastic journey through a world in which nothing is quite as it seems.

As the game begins, Manny is working for the Department of Death, situated on top of an office tower that looks like a cross between an Aztec pyramid and the Empire State Building. The unique visual style of the game, blending Mexican folklore, film noir and art deco, is one of its most outstanding features. And the slightly macabre mood of the game is further enhanced by its excellent soundtrack, made up of smooth jazz and Mexican folk music.

Unusual for an adventure game, *Grim Fandango* represents space in 3D, but the characters betray the genre's 2D roots. As the game's creator, Tim Schafer, once explained in an interview, the character design was modeled on the *calacas* traditionally made for the Mexican Day of the Dead. He points out that the skeletons are built as "tube-shaped bodies with the ribcage painted on," and that this technique reminded him of "cheap texture-mapping."

This low-tech approach was used to great effect in *Grim Fandango*. Rather than aiming for realism, the game reduces the characters' faces to cartoons, but the range of emotions these faces can express is remarkable. And the contrast between the crudely shaped bodies of the characters and their environment serves as a constant reminder that this is a game whose designers confidently chose the road less traveled.

An even more expressive style was chosen for the Land of the Living, where Manny travels early on in the game. The here and now is represented as a surreal collage of what seem to be 1950s mail-order catalogs, and the alienating effect of this depiction serves to make the outlandish world of the hereafter feel like home to the player. Indeed, one of the most striking things about *Grim Fandango* is how it manages to make the Land of the Dead feel so alive.

Nowhere is this experienced more intensely than in the city Rubacava, a stylish Las Vegas on the coast of the Sea of Lament. The city is dotted with memorable locations such as the Calavera Café, The Blue Casket (a favorite with the local dead-beatniks), the Feline Meadows racetrack and the High Rollers Lounge. The city feels forlorn and cheerful at the same time, a transient place that has learned its lessons from Robert Venturi. For the sake of Rubacava alone, the Land of the Dead is worth a visit.

PSYCHONAUTS
The Final Frontier and Beyond

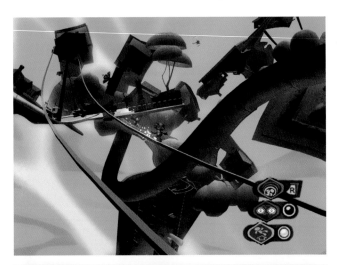

Psychonauts was released for the XBox in 2005. In it, you play Razputin, a young boy with psychic powers who shows up unexpectedly at a camp for psychic kids. The camp is staffed by psychic adults who train the kids and help them learn how to use their powers. Pretty soon, though, things go awry, and the player has to develop and use Razputin's powers in order to set them right. To do this, he must enter the minds of other characters in order to solve puzzles that can only be found in their heads.

Given this premise, the mind becomes the physical space that you as Razputin have to explore. This allows for some amazingly diverse spatial levels that don't have to adhere to any set of rules beyond those of the crazy worlds within the characters' minds. Each level thus features physical quirks based on the characters' personalities. Space becomes a representation of emotions, thoughts and character traits. The trick is to figure out how to plat-form-play your way through these spaces while also figuring out clues about the characters' personalities. These will help you successful-ly get through their minds and find the information you need in order to progress outside of the mental/emotional spaces, inside the world of the camp.

Psychonauts does a great job of altering the player's sense of space again and again and again. The world of the camp does, in fact, conform to some sense of reality, but this can be altered based on your – the player's – mental/emotional state, which, in turn, can be altered by using some of the abilities you gain throughout the course of play, by getting attacked by creatures in the campgrounds or by using some of the power-ups you can purchase from the camp store. These alter-ations are represented visually on the screen, thereby clearly demon-strating how the world bends to your perceptions and how this direct-ly affects gameplay.

Beyond that, the fact that each level exists within the minds of the other characters and is its own unique world with its own unique rules means that you the player must learn new rules in order to navi-gate each level successfully. And because the worlds are directly relat-ed to the personalities, emotions and thoughts of the characters, each one has a different look and feel and requires you to build on your abil-ities in order to platform through its spaces and solve its puzzles. The mental and the emotional becomes the virtually physical.

The idea of space in *Psychonauts* is thus extremely fluid, and you have to discover different ways to get around depending on where you are (or whose mind you're in). The real world is actually a less cru-cial part of the game; the most important part is the mental/emotional worlds you have to play through and use in order to learn about the char-acters. This underlines a general sense of how important perception and perspective are to our understanding of the world around us.

NARRATIVE ENVIRONMENTS
From Disneyland to World of Warcraft

In 1955, Walt Disney opened what many regard as the first-ever theme park in Anaheim, California, 28 miles southeast of Los Angeles. In the United States, various types of attractions had enjoyed varying degrees of success over the preceding 100 years. From the edgy and sometimes scary fun of the seedy seaside boardwalk to the exuberant industrial futurism of the World's Fair to the "high" culture of the museum, middle class Americans had plenty of amusements. More than the mere celebrations of novelty, technology, entertainment and culture that preceded it, Disneyland was a synthesis of architecture and story (Marling 1997). It was a revival of narrative architecture, which had previously been reserved for secular functions, from the royal tombs of Mesopotamia and Egypt to the temples of the Aztecs to the great cathedrals of Europe.

Over the centuries, the creation of narrative space has primarily been the purview of those in power; buildings whose purpose is to convey a story are expensive to build and require a high degree of skill and artistry. Ancient "imagineers" shared some of the same skills as Disney's army of creative technologists: they understood light, space flow, materials and the techniques of illusion; they could make two dimensions appear as three and three dimensions appear as two; they understood the power of scale, and they developed a highly refined vocabulary of expressive techniques in the service of awe and illusion (Klein 2004). Like the creators of Disneyland, they built synthetic worlds, intricately planned citadels often set aside from the day-to-day bustle of emergent, chaotic cities or serving as a centerpiece of escape within them. Narrative space is not new, nor is it an aberration of 20th-century capitalism and commercialism. In fact, architecture has functioned as a narrative medium for millennia.

Cities themselves also have a rich, emergent folk narrative of their own – a messy, unplanned story of ad-hoc expansion, a stark contrast to the highly controlled schema of narrative spaces (Mumford 1961, Brand 1994). Different stylistic motifs were layered upon each other. Against a scenography of a rich historical cityscape and a lineage of narrative spaces, European modernism must have seemed refreshing in its vision to shed the shackles of hegemonic ideologies and aesthetic eclecticism to create a new, purer form of space. Yet for places with little of their own historical backdrop, such as the newer, postautomotive settlements of the US, modernism ultimately became more blight than revolution.

Los Angeles is one such settlement. Barely 100 years old as a municipality when Disneyland was built, by 1955, the systematic erasure of its already meager history was well underway. Adobe missions and Victorian mansions were being razed to make way for steel girders and curtain walls. As cultural critic Norman Klein brilliantly and poetically explains, through the combined machinations of Hollywood and efficiency real estate, Los Angeles' short and less glamorous *real-life* history of immigration, agriculture and boosterism was supplanted by a *mise en scène* of movie backdrops, a "social imaginary" of the fictional histories of Los Angeles (Klein 1997).

It was in this sociocultural milieu, at the crest of the 20th century, against the backdrop of a systematically dehistoricized, increasingly sprawling, automobile-enraptured Southern California, that Disneyland was born. It is generally assumed that Disneyland was conceived as a mecca for Disney animation, the vehicle for the first modern entertainment mega-brand and the prototype for transmedia. Quite to the contrary, in its initial conception, the theme park contained no references to Disney animation at all. Disneyland was envisioned as a kind of "locus populi" of narrative space, a pedestrian haven for families, traversable only by foot or by train (Hench et al. 2003). It was a return to a more innocent past and perhaps a reaction *against* the suburban, freeway-interlaced sprawl that Southern California had become.

In places like Paris, London, Athens or even New York or Boston – urban centers rich in history and interwoven with centuries of narrative – there was no need to create synthetic stories in the architecture. Cathedrals and castles are the narrative structures of Europe. New York's emergent stories are inscribed in the wrinkles of its weatherworn edifices. Disneyland was created to fill a vacuum that did not exist in cities with a history, a vacuum that was uniquely regional and historical or, more accurately, ahistorical. In some sense, Disney was trying to rehistoricize Southern California. While Disneyland's value as high design or low design is certainly arguable, what cannot be argued is that it fulfills a deep need in contemporary mass culture – particularly in the United States – for a human-scale, pedestrian experience of immersion in a three-dimensional narrative. In Europe and even in the northeastern United States, such immersion is commonplace; in Southern California, it's not.

From Theme Parks to Games

Thanks in part to the advent of 3D and eventually real-time 3D in the 1990s, video games have come increasingly to resemble theme parks in terms of both design and culture. Both can be classified as "spatial media" (Pearce 1997). Digital games, with their conventions of real-time 3D and highly spatialized storytelling techniques, can be viewed as one step in the development of narrative environments with their own unique poetic structures (Klastrup 2003). In addition to making use of the major facets of theme park creation – spatial narrative, experience design, "illusion of authenticity" and immersion – digital games and networks also introduce three new key dimensions to spatial media: Agency, Identity and Persistent Community.

Glimmerings of theme-park-style craftwork can be seen in seminal single-player titles of the early 1990s. While spatial gaming has its precursors in text-based adventures, i.e. MUDs and MOOs, it began to emerge in visual form in games like the *Monkey Island* series (1990-2000), the landmark *Myst* (1993) and creative masterpieces like *Blade Runner* (1997) and *Grim Fandango* (1998). In these, the illusion of authenticity and the integration of space and story are at their highest level of artistry. In addition to richly articulated themes and narratives, these games also introduce the added dimension of player agency, although they tend to constrain it to physical navigation and limited interaction with the world and its inhabitants. Unlike visitors to Disneyland, which is a highly controlled environment, the players of these games can begin to engage with the gameworld, enacting their own agency in a more dynamic way. Yet this has its shortcomings: in *World of Warcraft* (2004), for example, unlike in Disneyland, aberrant behavior such as public disrobement is commonplace due to the lack of social controls. But in spite of such drawbacks, Disney has also attempted to add increased agency to the experience of its kingdom through experiments such as the *DisneyQuest* Virtual Reality attraction and the recent *Kim Possible* Alternate Reality Game based on the popular children's television show.

The greatest parallels between theme parks and games can be drawn from the advent of graphically based Massively Multiplayer Online Games (MMOGs). First and foremost, they are public places that thousands of people enter simultaneously to share an entertainment experience. Most MMOGs are themed, and it is interesting to consider the history and significance of that theming. Starting with the tabletop role-playing game *Dungeons & Dragons* (1979) and some of its offspring (such as *Warhammer* (1983), for example), the vast majority of online role-playing games have been and continue to be based on or inspired by J.R.R. Tolkien's *The Hobbit* (1937) and *The Lord of the Rings* trilogy (1954-55). Peopled with elves, dwarves, orcs and all manner of fantastical monsters, these virtual worlds rival Disneyland in both scale and audience. According to the independent website *MMOG Chart*, 93.5% of the major MMOGs revolve around *Dungeons & Dragons*-style themes (http://www.mmogchart.com/). The medieval fantasy theme is nostalgic in a sense, but it also imbues games with features like alternative races, monsters and magic. The growing appeal of these themes on a mass level cannot be denied; in 2004, the Korean game *Ragnarok Online* (2002) surpassed 17 million subscribers, and as of this writing, the number of *World of Warcraft* participants has passed the eight million mark. By way of comparison, the average attendance in Disney Parks is about 15 million annually (Niles 2005); Disneyland's admission price is about three times the monthly subscription to *World of Warcraft*.

Like Disneyland, the bulk of Massively Multiplayer Online Role-Playing Games (MMORPGs) – starting with *Meridian 59* (1996) and *Ultima Online* (1997), which are among the earliest, all the way up to *World of Warcraft* and *Ragnarok* – play host to primarily pedestrian cultures. *World of Warcraft* allows travel by mount (high-level players can purchase a horse or other suitable creature), rental of a griffin to fly from one place to another (via a network of fixed "flight paths" throughout the world) or subway transport between the major "Alliance" cities. Also like Disneyland, *World of Warcraft* contains different "lands" with unique themes: on the "Alliance" side (the good guys), there are human areas, elven areas, dwarf areas and gnome areas, while areas such as "The Barrens," "Desolace" and "Mulgore" are dominated by the "Horde" (bad guys).

In addition to extending the player agency of the earlier spatial games through features such as added navigation, interaction with nonplayer characters, quest-based gameplay and dynamically interactive battle scenes, the integration of a network into MMOGs creates two additional dimensions of gameplay: Identity and Community.

Unlike at Disneyland where every visitor is a "guest," in MMOGs, every guest is a "resident," a citizen of the online world, if you will. Following a model more akin to Renaissance fairs and live action role-playing, players are not simply spectators, but rather take the *roles* of elves and orcs fully engaged with the narrative and conflicts of the game. Unlike at a costume party or on Halloween, however, these identities are "persistent," meaning the player maintains the same role over time. One game that has tried to walk the line between players having a "role" and playing "themselves" is the recently relaunched *Myst Online: Uru Live* (2003/2007). In this game, players take the role of explorers who, presumably playing themselves, have come together to uncover the mystery of the abandoned underground city of *D'ni Ae'gura*. This kind of persistent identity is a prerequisite for the last and final game dimension created by digital networks: Community.

Although Disneyland has generated a fan community, it fails to fully realize Walt's aspiration to recapture the small town of his youth. The lack of a persistent identity amongst visitors is one key reason for this. Community can only occur in a context that blends agency with persistent and recurrent attendance and an ongoing sense of participation, neither of which is afforded by the infrequent visitation scheme of theme parks. By moving players beyond the role of spectator and towards the role of a full participant in the narrative, MMORPGs allow players to "live" in their magical worlds as citizens, rather than simply visit them as guests once or twice a year.

From Games to Virtual Themed Cities: The Fourth Dimension

Finally, we see a fourth dimension emerging in new virtual worlds such as *There* (2003) and *Second Life* (2003). In these worlds, players are not merely citizens of someone else's fantasy world, but actually have a hand in constructing the fantasy themselves. I term this "productive play," in which play merges with creative production (Pearce 2006a/2006b). In *There*, players can design their own houses, vehicles and fashions, which then become part of the world and can be acquired by other players. In

Second Life, virtually everything in the world is created by players. Many players even buy their own islands on which to build, in a sense, their own theme parks. These "co-constructed" worlds merge MMOGs with user-created content such as that seen on websites like MySpace and YouTube, yet they go beyond the scope of these sites by combining all player creations in a single, contiguous virtual world.

An interesting confluence of the former and latter type of world is the emergence of an *Uru* fan culture within the player-created worlds of *There* and *Second Life*. When *Uru* closed in early 2004, not wishing to see their communities destroyed, players from the game immigrated en masse into other virtual worlds where they began to re-create numerous cultural artifacts of their former "home." Members of the "*Uru* diaspora" in *Second Life* created a near-exact replica of *Uru*, while another group of *Myst* fans created a totally original *Myst*-style game. In *There*, players continue to create *Uru* and *Myst*-inspired artifacts and environments, such as a recreation of the "Channelwood Age" (a game level) from the original *Myst* game.

Are MMOGs the new theme parks or are they the new cities? Perhaps, in some respect, they are both. On the one hand, they provide the human-scale pedestrian fantasy of Disneyland, a respite from the modern, homogenous, cookie-cutter reality of suburban sprawl. On the other hand, they provide the level of ongoing participation and contribution afforded by cities. And when players can contribute to the world itself, they become more like themed cities in which players bring their own fantasies to bear on the environments. Whether highly synthetic and predesigned like *World of Warcraft* or player-created and emergent like *Second Life* and *There*, these virtual themed cities clearly fill a longing that parallels Walt Disney's initial inspiration over half a century ago: the desire to be part of a "small town," a community to which one can belong and, in the case of digital virtual worlds, potentially contribute.

◆ *Blade Runner* (1997), developed by Westwood Studios, published by Virgin Interactive. ◆ Brand, S. (1994), *How Buildings Learn: What Happens After They're Built*, Penguin, New York NY. ◆ *EverQuest* (1999), developed by Verant Interactive, published by Sony Online Entertainment. ◆ *Grim Fandango* (1998), developed and published by LucasArts. ◆ Hench, J., Lefkon, W. & Van Pelt, P. (2003), *Designing Disney: Imagineering and the Art of the Show*, Disney Editions, New York NY. ◆ Klastrup, L. (2003), "A poetics of virtual worlds," *Proceedings from Digital Arts and Culture Conference*, Melbourne, Australia. ◆ Klein, N.M. (1997), *The History of Forgetting: Los Angeles and the Erasure of Memory*, Verso, New York NY. ◆ Klein, N. M. (2004), *The Vatican to Vegas: The History of Special Effects*, Verso, New York NY. ◆ Marling, K.A. (ed.) (1998), *Designing Disney's Theme Parks: The Architecture of Reassurance*, Canadian Centre for Architecture/Flammarion, New York NY. ◆ *Meridian 59* (1996/2002), developed and published by 3DO/Near Death Studios. ◆ *Monkey Island* series (1990-2000), developed and published by LucasArts. ◆ Mumford, L. (1961), *The City in History: Its Origins, Its Transformations and Its Prospects*, Harcourt, Brace & World, Inc., New York NY. ◆ *Myst* (1993), developed by Cyan, published by Brøderbund Software. ◆ Niles, R. (2005), *Disney slams Universal in 2005 theme park attendance*, Retrieved December 27, 2005, from http://www.themeparkinsider.com/flume/200512/2/ ◆ Pearce, C. (1997), *The Interactive Book: A Guide to the Interactive Revolution*, Macmillan, Indianapolis IA. ◆ Pearce, C. (2006a), "Productive Play: Game Culture from the Bottom Up," *Games and Culture*, Issue 1, vol. 1. ◆ Pearce, C. (2006b), *Playing ethnography: A study of emergent behaviour in online games and virtual worlds*, Ph.D. Thesis, SMARTlab Centre, Central Saint Martins College of Art and Design, University of the Arts London. ◆ *Ragnarok Online* (2002), developed and published by GRAVITY Co., Ltd. ◆ *Second Life* (2003), developed and published by Linden Lab. ◆ *There* (2003), developed and published by Makena, Inc. ◆ *Uru: Ages Beyond Myst* (2003/2007), developed by Cyan, originally published by Ubisoft, re-released in 2007 as *Myst Online: Uru Live* by Gametap. ◆ *Warhammer* (1983), developed and published by Games Workshop. ◆ *World of Warcraft* (2004), developed by Blizzard Entertainment, published by Vivendi.

PLAYING WITH URBAN LIFE
How SimCity Influences Planning Culture

"Is it time – to be Mayor? Do you have the empire-building skills to develop a metropolis of soaring skyscrapers or the aesthetic sensibilities to create a city that delights the eye? Do you enjoy tinkering with an entire world – widening a riverbed there, increasing a tax rate here – to see the effects on the inhabitants under your sway? Or do you want to get down and dirty with The Sims in your streets, taking on missions that have you hurtling down highways in a tank?"

These are the welcome lines to *SimCity* (1989), one of the most influential strategy games in the history of urban planning. While designing the game *Raid on Bungeling Bay* in 1984, Will Wright discovered that flying an attack helicopter over a swath of islands wasn't half as fun as designing the islands themselves. Out of an interest in city planning and computer modeling theory, he conceived of a game that would let players build cities and watch them function. The first *SimCity* was published in 1989. Since then, the *SimCity* series has paralleled and influenced the now omnipresent, if not always well-conceived use of computer simulation in contemporary urban planning.

Early Influences

Wright acknowledges the influence on *SimCity* of systems dynamics, an approach to analyzing how complex systems change over time. Its "founding father" and an outsider to city planning, MIT Professor of Management Jay Forrester, laid the foundations for computer simulation in his 1969 book *Urban Dynamics*. Instead of simple intuitions about urban policy that treated symptoms instead of causes of urban decay, he advocated a balanced, multivariate assessment of existing conditions and how they might fluctuate with changes in job training, new enterprises and low-income housing. If his proposal was not entirely successful, it was because not all behaviors could be modeled and because of the large scale of his assumptions. Even the smallest systems are hard to predict, and his model applied statistical data to the city as a whole, rather than treating more localized areas; later versions of *SimCity* remedy this problem.

Architect and mathematician Christopher Alexander is the next key influence on in the creation of *SimCity*. His work in the 1960s and 1970s advocated an idealistic departure from the then-popular top-down modernist models towards what he called a universal way of design and development based in the logic of human–city interrelations. In his essay *A City Is Not a Tree*, he denounced cities designed to fit a "tree" pattern – cities that are compartmentalized so that individual sections function independently of each other – and celebrated cities that fit a "semi-lattice," in which each section bleeds into the others by virtue of overlapping functional systems. His following work applied his planning theories to the basic elements of architecture, suggesting that universal principles could be found that are applicable to everything from the organization of an entire countryside down to the construction of a home.

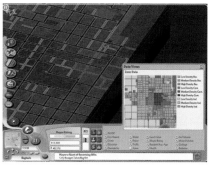

The original *SimCity*.

SimCity also has a strong colonial underpinning. Witold Rybczynski, Professor of Urbanism at the University of Philadelphia, has demonstrated that *SimCity* resonates with certain early colonial assumptions about cities. In his 1995 book *City Life*, he argues that the American city is different from the European city because its early planners were faced with an abundance of open space and worked accordingly. They often allowed laissez-faire consumption of undeveloped land. The principles of freedom, equality and respect, the theory went, would arise naturally in a world that had the social and physical space for individuals to vote with their actions and real estate purchases. Early planners also tended to envision continued growth. To the extent that planning happened, it was done in a way that left room for later expansion, often by means of a grid that could grow proportionately with the population.

SimCity's Black Box

The works of Forrester, Alexander and Rybczynski serve as *SimCity's* foundational ingredients. One can see the influence of systems dynamics in the game's rating of player performances based on whether all "goods" – from industrial land to public schools – are being supplied at levels that satisfy a computer-calculated model of demand. Alexander's influence is found in the fact that the game allows for numerous configurations of a limited number of categories of building design and zoning and thereby imposes a universal aesthetic on the cityscape. This aesthetic favors segregated zoning over mixed use and stresses homogenous, class-segregated neighborhoods. Finally, an inherited colonial view shows land as existing in infinite supply by allowing players to settle in areas of land devoid of cities or inhabitants and by favoring urban grid structures over organic development.

An emphasis on the power of the mayor (i.e. the player) is also a key feature of the game. The only way that SimCity will eject a mayor is if he severely bankrupts the city budget. Otherwise, the player will never have to face questioning by the local council, campaign for reelection or experience the pressures of any other democratic process. The mayor has absolute power to build, demolish, tax and spend. Unwieldy growth and megalomaniacal destruction are the two poles of city development and the player's most likely courses of action. Thus the heart of the game is much less a universal vision of city design than it is a reflection of the most extreme tendencies of development in the USA.

Land zoning analysis.

The many aspects of urban planning and development that do not reflect this model of total control over virgin territory get short shrift. *SimCity*'s narrow lens only captures half of the story of urban development. Nevertheless, aspiring and practicing urban planners have been looking through this lens for several years, with influential results.

Not Just a Game

From the beginning, *SimCity* stressed a desire to influence policy and especially education by nurturing reflection on the nature of "ideal cities." No other game has been used so widely at so many levels of schooling to help illuminate the different elements of local government. For example, David Lublin, Professor in the Department of Governance at American University, used *SimCity* to teach 20th-century local government. After creating a SimCity of their own, his students had to write a paper analyzing the game's underlying principles. "A fundamental aspect of the paper was to stress how it reflected real world conditions, and what aspects were ignored or sent to a second plane," explains Lublin. Because of the widespread use of *SimCity* in schools and homes, it is easy to make a case, as public affairs expert Paul Starr of *The American Prospect* has, that *SimCity* provides a more influential introduction to city planning than any book on the subject.

The differences between SimCity and a real city seem to be narrowing as new versions of the game take more sophisticated real-life issues into consideration. Such features as, for example, regional planning and bedroom communities that resemble facets of real-life urbanism have been incorporated. But more importantly, real-world planning increasingly resembles *SimCity* planning thanks to a growing use of technology, often in support of a *SimCity*-like top-down model of local government. Geographic Information Systems (GISs) have replaced paper maps as the main medium of geographic analysis in government agencies across the USA. A GIS integrates different sets of geographic data by, in effect, allowing a user to overlay transparencies. The system can then show, for example, which homes are within a five-minute drive of a fire station. While their roots are in evaluating how environmental conditions limit potential developable land, GISs are now used by planning departments to evaluate social elements of city life. For instance, many departments overlay census data to make zoning decisions relative to income, class, education levels and development desirability. *SimCity* uses the same basic analytic mechanisms; consequently, when schools use *SimCity* to teach urban planning and politics, they are teaching the framework of analyzing environmental and social relations via a GIS.

A GIS by itself cannot make choices on issues like gentrification, race inequality or immigration. It can tell planners what a policy's likely effects will be (for example, how many existing residents might be displaced as a result of a redevelopment project), but cannot say whether those effects are desirable. This *SimCity*-like analysis can blind city leaders to problems that lie outside of the system's geographic or political scope. Washington, D.C. Mayor Tony Williams, for example, placed much faith in advanced GISs and data systems, which led him to the conclusion that to solve budget woes, he has to attract 100,000 new, wealthy workers who will provide high taxes. Other solutions may be viable, such as restructuring local taxes in a city in which 66 percent of the local income is not taxed

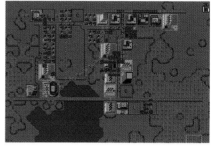

SimCity traffic analysis.

and the Federal Government owns 42 percent of the real property. But such options remain unconsidered if the city model takes these fiscal factors for granted. The alternatives may be rejected for sound reasons, but they should at least be subject to open debate, not hidden in the black box of model assumptions.

Power-Trip Planning

The family of *Sim* games has always featured subtle ironies that combine experience with a witty sense of humor. But new versions of the game add power-trip possibilities that would give any real city planner a God complex. In a return to Wright's original helicopter attack game, not only can players now demolish buildings from a tank, but they can also run "vehicle missions." The mayor can drive to an area of low mayoral popularity that threatens to strike or revolt; hold down the space bar, et voilà, the mayor is throwing bills from the limo that stop the demonstration. The mayor's rating is

Crowd control: the mayor throws money to demonstrators.

restored. Of course, this scenario reflects the reality of some cities. But shouldn't a game of influence not just teach power accumulation but at least attempt to instill a sense of what civic development can and should do? Some sense of values that transcend a narrow interpretation of supply and demand?

◆ Alexander, C. (1965), "A city is not a tree (Part II)," *Architectural Forum*, vol. 122, no. 1&2. ◆ Forrester, J. (1969), *Urban Dynamics*, Productivity Press, University Park IL. ◆ *Raid on Bungeling Bay* (1984), developed by Will Wright, published by Brøderbund Software. ◆ Rybczynski, W. (1995), *City Life: Urban Expectations in a New World*, Scribner, New York NY. ◆ *SimCity* (1989), developed by Maxis, published by Maxis et al.

SIMCITY
Simulating Nothing

Since its release in 1989, no video and computer game has done more than *Sim-City* to advance the notion that entertainment could be wrung from any topic, even one as apparently pedantic or banal as city planning and management. Void of obvious narrative conflict, *Sim-City* pushed the possibilities of games to the limits, ironically by presenting gamers a construction set with few building parts and an even more limited set of outcomes.

And yet fans flocked to the game by the millions, making *SimCity* a commercial hit that spawned a whole new game genre – the sim. After *SimCity*, games no longer needed clear goals or narrative action; if a game was classified as a "sim," it had the potential to sell.

Educators long interested in the pedagogical potentials of the computer saw *SimCity* as an obvious argument for how games could teach. The seemingly serious nature of a game based on urban planning appeared to link objective content with motivated engagement, all the more so because it was shelved next to titles about defeating space aliens and dragons. It appeared as though people were paying to play while they learned.

What successive iterations of the series and critical scrutiny have revealed is that *SimCity*, in fact, simulates nothing other than itself.

This realization provides the key to understanding both *SimCity*'s value as an educational tool and its perennial appeal as a video game.

SimCity demonstrates the fundamental appeal of observing and interacting with systems. Like a lava lamp that accepts input, *SimCity* allows players to test theories and construct mental models of a hidden system. The rhetorical layering of the city provides a frame of reference and, to a degree, constrains the possibilities of that system. But ultimately, *SimCity* reproduces the basic structure of all "sandbox games," encouraging players to experiment with the computer game medium and enjoy the play of system elements in motion.

Whether one is attempting to build a city "like the one on the box" or actively destroying a successful town with one of the game's built-in disasters, the joys of *SimCity* are not found so much in the inherent pleasures of city planning and governance, but rather in seeing how the game models the connections between its parts. Building roads creates pollution, stimulates industry and increases housing demands. Flying saucer attacks ravage the city core, but also provide fascinating potentials for brown field development and rewiring the operation of the city system.

SimCity's central deceit is that it simulates urban life. Its central pleasure is that it only simulates *SimCity*.

Game Review	Text	Developer	Publisher
	Kurt Squire	Anim-X	Electronic Arts, 2001

MAJESTIC
Blurring the Lines between Computer Games and Reality

Majestic, released in July 2001, was one of the first commercial Alternate Reality Games that sought to blur lines between computer games and reality. A science fiction thriller in the tradition of *The X-Files* (20th Century Fox TV 1993-2002), *Majestic* opened with a news video feed explaining that the building of an Oregonian game developer, Anim-X, had caught on fire and that *Majestic* was thus going to be discontinued. Shortly thereafter, players received a mysterious email message with a link to an underground website suggesting that the fire was no accident; the building had been blown up because the game developer was "getting too close to the truth" about the nature of a governmental conspiracy. Your job as player was to figure out what this conspiracy was all about.

The gameplay itself consisted of somewhat traditional adventure mechanics, with players given an overarching challenge – i.e. "track down the conspiracy" – via various clues – e.g. "a mysterious black helicopter was seen near the fire." Most of the game was played via a simple AOL-style chat client that integrated chatrooms, email, a buddy list and a Web browser, although players could sign up to receive phone calls, faxes and text messages as well. Each message contained narrative pieces, which functioned as clues that needed to be assembled in order to unravel the mystery.

When it worked, *Majestic* produced some of the most memorable game experiences of the year for its players. Imagine being at the

212

SPACE TIME PLAY

bank and your cellphone rings. You hear a whispery voice telling you that "they" are on to you and know what you're doing. Or a confused secretary runs into your office with a mysterious fax in hand. When it worked, *Majestic* turned the mundane of the everyday into the sublime.

But the game never reached widespread commercial success for a variety of reasons. First, it had the misfortune of shipping six weeks before the terrorist attacks of September 11, 2001, which caused Electronic Arts (EA) to pause its service for fear of backlash or confusing players. It is also likely that the attacks – at least in the short term – reduced consumer demand for a government conspiracy game. Second, the game was initially only purchasable via the Internet, and EA reported that technical glitches prevented a large number of would-be buyers from successfully downloading it.

Aesthetically, the game suffered from a mismatch between its story/narrative, its core target audience and its gameplay mechanics. Players received new clues on a "timer" (messages were doled out a few per day), which meant that hardcore players were unable to play for more than ten or 20 minutes daily. Furthermore, the clues themselves were relatively simple for those who had played adventure games in the past; to them, most of the conversations and content appeared "shallow" in comparison to games on traditional platforms. Thus *Majestic* suffered from too mixed a set of features, some of which appealed to a hardcore audience (i.e. the innovative game style, the download-only availability, the marketing campaign (the game plays you) and the pervasiveness), yet others of which appealed to a more mainstream player (i.e. accessible content/themes, a not too difficult challenge, limited play sessions).

NEW PUBLIC SPHERE
The Return of the Salon and the End of Mass Media

Denizens of the Internet have long noted that many online meeting places have served roles similar to those of the literary salons and coffee houses of the 18th century. Online conferencing systems like *The WELL* (1985) and *MindVox* (1991), MUDs and MOOs like Xerox PARC's *LambdaMOO* and MIT's *MediaMOO* and graphical social spaces like *The Sims Online* (2002) and *Second Life* (2003) have become places where robust and innovative political, social and artistic ideas are discussed and debated. In this note, I will say a bit about why such "cybersalons" are important, raise the question of whether they are endangered and ask whether there is anything we must do to preserve them.

It is interesting that in the decades during which the cybersalons emerged on the scene, the philosopher Jürgen Habermas has written extensively on the concept of the "public sphere" and its demise. For Habermas, the 18th-century French coffee houses and salons formed a kind of paradigmatic model of the exchange of ideas in the public sphere, and in his view, it was the critical exchange of ideas in these 18th-century venues that led to parliamentary democracy and other great social advances in western culture. In Habermas' view, however, this model of the public sphere has been crippled by the rise of mass media – the problem with mass media being that it turns media into a consumable commodity rather than a forum to critically debate important ideas.

Clearly, Habermas has not been spending a lot of time online. If he were, he might have sounded more optimistic. Of course, the discourse that takes place on chat boards and in online worlds like *Second Life* is not always of the highest order, and it certainly has its share of intolerant "trolls" and unreflective, self-important spammers, but no doubt the literary salons of the 18th century had to suffer through these as well. The key point is that the "structure" of the online salons is conducive to the exchange of ideas – it is not a format conducive to mass media, but rather to word-of-mouth exchanges between small groups of individuals.

Has the literary salon returned to its old glory? And if it has returned in the form of online communities, is its new incarnation sustainable or will it be absorbed ("borged") by the mass media? There is certainly some cause for concern. In the first place, most of these new online spaces are owned by private corporations, and the corporate owners have not always been tolerant of criticism and controversy. Most of the corporations insist that their users sign onerous "terms of service" agreements, which, in some cases, require the user to not criticize the platform owner and often allow the platform owner to ban a user "for any reason or no reason."

In the second place, large media companies have seen the rise of Web 2.0 social spaces ranging from MySpace and YouTube to *Second Life* and have registered concern that this new social iteration of the Web is undermining traditional "push media" like television and mass market newspapers in which a single source broadcasts ideas to a passive audience. The media companies have accordingly attempted to control the content in social spaces so as to monetize it on the mass media model (for example, by hiring people to write Wikipedia articles or paying people to post entries on blogs – or even create fake blogs – to advance ideas).

The first bit of good news is that platform owners like Electronic Arts Corporation and Linden Lab have discovered that enforcing the terms of service to silence critics simply doesn't work; at best, it is counterproductive, generating more negative publicity in the blogosphere than the critic ever did when s/he was protesting "in world." Furthermore, there are many platforms in which users can participate, and users have shown a willingness to abandon platforms that are restrictive and move to more liberal and accommodating spaces. Indeed, platforms like *Second Life* are currently moving to an "open source" format, and many other new virtual platforms are being developed as of this writing. In other words, there is good reason to expect that users will be able to vote with their virtual feet. Not *every* café must tolerate the open and free exchange of ideas. It is enough that *many* of them do.

The other bit of good news is that attempts to commercialize the social media forums have not been successful and, indeed, have been met with near universal derision. So far, the social Web has successfully fought back against the mass media model – or perhaps more accurately, the mass media model simply does not work for social spaces. There was no need to fight at all; the mass media model of pushing information at thousands or millions of captive eyeballs failed all by itself.

The mass media model fails particularly badly in online graphical spaces like *Second Life*, which are currently limited in the number of people that they can support. At present, no more than 40 to 50 people can simultaneously attend an event at a single location in *Second Life*.

Given this truth, what replaces the mass media model? In *Life After the 30-Second Spot*, Joseph Jaffe (2005) argues that the age of push media and mass media may be fading and businesses must now rethink their marketing strategies. Broadcasting to a large Superbowl audience may have to give way to one-on-one contacts, word of mouth marketing, the cultivation of quality contacts and playing the "long tail" for an eventual payoff.

If Jaffe is right, then we needn't man the barricades to protect the new online spaces. The giant media corporations will not be swallowing them up. Paradoxically, contemporary marketing will not destroy the virtual salons; the virtual salons are destroying contemporary marketing strategy and replacing it with something altogether new. Or rather, with something altogether old: the very sorts of forums for the exchange of ideas and information that led to the revolutionary modes of thinking that emerged in the 18th century.

◆ Jaffe, J. (2005), *Life After the 30-Second Spot: Energize Your Brand with a Bold Mix of Alternatives to Traditional Advertising*, John Wiley & Sons, Hoboken NJ. ◆ *MindVox (1991)*, created by Bruce Fancher & Patrick K. Kroupa. ◆ *Second Life* (2003), developed and published by Linden Lab. ◆ *The Sims Online* (2002), developed by Maxis, published by Electronic Arts. ◆ *The WELL* (1985), created by Stewart Brand & Larry Brilliant.

UBIQUITOUS GAMES

ENCHANTING PLACES, BUILDINGS, CITIES AND LANDSCAPES

Level

3

NEW BABYLON RELOADED
Learning from the Ludic City

> "With no timetable to respect, with no fixed abode, the human being will of necessity become acquainted with a nomadic way of life in an artificial, wholly 'constructed' environment."
> *Constant Nieuwenhuys (1974)*

Cities are dynamic places of change and transformation. Dense and heterogeneous, they offer a general framework for individuals to create personal patterns and act on them. Within the game of urban possibilities, the city is a constantly changing stage, forever reinventing and redefining itself on the basis of its performers' creativity and interactions.

The Ludic City

Pushing the playful and performative interplay of cities and their inhabitants to extremes, the Dutch artist-architect Constant Nieuwenhuys developed an urban utopia over the course of more then 20 years starting in the 1950s with the aim of liberating people's ludic nature and lending it spatial form. Constant's *New Babylon* is a labyrinthine vision – comprised of writings, collages, models and other projects – of a dynamic metropolis divided into endless sectors, subject to constant change through the use of mobile modules, with a shape and form determined by spontaneous actions. Wall, floor, light, sound, color, surface and smell are in a state of perpetual transformation. This boundlessly fluctuating world does not conform to any master plan; it is abandoned entirely to its inhabitants' collective and creative play instincts.

Operating at the interface between art, politics, architecture and social criticism, *New Babylon* positions itself as a Situationistic counter-design to Modernism's functionalization and realization mechanisms for architecture and town planning. Constant's appeal for a different city for a different life ("Une autre ville pour une autre vie" (Nieuwenhuys 1974)) did not go unheard. *New Babylon* represents one of many preliminary tremors of a creative shockwave in architectural history whose traces and fractures extend right down to the present day.

Architecture Without Architects

In the mid-20th century, at almost the same time as Constant, architectural theory and practice discovered new scopes for undermining urban rules and functions, taking risks with architectural experiments that differed radically from traditional, reactionary approaches and tried to fundamentally redefine the role of architecture.

This trend includes Bernard Rudofsky's influential MoMA exhibition and publication of *Architecture Without Architects* (1964) – about historic and prehistoric amateur architecture beyond the rules of classical building – as much as it includes the busy and provocative utopias of a young generation of architects like Yona Friedmann, Archigram, Superstudio and Archizoom Associates who used their eclectic working methods to transform and redefine existing spatial and intellectual structures. This work is still influential, but almost all of it remained at the design stage and was not implemented in real space.

Extended Space

Developments in technology and the media have not failed to influence our ideas and perceptions of space and time. Global networking, the application of electronic and digital media in all spheres of life and the establishment of virtual worlds of simultaneous information exchange in the last decade of the 20th century confront architects today with unimagined challenges in terms of creating space that extends far beyond the traditional horizons of their discipline. But this does not apply to architecture alone; it increasingly affects all disciplines and generally constitutes a contemporary phenomenon. A glance beyond one's own disciplinary limitations therefore provides inspiring insights.

Today, *New Babylon* seems almost like a spatial-pictorial prototype of the computer-generated worlds of the World Wide Web. Both define models of liberated, collective creation and interaction within apparently open and incomplete systems by dissolving linear and hierarchical order structures. On the Web, the layman at play becomes, in the collective, a designer of nomadic space. The comparison between the architectural concepts of Constant & Co. and the extended spaces of computer worlds can also be carried further using contemporary developments in computer game design. It almost seems as though things are possible in computer-generated worlds that were not possible in the architectural world of Constant and his contemporaries.

The Architecture of Ludic Space

Any discussion of the architecture of ludic spaces in computer games must distinguish between architecture as a general play structure and as the actual design of virtual space. The former defines the internal setup of a game that provides the basis for the actual actions possible within that game. Recourse to architectonic terminology as figurative device refers in this context to the universal power of architectural imagery. Applying architectural metaphor to nonarchitectural matter seems to express a widespread longing for order and stability. Apparently, even the age of fluid cyberspace cannot manage without the static sense conveyed by architectural form to express the structure of its virtual worlds appropriately.

Various narrative models emerge within these "play architectures": a) games that follow a linear and final course of action and offer the player no scope for action outside this fixed framework (e.g. *Super Mario Bros.* (1985)); b) games with a linear but nonfinal course of action that offer players a certain amount of room for maneuver within a clearly defined action field (e.g. *The Elder Scrolls* (1994)); and c) games following a nonlinear, nonfinal course that are designed and modified by the players (e.g. *Second Life* (2003)). The "play architectures" in the latter are open in principle and develop without a central game designer. Here, in the ludic space of computer gameworlds, something is happening that Constant earlier envisioned in his design for the ludic city. His description of the *New Babylon*ians very much applies to today's game designers and players: "They wander through the sectors of *New Babylon* seeking new experiences, as yet unknown ambiances. Without the passivity of tourists, but fully aware of the power they have to act upon the world, to transform it, recreate it." (Nieuwenhuys 1974)

As virtualized spatial impressions, these computer-generated worlds are not localized topographically. They are genuinely placeless. By shrinking time-space distance by dissolving the physical presence of the place where events occur, they recruit their players beyond social, factual, spatial and time boundaries. At the same time, they make it possible for them to become master builders of their own virtual spaces. This is a possibility that real space, on the grounds of its structural mass alone, can never provide.

Against the backdrop of this creative democratization process à la Constant ("Now, it is as a creator, and only as a creator, that the human being can fulfill and attain his highest existential level" (ibid.)), the question arises of what role architects are and will be allotted for the spatial design of virtual worlds and of what responsibilities they see themselves taking. Certainly, designing cyberspace is one of the 21st century's great aesthetic and political challenges. The liquefaction of once clearly defined interfaces between the real and the virtual, between "meatspace" and "cyberspace" (Gibson 1984), through the ubiquitous integration and miniaturization of digital network technologies in physical space increasingly questions physical space's role as the fundamental model for ordering human experience and as the primary architectural medium.

Architecture Plus

As a space-creating practice, architecture concerns itself with defining, arranging and formally shaping space. If space is seen as electronically extending beyond physical and geometrical boundaries, it starts to present challenges for contemporary architecture that have to be taken seriously. Acknowledging the possibilities of immaterial architecture opens the door for action that penetrates, extends and dissolves material space as a classical field for architecture. Due to the influence of new media and digital technologies on architecture, approaches are once again being formulated that are increasingly turning to the dynamic, transversal and performative character of architecture and urban development.

In this context, performativity has become the secret key concept in a slew of new research perspectives that are examining architecture as a cultural statement in terms of its dramaturgical and scenical effect. This view embraces both architectural projects that explore new possibilities in the architectural design and production process by the use of new technical means and also those that shift their attention from strategies for ordering space to complex contexts relating to effect and action in the built environment. Architectural utopias from the 1960s like Constant's *New Babylon* or Archigram's *Plug-In City* thus unexpectedly become relevant again in that they accentuate architecture's transformative and activist potential. Even though they existed in a different context, their fundamental and provocative analyses of architecture's and space's performative surplus now, as then, point beyond the boundaries of architectural practice to its social dimensions and responsibilities. Or, to conclude with the words of Constant, "Space as a psychic dimension (abstract space) cannot be separated from the space of action (concrete space)." (Nieuwenhuys 1974)

◆ Gibson, W. (1984), *Neuromancer*, Ace Books, New York NY. ◆ Nieuwenhuis, C. (1974), "New Baby-lon" in Haags Gemeentemuseum (ed.), Exhibition catalogue, The Hague. ◆ Rudofsky, B. (1964), *Architecture without architects*: An Introduction to Non-Pedigreed Architecture, Museum of Modern Art, New York & Doubleday, Garden City, NY. ◆ *Second Life* (2003), developed and published by Linden Labs. ◆ *Super Mario Bros.* (1985), developed and published by Nintendo. ◆ *The Elder Scrolls* (1994), developed and published by Bethesda Softworks.

GEOCACHING
The Combination of Technology and the Outdoors

In one of the fasting growing modern sports in history, players use GPS receivers to find hidden caches around the world.

In May 2000, *geocaching* had its beginnings in the Oregon woods. Six years later, it is now played in over 220 countries around the world. No one is completely sure how many people play, but the number is in the hundreds of thousands. *geocaching* is popular because it combines two unique elements: technology and the outdoors. The game takes you to great outdoor locations using the multibillion dollar government satellite based Global Positioning System (GPS).

Participants log onto the site www.geocaching.com to select hidden caches. A GPS receiver is needed, but there is no charge to play. A cache can be a physical container such as a small box or a virtual cache, i.e. a special location. Players attempt to find the hidden caches by their latitude/longitude coordinates entered into a GPS receiver and by following other clues. GPS provides the distance and pointer arrow to the location; it is up to the player to find the correct road and path to the target. Once the cache is found, the player signs the cache's logbook and often trades trinket items (this is the treasure part) that are left in the container. Caches are rated for difficulty to get to and difficulty to find. This allows cachers to plan for the ideal targets to go after. Once a cache is found (or not), players can leave feedback of their adventure on the *geocaching* website.

Caches are hidden everywhere from wilderness areas to city parks in nearly every country in the world. And *geocaching* is also a social game in which cachers participate with friends, family and clubs. They also throw event caches to bring fellow geocachers together at a pizza parlor or backyard barbecue. These are great ways to meet the cacher behind the screen name and trade tales of the hunt. Cachers track the number of caches they have found for bragging rights. Some have logged over 1,000 finds.

Geocaching continues to evolve, driven by player creativity and improved technology. Participants continually think of new ways to modify caches, such as making them multi-staged or converting them into Travel Bugs that you take with you to hide at another cache location. Mobile computers have also improved a cacher's efficiency through improved digital mapping and the ability to load hundreds of targets at a time. And the GeocacheNavigator application allows caches to be acquired through a GPS-enabled cell phone. Fun? Yes. But don't take my word for it: there's a cache waiting to be found near you!

Project Description	Text	Project	Affiliation
	Benjamin Joffe	Mathieu Castelli, Benjamin Joffe, Ignazio Mottola et al.	Newt Games, Paris, FR, 2003

MOGI
Location-Based Services – A Community Game in Japan

Mogi Genesis: It was in 2000, in the heart of Tokyo's nightlife district, witnessing people carrying mobiles and thumb-typing casually, that the idea of creating a layer on top of reality came to the mind of Mathieu Castelli, founder of Newt Games and *Mogi*'s creator. The objectives were to create a first-of-its-kind mobile massively multiplayer location-based Role-Playing Game (RPG) that promotes teamwork through physically positioned "missions" and to launch it first in the country where mobiles are the most advanced – Japan.

Of course, things rarely work as planned, and financial shortage combined with investor pressure led to a simplified type of collection game with communication features. It went live with the Japanese telecommunications operator KDDI over a third-generation mobile phone standard CDMA 1x in April 2003.

What sets *Mogi* apart from other location-based games?

Gameplay: no killing, no running, easy-to-start for new users, deepness of features and gameplay according to users' styles, accommodating everyone from social nongamers to hardcore gamers

Technical: mobile and Web interfaces with complementary use, real map data (GIS)

User base: much wider in age and more gender-balanced than most games, *Mogi* is closer to "casual games" in terms of audience

Core features: messaging, avatars, one-hand play, seeing other users

LBS specifics: location and privacy management

But what really sets *Mogi* apart are the emotions it triggers. A strong sense of "reality" and "feeling connected" comes from seeing and being seen by other users. New communication patterns emerge from playing at the same time or in the same area. Those two elements along with the friendly gaming environment of *Mogi* trigger contacts between users. Relationships established in the game ensure *Mogi*'s stickiness and bring its perceived value well beyond a normal game's.

Mogi explores new ways to interact with both space and time and, in doing so, generates an eerie sense of being in an augmented world only shared by *Mogi* users.

What to remember? Despite the game's appeal and addictiveness, the lack of marketing and the prohibitive data pricing prevented the spread of *Mogi*. Nevertheless, new usage patterns pioneered by *Mogi* could today succeed thanks to the improved environment in terms of handsets, networks and users' more mature relationship with mobile services and social networking software. Online and offline activities and realities are connecting.

www.mogimogi.com

Project Description	Text	Affiliation
	Mirjam Struppek, Katharine S. Willis	It's Alive Inc., SE, 2002

BOTFIGHTERS
A Game that Surrounds You

The 2002 launch of the game *Botfighters* – a mobile version of *Counter-Strike* (Valve 2001) – marked the beginning of the invasion of urban space by real-time location-based mobile games. In *Botfighters*, a mobile device becomes a weapon, and the real urban landscape is transformed into a battlefield for a computer-supported action adventure. To play the game, a player needs to visit the *Botfighters* website and create a robot warrior character, which, along with the mobile device, enables him to slip into the gamespace. The object is simple: to destroy or kill as many other players as possible. The mobile platform constantly scans the city for opponents. When an enemy moves into a 500-meter radius, then the game can begin with a text-message-based exchange of shots. The ability to shoot is based on the players' proximity to one another, which means that the game often develops as a chase through urban space with players simultaneously trying to locate their enemies and hide from their assailants. To make the chase more challenging, the game designers have inserted imaginary items into the real-world terrain so that as players wander through the city, they can gather help in the form of weapons and power-ups. When gamers walk around a certain street corner, for example, they might discover a first-aid kit; or, when standing at an intersection, a hidden gun.

All game interactions take place via text messages. The mobile positioning of the players and objects is calculated through locational proximity within the cells of the GSM phone network. The game website lets the players gather points and initiate new missions, thereby enhancing their sense of immersion in the outdoor fantasy world. It also contains a community platform, where the players can exchange information with one another or affiliate themselves with a team or clan.

When players enter the game, they start to create their own personalized world, a space where concepts of identity and presence are more flexible than they are in the physical world. As player Niklas Wolkert explains in *The Guardian* (London, 15 August 2002), "It's a game that plays with your mind. It uses the best images you can get – those of your own imagination. My opponent probably doesn't have the slightest similarity to my idea of what the game looks like to me, but that doesn't matter to me." Since the player's physical location influences how the game evolves, it's not always easy to distinguish reality from fiction. This means that the gameplay can have some drawbacks, including privacy issues as well as more practical problems such as those that occur when a player's attention is distracted from the everyday dangers of city life.

Botfighters is a bodily experience and a pervasive game that is always and everywhere present. It enables old game genres such as role play, treasure hunt and hide-and-seek to be rediscovered and reinterpreted through new technologies. Inspired by the players' own individual fantasies and enabled by mobile applications and devices, the everyday environment becomes overlaid with the virtual gameworld, creating a form of augmented reality. Architecture becomes the virtual canvas for the virtual world, stimulated by the imagination of the player. Urban space and virtual space, like everyday life and gameplay, merge together – and adventure lurks everywhere as a result. The manner in which the environment supports and enhances the gaming experience changes players' long-term appreciation of urban space and stimulates the recapture of the city as a site of socialization and interaction.

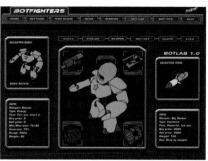

Project Description	Text	Project	Affiliation
	Dave Szulborski	Jordan Weisman, Elan Lee, Sean Stewart	Warner Bros., Microsoft Game Studios (later 42 Entertainment), US, 2001

THE BEAST
An Alternate Reality Game Defines the Future

In 2001, a group of Microsoft developers working with Steven Spielberg to promote his new film *A.I. Artificial Intelligence* (Warner Bros. et al. 2001) began to envision what they were doing as a new form of storytelling and interactive entertainment. The campaign they created came to be called *The Beast*, and it did indeed spawn an entirely new genre of games in which such things as traditional gamespace, gametime and game rules no longer seemed to apply.

Although it had been set the task of creating a virtual world based on the film, the design team decided early on that the campaign wasn't going to be just virtual and immediately began crafting a narrative that the audience would experience as a game – but unlike any other game that came before. Instead of creating either a representational or abstract gamespace for the players, the designers overlaid their narrative and gameplay atop the real world, effectively making reality the gamespace for the experience.

The Beast was delivered primarily via the Internet. It was essentially a platformless game in that it adapted any media, entertainment platform or communication method it could to tell its tale. The first entry points into the game were grounded in the real world, with clues hidden in the trailers and posters for the film and in a voicemail message discovered by following them. Though these led eventually to a complex virtual world consisting of 30 fictional websites, the real-world elements of the campaign launch set the game firmly in the actual world of the audience right from the start.

The Beast began as a mystery story that asked the question, "Who killed Evan Chan?" but quickly evolved into an epic tale about the emergence of robots and artificial intelligence (A.I.) as a new sentient life form. In many ways, the story of *The Beast* foreshadowed the world that the film itself would present. The game anchored its narrative in reality by using everyday methods of communication as story-delivery mechanisms. There was nothing inherently artificial in the emails, phone calls or instant messages that players received, so interactions conducted using them felt real; this meant that the spatial parameters of the game were defined as any and all forms of communication coming into players' homes.

The gameplay involved the discovery and reassembly of the narrative fragments that had been scattered around the Internet like artifacts of an ancient civilization from an archeological dig. As the players progressed through the puzzles, interactions and multimedia pieces, they learned more of the story. Since the progress of the game was largely dependent upon the players' interaction with the content, their progression through it in many ways mirrors the progression of a player through both gamespace and gametime in more traditional game formats.

www.cloudmakers.org
http://42entertainment.com/beast.html

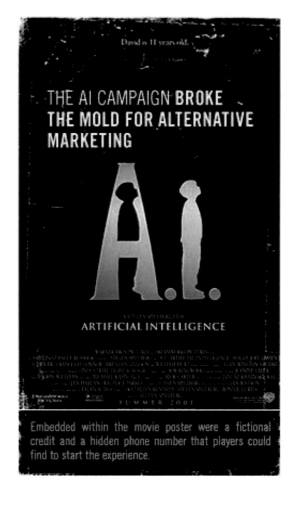

David is 11 years old.

THE AI CAMPAIGN BROKE
THE MOLD FOR ALTERNATIVE
MARKETING

A.I.

ARTIFICIAL INTELLIGENCE

SUMMER 2001

Embedded within the movie poster were a fictional
credit and a hidden phone number that players could
find to start the experience.

PLAY AS CREATIVE MISUSE
Barcode Battler and the Charm of the Real

In March of 1991, at least for two summers, the world itself became playable. A little computer game of simple construction – which many fanpages continue to mourn to this day – broke the rule according to which gameworlds are only successful to the degree that they maximally exclude real-world annoyances. For dance mats, samba rattles and similar ineffectual motivating accessories could never really make us forget that computer games call for maximum adaptive performance and hence forbid all distraction, deviation and creativity. As such, computer games are the opposite of that which developmental psychologists such as Jean Piaget regarded as the core element of human play – namely the option of allowing everything to become an object of the game, to assimilate "all objects to the ego."

Barcode Battler (1991) was the name of an inconspicuous black handheld with a text-based LCD display, a small number of buttons and a narrow slit through which the world suddenly appeared dif-

 VS

ferently. This slit concealed a barcode-reading device, which is used to scan the playing cards (also included with the device), allowing warriors, magicians and other role-playing personnel to "fight" against one another singly or in teams of two. The options are minimal, and the game soon comes to an end: you simply load the warrior with a card only to see it attack, cure or flee. In a fraction of a second, everything has been decided, evaluated on the display, and the potential combinations of supplied cards are already calculable.

But with this little handheld in your pocket, there exists the prospect of a "new legibility of the world" – or at least the commodity portion of it. For after June of 1974, when a legendary packet of Wrigley's Spearmint chewing gum was passed successfully across a register scanner in an Ohio supermarket, the world of commodities came to be systematically superimposed with a symbolic layer of barcodes. And all of them – at least within certain limits – are readable by the *Barcode Battler* and deployable to different degrees of success as gaming material. Now, playing means going out into the real world, suspending the logistics of commodity economics and shelf-lives for which these barcodes were originally designed and diverting them experimentally in the direction of the logic of the game. For anything that can be purchased can be also played via its digital signature. Not money, but barcodes suddenly allow the universal exchange of anything with anything. How could we possibly know whether cornflakes are more powerful magicians than sweaters or socks? Why should we assume that red wine possesses greater curative powers than a book of poetry by Trakl or a packet of sparkplugs? Certain sources – which should be granted at least a modicum of poetic justification – have even told of certain Japanese soups that possess unsuspected powers.

But the charm of *Barcode Battler* does not lie solely in this juvenile delight in experimentation and collecting. Also implemented when testing a given commodity for its gaming effectivity is a kind of "revaluation of all values." Quantitative and qualitative distinctions between large and small, cheap and expensive, foodstuffs and electronic devices, clothing and household appliances, suddenly become invalid, and all use and exchange values become reconfigured. The difference between Coke and Pepsi is no longer a question of taste, conviction or lifestyle, but can be decided objectively in a contest between the two products. Your favorite chocolate bar may turn out to be a pitiful warrior when examined for its effectiveness in the game. Determining the strengths and weaknesses of various products in this "realm of signs" – which established itself primarily, and not by accident, in Japan – are no longer image consultants, but instead arbitrary barcodes. In itself, a product is characterless; but now, it literally becomes a character. And while clever consultants are convinced they have made the products lining supermarket shelves irresistible according to the criteria of "ontology engineering," the players of *Barcode Battler* rearrange them in an almost fantastical manner, in the process disclosing another, hidden "order of things." The ontology of products is thoroughly disarranged in a way that happens

elsewhere only in the word salads of schizophrenics, who – assuming Gregory Bateson is right – must learn for the first time in therapy to distinguish between play and nonplay.

The deliberate muddling of registers and levels is the systematic foundation of *Barcode Battler*. Those playing it long enough unavoidably become themselves barcode readers. Through this unnerving training, which probably only children can withstand, a human *Barcode Battler* becomes a scanner, gradually becoming capable of deciphering codes that were never intended to be read by human eyes.

He no longer registers the codes of commodities according to an informational level involving names and images, but instead according to the level that coordinates their administration. This leap is somewhat comparable to the activities pursued a generation earlier by the so-called "phone phreaks" when they no longer telephoned normally, but instead eavesdropped on and imitated the coded tone sequences of telephone technology that make telephone calls (even and especially free ones) possible in the first place. The difference is simply that with *Barcode Battler*, there is no threat of punishment, since its parallel gaming economy is incapable of doing any damage.

The brief flourishing of the barcode games – of which *Barcode Battler* did not remain the sole instance – is long past, and it remains today as a whimsical fashion with antiquarian charm. While its soon-to-follow and infinitely more successful successor *Pokémon* (1996) took over the idea of collecting and exchanging characters and was expanded into the areas of reproduction and upbringing, *Pokémon*'s world of play was nonetheless systematically closed. Media art, too, tried out the transformation of codes into characters – for example, with *Life Spacies II* by Christa Sommerer and Laurent Mignonneau (1999), which reads emails as a kind of "genetic code" according to which graphic creatures are then generated for computer screens. In the process, however, the charm of the real becomes lost. Perhaps the most explosive successors today can be found in games like *Second Life* (2003), which are characterized not least by the conversion of virtual into real currencies. Compared to them, *Barcode Battler* – which could also have been a bonus point game offered by supermarket chains – was not only more innocent, but also more intelligent.

◆ *Barcode Battler* (1991), developed and published by Epoch Co. ◆ *Pokémon* (1996), developed and published by Nintendo. ◆ *Second Life* (2003), developed and published by Linden Labs.

Essay | Text

Jane McGonigal

UBIQUITOUS GAMING
A Vision for the Future of Enchanted Spaces

Introduction

Ubiquitous computing, or ubicomp, is the emerging field of computer science that seeks to augment everyday objects and physical environments with invisible and networked computing functionality. Experimental game design is the field of interactive arts that seeks to discover new platforms and contexts for digital play. The convergence of these two fields at the turn of the 21st century has produced a significant body of games that challenge and expand our notions of where, when and with whom we can play. This short essay explores how and to what ends these playful projects reconfigure the technical, formal and social limits of games in relation to everyday life.

Already, three distinct and competing visions have emerged for the future of ubiquitous play and performance. In *ubiquitous computer gaming*, academic research games such as *Can You See Me Now?* (2001) and *You're In Control* (2003) are deployed to colonize new objects, environments and users in the name of ubiquitous computing. In *pervasive gaming*, spectacular art games such as *Big Urban Game* (2003) and *PacManhattan* (2004) aim to critique and disrupt the social conventions of public spaces. And in *ubiquitous gaming*, commercial, massively multiplayer games such as *I Love Bees* (2004) and *Perplex City* (2005) work to materially replicate the interactive affordances of traditional digital games in the real world. Most of these projects are described in *Space Time Play*.

These three approaches work in favor of different ends: toward the mutual research and development goals of digital games and ubiquitous computing; toward techno-critical ruptures of the magic circle of play; and toward the discovery of more platforms for meaningful interaction in everyday life, respectively. Accordingly, each vision adopts a different metaphor for the work of games in society: *colonization* through gameplay (the ubiquitous computing games); *disruption* through gameplay (the pervasive games); and *activation* through gameplay (the ubiquitous games). Each also has its own distinct reproductive practices: the proliferation of gameplay *citations*, the situated proliferation of gameplay *spectacles* and the proliferation of gameplay *affordances* – without necessarily embedding computing technology.

Here, I want to focus in particular on the category of ubiquitous gaming, which, of the three, has to date produced the most scalable, reproducible and popular vision of a games-infused, everyday life. My analysis of this category draws heavily on a close reading of seminal ubiquitous computing manifestos by digital artist and Xerox PARC researcher Rich Gold, whose perspective as an artist and former toy developer yields an unusually performative and playful understanding of the phenomenological implications of invisible, embedded and everywhere computer networks.

The Secretive Affordances of the Ubicomp World

Design critic Donald Norman first introduced the term "affordance" to the field of everyday object design in *The Psychology of Everyday Things*, published in 1988 and then republished in 1990 under the new title *The Design of Everyday Things*. Norman's user-oriented philosophy emphasizes the importance of sensory cues that help users understand how to interact with designed things and built environments. In other words, the perceivable properties of things – not only their physical shape, size and position in space, but also their culturally recognizable form as something one traditionally pushes, pulls, dials, detaches, grabs or sits on – tell us exactly what to do with them in order to make them work. Ubiquitous computing adopts Norman's notion of affordance and seeks to transform the reproductive culture of electronic media from the replication of data to the replication of affordances – that is to say, the replication of embedded signals that prompt specific modes of engagement.

There is, by design, a kind of secretiveness inherent to the ubicomp proliferation of embedded affordances. Not all in an ubicomp world is what it seems. In 1993, Gold defined his vision for the nascent field in his short text, "This Is Not a Pipe," stating that "ubiquitous computing is a new metaphor in which computers are spread invisibly throughout the environment, embedded and *hiding* as it were, within the objects of our everyday life" (Gold 1993, p. 72). Gold envisions that features and connectivity go undercover. Interactivity and active networks hide where we least expect them. "The everyday objects themselves become a kind of ruse," explains Gold (ibid.).

One way to think about this move in computing design philosophy, away from perceptible surfaces towards imperceptible functionality is to view it as a shift from powerful *simulation* to masterful *dissimulation*. In both cases, what you see is not necessarily what you get, but for very different reasons. In a world of computer-

Public cemetery play during the ubiquitous, or alternate reality, game *Tombstone Hold 'Em* (2005) courtesy of 42 Entertainment.

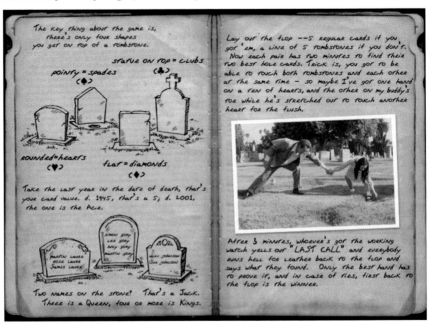

driven simulation – that is to say, in the "skins" scenario – appearances *make empty promises*. The image is not, in fact, the thing itself, the referent, but rather simply one of infinitely many cognitively convincing references. However, in a world of computer-driven dissimulation – that is to say, in the secret "inner life" scenario – appearances *feign a lack of promise*. The seemingly ordinary object conceals its own extraordinary capabilities. The simulation, the reproduction of semblances, likes to show off. It aggressively and proudly demonstrates its mimetic charms to you. The dissimulation, the reproduction of systems, on the other hand, is coy. It reveals its true affordances only to those who pay special attention, who investigate more than just its surface properties.

Ubiquitous computing aims to reproduce not appearances, but network structure and computational functionality, embedding *systems* rather than *semblances* within nearly any context. It is not the mimetic references or cognitive concepts that ubicomp wants to proliferate; it is, rather, interactive experiences and phenomenal affordances that will be made pervasive.

The "Enchanted Village" of Distributed Networks of Play and Performance

Ubiquitous gaming today is the design philosophy and practice that represents the most direct legacy of the play and performance roots of early ubicomp manifestos such as Gold's. For ubiquitous gaming asks the question: What are the secret gaming affordances of everyday objects and spaces?

Gold closes his essay by describing the world of ubiquitous computing as an "enchanted village, in which common objects have magically acquired new abilities, a village where toy blocks really do sing and dance when I turn out the lights" (ibid.). I want to linger on this fanciful notion, these closing words. What does it mean to compare computing-enhanced objects to inanimate props that secretly come to life? Why leave the reader with a vision of technologies as *toys*, as playthings? What does it mean to end with the performing arts, the singing and the dancing?

Gold's vision for ubiquitous computing is fundamentally a vision of distributed networks of play and performance. His professional biography before joining the Xerox PARC research group for ubiquitous computing includes the distinction of having cofounded, in the 1970s, the League of Automatic Music Composers, the first network computer band, as well as several years spent in the early 1980s as the director of a design group at Sega USA's Coin-op Video Game division and later, several years as the head of an electronic and computer toy research group at Mattel Toys. Gold's background drives home an important fact often overlooked by those working in or writing about the field – namely that the original design philosophy and goals of ubiquitous computing were constructed in part by someone with a lifelong interest in playful objects and collaborative performance. That Gold brought to the original ubiquitous computing team a tremendous amount of experience with interactive toys, video games and networked performance has been ignored,

I think, because of the work-focused research context in which ubicomp was first conceived. Ubiquitous gaming is, essentially, a reclaiming of the distributed play and performance ethos of early ubiquitous computing as first theorized by Gold.

Core Mechanics of Ubiquitous Gaming

What would real life be like if game designers applied the ubiquitous computing vision of secret affordances to everyday objects, places and sites? Ubiquitous gaming

seeks to answer this question. Rather than focusing on specifically technological platforms, ubiquitous gaming seeks to make everything in real-life environments as satisfyingly interactive as the objects and characters encountered in virtual gameworlds. Instead of "wherever hardware, there'll be games," the traditional philosophy of experimental game design, we have "wherever *whatever*, there'll be games."

Ubiquitous gaming asks players to take up two core mechanics: first, searching for and experimenting with the hidden affordances of everyday objects and places; and second, exhaustively seeking to activate everything in their immediate environment. This activation is, in fact, mutual. Game structures activate the world by transforming everyday objects and places into interactive platforms and also activate players by making them more responsive to potential calls to interaction. This is because the act of exposing previously unperceived affordances creates a more meaningful relationship between the actor and the object or the space in the world.

Ubiquitous games typically are played persistently (without stop) over long periods of time – anywhere from several months to indefinitely. During this extended gameplay period, particular game missions, challenges and other ludic events are iterated hundreds, thousands or tens of thousands of times. And if a ubiquitous game is not persistent, then as a live event, it is deployed on a much higher order than the other two categories: say, thousands of games produced over the course of several years. The number of players across the three categories of games also shifts dramatically upward when it comes to ubiquitous games.

Ubicomp playtests and pervasive gaming events typically engage, directly, a few dozen players at a time – maximally, a few hundred. Ubiquitous games, on the other hand, engage players by the hundreds or thousands at minimum, more typically by the tens of thousands and, in the most successful ubiquitous games, by the hundreds of thousands at a time. An excellent compilation of player statistics for ten major ubiquitous games has been compiled by new media researcher Christy Dena and is available at http://www.cross-mediaentertainment.com/index.php/2006/03/04/top-args-with-stats/.

Conclusion: The Emerging Culture of Ubiquitous Gaming

On the fringes of experimental game design and performance practice, Rich Gold's vision for distributed networks of play is both manifest and profoundly changing the technological habits, perceptual techniques and social identities of millions of players worldwide. In this context, I present the shared characteristics of the experiences that comprise this emerging culture of ubiquitous gaming and that define the enchanted spaces of techno-social play in the ubicomp era:

1. Ubiquitous games are designed experiences with a strong potential for emergent, that is to say, unexpectedly complex, group play and performance.
2. They are distributed experiences: distributed across multiple media, platforms, locations and times.
3. They have a significant *physical* component, phenomenologically speaking and a significant *material* component, ontologically speaking.
4. They are embedded at least partially in everyday contexts and/or environments, rather than in marked-off gaming contexts and spaces. They prefer to adopt everyday software, services and technologies rather than exclusively gaming platforms.
5. They have the effect of sensitizing participants to affordances, real or imagined. That is to say, they increase perception of opportunities for interaction.
6. Many, if not most, of their distributed elements are not clearly identified as part of the experience. Thus active investigation of and live interaction with both ingame and out-of-game elements is a significant component of the experience.
7. They have the effect of making all data seem connected or at least plausibly connected.
8. They make surfaces less convincing. Underlying structures are what matter.
9. They establish a network of players who are in the know. They intentionally involve or engage others who are, at least temporarily, in the dark.
10. Through the relationship rhizome, they aspire to a massively multiplayer scale.
11. They inexorably create community.
12. They structure player relationships with each other according to relevant computing metaphors.
13. They encourage collective magical thinking.
14. They aspire to persistent and perpetual gaming.
15. They encourage players to construct, consciously, a more intimate relationship between gameplay and everyday life.

For further elaboration on this subject, see the dissertation on which this essay is based, published at www.avantgame.com/dissertation.htm; the dissertation was accepted by the University of California, Berkeley in 2006.

◆ *Big Urban Game* (2003), developed by Nick Fortugno, Frank Lantz & Katie Salen, commissioned by University of Minnesota Design Institute. ◆ *Can You See Me Now?* (2001), developed by Blast Theory & The Mixed Reality Lab, University of Nottingham. ◆ Gold, R. (1993), "This Is Not a Pipe," *Communications of the ACM*, vol. 36, no. 7, p.72. ACM Press. ◆ *I Love Bees* (2004), developed by 42 Entertainment, published by Bungie Studios/Microsoft. ◆ Norman, D. (1990), *The Design of Everyday Things*, Doubleday, New York NY. ◆ *PacManhattan* (2004), developed by Frank Lantz with students, Interactive Telecommunications Program, New York University. ◆ *Perplex City* (2005-07), developed and published by Mind Candy. ◆ *You're In Control* (2003), developed by Dan Maynes-Aminzade & Hayes Solos Raffle at MIT Media Lab.

CREATING ALTERNATE REALITIES
A Quick Primer

> "I once jokingly said that if Moby Dick was an ARG, 1. you'd see a whale swim by outside your window, 2. Ahab would call you on the phone, and 3. a harpoon would come flying out of your television set."
>> *Stewart (n.d.)*

At present, the most that creators of Augmented Reality Games – ARGs, for short – can offer is a call from Ahab; the rest of Stewart's vision will have to be left to play-ers' imaginations, some hallucinogenic assistance or time travel to the future. The sentiment behind his words, however, holds true. ARGs surround a player and are immune to boundaries. ARGs are transmedial in that the experience they provide is expressed through a variety of media platforms, with each component provid-ing unique information. They are designed to be collaborative by being too large for one person to play and requiring a variety of skills and knowledge that only collective intelligence can provide. ARGs have high degrees of both narrative and game elements. They are tiered so that players can participate to different degrees, sometimes relying on the efforts of others. ARGs have inspired what has become known as the alternate reality design aesthetic.

Alternate Reality Creation

This alternate reality design aesthetic is one of the key elements that distinguishes ARGs from other cross-media games (McGonigal 2003). Essentially, the design goal is to reduce signs of the game's fictional status while enhancing elements that trigger gamers to treat it as they would real life. To facilitate the belief that the ARG is a reality, everyday technologies such as email, billboards and faxes are employed in the gameplay. They are run in real time, with the hours and days of the gameworld running concurrently with our own. Real-life websites, events and people are ap-propriated for game purposes in order to root the game's fiction in the real world of the player. They are expressed mainly through a nonfiction discourse, and so the narrative aspects are enunciated through clever dialogue and plot structure rather than poetic language or a narrator (unless a character creates a story or comic). The exception to this rule is the employment of a magic realism approach in which unusual events (such as visitors from the future) are treated as normal. The world of the ARG, however, is usually set in the time and space of the player and adheres to the laws of nature. Challenges are sometimes issued in line with the reality of the world created: players must, for example, hack into game characters' emails, conduct DNS lookups and retrieve objects from real-world locations like a car dealership. The ultimate challenge, which supports the alternate reality ideal, is for players to find or to stumble upon the fictional world. Because the gameworld is real, it reacts to the input of the players thanks to manual adjustments made by the puppet masters (PMs, or those who run the ARG) during their real-time monitoring of the gameplay.

From a player's perspective, ARGs have no event horizon. The potential mediums for the expression of an ARG are limitless; players could see an in-story advertisement in *The New York Times* or be called at home in the middle of the night. For ludologist Eva Nieuwdorp, this "means that the realized resources in the game world are potentially seemingly infinite to all players, because they can-

not be sure what objects are intended to play a role in the game world and which do not" (Nieuwdorp 2005, p. 7). It also means that players assign elements of the real world, parts that are not part of the game to the ARG. This is encouraged by the puppet masters, but quashed if the appropriated material causes confusion or affects a nonplayer.

Each element of an ARG contributes to the detail that is needed to facilitate the belief that an alternate world exists. In-story newspapers, advertisements, blogs, companies and locations are created and published on their own sites or on already-existent sites. Just about everything a city would have is created either by the producers or players. In the ARG *Perplex City* (2005), for example, a player called Daffy created an entire city map.

And as for the game's producers, they provided a tourist guide to the fictional city complete with a subway map.

The creators of *Chasing the Wish* (2006) also provided a map of their fictional town, *Aglaura*. These visualizations help cement the fictional world as real, but how do they justify live meetings between people from our reality (players) and people from another reality (the

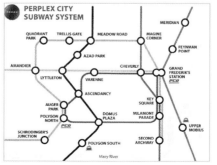

Google Map of Perplex City assembled by Daffy, player of *Perplex City* (2006). Available at www.perplexcitymap.com

Scan of "Perplex City Subway System" from *24 hours in Perplex City* tourist guide (n.d.).

characters)? Creators integrate the current time on Earth into the ARG world. ARG designer Dave Szulborski advises that "the goal is not to immerse the player in the artificial world of the game; instead, a successful game immerses the world of the game into the everyday existence and life of the player" (Szulborski 2005, p. 31).

From Setting the Scene to Creating Rabbit Holes

Since the world of an ARG is meant to have always existed, the commencement of an ARG is not the beginning of the world, but rather the first time that the game-world and our world touch. An ARG is therefore a short window of interaction with another world that is mediated by the PMs. PMs, then, could perhaps be better described as portal masters. The gateway to an ARG is opened by PMs in the form of a "rabbit hole." The rabbit hole, a term appropriated from Lewis Caroll's *Alice in Wonderland*, is a mysterious opening to another world that is stumbled upon and then entered. The world of *The Beast* (2001), for example, was stumbled upon through the film credits of Steven Spielberg's film *A.I. Artificial Intelligence* (2001), in which a "Sentient Machine Therapist" named Jeanine Salla was listed. This in-story element in the paratextual layer inspired players to pounce on their search engines. There, they uncovered websites that detailed the mystery of murdered Evan Chan.

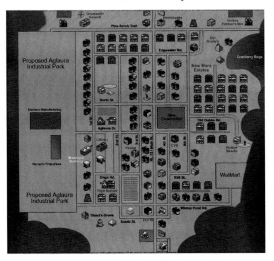

Scan of map of *Aglaura*, NJ from *Chasing the Wish Book One*, Vol 1, Issue 1, New Fiction Publishing, April 2006.

More recently, the ARG for the *Lost* (2004) TV series, *The Lost Experience* (2006), was launched with an in-story advertisement during the airing of an episode. The advertisement provided a call to action in the form of a phone number to the Hanso Corporation. This launch was stumbled upon by some, but most were made aware of its existence through media coverage. Indeed, most rabbit hole discoveries are facilitated by ARG communities such as ARGN.com and Unfiction.com; PMs send an announcement or gifts to such communities or to their players directly.

Photo of the contents of a wooden box sent to launch *Sammeeeees* (2006).

Previous examples of gifts include jars of honey with sticky clues, which were sent for *I Love Bees* (2004), and tin-foil-wrapped wooden boxes with rose petals and written clues, sent for *Sammeeeees* (2006).

In *Sammeeeees*, as in most ARGs, the rabbit hole was meant to surprise, delight, confuse and inspire action. At the crucial stage of inspiring cross-world migration, the rabbit hole also represents a slippery slope of inter- and hypertextual links. For instance, within hours of a player publishing the contents of the *Sammeeeees* wooden boxes at the Unfiction.com forum, a phone number, numerous websites, flickr images and in-story advertisements were found scattered throughout cyberspace. The altruism of players is often accompanied by a plea for other players to uncover some truth, find a murderer, save a person or save the planet. Players do, however, expect some reward for their good work in the form of a compelling entertainment experience. Some ARGs do provide an in-story reward as well, to motivate audiences to participate initially and to continue to do so over time. *Perplex City*, for example, is a perpetual ARG with no end in sight, in which the residents of Perplex City offer a substantial cash prize (in Earth currency) for the retrieval of their "Receda Cube." Most ARGs, though, do end, and the fact that access to their worlds is short, occurs in real time and cannot be replayed impels participation.

Shared Play

As stated earlier, ARGs are collaborative. PMs facilitate this characteristic by creating a world that is too large for any one person to traverse: dispersed across cyberspace and other media and with unique content in different countries. They provide a range of ways of participating by creating pure game activities as well as narrative ones, and they include a range of subjects in which no single person could possibly have expertise. This encourages what many have called "collective intelligence." Unlike in most games, in ARGs, players can choose what parts of the game to participate in and can still be privy to other parts through the resources produced by their peers. Listings of sites found, solutions to challenges and speculation about the plot are always shared globally through forum posts, listservs, wikis, blogs, Trails (listings of puzzles) or Guides (narrative recounts of the discovery of components in real time).

Another aspect of the multiplayer experience is the fact that ARG players play as themselves. They do not need a supernatural ability, a cape or a time-traveling device. Everything they are is valuable and needed immediately; the only requirement is the ability to step into an alternate reality. And in the word of ARG designer Elan Lee, "There's something very empowering about saying there's a little bit of magic in this world, and if you pay attention you'll find it" (Ruberg & Lee 2006). If you believe in ARGs, clap your hands.

◆ *A.I. Artificial Intelligence* (Movie)(2001), produced and distributed by Warner Bros. Pictures & DreamWorks. ◆ *The Beast* (2001), developed by Microsoft, published by Dreamworks. ◆ Carroll, L. (1865), *Alice in Wonderland*, Mcmillan, London. ◆ *Chasing the Wish* (2006), developed and published by Dave Szulborski et al. ◆ *I Love Bees* (2004), developed by 42 Entertainment, published by Bungie Studios / Microsoft. ◆ *Lost* (TV-Series) (2004 - ongoing), produced by Touchstone TV & ABC TV Studio, various distributors. ◆ *The Lost Experience* (2006), developed and published by ABC Entertainment. ◆ McGonigal, J. (2003), " 'This is not a game': Immersive Aesthetics and Collective Play," *Proceedings of the 5th International Digital Arts and Culture Conference, RMIT*, Melbourne, Australia, pp. 110-118. Retrieved December 20, 2003, from http://hypertext.rmit.edu.au/dac/papers/McGonigal.pdf ◆ Nieuwdorp, E. (2005), "The pervasive interface: tracing the magic circle," *Proceedings of DiGRA 2005 Conference: Changing Views – Worlds in Play*, Vancouver, Canada. Retrieved December 10, 2006, from http://www.digra.org/dl/db/06278.53356.pdf ◆ *Perplex City* (2005 - ongoing), developed and published by Mind Candy. ◆ Ruberg, B. & Lee, E. (2006), *Elan Lee's Alternate Reality*. Retrieved December 7, 2006, from http://www.gamasutra.com/features/20061206/ruberg_02.shtml ◆ *Sammeeeees* (2006), developed and published by Jan Libby. ◆ Stewart, S. (n.d.), *Alternate Reality Games*. Retrieved December 13, 2006, from http://www.seanstewart.org/interactive/args/ ◆ Szulborski, D. (2005), *This Is Not A Game: A Guide to Alternate Reality Gaming*, New Fiction Publishing, Macungie PA.

I LOVE BEES
Hijacking Payphones for Play Experience

In the spring of 2001, a small team working out of the Microsoft offices built an Internet-based story orbiting around the Steven Spielberg film *A.I. Artificial Intelligence* (Warner Bros. 2001). The story engaged a large number of people, each of whom could contribute to the entire community's understanding based on "what he knew."

In 2004, we wanted to transfer our kind of online storytelling from the Web to the real world. So we set out to build a game in which a player would feel special and able to contribute based on his location instead of his knowledge base.

Our story took place in the world of the video game *Halo 2* (Bungie Studios 2004). For both practical and artistic reasons, we did not incorporate visual assets from the game into our story, whose core was a radio-play-like audio drama. The main event in the title was the arrival of aliens on earth, so we decided to use Orson Welles' *War of the Worlds* (1938) broadcast as a touchstone.

Now we needed to come up with a game that met our two design parameters: delivering an audio drama and simultaneously cutting it into pieces so that people who lived in different places would be motivated to leave their computers, go out into the real world and search for the different bits and pieces of the story. Building our own radio towers all over the world seemed impractical. Instead, Elan Lee, the lead designer on the project, pointed out that there was a huge base of audio delivery platforms already installed all around the world, waiting to be hijacked: payphones.

By the end of the 16-week play experience, we had broadcast a five and a half hour long audio drama in 45 second snippets, making more than 75,000 calls to payphones. Players in the game were given GPS coordinates, which they would use to find a real-world payphone. They would then have to stand at that payphone at a given time and answer a phone call. Players eventually became the driving force behind certain parts of the story, as is always the case in good interactive fiction, and performed numerous real-world "missions" in response to the calls.

PERPLEX CITY
An Alternate Reality Treasure Hunt

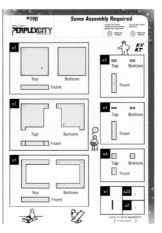

In April of 2005, Mind Candy launched *Perplex City*, an Alternate Reality Game (ARG) meant to promote its line of *Perplex City* puzzle collector's cards and games. The ARG is a new genre of storytelling that combines the Internet with real-world events, locations and channels of communication to blur the lines between fiction and reality. *Perplex City* is the world's first for-profit, ongoing Alternate Reality Game. Episode One spanned almost two years and utilized blogs, websites, tricky puzzles and live events to tell the story of "the Cube" —a mysterious artifact from a parallel universe – while encouraging players to collect a vast array of puzzle cards. The game's plot centered on the theft of this so-called "Receda Cube," a real-life, tangible object (albeit from a fictional universe) that was stolen while on display at the Perplex City Academy in *Perplex City*, a fictional metropolis belonging to the parallel universe. It was discovered that the Cube had been hidden somewhere here on earth, and it was up to players to find and return it. The result was a global treasure hunt with a reward of www.perplexcity.com

200,000 US Dollars, in which players solved puzzles, coordinated efforts and sought out clues to the Cube's whereabouts in actual real-world locations. Along the way, they met up at actual locations in England and North America, where the game expanded beyond the fictional world to reach out and touch our's.

Early in the game, for example, players were instructed to make their way to Imperial College in England, where they found posters for a band (Receda Approach), along with its website address. On this website, they found instructions to be at one of five movie theaters in Toronto, Canada on a certain date. Canadian players jumped in to contribute, heading to the appointed theaters to see an actual trailer for a fictional film (The Receda Sign) and its accompanying website. This website then gave them a phone number to call that revealed the location of yet another clue in an actual real-world location.

In addition, *Perplex City* sponsored numerous "Academy Games," which were high-tech urban scavenger hunts held in London and New York City. Players were given instructions and asked to send evidence of their completion in the form of photos and text messages via mobile phones back to the *Perplex City* "base camp," which responded with trivia questions and pop-quiz tasks throughout the day. Many tasks included creating mini-spectacles (such as forming choirs or conga lines in Trafalgar Square) that transformed public space into gamespace – much to the surprise of innocent passersby.

After following a trail of online and offline puzzles and events, completing tasks that triggered new story chapters and putting resultant clues together, one player finally found the "Receda Cube" in February 2007 buried in Wakerly Great Wood in England.

3 | UBIQUITOUS GAMES

245

Project Description	Text	Project	Affiliation
	Dave Szulborski	Dave Szulborski, Steve Wax, Mike Monello, Gregg Hale et al.	Campfire, New York, US, with Chelsea Pictures, Haxan Films and GMD Studios, McKinney Silver, Durham, US, 2005

THE ART OF THE HEIST
An Alternate Reality Game as Advertisement

In 2005, I was the puzzle designer for an ambitious Alternate Reality Game (ARG) campaign commissioned by McKinney Silver and its client Audi that found new ways to transcend the primarily web-based format of the genre by presenting a fictional adventure story set in the real world. *The Art of the Heist* immersed the audience in the story of a stolen Audi A3, a planned multimillion-dollar art theft and a video game designer desperately trying to craft a career comeback. But despite its fictional basis, the game powerfully and persistently declared its gamespace to be the real world by seamlessly blending real-world assets, locations and events into the narrative.

Immediately upon launch, *The Art of the Heist*'s developers presented the game's setting as reality itself, embedding game assets and artifacts conspicuously into the real world. Initial ads or "rabbit holes" weren't just on the Internet; they appeared as actual magazine ads or as legitimate Audi TV commercials. Likewise, the game's fictional car theft wasn't just staged for video purposes. Instead, it was produced and presented simultaneously – with Hollywood production costs – at two hugely visible real-world venues. The new Audi A3 models on exhibit at the NYC Car Show and the prestigious Park Avenue Audi dealership actually did disappear at the start of the game; two broken showroom windows and signs declaring the car stolen were all that was left behind.

Actors portrayed the three main characters and were actively involved at the multiple real-world events staged for the game. Even the fictional in-game websites, which could be considered the most traditional representative gamespaces of the campaign, were carefully crafted and loaded with content so as to appear as real as possible. Finally, the narrative and gameplay unfolded in real time and were anchored by real-world milestones, including the NYC Car Show and live events at the E3 Convention and Coachella Music Festival. Merging a player's sense of gametime and real time was a key technique used to set the game firmly in the everyday world. The gameplay did consist of working through the deep levels of online story content, but even that was triggered by the players' involvement in the real-world events. The end result was to transform the player's everyday world into a game board where gamespace and gametime effectively became real space and real time.

246

Steve Benford,
Carsten Magerkurth,
Peter Ljungstrand

PERVASIVE GAMES
Bridging the Gaps between the Virtual and the Physical

What Are Pervasive Games?

Pervasive games extend gaming experiences into the real world – be it onto city streets, remote wildernesses or living rooms. In pervasive games, players with mobile computing devices move through the world. Sensors capture information about the players' current context – including their location – and are thereby able to deliver gaming experiences that change according to where the players are, what they are doing and even how they are feeling. The players become unchained from their consoles and experience a game that is interwoven with the everyday world and potentially available at any place, at any time.

This is an exciting idea. From a commercial viewpoint, pervasive games extend current wireless games in that they are more deeply connected and bound up with real locations and activities. This means that they hold the potential for delivering much-needed content for 3G mobile telephony. Pervasive games are equally exciting from a research viewpoint because they open the door for new technical and human challenges.

There are already various forms of pervasive games in existence. One approach is to reinterpret classic computer games, mapping them onto real-world settings so that players have to physically run about in order to control their avatars. An example of this game incarnation is *Human Pacman* (Cheok et al. 2004). Other games focus strongly on social interaction; examples include *Pirates!*, a fantasy game about trading and fighting at sea (Björk et al. 2001) and the *STARS* platform for augmented tabletop games, which preserves the rich social interaction found in traditional board and tabletop games (Magerkurth et al. 2004). Touring artistic games, for their part, combine players on the streets of a city with those who are online in a parallel virtual city, requiring them to exchange perspectives. Some examples of this type include the chase game *Can You See Me Now? (CYSMN)* (Flintham et al. 2003) and *Uncle Roy All Around You* (Benford et al. 2004b), which explores the theme of trust amongst strangers.

Pervasive games such as *CYSMN* build upon three core technologies: displays that can make digital content available to players as they move through the physical world, including mobile phones, handheld computers, earphones, wearable computers and interactive projections and tangible interfaces that are embedded into the surrounding environment; wireless communications that enable players to communicate with remote servers and other players; and sensing technologies that capture players' contexts, including positioning technologies such as GPS, cameras, microphones and potentially even physiological sensors. This blend of technologies combined with the location-based and often public nature of gameplay gives pervasive games their distinctive identity. At the same time, it also poses significant new challenges, five of which we now briefly discuss.

Challenge I: Dealing with Uncertainty

The first challenge arises from the considerable uncertainties associated with sensing and wireless communications. Both are constrained by limited coverage, especially in built-up urban areas, so that players may often be unable to obtain a fix on their position or communicate with others. Sensing technologies are also associated with further uncertainties such as error and jitter, which can vary with both location and time. Previous research has proposed different approaches to dealing with uncertainty (Flintham et al. 2003): removing it (by carefully choosing game locations and times, for example); revealing it so that players are able to understand and adapt to it; and even exploiting it by deliberately incorporating uncertainty into the structure of a game (enabling players to "hide in the shadows" by moving out of network coverage, for example).

Challenge II: Hybrid Architectures

The second challenge involves reconciling client-server and peer-to-peer architectures. Whereas a client-server setup enables players to share a consistent game experience, a peer-to-peer setup supports highly localized and ad-hoc gameplay that occurs during encounters on the streets. The challenge here is to integrate these two approaches. For example, can we design games in which publicly visible and "legitimate" actions take place at central servers but in which the exciting possibility of more secret or private interactions occurring in peer-to-peer mode also exist (pick-pocketing other players, for example, or trading on the black market without revealing sources)?

Challenge III: Hefting Domains

Game elements in computer games are mostly tied to the virtual world while traditional games reside in the real, physical world. Since pervasive games take elements from both the real and the virtual worlds, their design requires careful consideration; which elements should be represented virtually, which physically and which as a blend of both?

Challenge IV: Configuration

A pervasive game may need to be configured to work at many different locations. For a game that is intimately tied up with its local setting, the challenge is to quickly integrate rich local information – maps, plans, images and sounds – into the game content. Pervasive games that are less integrated into a local setting – for example *Savannah*, which takes place on an empty playing field (Benford et al. 2004a) – may still require considerable configuration of network and sensing technologies.

Challenge V: Orchestration

The final challenge concerns orchestration, the real-time management of a live game from behind the scenes, an important issue when game providers assume responsibility for the safety of players who are on the streets of a strange city. Successful orchestration requires tools for managing the status of players – for example, being always aware of their connection statuses and last known locations – and also for subtly intervening without disrupting the game – by improvising game messages, for instance.

Future Challenges

The pervasive game is both an exciting and commercially promising new form of computer game that builds on a combination of hybrid interfaces, wireless networking and context-sensing technologies. However, while recent projects hint at a wide variety of potential gaming experiences, they also reveal some of the research challenges that need to be addressed if pervasive games are to move forward, including designing for uncertainty, exploiting hybrid architectures and developing sufficient support for configuration and orchestration. Once these challenges are tackled and we understand the implications of bringing gaming experiences back to the streets, we will even be able to draw empirically valid conclusions for the design of the urban spaces that host our games. Until then, pervasive games will be an attractive testbed for gaining insight on the perception of space and the orchestration of architecture in entertainment applications.

◆ Benford, S., Rowland, D., Flintham, M., Hull, R., Reid, J., Morrison, J., Facer, K. & Clayton, B. (2004a), "Savannah: Designing a Location-Based Game Simulating Lion Behaviour," *Proceedings of ACM Advanced Computer Entertainment (ACE)*, Singapore, July 2004, ACM Press, New York. ◆ Benford, S., Seagar, W., Flintham, M., Anastasi, R., Rowland, D., Humble, J., Stanton, D., Bowers, J., Tandavanitj, N., Adams, M., Row-Farr, J., Oldroyd, A. & Sutton, J. (2004b), "The Error of Our Ways: The Experience of Self-Reported Positioning in a Location-based game," in N. Davies (ed.), *UbiComp 2004: Ubiquitous Computing, Proceedings of 6th international conference*, Nottingham, UK, September, 2004, Springer, Berlin. ◆ Björk, S., Falk, J., Hansson, R. & Ljungstrand, P. (2001), "Pirates! – Using The Physical World As A Game Board," *Proceedings of Interact 2001, 8th IFIP TC.13 Conference On Human-Computer Interaction*, Tokyo, Japan, July 2001. Retrieved from http://Play.Tii.Se/Publications/2001/Piratesshort.Pdf ◆ Cheok, A., Goh, K., Farbiz, F., Fong, S., Teo, S., Li, Y. & Yang, X. (2004), "Human Pacman: A Mobile, Wide-Area Entertainment System Based On Physical, Social And Ubiquitous Computing," *Personal And Ubiquitous Computing*, 8 (2), pp. 71-81, May 2004, Springer, Berlin. ◆ Flintham, M., Anastasi, R., Benford, S., Hemmings, T., Crabtree, A., Greenalgh, C., Rodden, T., Tandavanitj, N., Adams, M. & Row-Farr, J. (2003), "Where On-Line Meets On-The-Streets: Experiences With Mobile Mixed Reality Games," *Proceedings of the 2003 CHI Conference On Human Factors In Computing Systems*, Florida, pp. 569-576, ACM Press. ◆ Magerkurth, C., Engelke, T. & Memisoglu, M. (2004), "Augmenting the Virtual Domain with Physical and Social Elements," *Proceedings of 1st International Conference on Advancements in Computer Entertainment Technology (ACM ACE 2004)*, Singapore, pp. 163-172, ACM Press.

THE POETICS OF AUGMENTED SPACE
The Art of Our Time

How is our experience of a spatial form affected when the form is used to display dynamic and rich multimedia information? (Think of *urban spaces* such as the shopping and entertainment areas of Tokyo, Hong Kong and Seoul as well as of *any human-constructed space* where a subject can access information wirelessly via cell phone, PDA or laptop.) Does the form become irrelevant, reduced to functional and ultimately invisible support for information flows? Or do we end up with a new experience in which the spatial and information layers are equally important?

Since these environments do not have a recognizable name yet, I will call them *augmented spaces*. Augmented space could be defined as physical space overlaid with dynamically changing information. This information is likely to be in multimedia form and is often localized for each user.

Augmentation and Monitoring

The 1990s were about the virtual. We were fascinated by the new virtual spaces made possible by computer technologies. Images of an escape into a virtual space that exists parallel to our world dominated the decade. This phenomenon began with a media obsession with Virtual Reality (VR). In the middle of the decade, graphical browsers for the World Wide Web made cyberspace a reality for millions of users. During the second part of the 1990s, yet another virtual phenomenon – the dot-com – rose to prominence, only to crash in the face of real-world laws of economics. By the end of the decade, a daily dose of cyberspace became so much the norm that the original wonder of cyberspace was almost completely lost.[1] The virtual became domesticated. To use Norman Klein's expression, it became an "electronic suburb."

At the beginning of the 21st century, there is a new agenda: physical space filled with electronic and visual information. The previous icon of the computer era, a VR user traveling in virtual space, has been replaced by a new image, that of a person checking her email using her PDA/cell phone combo at the airport, on the street or in any other actually existing space. But this is just one example of what I see as a larger trend – namely, technological applications that *dynamically deliver dynamic data to, or extract data from, physical space*:

Video surveillance is becoming ubiquitous; cheap, tiny, wireless and Net-enabled video cameras can now be placed by almost anyone, anywhere. The installment of such technology translates a physical space and its dwellers into data.

Cellspace technologies (mobile, wireless or location-based media) work in the opposite direction, delivering data to mobile physical-space dwellers. Some of that

<1

VRML stands for the Virtual Reality Modeling Language. In the first part of the 1990s, the inventors of this language designed it as a means to model and access 3D interactive virtual worlds over the Internet and promoted it as the material realization of the idea of cyberspace. (See, for instance, "Ontos, Eros, Noos, Logos," **(Pesce 1995)**) As of this writing (May 2007), Internet-based 3D virtual worlds have failed to become popular.

data may come from global networks such as the Internet, some may be embedded in objects located in the space around the user.

We can think of *cellspace* as the invisible layer of information that is laid over physical space and is customized by an individual user. Publicly located *computer/video displays* present the same visible information to passersby.

If we consider the effect of these three technologies on our concept of space – and, consequently, on our lives in so far as they are lived in various spaces – I believe that we will see that the three very much belong together. They make physical space into a dataspace, which can be augmented by data (*cellspace*, computer displays) or from which data can be extracted (surveillance). It also makes sense to conceptually connect the surveillance/monitoring of physical space and its dwellers and the augmentation of this space with additional data because, technologically, these two applications exist in a symbiotic relationship. The close connection between surveillance/monitoring and assistance/augmentation is one of the key characteristics of the high-tech society. *Augmented space is also monitored space.* Augmented space is physical space that is "data dense," as every point in it potentially contains various information delivered to it from elsewhere. At the same time, video surveillance, monitoring and various sensors can also extract information from any point in space, recording face movements, gestures and other human activity as well as temperature, light levels and so on. Thus we can say that various augmentation and monitoring technologies add new dimensions to a 3D physical space, making it multidimensional. As a result, physical space now contains many more dimensions than before, and while from the phenomenological perspective of the human subject, the "old" geometric dimensions may still have priority, from the perspective of technology and its social, political and economic applications, they are no longer more important than any other dimension.

Augmentation and Immersion

I derived the term "augmented space" from the already established term "Augmented Reality" (AR).[2] Coined around 1990, Augmented Reality is normally used in opposition to VR. In a typical VR system, all work is done in a virtual space; physical space becomes unnecessary, and the user's visual perception of it is completely blocked. In contrast, an AR system helps the user to work in a physical space by augmenting that space with additional information. This is achieved by laying information over the user's visual field. An early possible AR application developed by Xerox PARC, for example, involved a wearable display for copier repairman, which overlaid a wireframe image of the copier's insides over the actual copier as it was being repaired.

Today, additional AR scenarios for everyday use can be imagined – AR glasses for a tourist, for example, which layer dynamically changing information about the sites in a city over the tourist's visual field. Military and artistic applications are also being developed, as presented, for instance, in the exhibition showcasing AR projects developed by Ars Electronica Futurelab (Ars Electronica Festival 2003). In this new iteration, AR becomes conceptually similar to wireless location services. The idea that governs both is that when a user is in the vicinity of particular objects,

2 >
For AR research sites and conferences, see http://www.augmented-reality.org

buildings or people, information about those entities can be delivered to her. But while in *cellspace* this information is displayed on a cell phone or PDA, in AR, the information is laid over the user's visual field.

The decrease in the popularity of VR in mass media and a slow but steady rise in AR-related research in the last five years are two examples of the ways in which the augmented space paradigm is now overtaking the virtual space paradigm. Interestingly, this reversal was arguably anticipated in the very origins of VR. In the late 1960s, Ivan Sutherland developed what came to be known as the first VR system. The user of the system saw a simple wireframe cube whose perspectival view would change as the user moved his head. The wireframe cube appeared over whatever the user was seeing. Because the idea of a 3D computer graphics display whose perspective changes in real time according to the position of the user became associated with subsequent virtual reality systems, Sutherland is credited with inventing the first one. It can be argued, however, that this was not a VR, but rather an AR system because the virtual display was laid over the user's field of vision without blocking it. In other words, in Sutherland's system, new information – a virtual cube – *was added* to the physical environment.

In the case of VR, the user interacts with a virtual simulation; in the case of AR, she interacts with actual things in actual space. Because of this, a typical VR system presents a user with a virtual space that has nothing to do with that user's immediate physical space; in contrast, a typical AR system adds information that is directly related to the user's immediate physical space. But we don't necessarily have to think of immersion in the virtual and augmentation of the physical as opposites. On one level, whether we think of a particular situation as immersion or augmentation is simply a matter of scale – i.e. the relative size of a display. When you are playing a computer game on a game console that is connected to a TV, you are hardly aware of your physical surroundings. You are immersed in virtual reality. But when you play the same game on the small display of a cell phone, the experience is different. You are still largely present in physical space, and while the display adds to your overall phenomenological experience, it does not take it over. Thus whether we should understand a particular situation in terms of immersion or augmentation depends on how we understand the idea of addition: we may add new information to our experience or we may add an altogether different experience.

Augmentation as an Idea

What is the phenomenological experience of being in a new augmented space? What are the possible poetics and aesthetics of an augmented space?

One way to begin thinking about these questions is to approach the design of augmented space as an architectural problem. Augmented space provides a challenge and an opportunity for many architects to rethink their practice, since architecture will have to take into account the fact that from now on, virtual layers of contextual information will overlay built space.

But is this a completely new challenge for architecture? If we assume that the overlaying of different spaces is a conceptual problem that is not connected to any particular technology, we may begin to see that certain architects and artists have already been grappling with this issue. The layering of dynamic and contextual data over physical space is a particular case of a general aesthetic paradigm: how to combine different spaces. Of course, electronically augmented space is unique; because the information it contains is personalized for every user, it can change dynamically over time, and it is delivered through an interactive multimedia interface. Yet it is crucial to see the problem of combining spaces as conceptual rather than just technological and thus as something that in part has already been featured in other architectural and artistic paradigms.

Augmented space research gives us new terms with which to think about earlier spatial practices. If we consider the case of a past architect, fresco painter or display designer working to combine architecture and images or architecture and text, we can now say that all of them were working on the problem of augmented space – the problem, that is, of how to overlay physical space with layers of data. Therefore, in order to imagine what can be done culturally with augmented spaces, we may begin by combing cultural history for useful precedents. I have chosen two well-known contemporary figures as my examples. The first is Janet Cardiff, a Canadian artist who became famous for her "audio walks." She creates her pieces by following a trajectory through a space and narrating an audio track that combines instructions to the user (e.g. "go down the stairs") with narrative fragments, sound effects and other aural "data." To experience the piece, the user dons earphones connected to a CD player and follows Cardiff's instructions.[3] Even though Cardiff does not use any sophisticated computer, networking or projection technologies, her "walks" represent the best realization of the augmented space paradigm so far. They demonstrate the aesthetic potential of laying new information over a physical space. Their power lies in the interactions between the two spaces.

The Jewish Museum Berlin by Daniel Libeskind can be thought of as another example of augmented space research. Libeskind uses existing dataspace to drive the new architecture that he constructs. After putting together a map that showed the addresses of Jews who lived in the neighborhood of the museum site before World War II, the architect connected different points on the map and then projected the resulting net onto the surfaces of the building. The intersections of the projected net and the museum walls gave rise to multiple irregular windows. Cutting through the walls and the ceilings at different angles, these windows evoke many visual references. Just as in the case of Cardiff's audio walks, here the virtual becomes a powerful force that re-shapes the physical. In the Jewish Museum Berlin, dataspace is materialized to become a sort of monumental sculpture.

The Poetics of Discontinuity

Before we rush to conclude that the new technologies do not add anything substantially new to the old aesthetic paradigm of overlaying different spaces together, let me note that in addition to their ability to deliver dynamic and interactive information, the new technologically implemented augmented spaces also differ in one important aspect from Cardiff's walks, Libeskind's Jewish Museum and other similar works. Rather than laying a new 3D virtual dataspace over the physical space, Cardiff and Libeskind overlay only a 2D plane or, at most, a 3D path. In

3 >

I have only experienced one of her "walks," one that she created for P.S. 1 in New York City in 2001.

254

contrast, augmented space technologies define dataspace – if not in practice, then at least in theory – as a continuous field that completely extends over and fills in all physical space. Every point in space has a GPS coordinate that can be obtained using a GPS receiver. Similarly, in the *cellspace* paradigm, every point in physical space can be said to contain some information that can be retrieved using a PDA or similar device. And as far as surveillance goes, while in practice video cameras, satellites and other technologies can so far only reach some regions and layers of data, but not others, the ultimate goal of the modern surveillance paradigm is to be able to observe every point at every moment. It is important to note that in practice, dataspaces are almost never continuous: surveillance cameras look at some spaces, but not at others, wireless signals are stronger in some areas and nonexistent in others and so on. The contrast between the continuity of *cellspace* in theory and its discontinuity in practice should not be dismissed. Rather, it itself can be a source of interesting aesthetics strategies.

I think that we can give a provisional answer to the questions I posed at the beginning of this essay. The arrival of augmented space does not mean that physical form has or will become culturally irrelevant. On the contrary, as the work of Cardiff and Libeskind shows, it is through the interaction of physical space and data that some of the most amazing art of our time is being created.

This is a short version of a longer text. A full version is available at: www.manovich.net.

◆ Pesce, M. (1995), "Ontos, Eros, Noos, Logos," Keynote Address, *International Symposium on Electronic Arts 1995*, Montreal, Canada. Retrieved from http://www.xs4all.nl/~mpesce/iseakey.html

Project Description	Text	Project	Affiliation
	Staffan Björk, Peter Ljungstrand	Staffan Björk, Jennica Falk, Rebecca Hansson, Jussi Holopainen, Peter Ljungstrand, Jouka Mattila, Eero Räsänen, Timo A. Toivonen	PLAYstudio Interactive Institute Göteborg, SE, Nokia Research Center Tampere, FI, 2000

PIRATES!
Using the Physical World as a Game Board

In *Pirates!*, players assume the roles of captains struggling to advance their reputations while keeping their ships manned and afloat. What makes *Pirates!* different from ordinary computer games is that the movement within the game is prompted by the player's movement in the real world. This simple innovation shifts the focus of gameplay from watching a computer screen to observing and navigating through one's real-world surroundings. By "sailing" (i.e. physically walking around with a handheld device) players can find and visit the islands of the game's fantasy archipelago setting to collect resources, fight monsters and natives and complete quest-specific tasks. Early in the game, captains are commissioned small and simple ships with low firepower. However, as they successfully complete missions, they are rewarded with larger and sturdier ships. These replacement ships allow them to have more cannons and crewmembers and to store more commodities in the cargo hold.

Pirates! is played on handheld computers that make use of wireless local area network (WLAN) and short-range radio. The WLAN allows for a client-server setup in which the server maintains all players' game stats as well as the global high score list. The short-range radio provides a robust system for determining when players are near to each other as well as when they are in the proximity of islands, which are marked by stand-alone beacons using the same radio system.

All interactions within *Pirates!* are initiated by players. That is, nothing happens in the game unless a player gives the game input. This input can be choosing one of the buttons on the handheld device or moving oneself across the area where the radio beacons can detect senders. The decision not to include system-initiated actions in the game was necessary in order to allow players to focus their attention on physically navigating in the real world. It also had the advantage of letting players move smoothly between playing the game and socializing with other people in the game environment. Indeed, the only case in which it is not the player that initiates an action in the game is when another player does so; by moving close to another player, one can activate the real-time sea battle play mode for both oneself and for the other player.

www.tii.se/play/projects/pirates

Project Description	Text	Project	Affiliation
	Steve Benford	Matt Adams, Ju Row Farr, Nick Tandavanitj, Steve Benford, Andy Crabtree, Martin Flintham, Adam Drozd, Mark Paxton, Rob Anastasi	Blast Theory, Brighton, UK, Mixed Reality Laboratory, University of Nottingham, UK, 2001

CAN YOU SEE ME NOW
Chasing the Virtual

Can You See Me Now (CYSMN) is an artistic pervasive game created by the artists' group Blast Theory in collaboration with the Mixed Reality Laboratory at the University of Nottingham as part of the Equator project. It premiered in Sheffield in 2001 and has toured internationally since then, visiting cities across the globe, including Sheffield, Rotterdam, Oldenburg, Cologne, Barcelona, Tokyo and Chicago. *CYSMN* is a game of catch, but with a twist. Up to 20 *online players* at a time are chased through a 3D virtual simulation of a city by up to four *street players*, who must run through the actual city streets in order to capture them. The four street players, referred to as runners, are professional performers who virtually chase the online players through the city streets. They are supported by a digital map that shows the current positions of all players and that is delivered to their handheld computers through wireless network connections (initially 802.11b, but more recently GPRS) and GPS receivers.

The online players can move through the virtual model of the city at a fixed maximum speed, can access various views of the city streets, can see the positions of other players and the runners and can exchange text messages with one another or send text messages to the runners.

The runners communicate with each other over a separate walkie-talkie channel. Online players can listen to this audio stream via the Internet and thus hear real-time descriptions of the experience of running through the streets, including reports of traffic conditions, accounts of local street scenes and the sounds of the physical action involved in tracking players down. Indeed, it is this audio stream that really defines the game; because they are privy to the runners' talk, online players are quite adept at avoiding their pursuers, effortlessly leading them up and down hills or through crowded public spaces.

Studies of *CYSMN* have combined feedback from players with ethnographic observations of activities on the streets and behind the scenes through the analysis of system logs. They have revealed the ways in which the various participants cope with the inherent uncertainties of the experience, which arise from the limited coverage and accuracy of GPS and Wi-Fi/GPRS. Such observations have inspired new design strategies for dealing with uncertainty in mobile experiences as well as the design of new mobile authoring tools that enable designers to visualize the behavior of the underlying technical infrastructure of their games.

www.blasttheory.co.uk
www.mrl.nott.ac.uk
www.equator.ac.uk

Project Description	Text	Project	Affiliation
	Steffen P. Walz	Steffen P. Walz, Thomas Seibert and Tim Ruetz with students	School of Art and Design, Zurich, CH, 2002

M.A.D. COUNTDOWN
A Game about Group Trust, Risk and a Bomb Threat

M.A.D. Countdown (MC) is one of the earliest examples of a site-specific multiplayer game. The game takes place in both the physical and virtual worlds at the Zurich School for Art and Design (HGKZ), which commissioned the game in 2001. Played by close to 20 gamers over five consecutive daylong sessions, *MC* served as the testbed for an empirical experiment concerning group trust, risk-taking and cooperative behavior in an emergency- and rescue-themed "hybrid reality" setting.

In the game, players – divided in teams of five – assume the role of emergency heroes who have to locate and disarm a tangible "atomic bomb" planted as part of an "anti-art conspiracy." The bomb has been secretly hidden somewhere in HGKZ's physical building. One of the players, however, is randomly chosen to play the self-interpretable role of saboteur. The saboteur's goal is to prevent the locating and disarming of the bomb. During one day, the "rescuers" have to consolidate their groups and find fragments of the bomb deactivation code both in the physical world and on the virtual "6th floor" of HGKZ's main building. The 6th floor is a two-dimensional point-and-click top-view world displayed on the wirelessly networked PocketPC with which each player is equipped. Players must explore the virtual floor, interact with the many dungeons, puzzles, objects and art- and design-related game characters found thereon and fulfill quests by collecting and manipulating objects to progress in the game.

Extending the treasure hunt beyond the PocketPC, *MC* incorporates many other media for the player – for example, puzzle websites, automated calls to a

physical phone booth, messages on answering machines and physical game objects such as lockers, dislocated books and poster-sized puzzles. In *MC*, player-to-player interaction may take place: (a) on the virtual 6th floor – players can, for example, flirt with or attack one another, or even choose to have sex with an alien exchange student; (b) via WiFi chat facilitated by a text-message-like interface on the PocketPC; or (c) face-to-face. Player-to-real-character interaction takes place in physicality when, for example, players have to ask briefed staff for passwords.

260

Project Description	Text	Project	Affiliation
	Frank Lantz	Frank Lantz with students	Interactive Telecommunications Program, New York University, US, 2004

PACMANHATTAN
The City as the Game's Playground

In 2004, I taught a class called "Big Games" in the Interactive Telecommunications Program at New York University. The purpose of the class was to explore the social, technological and creative possibilities of large-scale gaming. For their final project, all of the students in the class worked together to create *PacManhattan*. Inspired in part by the visual pun between the New

York street grid and Pac-Man's (Namco 1979) glowing maze, *PacManhattan* is a life-sized version of the arcade classic. The game takes place in a 5x6 block area around Washington Square Park. One player takes the role of Pac-Man; his goal is to traverse as much of the grid as possible before getting caught by any of the three ghost players who are pursuing him.

The students' original conception of *PacManhattan* was very technically ambitious, with custom GPS-enabled location-tracking devices powering the action. But the final game was far simpler in execution. It was managed from a central headquarters. Each player on the street had a corresponding "controller" player at HQ with whom he was in constant communication via cellphone. Every intersection in the game grid was labelled, and the street players would tell their controller whenever they arrived at a new intersection. The controllers had access to a networked map on which they would update the players' positions.

Adopting the simplest possible technical execution allowed the students to focus on what was (to me) the most interesting aspect of the project – the gameplay. At its heart, *Pac-Man* is about a wily hero outsmarting a flock of dogged but less intelligent foes. In order to recapture this essential quality, the designers of *PacManhattan* spent a lot of time thinking about informa-

tion management. The final game was built around an interesting form of information asymmetry: Pac-Man is aware of everything – including the positions of all the ghosts – while the ghosts themselves know each others' positions but are not told Pac-Man's location by the controllers at HQ, unless one of them actually sees the Pac-Man player in the flesh. The ghosts are, however, aware of whether or not their current location contains "dots" and therefore ofwhether or not Pac-Man has been there.

As a result, the ghost players need to coordinate their actions, setting up a dragnet around Pac-Man's most likely location while Pac-Man uses sprints, feints and reversals in an attempt to stay one step ahead of them. In actual play, the game is genuinely fun and compelling; the dramatic tension naturally builds as Pac-Man clears more and more of the "board" and the ghosts close in for the inevitable showdown. In the process, the city becomes the game's playground.

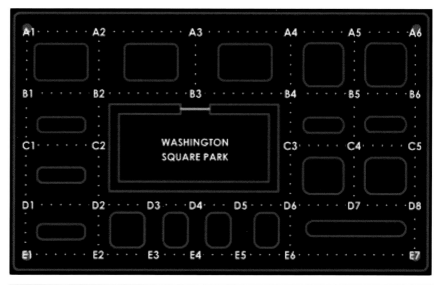

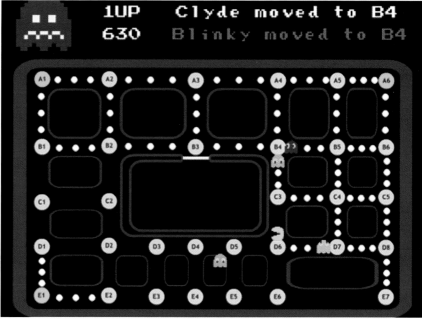

Project Description	Text	Project	Affiliation
	Gregor Broll	Gregor Broll, Steve Benford	Mixed Reality Lab, University of Nottingham, UK, Embedded Interaction Research Group, University of Munich, DE, 2005

TYCOON
A Seamful Game for Mobile Phones

Tycoon is a seamful location-based multiplayer game for mobile phones. Its gameplay is based on a simple producer-consumer cycle and is driven by competition between multiple players.

Tycoon uses the different GSM-cells of a service-provider network in a designated gaming area (e.g. a park, a mall or a city center) and virtually maps them to producers and consumers in the game. This mapping augments everyday locations with playful meanings and turns urban spaces into virtual playgrounds.

In this context, the metaphor of a gold rush scenario communicates *Tycoon's* central mechanisms of collecting resources in producer areas called mines and using them to buy objects in consumer areas called brokers, which have the names of cities or counties in California. Each mine produces an unlimited amount of one of the three resources in the game (gold, silver or copper). Players collect them by staying in an appropriate cell for a certain period of time. There are also brokers, each of whom has a list of objects, e.g. different buildings that players can buy with their resources. These objects are unique and limited; players compete against each other to claim them and collect their credit value. The objective of the game is to collect as many credits as possible until all objects have been claimed.

Tycoon's seamful design copes with different seams that are caused by the technical constraints of the mobile phone platform and are manifested as uncertainties, ambiguities or inconsistencies. For example, an alert is triggered whenever a player steps from one cell into another in order to visualize dynamic cell borders and decrease uncertainty about his or her position.

Mobile connections to the Internet are expensive yet necessary in order to synchronize mobile clients with the globally shared gamestate. Thus *Tycoon* puts an emphasis on offline play as its economic system gives players incentives for staying offline. The more time players spend offline, the more potential profit, but the greater becomes the probability of inconsistencies and missed claims. Therefore players have to adopt their own strategies and consider their chances for earning more credits against the growing risk of inconsistencies. Thus, *Tycoon* raises awareness of urban locations in a playful way. In order to succeed in the virtual world of the game, players have to use their spatial knowledge in order to find the best tactics for moving between cells in the real world.

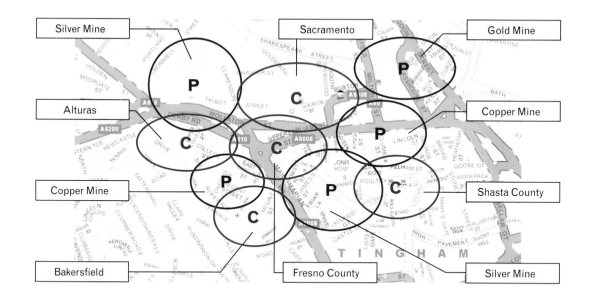

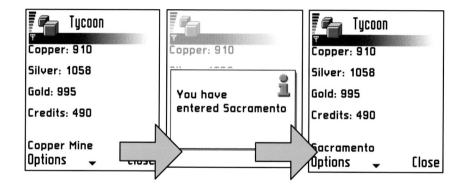

Text

URBAN ROLE-PLAY
The Next Generation of Role-Playing in Urban Space

The classical style of live-action role-playing (LARP) has its roots firmly in the genre of fantasy. Stereotypically, a LARP consists of players dressing up as medieval warriors and nobles, spending a day in make-believe fiction and acting out their characters' behavior in a forest setting. Diplomacy, drama and physical combat form the three typical pillars of the immersive and performative entertainment, which mixes improvisational theater with games of politics and swordplay.

That *Lord of the Rings*-induced stereotypical image of LARP started to crumble in the 90s as LARP based on anything from science fiction to Jane Austen began to emerge, taking gameplay from forests and castles into industrial halls, idyllic villas and city streets. Even though many long-term LARP players stuck with medieval fantasy, this change can be attributed to the maturing of the players and their culture: many players both became bored with the fantasy genre and grew to see and appreciate the uses of LARP in other settings as well.

A central forefather of urban outdoor LARP is *Killer* (1981), an assassination game played by university students worldwide. In the game, every player is assigned another player as a mark that he must "murder" during the weeks of play by, for example, pulling out a water gun and shooting the mark in an alley when no witnesses are present. As murders are conducted in daily life, proper playing takes hardcore efforts; players lurk in stairwells for hours or build prop bombs from alarm clocks, all while avoiding their own nemeses.

As competitive *Killer* is only occasionally role-played, only certain elements of ordinary reality are integrated into the game; the backstory is inconsequential, every player portrays an assassin, everyone is a target and the only real interaction is killing. In LARP, on the other hand, players are expected to have all kinds of theatrical social interactions with each other.

Social interaction with outsiders is a major design challenge for urban LARP: a player portraying a vampire can't bite random passersby, and potentially meeting their moms on the street while wearing funny clothes and fangs is usually a turn-off for people immersed in pretense play.

Pervasive LARP

The recent trends in experimental urban LARP transcend the limitations of "game" in many ways. While traditional LARP takes place at a dedicated time and in a dedicated space (Huizinga 1938), many recent games refuse these restrictions. *Prosopopeia* LARPs[1] seek to merge game and life seamlessly: an old mental hospital is

Prosopopeia Bardo 1: Dar vi foll (Stockholm, June 2005, by Martin Ericsson, Adriana Skarped, Staffan Jonsson & others) and Prosopopeia Bardo 2: Momentum (Stockholm, 2006, by Martin Ericsson, Staffan Jonsson, Emil Boss & others).

1 >

turned into a playground the moment players sneak inside it, a man at a graveyard becomes a game element the moment he's seen by the players.

The key innovation is an indexical relationship of gameworld and physical world. While tabletop role-players represent their gameworlds via symbols in speech and gestures, traditional LARPers also introduce iconic representation in the form of look-alike clothes, environments and other props (Loponen & Montola 2004). But in this new type of LARP, ordinary reality, exactly as it is, can represent the gameworld. In other words, a water pistol does not represent steel, oil and gunpowder, but rather, a plastic water pistol. More than that, my prop gun doesn't even stand for a generic prop gun, but for *my* prop gun; the social contexts of the ordinary world are used as source material for the gameworld.

From the players' perspective, this style of creating scenography solves the problem of outside-world interference, as everything can be directly read into the game. Certainly, it also imposes restrictions on game design, as indexical scenography is expensive to produce, and the real police (unconsciously portraying fictional police) put the players in real prison if they commit real crimes. But this problem is only relevant for Hollywood-like action, not minimalistic drama.

As David Fincher's 1997 movie *The Game* illustrates, sometimes the lines between LARP and real life can become dangerously blurred. It sometimes startles LARPers to realize that no "magic circle of gameplay" (Salen & Zimmermann 2004) protects them. In a computer game, the player can always try out different alternatives and play with different options, but stealing a real painting from a real art gallery is not one of them. Indexical LARPing is the extreme sports of performative play, as players never know where ordinary ends and ludic begins, and screwing up that distinction might hurt.

Secret Roles

Pretense play with characters differentiates role-play from other forms of play. Pretending to be someone else gives a player an excuse to act out in a strange fashion and enables him to engage in new styles of interaction with other players. In urban LARP, character play must contend with the fact that the environment is used as a game material.

One strategy for successfully balancing the two is by hiding gameplay from the outside world like characters of *Vampire* and *Killer* do. The environment is used as a challenge; players are expected to interact with each other while avoiding outsider attention.

The *Prosopopeia* way of combining character play and indexical representation is called the "possession model." It is used in order to allow very long urban LARP while mitigating the problems that occur in conflicts with the outside world. In this model, every player has three identities during the game. The first is the player's identity that exists outside the game – that is, the identity of the person participating in the LARP. This person then role-plays a *copy* of himself within the fiction – the second identity. This identity is expected to pretend, at all times, that everything happening in the game is real. Finally, the third identity is a *ghost* possessing the player-in-game. The premise of *Prosopopeia* was that dead spirits of real historical revolutionaries came back to life by possessing others' bodies in order to pursue agendas they had had in their own lives. All the world was source material for those playing the game; any information related to those historical figures could be used as game material.

In a LARP that runs 24/7 for many weeks, the benefit of the possession model is clear: when you see a friend on the street, you don't need to quit the game entirely. Just shove the possessing spirit to the back of your mind and be the player-in-game for a moment. This allows you to combine your whole life with the game in a seamless fashion.

Redefining Environment

Taking a role-playing game to the streets is a powerful way of questioning conventions and social codes embedded in space and architecture. Mike Pohjola (2004) views role-playing as a practice that enables the creation of *temporary autonomous zones* in which "willing participants agree on a new set of rules that are in effect within the zone." Urban LARP also imposes those rules on unaware bystanders, making it an empowering means by which to question implicit social contracts by first providing an *excuse* to break them and then allowing *insight* into their nature by exposing our unconscious beliefs regarding "proper behavior." Only when you play the role of a petty criminal and actually eat a steak in a posh restaurant with your bare fingers do you realize how hard-coded our social interactions really are.

Urban LARP allows experimentation in social interaction. The reality TV show *Candid Camera* is interesting because it offers a view of the strange behaviors of everyday people in strange situations. Urban role-play toys with the same theme but on a smaller, more personal scale. While *Killer* treats game outsiders as potential witnesses to be avoided, *Prosopopeia* takes the everyman "as is" by integrating the fiction of the game completely and seamlessly with the reality of life.

An example from the second *Prosopopeia* illustrates this. As part of the LARP, the players had to get a painting from a commercial art gallery planted by a game master who never informed the gallerist about the ludic nature of the event. "Give or sell this painting to whomever shows genuine interest for it," he said. The players did not know whether or not the gallerist was a player, and the gallerist only later came to suspect that the strange encounters were actually part of a game. But in the end, both parties loved the ambiguous and strange interactions they experienced.

Urban Playground

Urban exploration is fertile soil for this gaming style, and the urban landscape is a prime replacement for plastic swords and water guns as a means by which to infuse games with action. Instead of fighting, players can explore factory ruins, abandoned hospitals and underground tunnels. Indeed, the great hit of the second *Prosopopeia* was an empty reactor hall under Stockholm that served as a base of operations during the players' five weeks of ceaseless play.

While three decades of the role-playing game *Dungeons & Dragons* have rarely managed to convey the intended feeling of immersion, urban LARP is the perfect way to satisfy exploratory urges in urban space. Finding well-prepared game locations amidst a jungle of graffiti and concrete is a wonderful experience.

Urban exploring also includes the thrill of danger because it does not provide the protection that more traditional games do. Adventuring in ruins and caves gets clothes dirty and may leave minor scratches. The legality of exploration depends on where you go and in which country, but even perfectly legal areas are often guarded; this presents players with fun and satisfying challenges. Ideologically, urban LARP is often about reclaiming the streets in the name of playfulness, bringing ludic interaction to the public, predominantly serious sphere.

The historical significance of city locations plays a central role in a LARP's utilization of the city environment. If properly integrated into the fiction of the game, places such as the murder site of Olof Palme or the last elm trees of the old forest in the middle of Stockholm can be used to enhance meaning. The way that urban play can thus transform movement through everyday environments into a sightseeing tour has also been utilized in some other location-based games for its educational value.

Urban role-play holds great potential for allowing players to see their environment with new eyes and to better understand their interactions with other people. Its compelling selling point, though, is the thrill of danger it provides.

◆ Huizinga, J. (1938), *Homo Ludens: A Study of the Play-Element in Culture*, Beacon Press, Boston MA. ◆ *Killer* (1981), developed and published by Steve Jackson Games, Referred to 1998 edition. ◆ Loponen, M. & Montola, M. (2004), "A Semiotic View on Diegesis Construction," in M. Montola & J. Stenros (eds.), *Beyond Role and Play*, Ropecon, Vantaa. ◆ Pohjola, M. (2004), "Autonomous Identities," in M. Montola & J. Stenros (eds.), *Beyond Role and Play*, Ropecon, Vantaa. ◆ Salen, K. & Zimmerman, E. (2004), *Rules of Play. Game Design Fundamentals*, MIT Press, Massachusetts MA.

Project Description	Text	Project	Affiliation
	Staffan Jonsson	Pär Hansson, Karl-Petter Åkesson, Annika Waern, Jonas Söderberg, Markus Montola, Staffan Jonsson, Martin Ericsson, Jaakko Stenros, Adriana Skarped	IPerG (Integrated Project on Pervasive Gaming), 2005

PROSOPOPEIA 1
A Pervasive City-based LARP

Prosopopeia 1 was a pervasive Live-Action Role-Playing (LARP) game first staged in Stockholm in June 2005 with 12 players. After two weeks of dormant gametime, the game culminated in a 52-hour continuous role-play experience.

The central storyline of the game was a ghost story. The players role-played long-dead ghosts traveling back to the land of the living. All of them had been friends with the same person, who had also died but never made it to the world beyond. As the game progressed, the players gradually came to understand why their friend was trapped between the two worlds: each had wronged her in a different way and thereby contributed to her current state of depression and grief. Only by revisiting her and helping her untie her emotional knots could the spirits help their friend find her way to the other side.

Prosopopeia 1 followed a coherent storyline told through a number of scenes that took place at various urban locations at specific times. In between the planned scenes, the players were expected to freely move throughout the city, occasionally interacting with bystanders. Scenes were either initiated by the game masters or triggered by players solving puzzles and uncovering secrets.

The Myth: *Prosopopeia 1* combined real and fabricated story elements spun around urban myths, online legends, historical events, everyday stories and ghastly occultism. This ghost fiction was superimposed on the ordinary world in such a way that the border between the two was blurred.

City-based LARP, "Fabricating Reality": The whole city of Stockholm was the game's arena. This posed many challenges, particularly in terms of immersion; it is hard to maintain the illusion of an alternate world when you are constantly confronted with everyday society. To minimize the sense of being in the ordinary world, the chosen game locations were relatively secluded: examples include an underground cavern, a run-down harbor and a former mental hospital. These locations were used to stimulate the players' imaginations and provide them with an alternate view of their city.

The Possession Model of Role-Taking: In the *Prosopopeia 1* fiction, the core characters were ghosts who occasionally entered the living world by possessing mortals. The players participating in the event role-played their own personas as just such mortals, willingly possessed by ghosts. For the first two weeks of the game, they lived their everyday lives and personas. But pretty soon, they were confronted with messages from "beyond" and began to gradually encounter their ghosts. In the game's final weekend, they let themselves be possessed by these ghosts. Even then, they were able to participate in the game both as themselves and as their possessed selves. Indeed, many game puzzles required players to switch between these roles: the puzzles sometimes made use of their modern-day skills and at other times were based on the ghastly background of the possessing ghosts.

Alternate Reality Aesthetics, "This is not a game": *Prosopopeia 1* made extensive use of alternate reality aesthetics in terms of the background mythos, the way players were instructed and the game organization. The game was presented as a game only when the players signed up for it; immediately thereafter, their instructions were: "You should now do all you can to forget about this project until it contacts you again. This is the only time the game will be presented

as such. From now on every-thing is real." In keeping with Alternate Reality Game (ARG) aesthetics, the social boundary of the game was deliberately kept ambiguous. Players would frequently interact with other people unaware of whether or not they were also part of the game. Most of these people introduced themselves with their real names and professions, and they sometimes even had game-relevant information without knowing that the game existed, either because the game made use of all the myths and features of the real world or because the information was planted by the organizers in advance.

Extensive Game-mastering: In a typical LARP, the game mastering mostly happens prior to the game's beginning. In *Prosopopeia 1*, game masters were provided with extensive information on player activities and allowed multiple ways of influencing them. The technology used to achieve this had to be disguised or explained in the game mythos. In practice, this was mostly achieved by game masters role-playing via different electronic media, including posing as characters on the Internet and ghosts that communicated from the grave via a rigged reel-to-reel recorder. The advantage of game mastering is that it enables a more dynamic storyline – at least to the extent that it supports game masters' improvisations – and in general generates a joyful experience for players as well as game masters.

Project Description	Text	Project	Affiliation
	Karen Schrier	Karen Schrier	Massachusetts Institute of Technology (MIT), Cambridge, US, 2006

RELIVING THE REVOLUTION
Learn and Play with Augmented Reality

How can Augmented Reality (AR) games alter our perceptions of place? AR games mix the physical and virtual worlds to create hybrid game boards that can potentially affect the experience of a site. To study this phenomena, I created a novel AR game, *Reliving the Revolution (RtR)*, which uses PDAs and GPS to access virtual information embedded in real-world Lexington, Massachusetts.

To play *RtR*, participants physically explore present-day Lexington and go back in time to April 19, 1775 in order to figure out who fired the first shot at the Battle of Lexington. They use the PDA to interact with virtual historic figures, documents and artifacts, which are preprogrammed to appear in specific hotspots around Lexington Common. The participants work in pairs and receive conflicting evidence depending on their role in the game (e.g. Minuteman soldier, female loyalist, etc.). Afterwards, they collectively debate what happened at the battle based on the evidence they have gathered, shared and interpreted.

I tested the game with students ages 13 and up; results suggested that *RtR* fosters the practice of historic inquiry and critical thinking skills. Moreover, participants interacted deeply with the physical site itself. Lexington became an engaging, interactive playground, a living archive and historical laboratory where participants could search for spatial stories, exchange ideas, test hypotheses and construct narratives of the past. Firstly, by exploring an authentic landscape, participants could more easily envision how its contours shaped and were shaped by history. Secondly, the interpretive tasks of the game and the juxtaposition of virtual and physical information also compelled participants to look deeply at their surroundings and consider their historical context. Participants began to view the natural and built environment as sites of inspection rather than simply as ambient information, and they more easily recalled, analyzed and visualized the game's data in relation to the layout of Lexington. Houses, buildings and monuments suddenly took on cultural, historical and political significance.

In the process, participants remapped an unfamiliar public space with personally meaningful game narratives, historic interpretations and visions of the past. By creating personal paths in a public space, participants traversed boundaries of propriety and convention, which encouraged them to take intellectual risks such as creatively reimagining the past and critiquing traditional historical perspectives. Lexington became a safe environment where participants could more easily experiment with new narratives, identities and perceptions without fear of real consequences. The site also became a social space where participants could serendipitously exchange ideas and form spontaneous learning communities.

RtR transformed Lexington into a hypertextual stomping ground, a knowledge-sharing community, a networked collage of location-specific stories and discoveries and, but most importantly, a rich place to experiment, learn and play.

Welcome to Lexington

Investigate what is happening in the town of Lexington. Walk around and inspect the Lexington Common and the surrounding buildings and monuments. Talk to virtual people and pick up virtual items.

Start

Name: Captain John Parker2

Look what you and your men have done! You fired upon and killed ten of our men, without receiving any provocation from us.

View Document | Done

ID: Munroe House

The Munroe House. This is where Nathan Munroe and his father, Marrett Munroe, lived during April 17, 1775. It was built in 1729.

Inspect Item | Return

ID: New Belfry

This hill is the location where the Belfry was first built in 1761. The Belfry was moved to Lexington Common in 1768, where it rang the

Inspect Item | Return

Project Description	Text	Project	Affiliation
	Irma Lindt	Irma Lindt, Jan Ohlenburg, Uta Pankoke-Babatz, Wolfgang Prinz, Sabiha Ghellal	IPerG (Integrated Project on Pervasive Gaming), 2006

EPIDEMIC MENACE
Playing Across Different Gaming Interfaces

Epidemic Menace is a cross-media game in which players become medical experts and need to save mankind from a threatening virus epidemic. Craving for power, a villain scientist has created a lethal virus mutation and contaminated a physical university campus. From there, the virus is going to spread and infect all humans unless players do something to stop it; they have only three hours to avert the danger. To this end, teams of players are provided with different gaming interfaces to observe, hunt, catch and destroy the virus. Hunting interfaces include large stationary displays in each team's headquarter room, mobile phones and mobile Augmented Reality systems.

The game is played indoors and outdoors on an approximately 80,000-square-meter campus area with meadow, trees and bushes. There are technical constraints that determine where players can actively play the game: to use the mobile gaming interfaces, players must be within the reach of at least one of the five Wi-Fi access points that are used for the game. The gamespace of *Epidemic Menace* consists of the physical environment and of a virtual plane on which virtual viruses exist. The two are closely interconnected. On the one hand, the physical environment defines the frame in which the virtual viruses move and replicate. For example, environmental factors such as wind direction and strength influence the movement of the viruses. On the other hand, the virtual viruses influence the physical environment as well. If a player is close to a virus, she might

get infected, and her gaming interface will start to malfunction.

Each team of players has three interfaces it can use to hunt viruses. The first one is the stationary gaming interface in the team's headquarter room, on which the gamespace is shown as a graphical map of the physical environment overlaid with player and virus locations; players in this room communicate with mobile players. The second interface is the smartphone used by the mobile players. These phones show a fragment of the map of the gamespace as well as the viruses in their surroundings, thereby helping the mobile players catch them. The map on the display updates when a player moves. The third interface is a mobile Augmented Reality system consisting of a laptop strapped onto a backpack with a monocular head-mounted display allowing the player to see the animated 3D viruses in her proximity overlaid on top of the physical space. Teams have to coordinate the hunt between team members.

Epidemic Menace was tested with 30 players between 19 and 60 years of age. Most players changed their gaming interface at least once during the game, though none of the three interfaces was clearly preferred over the others. Mostly, players alternated between interfaces because they were curious to try out the other devices. The gamespace was perceived as a coherent whole by 78% of the players despite the fact that different gaming interfaces showed different representations of the physical environment, players and virtual gaming artifacts.

274

CHANGING URBAN PERSPECTIVES
Illuminating Cracks and Drawing Illusionary Lines

In recent years, a new breed of game – the pervasive game – has appeared in a number of different manifestations. *Pirates!* (Björk et al. 2001) transferred gameplay from the screens of PDAs to the environments directly surrounding players. Games such as *Songs of the North* (Lankoski et al. 2004), *Treasure* (Chalmers et al. 2005) and *I Love Bees* (2004) took this one step further by using cityscapes as their playground, thus expanding gamespace locally and even globally. This trend was continued by games such as *The Beast* (2001), which some argue was played in both physical and virtual environments in that it included spatial interpretations of the Internet; a similar claim can be made regarding *Can You See Me Now?* (2001). By contrast, it was never quite clear when one was and wasn't playing *Majestic* (2001) because the game often seemed dormant for long periods of time; similarly determining the exact starting point of *Prosopopeia* (Jonsson et al. 2006) is problematic since nongame events are retroactively redefined as parts of the game.

In all these new games, it can be difficult to judge which objects belong to the game and which people are playing it. In *Whirling Dervishes* (McGonigal 2005), for example, people are enticed to begin whirling even as they are unaware of the game's rules and objectives and even if they are not game participants. In the game *Killer: The Game of Assassination* (1981), players may not know who is hunting them, and everyday objects may be converted into game objects. Organizers of *Prosopopeia* gave clues and artifacts to nonplayers, which meant that players had to interact with both prepared and nonprepared nonplayers in order to play the game. And identifying Bluetooth devices – and, in many cases, the people who carry them – is an important part of *Insectopia* (2006), in which players must repeatedly scan the same devices over periods of weeks.

A Definition for Pervasive Games

As shown by the examples above, pervasive games not only challenge the normal perceptions of where and when games are played, but also of what constitutes a game element and even a game player. The origins of these types of games can be found in the computer science research field of pervasive, or ubiquitous computing (Nieuwdorp 2007). In the context of these games, however, the meanings of "pervasive" and "ubiquitous" are different than they are in the computer science context: here, they refer not only to the technological features of a game, but also to aspects of gameplay. Focusing on the latter, the observation that pervasive games can affect the how, why, when and who of playing can be used as the basis for a definition. Hence the following:

Pervasive game: a game whose spatial, temporal, social or interface-related characteristics are ambiguous.

This definition, which is an expansion of Montola (2005), is built upon a distinction between four main categories in which the pervasiveness of a game can manifest itself. The first two, *spatial* and *temporal*, mirror the original vision of pervasive computing – that is, "anywhere, anytime" (Dordick 1998). They differ from pervasive computing, however, in that their pervasiveness is an ambiguous and dynamic characteristic rather than a static description: instead of seeing a pervasive game as one that can be played in a given area at all times thanks to pervasive technology, one should view it as a game whose core attribute is the distinction between where and when it can be played. The *social* and *interaction* aspects of the definition, for their part, illustrate that the ambiguity of pervasive games' spatial and temporal boundaries may make it difficult to judge if social interaction or interaction with artifacts are part of the game or not.

Most pervasive games take place in urban environments. Just as these games can change one's perception of what a game is, they can also change one's perception of a game context, thereby often changing one's perspective on an urban environment. The following four aspects of pervasive games provide a tool with which to explore how such games accomplish this.

Spatial Ambiguity

The ambiguity of a game's spatial boundaries can become the basis for a skill necessary to that game. As players test out a game's boundaries, their perceptions of the city in which the game is played change. Instead of only distinguishing different parts of the city, visual landmarks help define new areas, which tend to overlap with old ones. Examples of this include runners in *Can You See Me Now?* discovering the location of GPS shadows, areas full of shops with Bluetooth-enabled printers representing stable hunting grounds for insects in *Insectopia* and players of *Treasure* learning that certain physical areas are "hot spots." In addition, determining the boundaries of a game can be a reason in and of itself for players to explore unfamiliar areas of a city, thereby expanding their knowledge of the urban landscape.

Temporal Ambiguity

By restricting gameplay to a certain time period or by making it unclear when a game is or is not in play, it is possible to make a player question why he is at any given city location at any given moment in time. This means that the need to catch individual insects every eight days in *Insectopia* can make a particular ride on the subway, for example, distinctly more interesting for a player than the one before or after. This is because the duration of gameplay comes into question: is the player playing the game for the duration of the subway ride or is he only playing when he's technically interacting with the game's system?

Social Ambiguity

In pervasive games, it can be difficult to easily judge which people in one's vicinity are other players; there is not, after all, a social agreement amongst all people present in a certain area that a game is in progress within that area. Since social ambiguity can make players break the traditional boundaries between social groups, this aspect of pervasive games has a strong potential for making players change their views of other groups of people or at least question their preconceptions about them. This may be an intended side effect of game design or a serendipitous process that occurs during gameplay; either way, it may be described as *spontaneous social interaction* (Zagal 2000). These interactions may sometimes cause problems, mostly when a nonplayer is disturbed by the gameplay. Some thus argue that designers should take *social adaptability* (Björk 2005) into consideration when designing pervasive games.

Interaction Ambiguity

Although it may be clear where and when one is playing a pervasive game and even whom one is playing with, the fact that technology can be hidden makes game objects indistinguishable from other objects in the world. The result is that the nature of all perceived objects is potentially put into question. This changed perception of objects is probably the least developed aspect of pervasive games due to the problems that accompany changing infrastructures or placing new technology in public places. Hiding game objects was accomplished easily on the Internet for games such as *Majestic* or *Prosopopeia*, in which it was often impossible to determine if a web page had been created by the game designers or not. But such dissemination can even be accomplished in non-online games. In the game *Killer: The Game of Assassination*, for example, secrecy is a central concept: a player may not know if a letter received is a "mail bomb" or an ordinary mailing, or he may accidentally open a door that triggers a "bomb" when he only meant to open an ordinary door. *I Love Bees* can also be seen as making use of dissemination, as it provided players with no details about game objects (or rules, choices and resources, for that matter). As a result, players had to figure out for themselves what was part of the game and what was not.

Finishing Remarks

The field of pervasive games is still in its infancy; it is too early to tell which game designs will become archetypical, and the genre itself does not yet have a very large player base. What can be said with certainty is that whatever forms pervasive games take in the future, they will affect how players – and most likely nonplayers as well – relate to their surroundings. The definition presented in this essay provides a framework for analyzing existing pervasive games and the concepts on which they are based, as well as for understanding how these games can change players' perceptions of the cities in which they live. As a result, it can also be used to gauge the extent to which a pervasive game has met its intended design goals and made the fullest use of the spaces in which it is played.

◆ *The Beast* (2001), developed by Microsoft, published by Dreamworks. ◆ Björk, S., Falk, J., Hansson, R. & Ljungstrand, P. (2001), "*Pirates!* Using the Physical World as a Game Board," paper presented at *Interact 2001, 8th IFIP TC.13 Conference on Human Computer Interaction*, July 9-13, Tokyo, Japan. ◆ Björk, S., Eriksson, D. & Peitz, J. (2005), "Socially Adaptable Games," Lightning round presentation at *Changing Views: Worlds in Play, DiGRA conference 2005*, June 16-20, Vancouver, Canada. ◆ *Can You See Me Now?* (2001), developed by Blast Theory & The Mixed Reality Lab, University of Nottingham. ◆ Chalmers, M., Bell, M., Brown, B., Hall, M., Sherwood, S. & Tennent, P. (2005), "Gaming on the Edge: Using Seams in Ubicomp Games," short paper at *ACM Advances in Computer Entertainment*

(ACE) 2005, June 15-17, Portland, USA. ◆ Dordick, R. (1998), "The Convenience of Small Devices. How Pervasive Computing Will Personalize E-Business," interview with Mark Bregman, general manager of pervasive computing research at IBM, *IBM Think Research*, no. 3, 1998. ◆ *I Love Bees* (2004), developed by 42 Entertainment, published by Bungie Studios / Microsoft. ◆ *Insectopia* (2006), developed and published by Interactive Institute's GAME Studio. ◆ *Killer: The Game of Assassination* (1981), developed and published by Steve Jackson Games. ◆ Jonsson, S., Montola, M., Waern, A. & Ericsson, M. (2006), "*Prosopopeia*: experiences from a pervasive Larp," *Proceedings of ACM Advances in Computer Entertainment Technology (ACE 2006)*, ACM Press, New York NY. ◆ Lankoski, P., Heliö, S., Nummela, J., Lahti, J., Mäyrä, F. & Ermi, L. (2004), "Approaching Game Design: The Case *The Songs of the North*," *Proceedings of NordiCHI 2004 Conference*, October 23-27, Tampere, Finland. ◆ *Majestic* (2001), developed by Anim-X, published by Electronic Arts. ◆ McGonigal, J. (2005), "Supergaming! Ubiquitous Play and Performance for Massively Scaled Community," *Modern Drama*, vol. 48, no. 3 (Fall 2005), pp. 471-491. ◆ Montola, M. (2005), "Exploring the Edge of the Magic Circle. Defining Pervasive Games," in *DAC 2005*, Copenhagen. ◆ Nieuwdorp, E. (2007), "The 'Pervasive' Discourse: An Analysis of the Use and Definitions of the Term 'Pervasive',"*ACM Computers in Entertainment Journal*, vol.5, no. 1 (January 2007). ◆ Peitz, J., Björk, S. & Jäppinen, A. (2006), "Wizard's Apprentice – gameplay-oriented design of a computer-augmented board game," *Proceedings of ACM Advances in Computer Entertainment Technology (ACE 2006)*, ACM Press, New York NY. ◆ Zagal, J.P., Nussbaum, M. & Rosas, R. (2000), "A Model to Support the Design of MultiPlayer Games," *Presence: Teleoperators and Virtual Environments*, Vol. 9, No. 5, pp. 448-462.

URBAN FREE FLOW
The Individual as an Active Performer

As an international urban phenomenon and unique physical art, *Parkour,* or *Free Running*, has attracted much media attention in recent years, ranging from various television advertisements and news reports to entertainment pieces. *Parkour* originated from childhood games played by the founders of the movement, David Belle and Sébastian Foucan, in the suburbs of Paris some 17 years ago. It has by now developed into a worldwide sportive engagement with the physical topography of the City that playfully contests its spatial constraints. Its practitioners, so-called *traceurs*, strive to overcome obstacles in the built urban environment in the fastest and most direct manner possible by fluidly adapting their movement to any given spatial restraint.

To explain *Parkour* merely as the further enhancement of a suburban playtime activity of children, however, would be to ignore the various other sources that have shaped the practice. It is beyond question that *Parkour* defines and explores the urban realm as a concrete playground just like any other street game in that it is "played" on city streets rather than prepared fields. Yet in addition to the ludic and seemingly infantile urge to move, *Parkour* is also fundamentally formed by serious methods of physical schooling such as martial arts and military training techniques. Even the term *Parkour* is derived from "parcours du combattant," the name of the obstacle course used in French military education. Viewed in this context, the city is literally being charged as a potential opponent by the *traceur*. As a counterbalance to this offensive mode of operation, the practice of *Parkour* also includes more serene elements inspired by eastern philosophies; these are meant to create a fusion of mind and body in space and time as a path of freedom. It is fluidity of movement and smooth passage around barriers that come into focus in this side of *Parkour*, which is intended to foster self-improvement through spatial awareness.

Whatever its origins may be, the movement of the *traceur* is clearly very different from the detached and observant mode of spatial engagement of the *flâneur*, who drifted through the boulevards and arcades of late 19th-century cities. Instead, the newly emerging urban figure of the *traceur* embodies a more active and intimate urban engagement and situational positioning of the individual as an active performer on the ever-changing city stage.

http://parkour.net
www.urbanfreeflow.com
www.sportmediaconcept.com/parkour

Project Description	Text	Project	Affiliation
	Bruce H. Thomas, Wayne Piekarski	Bruce H. Thomas, Wayne Piekarski, Benjamin Close	Wearable Computer Lab, University of South Australia, Adelaide, AU, 2000

ARQUAKE
An Outdoor Augmented Reality Shooter

ARQuake was originally developed in the year 2000 as an outdoor Augmented Reality (AR) version of the first person shooter game *Quake* (idSoftware 1996). AR is the process of overlaying and aligning computer-generated images over a player's view of the physical world.

ARQuake is a first-person perspective application with the following characteristics:

1. The application is positioned in the physical world.
2. The point of view, that the application shows to the player is completely determined by the position and orientation of the player's head.
3. Germane information is displayed as AR information via an HMD (Head-Mounted Display).
4. The player is mobile and is able to walk through the information environment.
5. For input, the player requires only a handheld button gadget.

The gameplay is quite intuitive. The player moves by physically walking and can change the orientation of the view by simply moving his or her head and looking in a particular direction. Shooting is performed just as in the original game: you just look, press a trigger and shoot. A series of evaluations of the usability and playability of *ARQuake* have been performed, and it was determined that the game is quite enjoyable to play.

In *ARQuake*, there is a 1:1 mapping of a *Quake* 3D graphical model to the physical world. The AR information (monsters, weapons, objects of interest) is located in the physical world in reference to the *Quake* model. The *Quake* models of the buildings are not displayed to the player. The see-through nature of the HMD allows players to see the actual wall, ceilings and floors in the physical world. The registration of actual and virtual structures is the key to the game. This allows for the occlusion of game objects behind physical buildings. The game fuses the virtual and physical worlds, allowing monsters to jump out from around corners!

Project Description	Text	Project	Affiliation
	Frank Lantz	Frank Lantz, Mattia Romeo, Kevin Slavin, Dennis Crowley, Liz Cioffi	area/code, New York, US, 2005

CONQWEST
An Urban Treasure Hunt

ConQwest was designed by area/code in collaboration with New York advertising firm SS+K. The game was sponsored by Qwest, a large telecommunications carrier, as a way of promoting its wireless services. *ConQwest* originated in 2005 and is played in ten different cities over the course of two years. Each game session spans a single day and is a contest between five teams of 20 players each.

The game is built around a technology called Semacode, which is a type of barcode specifically designed to be readable by cellphone cameras. Prior to each gameday, hundreds of Semacodes are distributed throughout the city in a variety of formats – ads on billboards, the sides of buses and taxi tops, flyers stapled to telephone poles, posters in store windows and stickers hidden in various locations throughout the urban landscape. Some of the codes are highly visible, while others are hard to find, but all of them have the same visual appearance: a cryptic grid of black and white squares with no explanation attached. During a game of *ConQwest*, the city is transformed by these visual ciphers; they become a kind of "public secret," a ubiquitous but mysterious feature of the urban landscape whose true meaning is understood only by the players of the game. For them, each Semacode corresponds to a unique piece of "treasure" with a value of 30 to 75 points. The goal of *ConQwest* is to be the first team to collect 5,000 points worth of treasure.

But the game is more than a simple treasure hunt. We wanted to create a game that rewarded teamwork and strategic thinking. In order to achieve this, we divided each city up into eight different geographical zones. To collect the treasure in a zone, a team must first establish control over that zone. To do so, it has to make use of a special game piece called a Totem. The Totems are 20-foot high inflatable animal figures corresponding to the names of the five teams – Bear, Mountain Lion, Wolverine, Big Horn and Sea Lion. In order to take control of a zone, the players have to move their Totem to a special location within the zone called the zone base. The presence of these enormous figures moving through the streets adds an element of cartoony surrealism to the spectacle of the game, and the task of maneuvring them around urban obstacles adds a layer of complex tactical challenge to the overall gameplay.

Project Description	Text	Project	Affiliation
	Martin Budzinski, Henrik Isermann	Martin Budzinski, Henrik Isermann	School for Architecture and Urban Planning, University of Stuttgart, DE, 2005

WHAVSM?
A Pervasive Role-Playing Game

WHAVSM? was created for architectural students at the University of Stuttgart for use during their introduction weeks. It is meant to help them orientate themselves in their new city and university as well as to support networking amongst them. Further development of the game will integrate study scheduling abilities and a rating/evaluation system.

In our game, players have to collect barcode-like symbols with their cellphone cameras. These barcodes are spread out across the city of Stuttgart at stores and locations important to architecture students and their studies. When a barcode is scanned, the player's phone connects to the game server, and the location is "unlocked." As a reward for unlocking, players receive virtual resources such as glue or paperboard. By collecting locations and respective resources, players can fulfill the game's missions, which ask them to create deliverables consisting of diverse resources.

During the game, players must gain advanced skills; in order to do so, they must depend on each other for help. This sometimes causes conflict, but ultimately nurtures communication and cooperation. With the help of the game application, players can at all times check their stock of items, identify requirements for level-ups and deliverables, search locations on the Stuttgart map, trade their items and communicate with other players via a chat. To make this possible,

the game application is equipped with different modules. Through the location tool, the player gains access to unlocked places such as resource collection points, libraries and the mission center. The map tool provides geographic overview. The production tool is used to create items and to supply information about the number of items and resources available. With these, players can build models, present products or design drawings – if they meet the required skill level, that is. With the trading tool, items and resources can be exchanged, while the chat tool helps to breed accord amongst the players.

Thanks to Erwin Herzberger and Steffen P. Walz. Mobile application by Michael Rohs, FTH Zurich. Mobile sponsoring by Andreas Köhler, ChrisKeimCom.

www.mrhi.de/whavsm?

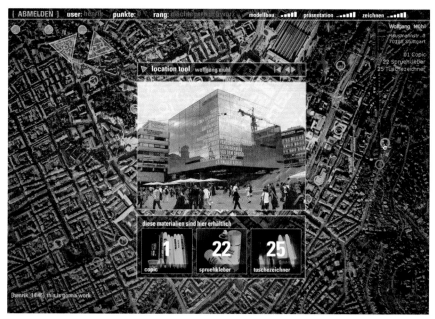

Project Description	Text	Project	Affiliation
	Claus Pias	Yishay Cohen, Jolanda Dekker, Arnout Hulskamp, David Kousemaker, Tim Olden, Cees Taal, Wouter Verspaget	Utrecht School of the Arts; Faculty Art, Media & Technology in Hilversum, NL, 2004

DEMOR
Egoshooter for the Blind

We write in the year 2066. Ghastly creatures spawned by miscarried genetic experimentation have seized control of Earth, transforming it gradually into a desert wasteland where no human life can survive. Yet the forces of resistance are never idle, and a small and intrepid band of elite fighters…

This is the apocalyptic (and hence typical for the genre) opening of the first-person shooter *Demor*. Except that in this case, the target cannot be seen, nor can the centrally perspectival vanishing point it customarily constructs; instead, they can only be heard. And *Demor* is, in fact, a so-called audio game or, to use Friedrich Knillis' wonderful expression, a "Schallspiel" (sound game). And you had better listen well, especially those of you who still think computer games are derived from video and hence refer to them as video games in the conviction that they must always be as visually realistic as feature films. *Demor*, developed by seven students at the Utrecht Academy of Arts especially for blind players, shows that, conversely, the main requirement for computer games is not photorealistic imagery, but instead the most advanced computer technology. Each player is supplied with a laptop, a headset, a GPS receiver, a head tracker and a joystick before being sent out onto the battlefield, which is an entirely real one. For in *Demor*, players move freely within physical space of which they see nothing, hearing only the sounds of the game. Via GPS and head trackers, the players' bodily coordination and head movements are transmitted continuously to a computer, which then uses them to generate a three-dimensional sonic landscape in real time. This allows players not only to hear the enemy, but to shoot him down with deadly accuracy.

"The new education of hearing," wrote Rudolf Arnheim about the introduction of the then novel medium of the radio, "consists in the way in which our ears learn to distinguish sounds, to tell the hissing of a snake from a hiss of steam, a metallic clang from the clatter of china. This involves an enrichment of the vocabulary of the ear, so to speak, with whose help the loudspeaker can describe the world to us." (2001) That this newly audible universe, or "soundscape," constitutes a functioning world of play points in the direction of philosophical questions concerning blindness, which – from Locke and Berkeley all the way to Cassirer and Glasersfeld – have always involved more than philosophical reflection, also addressing the question of artificial worlds. It was probably Denis Diderot in his "Letter on the blind, for the use of the sighted" (1749) who stated most pointedly that the problem of blindness resides not among the unsighted, but with us, who can see. The senses of hearing, smell and touch afford us (in their own way) a fully complete, self-sufficient and functional world along with a sense of identity available to the blind. Precisely this is the point of departure for games such as *Demor*.

The acoustic and sequential spaces of play available to the blind should at least heighten our awareness of the degree to which all of "our" computer games rely upon simultaneous perception. For the blind, the space of play is not a world of suddenly appearing visual images, but instead one of gradually elapsing time. All challenges can be met via temporalization and are based on time sequences. Space is reduced to the player's own body, and its position is defined by the sequence of objects past which it moves. Acoustic impressions – themselves occurring in time – fill in this space and empty it out again. Position and distance are determined by time intervals and the speed of movement – literally by durations of bodies and sound waves. As spatial entities, the mutants in this computer game for the blind are present only in a time-limited fashion: they approach silently out of nowhere, coming very near at a given moment, only to vanish back into silence the instant an accurate shot finds its target.

As fascinating as games such as *Demor* might be and as many questions as they raise about the absence of the remaining senses (touch, taste, smell), they also point back to the history of the technical media themselves. For that which appears now as playful shoot-up

and integrative offering originally began as a form of military discipline, as compulsory training in enemy detection. An artificial blindness imposed for drilling purposes led the so-called "listeners" of World War II, outfitted with earphones, into an artificially generated deep sea world where they learned to recognize the sounds of enemy U-boats and to aim missiles accurately in their direction. It is to such exercises that we owe stereo sound – and games such as *Demor*, in which electronic spatial acoustics and positioning technology find their way back to their point of departure. According to Marshall McLuhan's thesis

concerning the numbing and simultaneous enhancement of the senses via media technology, it is hardly astonishing to realize the degree to which the images in these games for the blind resemble those of the "electronic soldiers" found in Pentagon scenarios. With their laptops strapped to their backs, these soldiers are deprived of their sense of touch by full body suits, their sense of sight by head-mounted displays, their sense of hearing by headphones and their sense of bodily orientation by means of GPS. The space of play and that of the battlefield converge here, where we are deprived of both hearing and sight.

PERVASIVE GAMESPACES
Gameplay Out in the Open

Recent Massively Multiplayer Online Games – or "synthetic worlds," as they have been called – such as *World of Warcraft* (2004), *Second Life* (2003) and *EverQuest* (1999), join hundreds of thousands of users in shared quests and mystery solving. These games even have their own currencies and real estate markets. Massively multiplayer online games are not pervasive in the sense that they offer an exertion interface or allow the user to play in a physical, real world; and yet they obviously go beyond the traditional confines of level-oriented game design.

Interestingly enough, contemporary best-selling computer games like *The Sims* (2000) and the *Grand Theft Auto* series (1997-2006) clearly blur the difference between gaming in a closed, rule-based environment (the "board") and playing in a much more open, story-driven universe (the "gameworld"). Taking the newly established field of pervasive games as our point of view, it is exactly this difference that we will explore in the following pages.

The Importance of Space

It is characteristic of pervasive games that they expand the gaming space, often by reconfiguring the social landscape of cities into a dense grid of game objects, game goals and gameworlds, thus obscuring the demarcations between the real and the virtual. Pervasive games play with these demarcations.

Truly pervasive games – excluding traditional computer games intended for mobile phones – evolve around specific sites or locations. The public sphere of, say, a downtown area of a major metropolis becomes a social framework in which interactions with the game and its surroundings are crucial. What, then, is most important? Is it the game itself or is it rather the social and geographical infrastructure that supports it?

The pervasive computing evolution liberates the user from the screen. In addition, it allows for a more direct and physical interconnection of players. The evolution has two essential characteristics: first, there is the explicitness of *computational tasks*, and second, there is the overall importance of *physical space*.

The former implies that actions are carried out in ways that transcend the traditional Graphical User Interface (GUI). Mobile devices and many forms of wearable or embedded computing shift gamers' attention from metaphorical data manipulation to simulated, hands-on and direct interactions with physical objects. This is closely entwined with the second essential attribute of pervasive computing, namely, that objects obeying the laws of physics are responsive to digital manipulation

290

and thus take on a double meaning: they are objects in the outside (nongame) world, yet can also simultaneously be objects within a simulated world.

A growing number of games already run on mobile devices such as cellular phones or PDAs, but only a few of these devices can sense their physical environment. Massively Multiplayer Online Role-Playing Games (MMORPGs) such as *EverQuest* and *The Matrix Online* (2005) clearly aim at being pervasive in the sense of incorporating a wide spectrum of information and communication technologies. However, they do not fully exploit the potential of combining physical and virtual space.

In addition, we are witnessing a growth in the design of game systems that use ubiquitous computing techniques to propel player experiences that connect objects in the real world to objects of the virtual world. *SuperFly* (2005), by the Swedish game company It's Alive, is a good example, in which the player's aim is to become a virtual celebrity. So too are the projects *Can You See Me Now?* (2001) and *Uncle Roy All Around You* (2003), both created by the UK performance group Blast Theory and both of which use hand-held, digital devices, GPS location tracking and online agent technology so that location and mobility act as game features from within the real world. While one player stays at home and moves a virtual character around a representation of a real city, other players speed around the real streets trying to hunt down the virtual quarry.

Play-Space And Gamespace

There is a fine line between being somewhere and being there with a purpose. To explore a territory – whether in the real, physical world or in the flowing realm of one's fantasy – involves the incessant modification of intentions. It is an advanced process of trial and error set in a socio-semantic context. You go right. Not interesting. You move to the left. Wait, here's something. You rush straight forward. Now, that's where the action is. However, the elusive coexistence of presence – being there – and intentionality – moving around for a reason – is also known as *rules*. Mapping a place through adventurous discovery in order to figure out the stories underneath the space and possibly invent new ones in the same process is all about *playing*. Learning to move and advance in a space filled with discrete norms of orientation – meaning that you can do "this" but not "that" – is the art of *gaming*.

Thus, there are two tightly interwoven modes of gamespace: there is *play-space* and there is *gamespace*. Together they form the much-hyped and widely misunderstood term "gameplay." We call those games that mix tangible, everyday spaces with the closed information spaces found in digital computers *pervasive games*. Such games may be the next generation in computer games. They make people move around instead of gluing them to the computer screen. Moreover, these games are particularly captivating because they deliberately place the relation between rules and world voyaging, between gaming and playing, at the nucleus of the very rule system itself. In other words, you learn how to master the rules of the game by playing them out in the real world. Hence my subtitle: *pervasive gaming* is gameplay out in the open.

In the play mode, one does not want to fall back into reality (although there is always the risk of doing so). In the game mode, the important thing is to climb upwards to the next level and not lose sight of structure. Play is about presence while game is about progression.

Play-space could be a city, and gamespace could be the rules and informational network dictating what can and cannot be done during gameplay.

Falling Out of Play

Look at people playing. You will notice that their play always entails the inherent but fascinating danger of being "caught" in reality. Nothing is more disturbing to play than the aggressive interruption of reality, which at all times jeopardizes play *as* play or simply threatens to terminate the privileges of play. Then it's back to normal life.

This is, of course, a structural feature of all play and, hence, of all gameplay. This is true of chess and soccer. It is also apparent in *Doom* (1993-2004) and *Myst* (1993). In the unremitting pursuit of having fun, intermission and cessation must be avoided at all costs. But since they are inescapable, this is impossible. Instead, they must be *built into* the very "being" or ontology of playing games.

Now consider *pervasive gaming*, in which gameplay occurs out in the open. As a player, I sprint down a street in order to amass the next item to be uploaded via my PDA so that my game-buddy at home can keep track of my doings and goal-seeking thus far. It's 4:00 p.m., there is heavy traffic, and I am momentarily barred from reaching the corner with the momentum I wished for.

In chess, there are no strident interruptions between two or more discrete fields. I move my queen independently of physics, be it in the form of weather, traffic jams or the sporadically bad habits of my fellow citizens. In a game of soccer, you block your opponent, and he tries to tackle you. However, capitalizing on a nice set of training principles that provide guidance in steering clear of the physicality of blocking is always an option.

But in pervasive gameplay, which mixes play-space and gamespace, "real" problems, like the ones described above remain, well, real problems. The aesthetic production of eloquent game mechanics becomes a matter of ethics. I do not, in the quest of fulfilling the game's teleology, knock down the old – real – lady on the sidewalk only because she prevents me from targeting the "Pac-Man" farther down the road a little bit faster.

Therefore, we must be careful in judging the fun factor of gameplay in pervasive games. It is not only the city or social context in itself that is the locus of enjoyment. Yes, I can go explore and yes, I meet people and yes, the site of navigation has become much wider than a trivial board. But at times, the potentials of space become the constraints of the game. Serious gamers do not want to spend time in vain looking for "interesting" places to explore. They would much rather understand the structure of the game so as to move forward, revealing new areas, or climb upwards in the hierarchy of levels.

How Do I Get to the Next Level?

Play is centered on the discovery of open spaces that demand our complete presence and desire for interaction. However, there is an end point to all play, and eventually these spaces become permanent. Gradually, one learns how to pilot inside play, and since the completion of more and more successful tasks takes time, the learning curve corresponds to the distinctive forms that keep differentiating the play system into finer grades of subsystems. One inhabits spaces like these via certain as-if structures: one assumes a role and lives it out. When we play, we tend to measure the geometry of play-space. How big is the playing field? And where are its borders? These lengths and widths become, in turn, the source of the game's internalization of both geometrical space and discrete progression.

Play can also focus on investigations of semantics. When we play, we evaluate space, but we also discover ways to interpret or perhaps reinterpret the visible as well as hidden narratives of play. Not only do we explore a world while playing in it; the meaning we can potentially uncover and the stories we can invent also drive us. Play-spaces tend to expand either in structural complexity or in physical extent. This expansion is reflected in the praxis of play – for instance when players argue over the exact thresholds of a play domain.

As I pointed out earlier, another feature that distinguishes playing from gaming is the notion of presence. Obviously, the sensation of presence is tightly interwoven with phenomenological concepts like "immersion" and "flow." Play commands presence. We have to be there – not only *be* there, but also be *there*. We go with the flow; or rather, swallowed by the fact of playing, we are *in* the flow. A game's success is intimately tied to the way space and time is organized within it. Gamers need to trust this organization. Since a game hinges on a certain finite structure in order to promote infinite realizations of it – in other words, on the correlation of rules and tactics – the very articulating of presence so important for play must already be presupposed in a game. One already knows in a game that the mission is to *keep on gaming*, which in my vocabulary really means to *keep on playing* – that is, to prolong the sensation of presence. Energy can then instead be directed towards elucidation of the game's structure. The important question then becomes "How do I get to the next level?" not "Why do I play?"

In conclusion, although one should undoubtedly respect the ethical boundaries of pervasive games that transport gameplay out into the open, one does not want to wait too long for the old lady to cross the street. While waiting, the "Why do I play?" question might turn up, threatening to disintegrate the exquisite balance of gaming (to progress) and playing (to be present).

◆ *Can You See Me Now?* (2001), developed by Blast Theory and The Mixed Reality Lab, University of Nottingham. ◆ *Doom* (1993-2004), developed by id Software, published by Activision et al. ◆ *EverQuest* (1999), developed by Verant Interactive, published by Sony Online Entertainment. ◆ *Grand Theft Auto* (1997-2006), developed by Rockstar North et al., published by Rockstar Games et al. ◆ *The Matrix Online* (2005), developed by Monolith Productions, published by Warner Bros. ◆ *Myst* (1993), developed by Cyan, Inc., published by Brøderbund Software, Inc. ◆ *Second Life* (2003), developed and published by Linden Labs. ◆ *The Sims* (2000), developed by Maxis, published by Electronic Arts. ◆ *SuperFly* (2005), developed and published by It's Alive. ◆ *Uncle Roy All Around You* (2003), developed by Blast Theory and The Mixed Reality Lab, University of Nottingham. ◆ *World of Warcraft* (2004), developed by Blizzard Entertainment, published by Vivendi.

Project Description	Text	Project	Affiliation
	Johan Peitz, Staffan Björk	Johan Peitz	GAME Studio, Interactive Institute, Stockholm, SE, 2006

INSECTOPIA
Using the Real World as a Game Resource

Insectopia is a mobile phone game in which players strive to build and maintain the most valuable insect collection by catching and trading. *Insectopia*'s novel game mechanism is the use of Bluetooth devices to represent unique insects. Since not only mobile phones but devices such as photo kiosks and printers have Bluetooth, the game depends not only on who is in a player's presence, but also on the player's physical location. It is only possible to catch an insect every three minutes, but to encourage communal gameplay experience, *Insectopia* allows players in proximity of one another to team up for a double search and catch all the insects they find.

Captured insects must be refound at least every eight days or else they die; this motivates players to figure out which Bluetooth device represents which insect, but also allows them to keep insects they only find once a week – on a specific bus route, for example. The required recapturing of insects makes it difficult to get above a certain score and encourages new players to join the game because it means that their peers' advantage of an early start is mitigated within a week.

The main design goal of *Insectopia* was to create a game whose pace players can control and adapt to their real lives. This requires the game to support intermittent playing – i.e. to allow players to have ongoing play sessions but to let them decide for themselves when to take action within the game without incurring severe penalties for not playing. *Insectopia* achieves this by making an insect search a quick action to perform and one that cannot be immediately repeated. Thus intensive gameplay is made less efficient with the result that players do not feel that they have to play continuously in order to be able to compete with others.

Part of fitting a game into one's real life includes being able to choose whether and when to play with others. To ensure that users have this choice, *Insectopia*'s gameplay allows them to cooperate through collaborative searches and insect trading but does not itself mediate the coordination necessary for these actions. This allows players not only to maintain their privacy, but also to use their already existing communication channels and social networks. Thus *Insectopia* is fully playable as a single-player game but encourages players to try using it as a multiplayer game by coordinating with existing players or recruiting new ones.

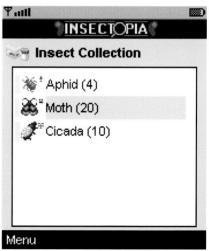

Project Description	Text	Project	Affiliation
	Stephen Boyd Davis, Rachel Jacobs, Magnus Moar, Matt Watkins	Matt Watkins, Rachel Jacobs, Zini Pandya, Robin Shackford	Active Ingredient, Nottingham University, UK, 2005

'ERE BE DRAGONS
Exploring the Subjective City

I used to walk to work every day but became so bored I took the car instead. Today the walk is different. I am wearing headphones and looking at a pocket PC, and I experience the city in a new way. Now my own body has become an engaging new companion, a soft machine whose physical response to my exertions I can sense and understand as I walk along.

In its simplest form, 'Ere be Dragons is experienced as follows. A player wears a heart rate monitor, and inputs his or her age into a pocket PC. Based on this input, an optimal heart rate is calculated, and the player then walks wherever and however he or she wishes. During the walk, an on-screen landscape is built, which uses GPS and corresponds spatially to the real one surrounding the players: if the journey revisits a place, players will see their new path cross the old one. If players do well, adequately exercising their hearts, the landscape flourishes. Insufficient exertion causes the local landscape to become impoverished, while overexertion leads to the growth of a dark, forbidding forest. The feedback includes sound.

The focus of 'Ere be Dragons is the relationship between art, technology and health. Health scientists despair of solving the current obesity crisis using conventional public health messages. There are already fitness programs available for use with portable devices (watches, phones and music players), some of which use heart rate monitors, but these are aimed at those already committed to fitness. Our target audience, on the other hand, is the rest of the population – the majority – that does not have this prior commitment.

'Ere be Dragons playfully recasts the players' relationships both with the space they inhabit and with the unseen space located within their bodies. The Situationist project, aimed at discerning the "precise laws and specific effects" of the geographical environment on the individual (Debord 1955), is implemented in 'Ere be Dragons both in its simple and inverse forms: the city is mediated through the subjective states of the body, while the body is mediated through perceptions of the city. As players move, they share the city with others, aggressively or collaboratively in the multiplayer version. But this is also a unique and personal city, one that unites the physical and symbolic in a truly "embodied interaction" (Dourish 2001).

'Ere be Dragons is built on the Mediascape architecture developed by Hewlett Packard, a tool for authorizing spatialized interactive media. The project was funded by the Wellcome Trust under the SciArt program in order to explore issues surrounding biomedical science. We are indebted to Richard Hull and Tom Melamed of Hewlett-Packard, Bristol, UK and to the Mixed Reality Laboratory, University of Nottingham, UK. Invaluable health science expertise was given by Chris Riddoch and Karl Cooke of Middlesex University.

◆ Debord, G. (1955) An Introduction to a Critique of Urban Geography. Retrieved from http://www.bopsecrets.org/SI/urbgeog.htm ◆ Dourish, P. (2001) Where the Action Is: The Foundations of Embodied Interaction, MIT Press, Cambridge MA, p. 205 - 7.

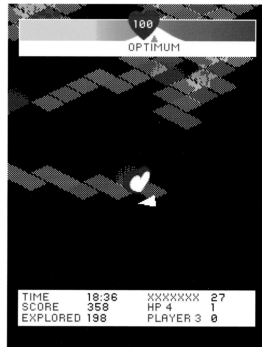

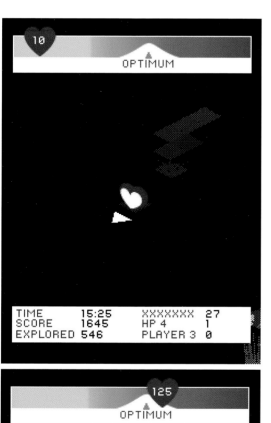

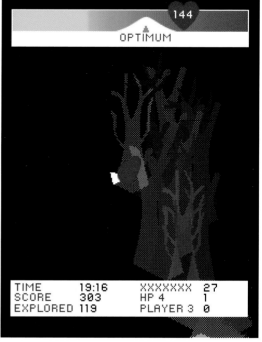

Project Description	Text	Project	Affiliation
	KP Ludwig John	KP Ludwig John, Gerhard Meixner, with students: Martin Böckenfeld, Daniela Buckel, Romana Fichtner, Maria Glas, Ulrike Hütte, Veronika Mika, Raphael Scheitza, Sarah Wiedenhöfer	Augsburg University of Applied Sciences, Augsburg, DE, 2004

FAUST – ACOUSTIC ADVENTURE
City Listening

Faust – Acoustic Adventure is a location-based adventure game that takes place in the city center of Augsburg. It was created as part of the "Mobile Experience" academic concentration at the Augsburg University of Applied Sciences.

In recognition of the fact that orientation and movement in urban areas today already overload the human senses, the game was designed such that the mobile technology is used as if it were "on the side."

Guidelines:
1. The gamers' attention should be focused on the real world – not on the technology.
2. During the game, the technology should be largely hidden from the gamers.
3. Gamers are guided exclusively via acoustic information.
4. System input from the gamers is derived from their spatial movements or by measuring their orientation with respect to the cardinal directions.
5. Standard types of input methods such as touch screens or buttons are not used at all.

Technology: PDA iPaq 5550, GPS receiver Garmin eTrex, headphones and Java-based software.

Implementation: The game was developed in cooperation with the Theater Augsburg and was inspired by a production of Goethe's *Faust I*. The theme is the contest between Faust and Mephisto about the preservation of the world. The player receives a "magic kit," a black-box device whose only accessible parts are headphones and an eTrex compass. Audio scenes from a radio play lead the gamers through Augsburg's city center and present them with tasks to complete and short games to play. The solutions always must be derived with the help of concrete artifacts in the cityscape. Along with the acoustic information, the compass plays an important role in the game. It enables gamers to provide detailed answers based on their orientation with respect to the points of the compass. It functions even when satellite reception is poor, substantially increasing the robustness of the system. Additionally, the compasses give the gamers an extra measure of confidence and security. They are the reference points for gamer interactions, and they supplement reality in an unobtrusive way.

Conclusions:
1. *Faust – Acoustic Adventure* requires gamers to move and orient themselves within the cityscape using normal human behavior patterns to explore a city.
2. The human tendency to orient primarily via visual clues is unobtrusively guided and supported by the acoustic information.
3. Knowledge absorbed by the gamers during their intensive engagement in location-specific tasks lasts long after the game is over.
4. The unusual forms of user input add to the fun factor of the game. The game becomes an experience.
5. Feedback solely via audio is unusual and offers both advantages and disadvantages. It requires support from visual and haptic elements of the interface.

www.village-global.de/Faust.html
www.acoustic-adventure.de

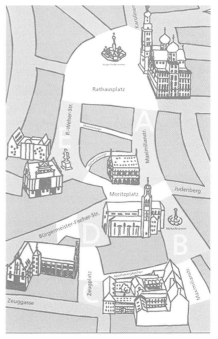

Project Description	Text	Project	Affiliation
	Nicolas Nova, Fabien Girardin	Nicolas Nova, Fabien Girardin	CRAFT – Swiss Federal Institute of Technology, Lausanne, CH, 2004

CATCHBOB!
Debord's Dérive and Pervasive Computing

Our stance with the *CatchBob!* project was that recent technologies (such as pervasive computing and location-based applications) provide game designers with the means to revisit the concepts formulated by the Situationists, an international group of avant-garde artists and thinkers formed in 1957. The Situationists developed their own theory of space, which considered the city as a playground in which to perform diverse activities such as Guy Debord's "dérive" – i.e. drifting through a city without any particular goal (1955). We believe that the integration of computing into the physical environment could enable the augmentation of the "dérive" by engaging people in new, creative and playful activities in urban space.

CatchBob! is a pervasive game in which groups of three players carry out a collaborative treasure hunt on a real-life university campus in pursuit of a virtual object. Completing the game requires the players to surround the object with a triangle formed by each participant's position in real space. To reach this goal, they run an application on their individual TabletPCs that allows them to see their own positions as well as those of their partners depicted as avatars on the campus map. Another meaningful piece of information given by this interface is an individual proximity sensor, which indicates whether the player is close to or far from the object by the number of red bars displayed at the top of the interface. In addition, the tool also enables communication: players can synchronously annotate the map with their styli. These annotations continually fade until they become completely invisible after four minutes. Even though a sole player could find the object alone, collaboration is necessary in the game because players have to coordinate to form the triangle surrounding the virtual object.

CatchBob! provided us insights on staging pervasive technologies in uncontrolled environments such as public spaces. The most significant problems that we encountered were technological: patchy networks and lower positioning accuracy, for example. Furthermore, we noticed that the limitations and flaws of the current technological infrastructures challenge the designers and developers to create engaging digital urban playgrounds. As a result, design strategies must be produced that deal with the social, economic, technological and physical constraints of the environment in order to successfully augment Debord's "dérive."

◆ Debord, G. (1955), "Projets d'embellissements rationnels de la ville de Paris," in Internationale Lettriste (eds.) *Potlatch #23*, Paris.

http://craftwww.epfl.ch/research/catchbob/

Project Description	Text	Project	Affiliation
	Christoph Schlieder, Sebastian Matyas, Peter Kiefer	Christoph Schlieder, Sebastian Matyas, Peter Kiefer	Laboratory for Semantic Information Technology Otto-Friedrich-University Bamberg, DE, 2004

GEOGAMES
Location-based Games as Infotainment

The first *Geogames* were conceived in 2004 by Christoph Schlieder and his team from the Chair of Computing in the Cultural Sciences at Bamberg University. Originally, the intention was to create a game-based testbed for studying algorithms that interpret the spatial behavior of users of mobile technologies, but soon *Geogames* became an object of research in their own right.

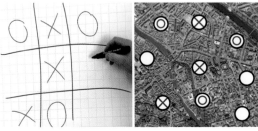

Geogames are a unique and novel type of location-based games because they are not restricted to single game concepts like other location-based games. Rather, they constitute a family of games produced through a computational method that generates location-based games using almost any existing board game, card game or puzzle as a template. A very simple example of a *Geogame* is *GeoTicTacToe*. In the paper and pencil version of "Tic Tac Toe," two players alternate in setting marks on a 3x3 game board. *GeoTicTacToe* transfers this idea to geographical space: two players move between nine locations, where they leave their virtual X- and O-marks. Navigation and communication is supported by software running on GPS smartphones.

Geogame technology is based on the scientific discovery that a specific type of spatiotemporal coordination mechanism is needed to map existing games onto geographical space. Anyone trying to build a location-based game without such a mechanism will necessarily produce a game that degenerates into a pure race: the fastest player always wins. This is because the *Geogame* coordination mechanism introduces short breaks into the game flow, during which individual players rest at a position on the geographic game board. A method to efficiently compute the optimal length of these breaks as a function of the spatial layout, the speed difference between players, the status of the game and so on is part of the *Geogames* technology.

These breaks provide the additional benefit of allowing integration of location-specific information content into the game. In a typical setup of a *Geogame* for tourists, for example, sites of high tourist interest are chosen as geographic game board positions, and the content presented during the game breaks relates to those sites. *Geogame* versions of different classical games have also been developed – *CityPoker*, for example, and *GeoRisk*. Furthermore, since January 2006, the *Geogame* concept and software technology supporting it have been used to communicate the idea of UNESCO World Heritage and to inform visitors about the architectural heritage of the city of Bamberg. Educational content for school children is developed in cooperation with the World Heritage Documentation Center of the city of Bamberg.

302

Test games in Bamberg,
Winter 2005/06

PERSUASION AND GAMESPACE

When we talk about places for persuasion, we are likely to think of bounded spaces like courtrooms, church sanctuaries and public pulpits. We may also think of less persuasive, more coercive spaces like interrogation rooms and auto lots. These spaces are stages for persuasion. They are the places in which activities like prosecution, campaigning and selling take place.

Games as Partial Reinforcement

Video games, too, can be seen as persuasive spaces. Researchers have paid much attention to the spaces in which video games are played, to how those spaces persuade players to play in the first place and how they persuade players to continue playing. In their classic study *Mind at Play*, psychologists Geoffrey R. and Elizabeth F. Loftus (1983, pp. 10-25) argue that video games are examples of partial reinforcement, a type of operator conditioning that explains how people become attached (and possibly addicted) to experiences. Unlike continuous reinforcement, partial reinforcement provides rewards at scheduled intervals. Loftus and Loftus argue that video games offer superlative examples of partial reinforcement, presenting incentives at just the right moments to encourage players to continue or try again when they fail.

Significantly, the video games Loftus and Loftus study are arcade games like *Pac-Man* (1980). As Loftus and Loftus well know (ibid., p. 11), arcade games derive directly from tavern and lounge games like pinball and indirectly from other games of chance like midway games and slot machines.

Atari founder Nolan Bushnell famously worked the midway as a barker before founding Atari, and his contributions to video games owe much to the principles of partial reinforcement. Midway games are more illusions than tests of skill, designed to offer the player just enough positive feedback to make him think that winning is easy – or at least possible. The midway barker must occasionally allow players to win, persuading onlookers and passersby that the game is a sure thing.

Casino, Tavern, Arcade, Pizza Theater

Slot machines internalize the logic of the midway barker, providing scheduled payouts of varying amounts based on complex mechanical (and later electronic) odds tables. But pinball machines and video games give the player partial control over the experience, making them much more like midway games than slot machines. In the taverns that first hosted Bushnell and Al Alcorn's coin-operated *PONG* (1972), the game became a social hub akin to darts, pinball and similar tavern sports. In *PONG* and its siblings, partial reinforcement operated on two levels. For one part, the game itself encouraged continued play and rematches; this is called "coin drop." For another part, the game encouraged players to remain in the bar ordering more food and drink. This notion of video games as instruments for enticing players to enter or remain in a particular space represents the main conceptual intersection between persuasion and space in the medium.

As tavern culture gave way to the video arcade of the late 1970s and early 1980s, secondary pursuits like ordering food gave way to the primary pursuit of additional gameplay. Arcades had more in common with casinos than taverns, and Bushnell, ever the entrepreneur, recognized this as a market opportunity: he would create an arcade space with the additional social and gastronomical goals of a tavern. While still at Atari, he founded Chuck E. Cheese's Pizza Time Theaters, a place for kids and families to eat pizza and play games. Here Bushnell combined all of his prior influences. Chuck E. Cheese's was an arcade: its games encouraged continued play and cross-cabinet play. It was a restaurant: food and drink drew players to the locale and kept them there longer. And it was a midway: players collected tickets from games of skill and chance like *skeeball* in the hopes of exchanging them for prizes.

Architecturally, the casino, tavern, arcade and pizza theater all share similar properties. They are enclosed spaces without windows in which participants can easily lose track of time. They are dark and constricted, with limited space for free movement. The games therein are provided not for their own sake, but as a means to an end, as a way of drawing players into spaces, keeping them there and taking their money (whether as payment for the games themselves or for other services).

Games as Rhetoric

The video games' tavern and casino game genealogy must not be ignored, especially as today's home console and PC marketplace diminishes cultural memory of the video arcade. But at the same time, we must not accept the tavern and casino as constituting the *only* possible intersections between persuasion and video games.

Despite the popularity and renown of coin-op games like *PONG* and *Pac-Man*, the content of arcade and tavern games is largely irrelevant. Beyond persuading players to insert (more) coins, these types of video games offer little in the way of design imperatives. Game designers Andrew Rollings and Ernest Adams (2003, p. 46) have discussed the negative effects of coin drop on the design of such games: "Arcade operators care little for richness, depth, and the aesthetic qualities of a game as long as it makes a lot of money for them. This requires some fine balancing. If a game is too hard, people will abandon it in disgust, but if it is too easy, they will be able to play for a long time without putting any more money in." Coin drop ignores the game medium's potential for persuading users to believe or act a certain way, not just to play again.

If the midway, the casino, the tavern, the arcade and the pizza theater persuade through capture and reinforcement – physical and psychological registers of human experience – then we must seek another register for video game persuasion, one more tightly coupled to deliberation and expression. In this sense, the space of video games is a conceptual one, constructed in the player's mind as he manipulates the representational system that comprises a particular game.

Game designers Katie Salen and Eric Zimmerman (2004, p. 28) offer a useful, abstract definition of *play* as "the free space of movement within a more rigid structure." Understood in this sense, play refers to the "possibility space" created by constraints of all kinds. Salen and Zimmerman use the example of play in a steering column: the meshing gears create "play" in the wheel before the turning gesture causes the gears to couple. The possibility space of play includes all of the gestures made possible by a set of rules. Imposing rules does not suffocate play, but rather makes it possible in the first place.

On a playground, the possibility space refers to the physical properties of the play space as well as to the equipment, time allotted and number and type of children. In traditional media like poetry, the possibility space refers to the expressive opportunities afforded by rules of composition, form or genre. In a video game, the possibility space refers to the myriad configurations the player might construct to see the ways the processes inscribed in the system work. This is really what we do when we play a video game: we explore the possibility space its rules afford by manipulating the symbolic systems it provides. Video games represent processes in the material world – war, urban planning, sports and so forth – and create new possibility spaces for exploring these topics. We explore this possibility space through play.

I suggest that we understand the representational characteristics of games in terms of the concept of procedurality, the authorship of rules that in turn create possibility spaces that we explore through play. In digital media scholar Janet Murray's words (1997, p. 71), procedurality refers to "the computer's defining ability to execute a series of rules." Procedurality in this sense refers to the core practice of software authorship; software is comprised of algorithms that model the way things behave.

I have previously suggested the term procedural rhetoric (Bogost 2007, pp. 28-29) to connect the inscriptive practices of procedurality with the persuasive practices of rhetoric, the art of effective persuasion. To write procedurally, one authors code that enforces rules in order to generate some kind of representation. Procedurality is a practice of model-building, and procedural rhetoric is a practice of model-based argument-building. To make procedural arguments, one builds models of a perspective on a subject. When players engage a game, they play in and with its possibility space. The persuasive space of games, then, makes arguments through conceptual models the player manipulates and then reflects upon.

While taverns and arcades stage persuasion between the game cabinet and the player's wallet, procedural rhetoric stages persuasion between the game's representation and the player's subjectivity. While partial reinforcement is meant to influence player action through psychological exploitation, procedural rhetoric is meant to persuade player action by inspiring deliberation. We play games in order to understand the possibility spaces their rules create and then to consider the implications of those possibility spaces and accept, challenge or reject them in our daily lives.

◆ Bogost, I. (2007), *Persuasive Games: The Expressive Power of Videogames*, MIT Press, Cambridge MA. ◆ Loftus, G.R. & Loftus, E.F. (1983), *Mind at Play: The Psychology of Video Games*, Basic Books, New York NY. ◆ Murray, J. (1997), *Hamlet on the Holodeck*, Free Press, New York NY. ◆ *Pac-Man* (Arcade) (1980), developed by Namco, published by Midway, US Release. ◆ *PONG* (Arcade) (1972), developed and published by Atari, US Release. ◆ Rollings, A. & Adams, E. (2003), *Andrew Rollings and Ernest Adams on Game Design*, New Riders, New York NY. ◆ Salen, K. & Zimmerman, E. (2004), *Rules of Play: Game Design Fundamentals*, MIT Press, Cambridge MA.

.WALK
The Universal Psychogeographic Computer (UPC)

Sitting in the park, I noticed something peculiar about certain passersby. They were all passionately studying a sheet in order to find out where they had to go, and they seemed pretty sure about where they were going. Yet they were taking the same streets over and over again like people usually do only when lost.

After a while of trying to work it out, the purpose of this strange behavior dawned on me. "Oh no!" I thought. "It's one of those experiments in generative psychogeography that seem to be going on everywhere at the moment." I mean, you can go to any random blog and within three double-clicks, you will find yet another report of a psychogeographic walk talking about "aimless wandering in memory of the *flaneur*."

I stopped a boy and a girl who were of the age when people really should be thinking about other things, like, if I may suggest, drinking beer and smoking marijuana (just like the real *flaneurs* did), instead of participating in a pointless [second left, first right, second left, repeat] walk. While talking to them, I found out that I had not been watching the stereotypical meanderings of psychogeographers walking in an algorithm, but instead the peripatetic processing of data within a ubiquitous computer in the truest sense of the word. The instructions resembled computer code, and the couple were calculating Pi by walking it. They where doing a *.walk*.

Apparently, it has to do with added functionality. The dot in the walk turns psychogeography into the Swiss army knife of nonelectronic computation. Because people were already executing algorithms by walking them for psychogeographical purposes, it occurred to the loonies of socialfiction.org that only a small step would turn an avant-garde walk into a retrograde computer.

All these people participating together produced the walktime – the execution – of the so-called UPC. The key moment in the functioning of this pedestrian computer is the random encounter. When two agents cross paths, the data generated during walking builds up within the system. But information only becomes intelligence when it can reach the individuals in the network that need it. When an agent receives new data, it doesn't need to be valuable at that time for that particular agent. But because it gets stored anyway, the information is copied and is increasingly likely to reach an agent who can use it. On top of such humble data management, the programmer only has to add logic to be able to solve, in theory, every computable problem, like chess or the flight control for the next Space Shuttle launch.

```
# Jigsaw.walk
# By Socialfiction.org
#
# Solving a jigsaw puzzle without thinking
# while having a walk
#
#
# info@socialfiction.org


Function direction():
            A=N{random_choice[„1st", "2nd", "3rd"]}+D{random_choice[„right", "left"]}
            B=N{random_choice[„1st", "2nd", "3rd"]}+D{random_choice[„right", "left"]}
            C=N{random_choice[„1st", "2nd", "3rd"]}+D{random_choice[„right", "left"]}
            route={A,B,C};
            if route.count(„left") or route.count(„right")==3:
                        direction();
            else: return route   # write down code:

Function exchange():
            for each piece of the puzzle:
                        if Pieces_match(piece, piece_other_agents)==TRUE :
                                    if agent_code.other_agent< agent_code.agent:
                                                piece_push_to_other_agent();
                                    else:
                                                if piece.other_agent == pushed_in:
                                                            piece=piece+1
                                                            pieces_snap_in_place()
            face(initial_pos)


Function walk():
while (Local_Time() < timer+1.5):
            if agent other_agent != in view OR pieces==0:
                        Iterate(route+1);
            else if other_agent == in view:
                        Approach(other_agent);
            else if other_agent == near:
                        exhange()

            Go_back(initial_pos)


pieces=Read_In                        # the pieces in your hand at start.
agent=YOU;
agent_code= [                ]
initial_pos=Read_Position_In
timer=Local_Time();

route=direction()
            # creates the route: (like: 2nd left, 1st right, 2nd right)

walk()
```

Project Description	Text	Project	Affiliation
	Jürgen Scheible, Ville Tuulos	Jürgen Scheible, Ville Tuulos	SensorPlanet, Nokia Research Center, 2006

MANHATTAN STORY MASHUP
Interactive, Collaborative Street Art

Manhattan Story Mashup is an urban storytelling game based on real-time interaction between mobile and Web users. In the game, stories written in the game's open website are illustrated by street players taking photos with camera phones on the streets of New York. The best of the resulting stories are displayed on eleven large public screens in Times Square and on the Web. The game was deployed in September 2006 with 184 players moving around Manhattan for 1.5 hours, shooting 3,142 photos in total. At the same time, 150 people were writing 115 stories on the Web using a specifically designed storytelling tool. *Manhattan Story Mashup* was organized by SensorPlanet, a Nokia research initiative on large-scale mobile-centric Wireless Sensor Networks.

Our motivation was to design a simple and engaging game that combines virtual and physical spaces. We wanted to inspire people's creativity in various settings to generate unpredictable and spontaneous visual stories in a collaborative manner.

The game website's storytelling tool consists of nine slots for sentences. In each slot, the player may either write a new sentence based on a given topic or copy-and-paste an already illustrated sentence written by someone else. Once the writer has constructed a story, the system chooses a random noun from each sentence and dispatches it in real time to a random mobile player in Manhattan for illustration. Shortly thereafter, the resultant photos are transmitted to the website, allowing the writer to see her illustrated story.

The nouns dispatched from the storytelling tool are presented to mobile players – one word at a time –

for the purpose of taking a matching photo with their camera phone within 120 seconds. For validation purposes, two other mobile players receive a newly taken photo together with four nouns, one of which is the original. They are asked to guess the original noun based on the photo and if they guess correctly, the photo is approved into the illustrated story. The players are awarded points for taking photos and for guessing correctly.

The final illustrated story consists of nine sentences, each imprinted on a photo. Selected stories were displayed live in Times Square. The large public screen served various purposes: it displayed to the public the street art generated from visual stories, it gave the web players the chance to see their own creative handprint exhibited to a large audience, and it showed the mobile players how their photos fit into the unpredictable context of the stories.

People enjoyed playing the game, and some features proved particularly engaging and important. One of these was the fast pace: players needed to think and act fast. Another was the emphasis on team play: if an abstract word was too hard for a mobile player to photograph, team mates were asked to physically act out the difficult concept in front of the camera. In doing so, some players crossed the boundaries of ordinary behavior in public places and enjoyed the chance to make spontaneous street performances. Overall, the opportunity to participate in a unique collaborative storytelling effort proved to be highly motivating – especially given the knowledge that the unpredictable results would be presented in an iconic location.

Howard Rheingold (HR)
in conversation with the Editors of Space Time Play (STP)

LIFE IS NOT COMPLETELY A GAME
Urban Space and Virtual Environments

STP **You were an early explorer of *The Well* (1985), an Internet-based communication platform that to some extent could be described as an ancestor of today's virtual environments like *Second Life* (2003). How would you compare the two?**

HR What was interesting about *The Well* was that in 1985, I had the ability to participate in many conversations. And I think you have to see that in the context of what else was happening in 1985, a good ten years before most people had heard of the Internet or the Web. I think in a lot of these discussions about technology, we are kind of missing historical context; everything moves so fast, and people forget what the last thing was about. What was exciting about *The Well* was that it afforded access to other minds at any time on a many-to-many basis. What's exciting about *Second Life* is that it looks like the beginning of a place in which we can play with masks and the visual sense of immersion in an environment. The problem with *Second Life* for me right now is that there's a big learning curve just to learn how to move your character around and navigate the environment and manipulate objects and move your avatar; all that takes some time to learn. And I have to do that. But it's not like typing words, which I already knew how to do, and which was essentially what you did on *The Well*. There were some kinds of commands you had to learn to navigate *The Well*, but nowhere near as complex as what you're seeing on *Second Life*. So *Second Life* requires a fairly serious commitment to climb that learning curve. But it looks pretty interesting in that there are all kinds of things that you can do in terms of constructing the environment. And that's one thing that you couldn't do in the world of text-only: you weren't able to construct objects and have behaviors and environments that you could navigate. That is what is so exciting about *Second Life* – you get the ability to create.

STP **How much of an impact could this ability to create something in a virtual environment have on how people behave in the "real world?"**

HR We need a very broad view of how people think of themselves in a world in which they are not just passive consumers of media, but have the capability of creating media. Yochai Benkler in *The Wealth of Networks* (2006) and Henry Jenkins in *Convergence Culture* (2006) are both advocating something very similar. They are saying that a citizen in a culture in which your only choice in regards to cultural production is as a consumer, you see yourself and your role in society very differently than you would in a society in which you see yourself as a creator. It is a big difference if your only choice is which channel you are going to turn on or if, on the other hand, you are able to make a video or create an online environment or write a blog post and have others in the world experience it. So I think the most important influence of virtual environments is the shift from the passive consumer to the active creator. I think that you have a very different relationship to master creators – even though you may not be one – if you yourself are an amateur creator, no matter how skilled.

STP **If you had to teach urban planners or architects, what would you say they have to learn from virtual communities?**

HR In virtual worlds, we're really at the beginning of being able to quickly create a model to give an experience of what experiencing that space is like. And that's a huge jump. Remember what the spreadsheet did for business? It enabled business modelers to ask "what if" questions that they weren't able to before because it took so long to make the calculations, to see "what if I change this variable and that variable?" And I think the same is true with modeling: sophisticated and three-dimensional modeling of space has been too much work to really use it as an interactive tool. What if we made the ceiling higher or we made this street longer? Those are not the kinds of things that architects and urban planners have been able to ask. It's just too much work. But now it's not so much work. And I think that as we see a literacy and a vocabulary manipulating simulation and modeling, we will see a similar augmentation of people's ability to try out different things.

STP **Hasn't the emergence of new media brought about a more fundamental transformation of urban space that architects and urban designers have to deal with?**

HR The most obvious change is that cities used to change when construction techniques and transportation technologies changed. The big changes in cities came from railroads and automobiles, the ability to build skyscrapers, elevators, steel. But those are things that take time, whose pace is rather slower. Now, the changes have to do with downloading something from your mobile phone (like a map of the city) or the ability to locate others who you know (through buddy lists, a locative media), which are all things that change at the pace with which software changes. And certainly, we've seen the way the Web has changed in ten years; that's a much more rapid pace. Urban planning used to have to do with the pace at which cities were planned by central planners. And now you can't really plan it in that way. You have to be able to *react*. These changes are things that are created by the people who use the technologies, and they are *emergent* from their activities, rather than something that some central planners plan, and contractors build it, and then people experience it. So there's a much more active element in the way that cities are used on the part of their actual inhabitants. So I think that planners and architects used to be somewhat removed from the people who used what they built. Now, in a sense, they have to become more like anthropologists and understand how people are using technologies in ways that they weren't designed for.

STP **On what changes should planners and architects focus first?**

HR By far the most sudden and radical change in the way people use urban space is the mobile telephone. It's visible everywhere in terms of people's behavior in public spaces: talking to people who aren't there. It has heated up the urban metabolism in that when you have a telephone with you, you are able to coordinate your activities with others in the city in ways that you weren't before. So people are able to do more things with more people in the same period of time – that's what I mean by heating up the urban metabolism (Townsend 2000).

STP **But isn't this new metabolism a mere western phenomenon, something which is only happening in the richer parts of the world? We are entertained when we use our mobiles in the city and when we use our mobile applications for gaming in the subway. We are entertained when we play around in** *Second Life.* **Seen in a global context, is there a widening of the technology gap?**

HR I actually believe that there's *not* a widening of the technology gap in a lot of ways. There are three billion mobile telephones in the world. If you are a relatively poor fisherman off the coast of India, you can get an SMS message that tells you which port has fish and where, therefore, you're not going to get a very good price for your catch, and at which port you're more likely to be able to sell your catch and feed your kids. Access to information about spot labor markets, commodity prices for the poorest farmers – those are pieces of information that people are getting on mobile telephones today. Now, that's not an immersive gaming environment, it's not a video iPod, but it *is* a way of participating in this information world that really was not possible with the PC-based Internet. So I really see the mobile phone as a way for people who weren't in on the information revolutions of the last ten years to get in on them. And that information is very active in the sense that it enables people to participate in their lives – in making a livelihood – in a much more informed way. So again, I go back to the idea of participatory culture: that the important thing is not so much that you're able to watch a movie that somebody else made while you're on the subway, but that more and more people are participating in journalism.

The constitution of the Senate here was really changed because one Senate candidate made a racist remark, and someone in the crowd had a telephone and made a video of that and put it up on the Internet. We're seeing instances of police misconduct recorded and put on the Internet. This is really active participation by citizens using media, rather than a passive experiencing of entertainment. So I certainly think that there are a lot of changes that come from those who can afford it being able to have mobile entertainment, but I think the most interesting change is the idea of people – even the poorest people – being able to use the technologies that they have with them to participate, to become citizen journalists, to get the kind of information they need to lead their lives and make a living in ways that they weren't able to before. It used to be that most people were only passive consumers of entertainment, and clearly we're seeing more and more of that. Also, gaming is very attractive to young people whether they're rich or poor. It is becoming more and more affordable to have handheld devices that game, and I think that the future of online games as a way of learning – gaming to learn – offers some real potential for people who don't have access to brick-and-mortar classrooms.

STP   **In the last chapter of *Smart Mobs* (2003), you cited an Amish gentlemen who said that the main question is what kind of people we will become through technology. So our question is: what kind of people will we become with all these entertainment environments around us?**

HR   Life is not completely a game. If you're walking down the street and you're too immersed in the virtual world, you could get run over by a bus. So I think there's some very important distinctions between the virtual world and the face-to-face world, but I also think that we need to pay attention to the way our relationships in the face-to-face world may be changing because of the number of people walking around who are in a virtual world. It used to be if you were in a virtual world, that happened because you were sitting at home behind a PC screen. But now people are walking down the street – they've got earbuds in, they've got their mobile phone screen, they may be playing immersive games. So the interpenetration of those two worlds, I think, is something that's just beginning to change public spaces. And we need to know more about that.

◆ Benkler, Y. (2006), *The Wealth of Networks: How Social Production Transforms Markets and Freedom*, Yale University Press, New Haven CT. ◆ Jenkins, H. (2006), *Convergence Culture: Where Old and New Media Collide*, NYU Press, New York NY. ◆ Rheingold, H. (2003), *Smart Mobs*, Basic Books, New York NY. ◆ *Second Life* (2003), developed and published by Linden Labs. ◆ Townsend, A.M. (2000), "Life in the real-time city: mobile telephones and urban metabolism," *Journal of Urban Technology*, vol. 7, no. 2, pp. 85-104. ◆ *The Well* (1985), developed by Stewart Brand and Larry Brilliant.

eXistenZ
From Fiction to Reality

The increasing popularity of mobile devices equipped with location awareness contributes to the design of new types of games: pervasive games. Pervasive games broaden the traditional game environment. Not only are they played beyond a board or computer screen, but they can also access the player unexpectedly, thereby eliminating a specifically delineated gameplay. The game environment never stops running. If in traditional Massively Multiplayer Online Role-Playing Games (MMORPGs) disconnecting from the Internet means leaving the game, how can one disconnect from a pervasive game given that its gamespace coincides with the space in which one lives?

In his 1999 movie *eXistenZ*, director David Cronenberg explored this lack of distinction between playful and nonplayful spaces. In the film, game designer Allegra Geller tests her new game *eXistenZ* with a focus group. She presents it as "not just a new game, but an entirely new game system." Apparently a virtual reality game, *eXistenZ* is intriguing because it merges physical and virtual spaces in a completely unexpected way – *eXistenZ* does not reveal what reality is.

Like *The Matrix* (Warner Bros. et al. 1999) and *The Thirteenth Floor* (Centropolis Film 1999), *eXistenZ* explores the idea of placing virtual spaces inside the user's mind by means of physical connections. But in the former, it was almost always clear what was reality and what was simulation. *eXistenZ*, on the other hand, makes no distinction between the two. In the beginning, it is apparently clear that users are playing a virtual reality game, having been invited to do so by the game's designer. Once players get into the virtual environment, however, they are faced with layers of games within the game, which make them move forward and backward inside *eXistenZ* and thereby completely merge reality and imagination. Until the last scenes of the movie, viewers are still fairly sure about the distinction between reality and gamespace despite having to keep track of the many games contained within *eXistenZ*. But then the players emerge on to one more level, which reveals another possible reality; that which had seemed to be real turns out to be yet another layer of the game. Again, viewers are supposed to think that they are finally in contact with the "real reality," but even at the movie's end, one character asks: "But tell me, are we still in the game?"

eXistenZ merges the physical and the virtual precisely because it does not distinguish between them. Reality can be playable, and a game can be more than mere imagination. All possible worlds might be different realities enfolded within one another yet all contained within "the real." At one point, a gas station worker says that he works at the gas station "only in the most pathetic level of reality," thereby pointing out that the game environment could be more real than reality itself, constituting a possible simulacra. And indeed, Cronenberg's movie is not about virtual reality as such. *eXistenZ* presents several levels of reality that are overlaid one on top of the other. These different levels can be perceived as virtualities that are no longer ready to emerge into our "real" world, but rather are already here.

If movies like *The Matrix* and *The Thirteenth Floor* are related to the future of traditional video (virtual reality) games, *eXistenZ* is definitely more concerned with the emerging field of pervasive and hybrid reality games, in which virtual and physical spaces merge to create a new concept of playable space: hybrid space.

Project Description	Text	Project	Affiliation
	Aram Bartholl	Aram Bartholl	Datenform, Berlin, DE, 2006

FIRST PERSON SHOOTER
Everyday Counter-Strike

The term first-person shooter refers to an independent computer game genre whose main characteristic is that it is played in the first-person perspective, with shooting as the main action of the game. The player moves his or her character in a three-dimensional world and perceives the digital environment through the eyes of this virtual character. A typical element within this genre is the virtual arm of the player, which remains in front at all times, and which represents the arm of the player reaching into virtual reality as a digital extension of his or her body. This virtual arm is attached to the character's head movements, which are controlled by computer mouse. No matter where the player looks, the arm holding the weapon stays at the lower right corner pointing toward the center of the screen. It is, in fact, impossible to lower the arm.

In the project *First Person Shooter*, the arm holding the weapon of the video game *Counter-Strike* (Valve 1999) is transferred into physical space. The project consists of a postcard that is also a do-it-yourself kit. Players who cut and glue all of the parts of the card together receive a pair of glasses bearing the arm with the weapon. These graphic objects, adapted from the game *Counter-Strike,* are visible both from within and from outside the glasses.

When a player wears the glasses, the arm holding a weapon always remains in the front, regardless of the direction in which the player moves his or her head. Attached to the eyes, the glasses reflect the strongly visual character of the game. The private space between the eyes and the gun is contrasted by public space in which the user of the glasses is identified from the outside as a first-person shooter.

The *First Person Shooter* glasses are, of course, a provocation and a comment on violence in video games. By transferring the typical first-person view to the real world, the player is confronted with his or her actions in the game. At the same time, the project shows how separate everyday life in the physical world is from virtual gaming space, with its own rules. A typical gamer would not confuse these two worlds. The *First Person Shooter* glasses are an attempt to indicate that violence happens primarily in people's minds.

www.datenform.de

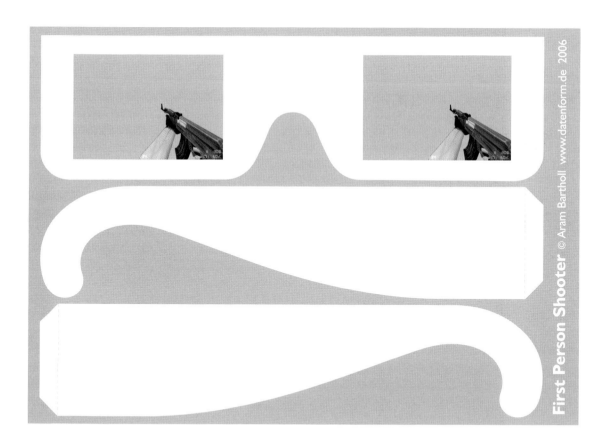

First Person Shooter © Aram Bartholl www.datenform.de 2006

SERIOUS FUN

UTILIZING GAME ELEMENTS FOR ARCHITECTURAL DESIGN AND URBAN PLANNING

Level

Project Description	Text	Project	Affiliation
	Jochen Hoog	Jochen Hoog	Faculty of Architecture and Planning, Vienna University of Technology, AT, 2005

ARCHITECTURE_ENGINE_1.0
Playing Architecture

Architecture_Engine_1.0 is a software game installation. It is a computer game that allows the player to act in a 3D virtual environment, as in a first-person-view game.

The focus of the project is to show how a game engine can be used in architectural design processes. As opposed to modifying computer games (modding) or using them as fast real-time rendering machines, the emphasis in this work is on the potential for using and running self-programmed scripts (behavior) within game engines. Therefore, the process of an architectural design task is divided into two parts: design-time and play-time. The first one breaks the specific design task down into rules and defines the environmental conditions of the virtual space, i.e. gravity, scale, time, the goal of the game, the perspective of the user, etc. That is a very useful way for an architect to approach the resources, time management, planning regulations and budget of a given project. During play-time, the architect becomes the player; he tries to win his own game.

In the *Architecture_Engine_1.0*, the player starts as a human being in the ego-perspective within a virtual space where four objects act and react both to him and to one another. Four simple cubes of various sizes always know where the player is, and they follow him. When they reach him, they stop and stay for a while; then the loop starts again. The player is pressed for time because he loses time-credits every five seconds and must perform an action in order to get them back again. He has to change the behavior of the cubes by activating them, after which they copy themselves around the player. Visitors appear randomly, and trees grow up around him as well. The player's perspective can be set to a cube (third-person view) or to a view from above (God-view). The player can also change the role he is playing and become the cube itself. The architect becomes architecture. The game has no goal except to avoid losing all of the time-credits because doing so means that the game is over. The result is reactive 3D virtual architecture within which the player can interact in runtime. The architect becomes part of an infinite, generative and reactive game. Even though the basic rules are very simple, the result is always different and always unpredictable. The possibility of altering perspectives within the game (which can even mean becoming the architecture itself) really changes the definition of an architect.

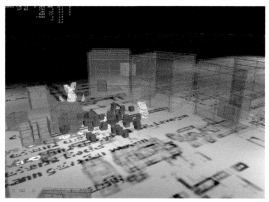
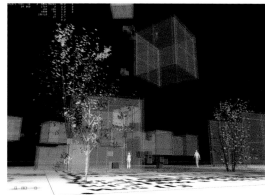

NOZZLE ENGINE
Need a Bot Skin Massage?

A cargo ship with a nozzle-driven engine – the *MS SUPAMIRA* – provides the playground for the following real space scenario. The engine that drives our game-generated architecture is the open-source *GoApe Game* engine, which provides gamespace for AI Action Bots with a fully implemented artificial neural network. The skin of this *Nozzle Engine* is a psychogeographic *GoApe Game* membrane (synthetic material mechanically manipulated by steel wires) installed inside the "Spielzimmer" (cargo hold) of the ship.

In psycho-organic system configurations, stress can be measured by the reaction and electric resistance of the skin. When playing the *Nozzle Engine*, all bots and players are connected to a "collective neuroactive membrane." The maximum stress (**Mühlmann 2005**) of Action Bots shooting in a game gives a pleasant massage to the players of a Second Life game in their first-life bodies. The *Nozzle Engine* plays with the skin of Action Bots. Following McLuhan (**1964**), the goal of the game is to trigger the medium as the massage in a self-referential ludic New Bachelor Machine.

The Nozzle Engine applies this notion in real time. Those players standing on the deck of the ship are the puppet masters of the game. Via the game, they are pulling and pushing the wires by a remote-controlled play interface (GoApe Chindogu 2006), generating a reflexive architecture. They play the game as it is projected on the Skin and visible from underneath the surface. The hypnotic flow of AC/DC turns into the creative flow of a game played on the supporting body of the Danube water stream. The Skin is a spatial boundary and the game's exchange surface

at once, interface to the bot world and the player's body skin.

The animistic nature of the signals mesmerizes the players who literally lie on the membrane and sense the bots' neural stress. Furthermore the alterability of the Skin's transparency allows the players to get an insight into the ludological game mechanics. The ludic heart of gameness, in the sense of Juul (**2003**), becomes lucid!

The level of the bots' current neural stimuli, their affection caused by shoots of human players or other bots, is indicated through the mechanical movement of the Skin's suspension armature. The concept of this "architecture of wires" can be seen as an analog to the networked realities of action bots, but also to their

role as collective avatar, similar to a Borg in Star Trek (1986) represented in a semi-technological collective consciousness. But also the role of the Action Bot as puppet, as "Super Mario-nette," becomes evident. In the essay "On the Marionette Theater," Heinrich von Kleist (1810) introduces the notion of the elegance of the puppet theater into ludic aesthetics.

Once one picks up the flow of the game, stress can be pleasure (Csikszentmihalyi 2005). The pleasure of *la plissure* (Ascott 1983), *le plis* (Deleuze 1992) of the Skin is changing according to the game's activity, rendering the *GoAPE Game* Skin as a dynamic architectural skinscape in real space.

Cruising on the flow of play, the *MS SUPAMIRA* travels along the Danube between Vienna and Istanbul.

The open-source game engine GoApe was developed at the artificial intelligence lab of the University of Zurich after an idea of the artists M. Jahrmann and M. Moswitzer. The specifics of the GoApe engine is the fact that a complete neural network was implemented as artificial intelligence element of the bots and that hardware devices connected affect the status of the bot intelligence. Ito Tsuyoshi, ETH Zurich, developed a graphical user interface to this game engine in 2005.

◆ Mühlmann, H. (2005), *MSC - Maximal Stress Cooperation: the driving force of cultures*, Springer, Vienna/New York. ◆ McLuhan, M. (1964), *Understanding Media: The Extensions of Man*, McGraw Hill, New York NY. ◆ Juul, J. (2003), "Looking for a Heart of Gameness," *Level Up: Digital Games Research Conference Proceedings*, Utrecht University, Utrecht. ◆ Csikszentmihalyi, M. (2005), "Flow," in A. Elliot & C.S. Dweck (eds.), *Handbook of Competence and Motivation*, Guilford Press, New York NY. ◆ Ascott, R. (1983), *La Plissure du Texte*, Electra, Musee d'Art Moderne, Paris. ◆ Deleuze, G. (1992), *The Fold: Leibniz and the Baroque*, University of Minnesota Press, Minneapolis MN.

Project Description	Text	Project	Affiliation
	Beat Suter, René Bauer	Beat Suter, René Bauer	AND-OR, Zurich, CH, 2005

GAMESCAPE
Generating Architecture from the Subconscious

AND-OR is looking to find and expose new ways of interactivity and concreativity between human user and machine. In *Gamescape*, behavior patterns of gameplay are used to visualize what lies beneath the digital surface and beyond the common limits of communication. *Gamescape* gives a visual form to existing communication patterns, which usually remain invisible to users. With this visualization, a whole new view of the real and virtual worlds is created. Furthermore, users get the opportunity to interact with a new type of spatial construction and may cooperatively create a new cityscape, which can be exported and used in 3D sotware and/or be entered in any geographical location of Google Earth.

Gamescape is a game art extension of the retro game *I1neum* (Ia1n 2005). It tries to capture the performative aspect of interactive gaming by representing the movements of a player as a 3D sculpture. While the movements of a single player make up a sculpture, every sculpture of every game played by every player is collected on a server and used to form an entire city – a city consisting of structures created by the gamers' movements. This assembly of structures constitutes an ever-expanding universe of movements – finished and unfinished. The different shapes of the buildings are related to the strategies of individual players; a player can in fact adapt his/her strategy in order to determine the shape of the buildings and the city and thereby engage interactively with the game on a metalevel. This metagame produces the game-based architecture.

All that usually remains after the end of a playing session in older games is the high score; most of the scores and games fade away once achieved or completed. *Gamescape*, on the other hand, uses the movements of players as creative material and not only builds sculptures out of traces, but also alters the concept of play by moving it onto a metalevel. By giving structural representation to transient movements that would normally go unrecorded and thus be forgotten, it is able to create an urban environment. When players realize they can shape an architectural building for a broader structure, they adopt new strategies for designing objects of their own imaginations. This means that players can take a playful approach to creating a new world and are for that reason more interested in concreation and interactivity than in getting fame by achieving new high scores.

www.and-or.ch/gamescape/
www.la1n.ch/l1neum/

PLAY STATIONS

STP   **Can computer games help us to understand questions of urban design?**

NL   Firstly, I would think that the notion of the "game" itself deserves to be taken seriously. Here the "game" should be perceived not simply as a leisure-time distraction, but as a logic of engagement that lies behind social life in general and capitalistic enterprise in particular. The concept speaks of competition and of certain rules of engagement. In that respect, I tend to agree with political theorist Chantal Mouffe's concept of an "agonistic" society. This is not so much a call for competition as such, for we have to be aware of the risks of a free-for-all libertarian existence, under which western capitalism itself would collapse without the safety net of social constraints. Rather, it is a warning against the often naïve – and to my mind somewhat dangerous – perception of society as having at its root a form of harmony. This perception is dangerous because it can generate expectations of society as a form of cozy, social fabric, leading to a false sense of community, which in turn engenders forms of fascistic behavior. [1]

1 >

I have discussed this issue at some length in "The Dark Side of the Domus" (Leach 1999).

Secondly, I think that society is based on certain implicit and explicit rules of behavior. These rules are set by social, economic and political conditions. In the context of the field of real estate, for example, it is precisely these rules that allow developers to predict the marketability of certain real estate projects based on certain formulas that have proven successful in the past.

If we combine this observation with an understanding of society itself as being agonistic, we can see that real estate can give us a good example of a form of rule-based competitive behavior, and that this can be modeled to some extent through digital simulations such as *SimCity*.

STP   **But can these digital simulations of urban development replicate analog realities?**

NL   It is important to bear in mind that computation may operate in both the digital and the analog domains. The word computation comes from the Latin verb, *computare*, which simply means, "to think together."

This process of thinking together lies at the heart of all forms of populational thinking, or swarm intelligence. Research by scientists at the Santa Fe Institute and MIT Media Lab has drawn comparisons between the behavior of insect colonies and that of other multiagent systems and demonstrated that all these behaviors depend upon interactive vectorial

2 >

See also *Swarm Intelligence* (Kennedy 2001) and *Turtles, Termites, and Traffic Jams* (Resnick 1994).

3 >

Collectively these ideas come under the heading of "emergence," a term popularized to describe a development in scientific explanations of the universe, but one which expands to all aspects of social life. It represents a shift in understanding from "low-level" rules to higher-level sophistication, a kind of bottom-up development of complex adaptive systems that self-regulate, in opposition to top-down overarching principles. It looks to patterns of behavior, though not ones which freeze into one single expression, but rather ones which are premised on dynamic adaptation. Constantly mutating, emergent systems are intelligent ones based on interaction, informational feedback loops, pattern recognition and indirect control. They challenge the traditional concept of systems as predetermined mechanisms of control and focus instead on their self-regulating adaptive capacity (Bonabeau et al. 1999, p. 11).

4 >

"Under the seeming disorder of the old city, where the old city is working successfully, is a marvellous order for maintaining the safety with the streets and the freedom of the city. It is a complex order. Its essence is intimacy of sidewalk use, bringing with it a constant succession of eyes. This order is all composed of movement and change, and although it is life, not art, we may fancifully call it the art form of the city and liken it to the dance — not to a simple-minded precision dance with everyone kicking up at the same time, twirling in unison and bowing off en masse, but to an intricate

forces that operate within a network, not in isolation (Bonabeau et al. 1999).[2] Such research falls within the theory of emergence and looks towards "the emergent collective intelligence of groups of simple agents" (ibid.).[3] According to the theory, connections may be made between any population that operates in this fashion, no matter how seemingly incommensurable the entities within that system. As Manuel DeLanda points out: "The dynamics of populations of dislocations are very closely related to the population dynamics of very different entities, such as molecules in a rhythmic chemical reaction, termites in a nest-building colony, and perhaps even human agents in a market. In other words, despite the great difference in the nature and behavior of the components, a given population of interacting entities will tend to display similar collective behavior" (DeLanda 2004).

Thus we can draw lessons from the behavior of ants and termites and apply those lessons to the ways that cities and brains function and even to the way in which computers operate. And, as Kevin Kelly has argued, through these applications, we can glimpse the complex nature of any form of cultural life, extending right through to social, political and even economic systems (Kelly 1994/1998).

There is an obvious parallel to be drawn between the self-organizing capacity of ant or termite colonies and the "natural" patterns of growth of human cities. Indeed, some of the early thinking by scientists on the theme of emergence was based on the observations of urbanist Jane Jacobs in her 1961 book, *Death and Life of Great American Cities* (Jacobs 1961). In a polemical attack on wholesale urban demolition and rebuilding, Jacobs recognizes the complex choreography of life in the city.[4] Since the time of her writing, however, a second generation of thinkers like DeLanda and Steven Johnson has taken up these ideas, developed them and extended them into an analysis of the very structures of our cities (DeLanda 1997/Johnson 2001). According to this line of thought, cities and towns themselves must be understood as amalgams of processes, as spaces of vectorial flows that adjust to differing inputs and impulses like some self-regulating system. John Holland sums them up as follows: "Cities have no central planning commissions that solve the problem of purchasing and distributing supplies (...) How do these cities avoid devastating swings between shortage and glut, year after year, decade ballet in which the individual dancers and ensembles all have distinctive parts which miraculously reinforce each other and compose an orderly whole." (Jacobs 1961), as quoted in *Emergence: The Connected Lives of Ants, Brains, Cities and Software* (Johnson 2001).

after decade? The mystery deepens when we observe the kaleidoscopic nature of large cities. Buyers, sellers, administrations, streets, bridges, and buildings are always changing, so that a city's coherence is somehow imposed on a perpetual flux of people and structure. Like the standing wave in front of a rock in a fast-moving stream, a city is a pattern in time" (Johnson 2001, p. 27).

This concept immediately opens up the possibility of seeing the city within the logic of material computation as a form of swarm intelligence. If the analog model of the city follows certain logics of development that are commensurable with the operations of digital computation, then digital simulations can offer certain insights into the behavior of the physical city.

STP **So how closely can the analog computation of the city be modeled through digital simulation?**

NL In fact, digital simulations offer us only a poor approximation of the very sophisticated material computations of the analog world. The limits of digital computation can be exposed, for example, when we look at questions of structural engineering.

Architect Frei Otto would often use techniques of material computation to analyze the structural behavior of forms by experimenting with materials such as soap bubbles. The astonishingly sophisticated material computation of the molecular behavior within the soap film coupled with the calculation of gravitational forces and internal and external pressures, gives the soap bubble a level of complexity that could never be matched by digital methods. Indeed, when we compare the material computation of nature with the digital computation that can be simulated, we must recognize the relative poverty of our knowledge within the digital domain.

STP **So does this mean that digital modeling techniques have a relatively limited scope in the area of architectural and urban design?**

NL I think that the real potential of digital technologies lies in the development of tools of optimization or search engines. This in itself is no small contribution. Architects and urban planners have often subscribed to what could be called a pseudocomputational logic, whereby they claim

330

5 >

On this, see "Directed
Randomness" (Shea 2004).

to have explored the range of possibilities without ever being very rigorous about the process. With these new digital tools – which can act as a
form of prosthesis to human operations, rather like the calculator – this
exercise becomes more rigorous. And within this limited sphere, the
digital technologies can operate as part of the design process itself, as is
the case with *eifFORM*, a design tool developed by MIT.[5] They can even
open up the range of aesthetic possibilities and broaden the architectural palette. Computer games themselves can even be employed as tools
within the design process. In fact, some of my students have used certain
software programs written for computer games in order to develop their
own multiagent systems for testing emergent patterns of behavior. By
ascribing agents certain characteristics and setting them certain goals
– such as walking to bus or subway stations or other targets – they can
mimic analog systems of path-making employed by ants laying phero-
mone trails and therefore generate optimized path layouts. I am sure
that there are many more possible ways in which software generated
for the computer games industry could be used in the architectural and
urban planning studio. But I think that we should be cautious of ascribing too much potential to the digital realm, as we did in the euphoric
early days of speculation; then, as now, this can too often border on a
form of science fiction.

◆ Bonabeau, E., Dorigo, M. & Theraulaz, G. (1999), *Swarm Intelligence: From Natural
to Artificial Systems*, Oxford University Press, New York NY. ◆ DeLanda, M. (1997), *A
Thousand Years of Nonlinear History*, Zone Books, Swerve Editions, New York NY. ◆ De-
Landa, M. (2004), "Material Complexity," in N. Leach, D. Turnbull & C. Williams (eds.),
Digital Tectonics, Wiley, London. ◆ Jacobs, J. (1961), *Death and Life of Great American
Cities*, Vintage, New York NY. ◆ Johnson, S. (2001), *Emergence: The Connected Lives of
Ants, Brains, Cities and Software*, Penguin, London. ◆ Kelly, K. (1994), *Out of Control*,
Perseus Books, Cambridge MA. ◆ Kelly, K. (1998), *New Rules for the New Economy*,
Fourth Estate, London. ◆ Kennedy, J. (2001), *Swarm Intelligence*, Morgan Kaufmann,
New York NY. ◆ Leach, N. (1999), "The Dark Side of the Domus," in N. Leach (ed.),
Architecture and Revolution, Routledge, London. ◆ Resnick, M. (1994), *Turtles, Termites,
and Traffic Jams*, MIT Press, Cambridge MA. ◆ Shea, K. (2004), "Directed Randomness,"
in N. Leach, D. Turnbull & C. Williams (eds.), *Digital Tectonics*, Wiley, London.

TACTICS FOR A PLAYFUL CITY

The playability of an enjoyable city is not confined to the existing interiors of buildings or to the way these have been conceived, but is rather an expanded field that incorporates the full range of possible architectures – that is to say, all kinds of objects, insertions, spaces, practices, ideas and emotions.

How, then, might this kind of space be constructed? I propose here a series of tactics that might be reused by designers, thinkers and urban residents.

Performance

Cultural expressions and critiques are often confined to the codified realm of texts, buildings and physical artworks – productions which speak of authority and imply a sense of stature and permanence. Yet, as theater, dance, poetry and music all tell us, there are other ways of being critical, of making statements without writing things down or making objects that exist in space. The life of the city should incorporate all manner of spaces where people can gyrate, glide and rotate, mime, perform and declaim, climb, descend and traverse – that is to say, where they can act out their opinions. Street poets, graffiti artists and skateboarders already know this much, and their actions should be encouraged and celebrated – for it is here that cultural acts can be performed, witnessed and heard.

Media

City spaces are often thought of too simplistically as being nothing more than parks and plazas. But what are parks and plazas if not meeting places, or rather *potential* meeting places where glances, touches, smiles, words, gossip, observations and opinions of all kinds can potentially be exchanged? City squares are information and relationship exchanges, allowing data and people alike to shuttle around in restless patterns of movement and copresence. This condition can be intensified by bringing nonphysical spaces into our cities, i.e., through screens, wireless networks, display boards, downloads and uploads, text messaging, podcasts and broadcasts of all kinds. In this way, cities become at once real and virtual, physical and ethereal, concrete and imagined – truly composed of media of all kinds, and accessible at all times. In this way, the city can be transformed from a dead archive where information is deposited and forgotten into a living flux of information and communication.

Uncertainty and Risk

There are some things we need to know: water supply, traffic flows, demand for housing, energy supplies, likely climate change. But there are other things it is best not to know, things that should remain uncertain, unclear and unknown. Our city spaces therefore need to be dual in character, spaces in which we encounter otherness and sameness, where we are at once confirmed and challenged: this comes from uncertainty, from not knowing everything around us, from a degree of surprise, from encountering the unusual as we go about our everyday lives. We need a city that we do *not* know, that we do not understand, that we have not yet encountered, that is simultaneously strange, familiar and unknown to us. This is a form of public space that is always a surprise, a unique place, a stimulation. This is the acceptable and indeed desirable risk of not always knowing what lies around the corner.

Provisional Identities

How do we define ourselves? Am I black or white? Are you gay, straight or bisexual? Is he a football, hockey or opera fan? Are we Italian, Bolivian, American, Korean or Kenyan? Is she a feminist or a socialist? Are they Conservatives, Democrats or Greens? Do not seek to answer these questions with any certainty or confidence, for many members of the global community no longer seek to proclaim permanent memberships in any solely determining form of identity. No longer do we have single identities that persist relatively unchanged throughout our lives, but rather multiple, fractured and provisional identities that shift and mutate according to our ages, bodies, cities of residence, cultural tastes and general attitudes. In short, just as our lives shift from year to year, week to week, even hour to hour, so too does our sense of who we are, who we might be, who we desire to become. This is the way people are constantly being reconstructed and reimagined in cities today, and this is the way that cities must be designed: not for predictable, monolithic sectors of the population (for these sectors are often but mirages, projections of the viewer rather than true representations of the city), but for various different and competing tastes, opinions and outlooks. The identities of our city spaces, like those of its inhabitants, should be multiple, diverse and dynamic, energetic, ephemeral and hybrid.

Fluidity

Boundaries mark social categories in space, inscribing the edges of territory, possession, authority, association and even opinion. Although undoubtedly necessary to demarcate our private homes and places of work, such boundaries do not have to be frontal and brutal in expression, not always challenging and confrontational to those who negotiate them. Boundaries can be thick, complex, gentle, staged, gradual and even invisible, using scenography, texture, materials, technologies and all manner of modulations in order to suggest to city dwellers whether or not they should traverse a given boundary. In this way, we ourselves are asked to regulate our behaviors in a subtle and responsible manner, which is much better than being immediately faced with an intimidating gate, guard or sign. Fluidity, not the creation of obstacles, is the key.

Interventions

Architecture, by its very nature, tends towards colonization and domination, taking over a particular space, imposing a certain social order that prevents other activities from taking place. And of course we need such domination, we need the security of hospitals, homes and schools, offices, factories and airports. And at other times, we need different kinds of architecture, those which appropriate rather than dominate, those which intervene and attach rather than impose and replace. We need architectures of an impermanent and temporary nature that appear for a few weeks, days or even hours, that do whatever it is that they need to do and then disappear without leaving a trace, except that they remain in the minds of all those who witnessed them. Architecture in this sense is like a seasonal flower, beautiful in its very ephemerality and provisional presence and appreciated not only for what it provides, but also in the knowledge that it will, very soon, be gone.

Play

Play is no laughing matter. Seemingly silly and superficial, play undoubtedly invokes the childish delights of being mischievous and of testing the boundaries of acceptability. Yet underlying its surface veneer of infantilism, play is much, much more: it tells us that aggression in cities is latent and not always detrimental, that being ridiculous is okay, that all of us are in some way children at heart and, above all, that our urban spaces are not there just for purposes of work, tourism, retail and other supposedly important affairs, but also for having fun, for letting go, for, in fact, being ourselves in our full range of emotions and bodily extensions. Play is *serious* fun, and we should all be able to take part.

If play is what we should do, then how does this occur? Here we have much to learn from children, who often see no separation between the world of imagination and fantasy and that of routines and chores. Rather, play exists everywhere – at home, in the schoolyard, in the back of the car – and at all times of the day.

Emotions

Nor need such thoughts always be logical, rational or considered. Our emotions, too, should be nurtured and cultivated. Hence the need for city spaces that make us glad and sad, happy and doleful, excited and calm, delighted and disgusted, pleased and angry, sympathetic and dismissive, intrigued and repelled, energized and relaxed. It is, after all, the quality of emotional life that, for many city dwellers, lies at the heart of urban existence. Without a full range of emotions – that is, without a full range of the meanings and possibilities of how it feels to be human – we are as yet unfulfilled, and the full life of the city is yet to be achieved.

A longer version of this text first appeared as "Thirteen Tactics for the Good Life," in Zoe Ryan (ed.) (2006), *The Good Life: New Public Spaces for Recreation*, Van Alen Institute and Princeton Architectural Press, New York NY.

WHY GAMES FOR ARCHITECTURE?

What do we stand to gain from using games for architectural purposes? The current architectural discourse is based on obsolete conceptions of technological realities. Current architectural practice is increasingly faced with economical, technological, ecological and, last but not least, formal and aesthetic problems. Architecture still has a mechanistic view of technology, despite the fact that it can provide the formal and theoretical ingredients necessary for innovation. Architects must develop new interaction schemes – more organic, but with comparable technological embedding in every respect. The construction of games can serve as a paradigm for this. We must expose builders, architects and users to individual measures of provocation, antagonism and reassurance so that modern buildings can be sensibly designed, built and operated.

Many well-known attempts by architects and game designers to capitalize on architectural games have been all too superficially presented and have thus been a welcome excuse for many architects to dismiss the genre as amateur. Yet through these games, palpably effective methods and technologies for more complex and dynamic systems of modeling, control and interaction were developed; these can achieve far more than what is currently possible in architectural practice. My interest lies not in the excited discourse of thrilling phenomenon, but in the search for mutually beneficial interfaces through which fundamental architectural structures can be linked to a game's modeling, production and interaction patterns. Unlike the focus of the majority of the discourse, these interfaces are geared towards everyday usage and demand an unusual amount of labor and patience to be understood.

Modern Architecture

Architects like to follow the "form follows function" design principle articulated in 1896 by Louis Sullivan, American architect and leader of the Chicago School. This maxim characterizes – often incorrectly – the idea behind the International Style, a term coined in a 1932 MoMA exhibition that refers to the minimalistic and functionalistic tendencies of European architecture in the 1920s and 1930s (the Bauhaus, for example), which shaped postwar architecture worldwide.

Sullivan's maxim follows the logic of cause and effect and is therefore an expression of modern thought. The most prominent representatives of modern thought are none other than Newton and his classical mechanics. In the modern way of thinking, objects are no longer described as matter, as they were in the Middle Ages, but as means to possible ends. The core idea in this worldview is energy, which, according to sociologist Daniel Bell *(1976)*, is the "central axis" of industrial society. Production systems no longer depend on people and places, but on machines and global infrastructures. The resultant architectural manifestations of this modern thought are the rastered buildings – disliked by most modern observers – that prescind from concrete matter and serve as a safeguarding system (i.e. infrastructure) for an industrialized, serialized production of buildings.

Information Technology as the Safeguard of Postmodern Thought

From a sociological point of view, the central axis of contemporary society is no longer energy, but rather information.

In physics, the notion of circuits and networks started catching on in the 20th century. Accordingly, the Object was no longer described by its outer, functional properties, but rather understood as belonging to a system of interdependent elements. The new notion thus placed the Object under a new heading: that of "information." In this context, information describes the accretion of improbability within a system (Shannon 1946), and communication is the accretion of information within a system.

Thus what we need for a successful modern system is no longer a trivial – in the mathematical sense – mechanism that functions predictably, but rather a nontrivial and therefore nonpredictable mechanism of adaptation, concentration, balance and provocation.

From the architectural viewpoint of an engineer, it is less interesting that this way of thinking has always been described as a myth, has long been formulated as a philosophy and has been defined for 60 years as a mathematically explicit theory, and more interesting that for the last 30 years, it has been a technical reality (Castells 2004) and thereby a potential tool for the practice of architecture.

This technical reality – which architects have barely even begun to understand – makes it possible to develop buildings with an enormous degree of freedom but without a loss of control, and it provides solutions to existing problems that will produce undreamt-of results. Grids as safeguarding systems are by no means still necessary, but a transformation in the way that buildings are drafted and constructed is.

From Monolithic to Constructed Element

Architects design buildings from "dead" elements. Modern information technology systems, in contrast, consist of objects with functions or even of agents with self-interests. Various examples of modern systems already exist in biology: things like cellular systems, neural networks, spring systems, evolution and emergence all describe systems behavior. The controlled, top-down, coarse-to-fine drafting of a building as a "lifeless" object must be supplemented through the only partially controlled, bottom-up "breeding" of a system performance from a score of far-reaching, largely autonomous, "flexible" elements.

From an information technology point of view, buildings can be happily constructed "from inside to out" on four relatively independent levels: reality, geometry, topology and ontology. This stands in stark contrast to Sullivan's "monolithic" dictum, "form follows function." It also stands in stark contrast to prevailing architectural practice, which is driven primarily by the formal and phenomenological criteria of surfaces while attaching little value to structural criteria.

336

In this layered system structure, the taxonomy or overall schematic of the building is governed by ontology. The entities and components of a concrete building as well as their shared nexuses are drafted topologically. Geometry determines the form of the building's individual components. And the last layer establishes the way in which the data structures will become reality. Whether it is presented as a photorealistic rendering, a simulation, a code for computer-run machines, a plan for manufacturers or a finished building is, from a structural point of view, irrelevant.

The virtual systematically supports the real. The real is systematically enhanced by the virtual. A division is no longer conceivable. The terms "virtual" and "real" are thus no longer expedient. We live in a postdigital world (Negroponte 1998).

Stageability and the Gateway to Games

In this context, the function of a system is to give its components as much liberty as possible in order to safeguard its coherence from changing surroundings (a building is built to survive more than 100 years). In other words, it must serve the demands of long-term stability and of daily change in equal measure. It is therefore useful to break down a building system into subsystems of various average lifetimes (as is often done in functionalist architecture): the most stable subsystem is the building's shell and possibly its façade, which on average changes only after 50 years. These represent the stage on which the elements of the next subsystem act; these include façade, walls, technical infrastructure, etc., which have an average lifetime of ten years and are, in turn, the stage on which the *next* subsystems act. These include furnishings, technical terminals and so on, which have an average lifetime of two years and serve as the stage for the building's daily use. If we want to anchor games in architecture, then, we must do so on many different levels (up until now, architectural games have only been considered in terms of the everyday level, or subsystem with a two-year lifespan). Because games can take place on various levels, the most important question is: to what extent does a game based on the level of one subsystem make possible a game on the underlying level? Or, in other words, how high is its degree of "stageability" (Walz 2007)?

A New Architectural Practice

When it comes to digital form, architect Frank Gehry is part of the avant-garde. He functions with virtuosity on the top levels of the schema described through ontology, topology, geometry and reality (O-T-G-R). Gehry suggests a consistency even in the lower strata, but only makes use of it in the field of digital media. Games can also be described in O-T-G-R terms. But unlike in Gehry's work, in games, the various layers of the self-contained model gameworlds are integrated as consistently as possible. Let us thus consider several everyday architectural tasks that are handled by, as an example, the CAAD professor at the ETH Zürich in a general O-T-G-R model and describe them in the form of a game.

The Spaces Game (cf. *SimCity, Second Life*)

Players are the prospective inhabitants of a new city district. They make their own choice of plot size, design, financing, neighborhood, particular requirements à propos noise, view and further development. Many of these desires are mutually exclusive. The goal of the game is to fully develop the given building area and thereby fulfill as many of the individual wishes as possible. The example of Heerhugowaard (2005-2007) brings the individual desires of 3,500 prospective inhabitants of a new city district into spatial equilibrium. This represents the solution to a problem with over 50,000 parameters, which could not be approached with the traditional notion of a top-down planning system designed by creative experts.

The Construction Game

In this game, players must construct a geometrically complicated building with a timber frame. They have at their disposal timbers of only one width and must build a stable, traditional timber-frame building without any metallic connections that will withstand varying alpine load, wind and snow conditions. The player who develops the construction with the least weight wins.

The Façade Game

A large structure plays host to many different types of spaces: living rooms, kitchens, offices, shops, hotel rooms... A shop needs plenty of visitors, a hotel room plenty of quiet... Some rooms face south and get a lot of sun, others face north and get all the noise of the train station. For every situation, there is an appropriate façade element. The goal of the game is to find the right façade element faster than the house undergoes reconstruction and the layout of its rooms is changed.

The Wallpaper Game (cf. *Pac-Man*) by Peter Kogler, 1993

In this game, decoration is approached in a new way. The rooms of a building must be wallpapered. In the process, the length of wallpaper may not be cut, but rather only folded. The goal is to fully wallpaper an apartment. With a little strategic planning, new types of ornamentation emerge (Reference example by Peter Kogler 1993).

The Energy Game

The goal of the game is for a house to "survive" one year without fossil fuels. The structure has various harvesting areas for sun and wind energy distributed across Europe. These must heat the house in the winter and cool it in the summer. Unfortunately, the weather doesn't always play along; this is because the game uses current, real-time meteorological data. Moreover, the inhabitants of the edifice have varying habits: they take long showers, leave windows open even in the winter, buy new electronic devices... The player has various technologies at his command, such as heat pumps, blinds, concrete core cooling units, batteries and flywheels, and is also able to praise and criticize the inhabitants. The goal is to procure the greatest possible comfort for the users at the least possible cost, without emitting CO_2.

Why Games?

All the games described operate according to the same principle: they are technical manifestations of the described ways of thinking, and they are more powerful and more adaptable than conventional engineering techniques.

All current techniques share a fundamental problem: they stagnate on a conventional performance level when the users don't challenge them or adequately learn to use them. As examples, one can cite energy-conserving houses, almost all of which degenerate to the performance level of conventional houses after a few years because the users have lost their daily interest in the system.

What we need is thus a new interaction model. Our environment can no longer be operated from the outside through chains of causes and effects like a simple machine. We need to embed the user in the system.

What does the technically supported reality described above have to offer the game? Unlike ways of life before the 1970s, it offers an element constitutive to the game. It offers the "experiment" of experiencing – without existential risk – ways of life limited temporally, spatially and in their content. It also offers, for the first time, the simultaneity of various such experiments. If the descriptions above are correct, an experiment of this kind was always existential and thereby limited neither temporally, spatially nor in its content. If the descriptions above are correct, our technological foundations need these experiments in order to avoid atrophying. For the technological systems, the experiments are the form of essential provocation or conflict necessary for stability.

What do we need from games for architecture? We need practice in the production of these temporally, spatially and content-limited experiments. We need rules, tension and reward in order to embed the user in the experiments. And in terms of the descriptions above, the users, too, need an individual measure of provocation, conflict and validation.

Gone is thus the time when one could hit the light switch, and the light would go on. Now we need esprit to go along with that and, as architects, believe that we can find it in games.

◆ Bell, D. (1973), *The Coming of Post-Industrial Society: A Venture of Social Forecasting*, Basic Books, New York NY. ◆ Castells, M. (1996), *The Information Age: Economy, Society and Culture, Vol. I: The Rise of the Network Society*, Blackwell Publishers, Malden MA & Oxford UK, (Second Edition 2000). / *The Information Age: Economy, Society and Culture, Vol. II: The Power of Identity*, Blackwell Publishers, Malden MA & Oxford UK, (Second Edition 2004). / *The Information Age: Economy, Society and Culture, Vol. III: The End of the Millennium*, Blackwell Publishers, Malden MA & Oxford UK, (Second Edition 2000). ◆ Negroponte, N. (1998), "Beyond Digital," *Wired* vol. 6 no. 12. ◆ Shannon, E. (1948), "A Mathematical Theory of Communication," *Bell System Technical Journal*, vol. 27 (July & October 1948), pp. 379-423 & 623-656. Reprinted in D. Slepian (ed.) (1974), *Key Papers in the Development of Information Theory*, IEEE Press, New York NY. ◆ Walz, S.P. (2007), "Pervasive Persuasive Play: Rhetorical Game Design Tactics For The Ubicomp World," in B.J. Fogg (ed.), *Mobile Persuasion: Perspectives on the Future of Influence*, Elsevier, San Diego CA. [in press].

GAME OF LIFE
On Architecture, Complexity and the Concept of Nature as a Game

A few years before Watson and Crick discovered the structure of DNA (Watson & Crick 1953) and shortly after the publication of Schrödinger's *What is Life?* (Schrödinger 1944), John von Neumann's famous 1948 lecture at the Hixon Symposium helped contribute to the convergence between computer and natural sciences. Based on aspects of information theory, von Neumann's ultimate goal was to create a cellular automaton as a biological machine. The difference between von Neumann's approach and earlier automata concepts was the idea of "information." He wanted to implement not only a determined plan of behavior, but also the capability to reproduce itself. Thus the goal of von Neumann's investigation was to develop mathematical rules that simulated the evolutionary principles of nature.

A simpler example of how basic rules can steer a complex entity is the mathematical game developed by John Conway in 1968, called the *Game of Life*. The game became widely known when it was mentioned in Martin Gardner's article, "The Fantastic Combinations of John Conway's New Solitaire Play of Life," published in *Scientific American* in 1970 (Gardner 1970). "*Game of Life* wasn't actually a game that you played," writes scientist Mitchell M. Waldrop. "[...] It was more like a miniature universe that evolves as you watched" (Waldrop 1992, p. 203). It represents a simplified version of cellular automata and is strongly inspired by the preliminary work of von Neumann. The latter was interested in the underlying rules of evolution and self-reproduction; Conway's goal of designing a set of simple mathematical rules able to generate complex patterns of life-like behavior is similar in spirit.

For a few years now, architects have been increasingly exploring self-organizational and evolutionary processes of complex structures in nature. "Is the new Nonlinear Architecture somehow superior, closer to nature and our understanding of the cosmos, than Old Modernism?" asks architect Charles Jencks in reference to the growing significance of irregular geometries in contemporary architecture (Jencks 1997, p. 7). Increasingly, modern architecture relates to the field of complexity science, which Stephen Wolfram recently titled, "A New Kind of Science" (Wolfram 2002). Nowadays, complexity in architecture is instead understood as the built emergence into nature. Both this new understanding of architectural complexity and the trend of Nonlinear Architecture require a specific conceptualization and view of nature. But a question inevitably arises from Jencks' characterization of Nonlinear Architecture as potentially "closer to nature" than Old Modernism – namely, what does "nature" mean to contemporary architects? In other words: what model of nature does the part of the scientific world that investigates self-organizing and nonlinear processes communicate to architecture?

Since the first half of the 20th century, models of nature in architecture have been mainly shaped by technical and conceptual progress in the natural sciences. Gyorgy Kepes' *The New Landscape in Art and Science* (1961) impressively illustrated how the visual language of modern art and architecture is linked to scientific images of microstructures scaled up with electron microscopes. On many levels, the technology of computation has changed the way we construct our world. The mathematical subject "nonlinearity" was introduced by Henri Poincaré in 1890, but has been further developed in recent years because new tools and computers allow researchers to simulate and visualize self-organizing and evolutionary processes in ways that were previously impossible. Such processes produce not only an architectural language of irregular geometries, but have been applied as a new type of "techne," primarily addressing problems of structural optimization in architecture.

Today, we live in a society frequently characterized as information-based; that is, one in which information serves as the basis for the ongoing course of cultural and technological globalization we are experiencing. Mathematician Benoît Mandelbrot argues that the idea of information will play a key role in understanding nature. And architect Antoine Picon argues further that "contrary to the traditional notion of structure, information ignores the distinction between the large, the medium, and the small, between the macro and the micro" (Picon & Ponte 2003, p. 300). Numerous processes in nature, such as growth and adaptation, are considered information-based processes described as a set of rules. Rules are also typical features of games, and laws of nature can be regarded as rules – rules of the game of nature. This means that rules of games can simulate laws of nature.

Playful Notions in Architecture

In the consideration of the fast-growing application areas of new computational technologies, there is an increasing interest in the question of how and by what means the interrelations between game, design and technology have affected spatiotemporal ideas in architectural planning.

The role of games in architecture and architectural discourse is based primarily on sociological concepts. Reconsidered today, the artistic manifestos of Jacques Fillon, Constant, Yona Friedman, Guy Debord and other Situationists can be seen as prominent examples of how the idea of "playful interaction" was employed by those seeking to reformulate social structures.

The notion of "game" is discussed frequently in the context of participating urban design, in which the design philosophy implicitly includes aspects of interaction, communication and cooperation. Such discussion derives from the similarity and comparability of certain features present in both processes: playing and planning. Architecture understood in this context is regarded as a collective game based on a set of constraints. It is important to note that in every such sociological model of gaming, there is an all-important subject who participates in the game, takes action, often collaborates and tries to reach a certain goal.

Separating the Subject from the Game

Philosopher Hans-Georg Gadamer has extensively discussed the subject's role and meaning for games from an epistemological point of view. In *Truth and Method*, he distanced himself from the subject-oriented approach argued by Kant (Gadamer 1960). Instead, he pleaded for a separation of the subject from the game itself and disagreed with what he called the "subjectification of play." Gadamer sought to change the object of investigation from the subject to the game itself: "Because the game has its own character, independent of the awareness of those playing it. And the game also intrinsically exists there where no independent being of subjectivity limits its thematic horizon, and where there are no subjects who comport themselves playfully" (Gadamer 1960, p.109). [1] Gadamer described the idea of play by means of motion, which implicitly exists within the play, and he assigned special significance to the process of back and forth, in and out: "The movement that is the game does not end with the achievement of some goal, but rather renews itself in constant reiteration. The seesaw movement is apparently so integral to the character determination of the game that it is irrelevant who or what carries out this determination. The game movement is such that it essentially exists without a substrate. It is the game that is played or happens – not a cleaved subject that plays it" (ibid., p.108).

All quotations from Gadamer were translated from the German by the editors of Space Time Play.

Nature as a Game

In the natural sciences, Manfred Eigen and Ruthild Winkler presented a similar concept meant to objectify the idea of game. As did Gadamer's, their approach went beyond the narrow definitions of game such as those, for example, used by historian Johan Huizinga. The crucial point in Eigen's and Winkler's approach is that game is considered as a natural phenomenon described as dynamical processes governed by the dialectical dichotomy between necessity (*Notwendigkeit*) and chance (*Zufall*). Gadamer's philosophical intention to objectify the idea of game anticipates in some way Eigen's and Winkler's concept of nature as a self-organizing system: "There is clearly an order to the game, by which the back and forth seesawing of its movement seems to arise of its own accord" (ibid., p.109).

To propose an answer to Jencks' opening question of whether contemporary architecture might be "closer to nature than Old Modernism," one would definitely need additional insights, particularly from history and the philosophy of science. Eigen's and Winkler's suggestion of regarding nature as nothing more then the interplay of chance and necessity as well as Conway's *Game of Life* are both based on rule-based concepts of play in which no subject is involved and needed. Eigen and Winkler reject the idea of nature as mechanistic and deterministic and provide instead a mathematical model of nature described in terms of complexity and dynamic, nonlinear, self-organizing features. A majority of scientists might not agree that this nonlinear paradigm provides new scientific insights into nature. But in architectural culture, the "New Kind of Science" still has influence. Jencks is correct when he demands that architects always explore new languages – but not only in terms of form. Architects, I would argue, must also explore new processes, processes that occur without the subject's control. The utilization of such processes is presently going to breed a new architectural methodology based on the technological conceptualization of evolutionary and self-organizing dynamics. In consequence, the conception of nature as a model of objectified game could mean that architecture, regarded as a kind of second nature, will be technologically designed and optimized to a certain degree autonomously. For the architectural discourse, this could be a productive point of departure in the future.

◆ Gadamer, H.G. (1960), *Wahrheit und Methode – Grundzüge einer philosophischen Hermeneutik*, Mohr, Tübingen. ◆ Jencks, C. (1995), *The Architecture of the Jumping Universe*, Academy Group Ltd, London. ◆ Jencks, C. (ed.) (1997), "Nonlinear Architecture: New Science = New Architecture?," *Architectural Design*, no. 129. ◆ Kepes, G. (ed.) (1961), *The New Landscape in Art and Science*, Paul Theobald & Co., Chicago IL. ◆ Picon, A. & Ponte, A. (2003), *Architecture and the Sciences: Exchanging Metaphors*, Princeton Architectural Press, New York NY. ◆ Schrödinger, E. (1944), *What is Life?*, Cambridge University Press, Cambridge UK. ◆ von Neumann, J. (1948), "The General and Logical Theory of Automata." Delivered at the Hixon Symposium in Pasadena CA, September 1948, first published in: L. A. Jeffress (ed.) (1951), *Cerebral Mechanisms in Behavior*, John Wiley, New York NY. ◆ Waldrop, M. M. (1992), *Complexity. The Emerging Science at the Edge of Order and Chaos*, Simon and Schuster, New York NY. ◆ Watson, J. & Crick, F. (1953), "A Structure for Deoxyribose Nucleic Acid," *Nature* 171. ◆ Wolfram, S. (2002), *A New Kind of Science*, Wolfram Media, Champaign IL.

Project Description	Text	Project	Affiliation
	Andreas Dieckmann, Peter Russell	Wouter van Oortmerssen	Guildhall of the Southern Methodist University in Dallas, Texas, US, 2004

SAUERBRATEN
The World is a Cube

What if the universe were cubic? What if the underlying structure of everything were based on a three-dimensional grid? What if every face of every object could be represented as part of a (possibly deformed) cube somewhere in that grid? If that were the case, then you'd have landed in the world of *Sauerbraten*, a first-person shooter with editing capabilities that is free and open source. In addition to these basic characteristics, there are a few distinct features that make *Sauerbraten* attractive for use in an architectural context: its ingame editing, coop editing, geometry concept and overall simplicity and quick learning curve.

The world structure of *Sauerbraten* is that of an octree: it is a giant cube that is subdivided into eight smaller cubes of equal size, which are in turn subdivided into eight cubes of even smaller size and so on. In other words, the subdivision of *Sauerbraten*'s geometry is recursive. Within each cube, every surface can be manipulated at its four vertices.

Editing in *Sauerbraten* is performed ingame: users can toggle easily between play and edit mode. Thus modeling is done entirely in perspective, rather than in plan or section, enabling the designer to check his decisions immediately. There is no GUI (Graphical User Interface), as editing is extremely simple. Geometry and textures can be altered by a combination of mouse-wheel actions and keyboard commands that can be memorized very quickly. For example, a cube's surface can be deformed by pushing its corners or the surface as a whole inward. With a few simple operations, complex geometry can be generated. Learning to work with *Sauerbraten* is a matter of hours.

Since multiplayer mode also supports most of the editing functionalities, *Sauerbraten* is an ideal environment for remote collaborative design. Designers can work simultaneously on the same model and use the game's built-in chat function to comment on each other's progress. Additionally, setting up a game server is easy and inexpensive, as all CPU-intensive operations are performed client-side, and any computer with a fast Internet connection will work as well as a server.

Sauerbraten is a game engine, not a full-fledged modeler. Its geometry concept doesn't allow for perfect spheres or complex organic forms, but these can be imported as separate 3D objects. At its core, it is an easy-to-learn, quick-to-use and, above all, fun design tool.

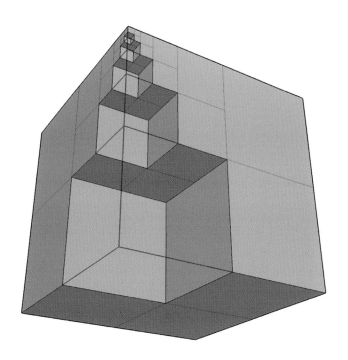

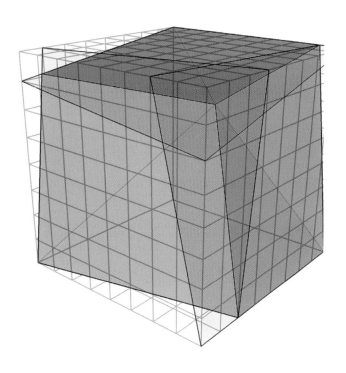

Project Description	Text	Project	Affiliation
	Wayne Piekarski, Bruce H. Thomas	Wayne Piekarski, Bruce H. Thomas	Wearable Computer Lab, University of South Australia, Adelaide, AU, 1998

TINMITH
Outdoor 3D Modeling Using Augmented Reality

The *Tinmith* system is a hardware and software platform that supports mobile outdoor Augmented Reality (AR). AR is the process of adding computer-generated graphics to a user's view of the physical world,
and *Tinmith* is an AR that provides its users with a
modified view of the physical world while allowing
them to move about freely in an outdoor environment.
With the *Tinmith* system, users are easily able to view
3D models of any structure while they are outside.
Users view the 3D data by using their body instead
of an input device. This is more intuitive than trying
to understand building plans on a piece of paper or
through a 2D interface on a desktop computer. The
user interface for *Tinmith* is based on a pair of cus-
tom-designed pinch gloves, that allow users to edit
information instead of just viewing it, unlike many
other AR systems. With the gloves on, the user is able
to select prefabricated objects such as trees and automobiles, place them down in the environment and
manipulate them intuitively – even when they are out
of arm's reach. The user is also able to create new geometry from scratch using a set of novel techniques
that we have termed *Construction At A Distance*
(CAAD). These allow users to freely create any kind of
outdoor object they desire by combining simple prim-
itives. They also enable users to form objects such as
buildings, outdoor features and sculptures with the
help of virtual carving tools. Possible applications of
Tinmith include help with town planning, previewing
new building designs and evaluating the environmental and aesthetic impact of new structures.

Project Description	Text	Project	Affiliation
	Wayne Ashley	Thomas Soetens, Kora Van den Bulcke with Patrick Bergeron, Jason Dovey, Matt McChesney	Workspace Unlimited, BE, CA, 2006

IMPLANT
Renarrativizing Architecture

Common Grounds: For the past five years, the artist collective Workspace Unlimited has been creating mixed reality events and installations that explore new forms of art, architecture and sociability. Conceptually tied to and physically installed in real places, the collective's 3D virtual worlds are part of an ongoing investigation into the immaterial architecture of information flows within physical space and its impact on notions of self, place and identity. Networked together via broadband Internet, these virtual worlds constitute an artist-driven platform called Common Grounds, an ongoing initiative for exploring the poetic possibilities of multiplayer gaming technology and augmented space and for developing critical dialogues and research opportunities in academia, industry and art.

The Hypermediated Building: Workspace Unlimited's newest work, *IMPLANT*, is situated inside the Art Nouveau building of Vooruit, a performing arts complex in Belgium. Navigating with a mouse and keyboard and projecting what they see onto various physical surfaces, online visitors from Montreal, Rotterdam and Gent together explore what first appears to be a sumptuous 3D simulation of Vooruit – a large maze of theater spaces, cafes, meeting rooms and offices. These can be traversed in much the same way that we move through physical space: walking upstairs, through doors, down corridors, around corners, inside and out.

But this logical order soon gives way to architectural and spatial inversions and reperceptions. As visitors move through the building, their glowing paths reveal a hypermediated environment of text, real-time chat, prerecorded and live streaming video of artists, activists and curators reflecting upon the conditions of urban life and technology, cultural hybridity and the virtual self. Each visitor's trajectory through *IMPLANT* renarrativizes the building and its function, offering multiple, simultaneous points of view that cannot be easily reconciled. Viewers share their real-time journeys with each other by using in-world virtual cameras that immediately project what they see onto specific walls located throughout the building. What appear to be mere projections, however, are actually entire 3D renderings of those portions of the world being filmed; viewers can instantaneously enter these images and join their fellow users in another part of the newly constructed world.

Augmented Space: Outside on the actual street, passersby peer into Vooruit's glass lobby only to see a projected simulation of the same lobby seamlessly integrated within Vooruit's façade. Instead of seeing the usual theatergoers purchasing tickets and socializing with friends, viewers observe the goings-on of *avatars* – real-time graphical representations of actual people in Vooruit – co-mingling and exploring the same simulated space with their counterparts. At the same time, a webcam outside Vooruit captures the scenery on the street, projecting the performances of everyday life back into the virtual world.

IMPLANT's power lies precisely in the interactions and gaps between these multiple spaces – in what the user in Gent is seeing and experiencing inside the virtual Vooruit juxtaposed to what (s)he sees and hears in the physical Vooruit. And even more, in what players in Rotterdam and Montreal experience inside the virtual Vooruit only and communicate back to those who are experiencing both spaces simultaneously.

www.workspace-unlimited.org/breakingthegame/vwa.htm

Project Description	Text	Project	
	Aki Järvinen	Aki Järvinen	2004

GAMEGAME
A Research and Design Process

–

In *GameGame*, players compete in designing games by collecting and trading cards in order to create a complete design. Throughout the process, one player gets to play a game publisher, while the other players try to sell their game concepts to her. In the end, the best game design is decided in a vote. *GameGame* tries to make Ludology – i.e. the academic study of games and their designs – accessible to the broader public in the form of a game. The game has another function as well: it can be used as a brainstorming exercise for coming up with new ideas for game concepts.

While playing and collecting the cards, players have to invent what the game elements represented on the cards mean for their game concept. What is the game's goal? What does the player do? What is the theme? And so on. Furthermore, players have to specify how the elements of their game interact because it is the interactions between the individual elements that put a game into motion. *GameGame* is essentially a theory that has become a game, and simultaneously a game that illustrates practical, applied theory.

Since 2004, I employed the game in a number of workshops both in industry contexts and in game studies and game design curriculums. In the play testing sessions and workshops I have been conducting, quite a number of wacky ideas have been introduced. Most importantly, playing the game has been fun for the participants.

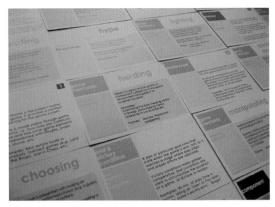

GameGame can also be applied to specific design topics if the players so desire. In the context of the themes of *Space Time Play*, for example, all *Game-Game* players in a given session of play could try to design a game about urban planning or agree that the environment cards should represent buildings. This kind of customization would give a particular focus to the playful brainstorming session.

http://gamegame.blogs.com
www.gameswithoutfrontiers.net

Statement | Text
_____

Jussi Holopainen,
Staffan Björk

DESIGN PATTERNS ARE DEAD
Long Live Design Patterns

The idea of design patterns originated in the field of architecture (Alexander et al. 1977). Aimed at making the design process more visible and thereby allowing nonspecialists to be involved in decisions, these patterns describe common design choices and how they relate to one another. Although the approach was not widely adopted by professional architects, it has remained popular among nonprofessionals and has proved even more popular in other fields, most notably in computer science, in which design patterns are an important part of understanding object-oriented programming.

The development of design patterns for gameplay was initiated in response to the lack and need of a design language for gameplay design. Using a slightly different template than for architecture, it resulted in a collection of 300 patterns (Björk & Holopainen 2004) dividable into several different areas. Perhaps the most concrete are patterns used for designing goal, action and information structures for the games. These subcollections of patterns are often used as the starting point for teaching game design patterns approach.

Since its development, the collection has been used in several workshops with students from several European universities to help them hone their analytical and practical design skills. After a brief introduction to the approach, students are given the task of identifying design patterns in games with distinct gameplay. This gives them a chance to gain first-hand experience in judging the success of a pattern as well as stressing to them that knowledge of how to work with patterns in general is as important as being familiar with a particular pattern collection. The patterns they identify, together with some from the main collection, are then used as design guidelines for developing a game concept, which, in turn, becomes more and more detailed through the incorporation of game patterns related to those originally chosen. Depending on the time available, this refined concept may then be turned into a low-fidelity prototype to allow feedback from others.

We believe that the workshops provide a feasible model for tutorials on patterns in general. These would be beneficial not only to professional game designers who can relate the approach to their current work, but also as applied in other fields – architecture, for example. In fact, working with more formalized design tools such as design patterns opens up possibilities for experimenting with creating rules for architectural design similar to those of games. In other words, these tools not only make it easy to incorporate nonspecialists into the design process, but potentially make it more fun.

◆ Alexander, C., Ishikawa, S., Silverstein, M., Jacobson, M., Fiksdahl-King, I. & Angel, S. (1977), *A Pattern Language: Towns, Buildings, Construction*, Oxford University Press, Oxford UK. ◆ Björk, S. & Holopainen, J. (2004), *Patterns in Game Design*, Charles River Media, Hingham MA.

Marc Maurer,
Nicole Maurer
Maurer United Architects

THE UNINHIBITED FREEDOM OF PLAYFULNESS

They lived in a very interesting time. Everything changed all the time. Nobody knew what given frames of culture to hold on to anymore. Maybe that was the reason why they were fascinated by nature so much. It was reliable, restful and all-embracing. Every time they examined or experienced it, it became even more beautiful. And they would gradually understand nature better. From time to time, they realized that *everything* was nature. Not only the leaves on the trees, but also the lampposts placed among the trees like steel columns, their glaring fluorescent light exposing at night the veined structure of the leaves. Their friends remained adamant that industrial products such as luminaries, cars, excavators and entire factories are the exact opponents of nature. However, they knew better.

It all began with the idea that human beings are superior and able to think independently – an arrogant idea that could only be conceived by humans them-selves. Of course, it might just happen to be true; but suppose it was not. They, on the other hand, argued that human beings are like all other animals, only capable of thinking within the framework nature has equipped them with, just like ants are capable of building anthills and otters, dams. And now, all of a sudden, it is supposed to be human beings' decision to mine iron ore and smelt it into lampposts in order to ensure safety in the streets of densely populated cities? Would it not be possible, after all, that it is nature itself that benefits from ore mining and ore processing? In a faraway future when any form of human civilization has disappeared, these new natural treasures might well be deployed for the benefit of other servants of nature. They would even venture to state that all actions undertaken by human beings would be by definition beneficial to nature. In their train of thought, environmental catastrophes would not be catastrophic to nature, but only to the environment of the human beings themselves.

This was their outlook on the world. They felt supported in this line of think-ing by the fact that not a single human being was personally involved in the *entire* trajectory, from ore mining up to and including the connection of lampposts to the electricity grid. After all, there was no one who steered all the decisions and all the stages of the implementation regulations of such a trajectory. Somehow, they took place in an organic way. They also saw their reasoning underpinned by their young son's huge mountain of toys in the colors red, yellow, blue and green. They themselves had only bought a fraction of the toys the child played with; most of them were presents from friends, or given on loan by parents whose children had outgrown them. No one would seriously claim that the plastic Lego puppets were a product of nature itself, the consensus being that plastic is a work of man and basically harmful to the environment. But they had not ordered these toys; they had just appeared of their own accord. Such natural processes fascinated them.

What could be the role of human beings in this whole scenario? They were convinced that the essential contribution of human kind to nature was *to play* with its materials and laws, to develop it a little further. Every child knows that nature only evolves by new and better combinations of already existing entities. The *act of playing* is very close to exploring and redefining existing boundaries. It supports innovation and evolution even more than classic science because it is based on experience but also on the uninhibited freedom of *playfulness*. "Like children, we play. Not to waste time, but to learn and develop skills until we find a more challenging field to conquer." This was, and still is, the motto of the architecture office they established some years ago. It shows immediately that this office is different from a conventional architecture office. Some of its projects have nothing to do with the building practice, but very much to do with architecture on the edge of its boundaries – in virtual reality.

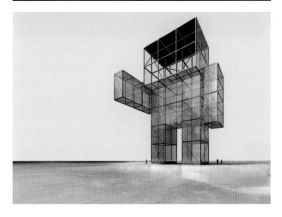

VIVA PIÑATA
Architecture of the Everyday

Before the Renaissance and before the invention of linear perspective, spatial experience was detached from imagery. Once the tools to depict three-dimensional space on a two-dimensional surface were developed, architecture and the understanding of space leaped into a new era. The possibility for a viewer to imagine him/herself walking around inside a painting opened up a whole new chapter in art as well as causing a fundamental shift in the experience of space. Earlier paintings used to put human activity, signs of power and emotional reflections in a symbolic relation. The experience of space was confined to the specific practice of building; architecture was media-specific. The genre Capriccio, which refers to paintings that depict architecture in idealist settings, is the first precursor of the representation of architectural ideas that computer programs have become so adept at creating. At the same time, Capriccio introduced the notion of virtuality, of something that is not real but can contain the properties of the real. This duality – this split between the real and the representation of the real or between the representation of objects as we see them and their measured description – has become more pronounced as each side is, in many ways unwittingly, mutually determined and transformed.

354

In 2002, in collaboration with the artist Palle Torsson, I initiated the "Production of Architecture" course for 4th year students at the Royal Institute of Technology in Stockholm. In the first years of the course, we used 3D tools bundled into games like *Unreal Tournament* (1999), *Doom* (1993-2004) and *Half-Life* (1998). But two years ago, we emigrated to the pervasive online platform *Second Life* (2003), where we have since been researching the limitations and possibilities of architecture. In a world like *Second Life*, where the production of desires has been completely overtaken by the market economy, the major influences on architectural thought are other media, as opposed to architecture itself. Rather than spatial experiences, architecture in such worlds is much more about images, television, movies and games. The image of space in virtual worlds bears direct relation to the fact that the image of architecture is becoming more and more dominant in contemporary architecture and the fact that we consume architecture as much through Hollywood, expensive coffee-table books and tourist information as we do through actually being in space. This contemporary obsession with external attributes and lifestyle aesthetics can also help explain the fact that in user-created virtual worlds, where one can do whatever one wants, design becomes so mainstream and totally predictable. The role model for housing and design in such worlds is more likely *MTV Cribs* – in which people also have the opportunity to do whatever they want as far as designing and building goes – than contemporary architecture and design.

Virtual online platforms are not breaking down any conventions as such, but they can help us to see things differently and maybe even think differently. This is not so much because they have changed something by celebrating its opposite; that would be more like continuing the same behavior but doing it in front of a mirror and producing a reflected image. Rather, because they may be able to change the way things change. A computer program like Excel has had a greater impact on contemporary architecture than have all star architects combined. When economic and architectural concepts become increasingly intertwined and opaque, the traditional role of the architect transforms, and the door to architectural decision-making is opened to professionals traditionally far removed from the design process. In virtual worlds, it paradoxically becomes possible to look beyond architecture as representation and instead discuss the underlying structures of architectural production. That is, virtual worlds are places where we can rethink social concepts, work, life and networks; they offer the possibility to stop thinking about what architecture looks like and start actually engaging in it.

In mainstream media reports on the phenomena of online worlds, the divide between the virtual and the real is most often presented as clear-cut. This black-and-white separation is somewhat problematic; it has been adopted from literature, especially from science fiction, based on a fantasy about parallel universes. Furthermore, it is only ever mentioned in relation to 3D worlds; no one really talks about being immersed in chatrooms or Web browsing. Since text-based experiences haven't been popularly inscribed into the idea of a cyberspace or a "Metaverse," they have avoided some of the oversimplifications attached to the preconceived understandings of 3D environments.

When it comes to architecture, there is a much greater difference between being an architect today and being one in the 1930s than there is between real and virtual architecture. Working with architecture in virtual worlds means that we have to re-search the specific properties of those worlds – how they are constructed, how their site and subjects are conceptualized and so on. In *Second Life*, the avatars take human form, can fly and have a unique visual ability, a kind of 100-meter-radius, 360-degree

way of seeing. The differences between virtual representations and real-life possi-bilities (one cannot fly in the real world) pose enormous problems when it comes to architecture. It is not until we fully understand this inequality that we can produce something that is really interesting. When architecture becomes more specific in how it relates to how we actually experience things then, maybe, we will see a completely new kind of architecture. But before that can happen, we really have to rethink al-most everything we know about architecture, which right now is almost completely grounded in how we operate in the physical world with all its limitations.

What we see now is, of course, only the beginning. We can choose to start mod-eling a type of architecture as similar as possible to the one in the physical world, but then we will miss the opportunity to engage in new ways of thinking about and experiencing architecture. Whether we like it or not, we live in a world where vir-tual architecture exists, with or without the help of architects. We would do best to prepare ourselves because this world is coming. With it come great opportunities to push the social aspects of architecture to the forefront, away from traditional models of representation and ill-disguised cynical trends towards a more down-to-earth, active and participatory approach to spatial questions – a world in which we are all architects, planners, engineers and builders of communities. It is a develop-ment that undermines a singular representation of the world in favor of a multitude of perspectives, shifting our understanding of inside and outside, producer and consumer, opportunity and annoyance. Most of all, it will set architecture in motion, allowing all kinds of individuals and groups to inhabit it.

◆ *Doom* (1993-2004), developed by id Software, published by Activision et al. ◆ *Half-Life* (1998), deve-loped by Valve Software, published by Sierra et al. ◆ *Second Life* (2003), developed and published by Linden Lab. ◆ *Unreal Tournament* (1999), developed by Epic Games, published by GT Interactive.

Statement | Text
_____

Kas Oosterhuis
Tomasz Jaskiewicz

798 MULTIPLAYER DESIGN GAME
A New Tool for Parametric Design

Designing architecture is serious play. It is a game whose goal is to create a great building. It is a game that designers need to play according to the rules of physics, economy and society. It is by nature a multiplayer game in which many specialists need to work together to increase their prospects to win. It is impossible to imagine designing contemporary architecture without computers. They have enormously accelerated many parts of the design process and opened up astounding new possibilities that have never been imaginable before. Parametric architecture, interactive architecture, mass customization and file to factory production: all these would not be possible without the use of digital technologies. Ironically, the common use of computers has also drawn designers away from meeting tables and stuck them into a single-player working mode. When we design, we are now confined to our screens and keyboards. We exchange information only when we *stop* designing.

The single-player way of operating in our digital workspaces makes cooperation between different specialists in the design process one of the most serious bottlenecks in a project's development. Each party involved in the design process has to wait for the work of other parties to be finished in order to continue with its own tasks. Thus it is absolutely impossible to verify all design variants or scenarios. Given that it already takes weeks to fully work out one design alternative, it would simply stretch the entire process into eternity if we were to investigate hundreds or thousands of design variations. As a result, designs are often just optimized from the point of view of one specialist, while others follow this dominant party, providing solutions for just one, very specific case. In this way, the whole range of design options that could be worth exploring is not even brought into consideration. The modern design process not only takes way too much time, but also hinders us from investigating all possible design alternatives. Given this, a new design method paradigm shift involving a change from single-player to multiplayer design has become an absolute necessity. The intention of the shift should be not only to accelerate the design process, but, more importantly, to enable the exploration of the whole possible spectrum of design alternatives.

Extensive research on this topic has been performed by the Hyperbody Research Group at the Delft University of Technology (TU Delft). The Protospace Lab, which soon will be located in the new iWEB pavilion on the university campus, will become a new kind of environment for multiplayer design. The research of Hyperbody at TU Delft is aimed at using real-time data exchange for serious play in architectural design. Various subprojects of Protospace have explored different ways of applying this concept. Protospace 1.1, for example, investigated the possibility of designing with many simultaneous views on one software application. COLAB project dealt with collaborating over the Internet. Protospace 1.2 and 1.3 involved research on the implication of interfaces that do not constrain our movement and communication abilities while working in a group. And the latest project, Protospace 1.4, along with the graph protocol, has managed to dynamically connect various applications used by different specialists working on one project. All this shows that multiplayer design is technically possible and within our reach, which will be definitively proven by a series of case study projects run in the final Protospace setup.

However, more important than all the technical issues of how to make things work is the whole new way of designing that these projects imply. Computers let us play together in real time. In a multiplayer game, the exchange of information happens instantly, many cycles per second. What will happen if design information gets exchanged immediately between different designers? We couldn't wait to see the answer to this question – that is, to see what implications such a radical change in design methodology will have. Thus, before the professional projects in Protospace started, we established a much simpler multiplayer design setup for our students in their design studio. The primary idea behind the project was to guide students in such a way that they would cooperate in an ambitious top-down-imposed master-planning scheme, but at the same time contribute their own bottom-up-designed subparts. These were meant to be designed concurrently, each one instantaneously negotiating with and mutually affecting its neighbors. Twenty-three students joined our design semester in September 2006. The design site we gave them was not the usual two-dimensional plot, but a large three-dimensional urban body. Each student was assigned to one of the 23 interlocking pieces of the three-dimensional puzzle. When put together, these pieces would form a giant sphere of 8,000,000m³ located in the middle of the 751 factory in Beijing, the eastern part of the 798 Art District. The sphere, partly submerged underground, would stand on small feet: a 20,000m² base. The rest of the 751 area was divided among a group of five students from the collaborating Southeast University in Nanjing. Their work proceeded in parallel to the one of the Delft students. Their designs, however, were based on a more conventional, two-dimensional starting point. Each of the students was encouraged to be creative and innovative; (s)he was allowed to develop any proposal as long as it obeyed the nine rules of the master plan:

1. Program is a mixed-use development of 1,000,000m² of built-up area.
2. Program is contained in a virtual sphere of 8,000,000m³, leaving 25% of open space for bringing light into the large urban body.
3. We provide the students with a three-dimensional puzzle of as many interlocking parts as there are students.
4. Each three-dimensional plot communicates and negotiates *only* with its immediate neighbors.
5. Each piece of the three-dimensional puzzle has a specific program of requirements (housing, offices, commercial, cultural, educational, leisure, etc.).
6. Location will be right in the heart of the 751 site.
7. Each plot administrates its data input, data processing and data output and communicates the parameters in a dynamic database with its immediate neighbors.
8. Each plot has to structurally support itself and communicate structural load data with its immediate neighbors.
9. The sphere must produce as much energy as it consumes.

The rules were designed based on the concept of swarm behavior. Each member of a swarm exclusively communicates with its immediate neighbor. The shape of the swarm is not imposed by any of the swarming members, nor does the swarm have any leader. Furthermore, members of the swarm have no awareness of the whole. The shape of the swarm is the balanced result of the bidirectional interactions between the acting members and of exterior climatic conditions that impose constraints on the swarm's size and direction. In the 798 master plan, the students are the bottom-up communicating swarm members, and the tutors represent the top-down control. The students from Nanjing working on the 751 area around the sphere were asked to approach their designs more conventionally. Their task was to react to the developments within the sphere and to provide facilities for those developments while accomplishing their particular design goals and creating an intermediate zone between the sphere and the rest of the 798/751 area and the sphere and Beijing. Three-dimensional plot distribution according to the master planning scheme dictated that some designs had to be located above others. This implied that some projects had to be structurally supported by others. It also meant that plots not directly connected to the ground level of the sphere had to be accessed through other plots. Thus students could not design without respecting what their neighbors were doing. Design decisions made by each one of them would always require adjustments in the design decisions of the others. As a result, the students saw for themselves that under such conditions, designing in a predefined, fixed way is extremely inefficient. The circumstances forced them to think and work parametrically so that projects could be changed instantly as their surroundings evolved.

Parametric design may be easy in principle – providing that designers can swiftly use all the technologies that the digital era has made available to them – yet it may still be difficult for those with a traditional, top-down educational background and a lack of needed technical skills. Therefore, students were split into three technical study groups to help them with particular technical difficulties that they encountered in their assignment. One of the groups was responsible for organizing the data exchange between all evolving designs. The second group concerned itself with the structural feasibility of all the projects. And the third group researched ecological issues, focusing mostly on energy use and consumption and making sure that the combined energy used and produced by all the projects together would balance out. The pressure put on the students in the data exchange group was the most intense, as they were the ones responsible for developing a means of exchanging information amongst the 23 designs – one that could be immediately applied to the design process. To do this, the students – with the help of their technical and design tutors – developed a database prototype for storing and exchanging design data and an interactive three-dimensional tool to locate points within the sphere where information was being exchanged. The information exchanged through this tool was related to structural loads, transportation and other custom-defined data, all of which combined acted as the instant parameters for mutual adaptation. Each design plot had predefined boundaries. This meant that all information potentially affecting a plot's neighbors was specifically related to a position on the sphere. Thus if structural loads were expressed as three-dimensional vectors anchored on a plot's surface, then the flow of people or cars would be simply a positive or negative value on that surface. This information could be easily structured in a database and immediately accessed by parties that were using it as parameters for their projects. It is not difficult to imagine more parameters being exchanged between the 23 complex adaptive systems to play the architectural design game to the full potential in real time.

The final result of the design project was astonishing. Together, all the designs successfully formed a giant structure. If built, this structure would have all the qualities of a small city, but instead of being spread over a two-dimensional ground surface, it would function in three dimensions on all detail levels. Even though the students were forming one large entity, each of their designs was absolutely unique as a separate concept. Some embodied well-defined, fixed architectural spaces. Others flexibly responded to the demands of their users. Many of them consisted of a high number of cellular elements, while others were just singular entities that combined all inner spaces under one skin. Together, they filled up the entire volume of the sphere.

Although the data exchange between the designers was not conducted in real time and was achieved with primitive technical means, the outcome of the studio showed that there is great potential for true, three-dimensional interactive urban design. It has proved that designing with instant communication between members of the design team produces far greater results than doing the same work in steps. In this particular case, each of the 23 designs became one part of a swarm that formed a whole much greater than just the mere sum of its parts. In the student project, everyone had the role of "designer." The only variation in their responsibilities stemmed from the unique three-dimensional boundaries and positions of their projects. The next logical step in the multiplayer design method is to introduce other specialists to the design process, who could validate and influence the concepts from structural, material, economic and other points of view. This would produce a more comprehensive result in the end. It would also guarantee that the final result is optimized in every respect. Only an architectural design game that takes this comprehensive approach will truly accelerate the design process and, more importantly, produce spectacular and sustainable results. This would definitely make all the design team players want to play another multiplayer round right away.

Project Description	Text	Project	Affiliation
	Winy Maas	Winy Maas with participants from the affiliated Institutions	MVRDV NL and Delft School of Design, TUD NL with the Berlage Institute NL, cThrough NL, MIT US, 2006-2007

SPACEFIGHTER
A Game for the Evolutionary City

SpaceFighter is a game meant to model the complexity of time-based competitive urban developments. It seeks to reflect on and compare imaginable, forecasted, interactive urban processes, actions and reactions. It compares series of selected and possible projective simulations, results and outcomes of urbanistic chain reactions. *SpaceFighter* builds on the accumulated knowledge of MVRDV's *Regionmaker* and *Climatizer* (Dekkers et al. 2004). But as a game, it can go beyond scenarios because an unlimited number of outcomes can never be produced by mere scenario making. And while the *Regionmaker* was focused on scenario building and the comparison of scenarios, *SpaceFighter* aims to model the interactive process beyond scenario making. Scenarios are based on a given, limited set of outcomes, while interactive models can generate outcomes that never could have been imagined beforehand. One can imagine that as soon as a scenario has been laid out, reactions occur. And as soon as these reactions have appeared, the planner is forced to interact in order to deal with these reactions. This, in turn, results in a new interaction, which in its turn triggers new reactions, and so on.

SpaceFighter seeks to model interactive urban development as an evolutionary process. The spatial "battles" that can be composed of or read through the spatialization of economic, demographic and sociological developments are, like battles in the biological world, about competition – survival even. This competition might lead, therefore, to the emergence of new urban configurations, new colonizations or entirely new urbanistic "species." *SpaceFighter* connects the biological model with urbanistic reality. It reveals the evolution within urban space – faster than fast in a competitive world.

In order to use *SpaceFighter* in planning, hypothetical interactive chains must be compared and can be validated. This means that they should be connected to a scoring device that can activate decision-making processes. Perhaps this is the core of the Evolutionary City – here software meets ideology, here it activates or motivates democracy.

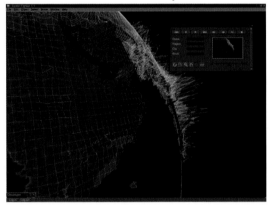

Last but not least, *SpaceFighter* is not just composed of one game; rather, it should be seen as a platform of emerging and competitive games. These games can be played simultaneously, but with different "clock-cycles." They are independent games played in the same arena that influence each other just as do events in the real world. In order to function as a collaborative platform, these games need a common representation and a common language, perhaps also accompanied by a new "translator" that continuously updates itself in order to fulfill these needs. A scoring device accompanies this platform so that the user can validate its action. Perhaps the "fittest" games are those that produce the most offspring games.

◆ Dekkers, D. & Wieland & Gouwens (2004), *MVRDV: The Regionmaker*, Hatje Cantz Publishers, Ostfildern.

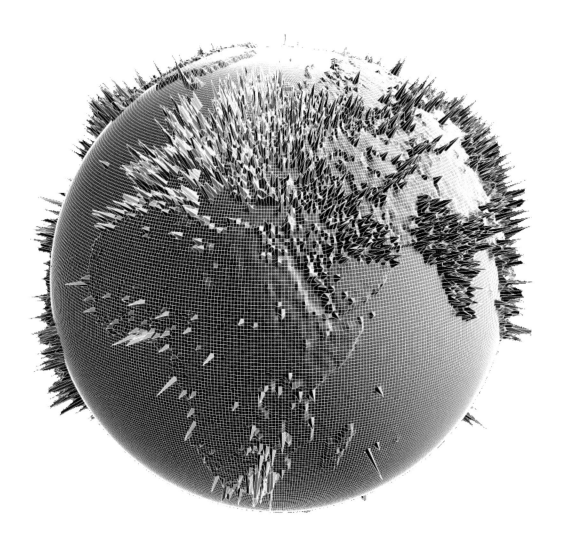

Project Description	Text	Project	Affiliation
	Alexander Lehnerer	Markus Braach, Oliver Fritz, Ludger Hovestadt, Alexander Lehnerer, Steffen Lemmerzahl, in cooperation with Kees Christiaanse	Chair for CAAD, Chair for Urban Design, ETH Zurich, CH, with changing partners, 2000

KAISERSROT
Roundtableware and Statistical Design

Based at the ETH Zurich, the *Kaisersrot* research explores the potential benefits of integrating the computer as active device into the urban design process. *Kaisersrot* combines method with technology, thereby enabling urban guidance beyond common geographical zoning and plan layout; the form, location and program of anticipated buildings, plots and infrastructures are not stipulated. Rather, urban material is guided by rules that require no fixed envelopes, but instead make room for individualized threshold negotiations along certain performance standards. Such "interplay" and its outcome are processed and synthesized by the computer.

Over the past years, *Kaisersrot* has developed design solutions ranging across various levels of granularity and different urban issues. It all started with the hope of letting future inhabitants participate in the design of their own neighborhoods. In *Kaisersrot*, the layout

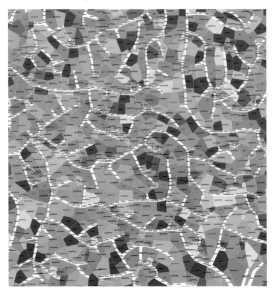

of inhabitants' parcels and their subsequent infrastructures are neither drawn nor designed, but rather arrange themselves according to the individual inhabitant's desired plot size, neighbors and proximity to public services, lake and forest. A potential layout crystallizes when each inhabitant's wish list is processed and the equilibrium of concurring interests is reached. In a study for the City of Zurich, we had to place a building on an extremely delicate area next to Zurich Main Station and the river Limmat. No matter how hard we tried, the building would always block important views to Zurich's churches, Lake Zurich or the Alps. So we designed software to generate and optimize the building's internal organization according to the specific requirements of all necessary functions depending on the building's maximum potential envelope and location. Thanks to this "consensus-machine," we were able to leave the locational decision up to the city's administration: it could choose any location and respective volume, and the program would always generate a building with a viable infrastructure – immediately. Thus this project clearly demonstrated *Kaisersrot*'s amazing capacity to play through scenarios according to changing conditions.

In the "Oceania" part of Dubai's "The World" project, we used this ability to test the compatibility of certain programmatic mixes with varying island layouts. These simulations provided an increased development accountability: they created worst-case envelopes or thresholds within which development might still take place – not via abstract Excel sheets, but via three-dimensional representations of potential building masses. With *Kaisersrot,* users immediately see what they get thanks to a seemingly bizarre hybrid of statistics and actual design measures.

www.kaisersrot.com

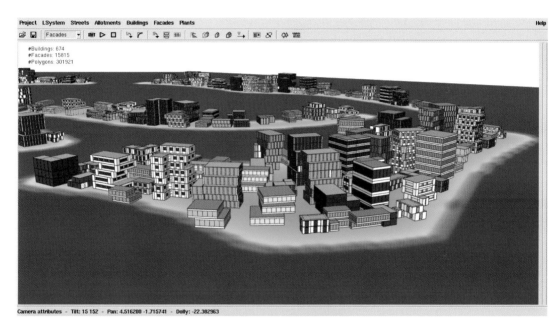

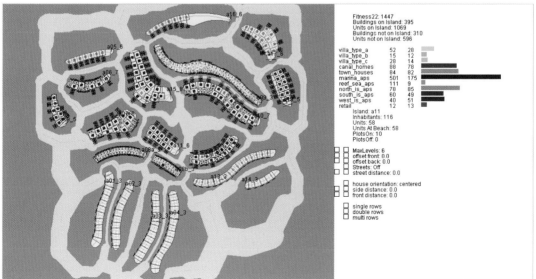

Project Description	Text	Project	Affiliation
	Rafael Ballagas, Steffen P. Walz	Rafael Ballagas, Steffen P. Walz	Media Computing Group, RWTH Aachen University, DE, Chair for CAAD, ETH Zurich, CH, 2007

REXPLORER
A Pervasive Game for Tourists

REXplorer is a mobile, pervasive spell-casting game designed for tourists visiting Regensburg, Germany. The game uses location sensing to create player encounters with spirits (historical figures) that are linked to historical buildings in downtown Regensburg. A novel mobile interaction mechanism of "casting a spell" (making a gesture by waving a mobile phone through the air) allows the player to awaken and communicate with a spirit. The game is designed to make learning history fun for young (and young at heart) tourists and influence their path through the city.

A new research field known as "Serious Games" attempts to channel the unique ability of video games to engage their audience to help inspire, educate and train their target user base (Prensky 2001). In *REXplorer*, the Serious Game concept is applied to tourism, helping young visitors engage with the history and culture of their destination.

The game's storyline is based on a mysterious tombstone engraved in a secret language whose symbols are linked to paranormal activity in the city. Fictional scientists have created a special measurement device (a packaged mobile phone available for rent) to research this relationship. Drawing the gravestone symbols in the air using the device excites medieval elements (wind, fire, earth and water) and establishes a communication channel to the spiritual world. As the players progress through the game, they encounter spirits that are located in front of significant buildings. The spirits reveal, through the phone loudspeaker, their "cliff hanger" stories related to significant events and periods in the city's history and then send the players on different quests. Points are rewarded for encountering new characters and completing quests and thereby influence players' movement by leading them from site A to site B.

The gesture recognition process is supported through camera-based motion estimation. As motion samples are collected, they are rendered on the screen, allowing players to see their gesture progress. *REXplorer* is the first pervasive and mobile game to enable magic-wand-style spell-casting.

At the end of the game, users are presented with a souvenir blog customized to show their personal experiences in the city. The blog includes an interactive map to indicate their path through the city and highlight points of interest that they visited.

◆ Prensky, M. (2001), *Digital Game-Based Learning*. Mc-Graw-Hill, New York NY.

www.rex-regensburg.de/im-stadtraum/rexplorer/
http://wiki.arch.ethz.ch/twiki/bin/view/Main/RexPlorer
http://media.informatik.rwth-aachen.de/REXplorer.html

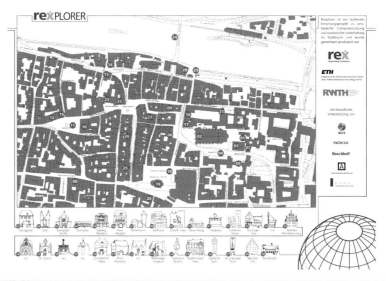

Game Review	Text	Developer	Publisher
	Ragna Körby, Tobias Kurtz	SCEE Studio London	Sony Computer Entertainment Europe, 2006

PASSPORT TO ...
The PSP as City Guide

Handheld game console with a 95x54 mm TFT LCD/480x272 pixel display, a 1-333 MHz power PC processor and a 166 MHz graphics processor. Storage options: UMDs and 8-3GB Memory Stick (PRO) Duo. Built-in stereo speaker, USB 2.0, IrDA, WLAN, GPS.

The PlayStation has become portable! In its new format, PlayStation Portable (PSP), the game console forsakes playrooms and living rooms and works its way into leisure time, working life and new city locales.

The PSP comes with a crystal clear LCD screen and excellent graphics so that virtual 3D gameworlds and even DVD-format films can be displayed in the highest quality. The Memory Stick gives users the additional power to play with their personal picture, audio and video data on the PSP.

The travel guides *Passport to...*, specifically designed for the PSP, enable the console to make a first foray into real city space. Together with Lonely Planet, Sony developed a software that is not a game, but rather a fact-based application that guides users through various cities with photos, street maps and thematic tours (so far, versions for Amsterdam, Barcelona, London, Paris, Prague and Rome have been released).

The *Passport to...* travel guides for the PSP are conventional as far as content is concerned, and they sort information according to the familiar categories (Eating, Sightseeing, Partying, Sleeping).

Impressive pictures combined with short descriptions of locations and facilities are directly linked to the most important map segments. As on Web browsers, chosen locations can be added to a Favorites list. An integrated daily planner takes on the job of generating day trips based on randomly selected data from the various categories. This function is enhanced by built-in WLAN and an accompanying Internet platform, which enable users to load itineraries from other users directly onto their PSPs or to make their own itineraries available to others. Periodic updates guarantee a consistently top-notch performance: the travel guide can read the ever-changing city, extract up-to-date information from it and connect the traveler directly with all it has to offer. The city is transformed into digital information communicated via the PSP interface, which serves as a link for the "player" between the abstract data and the real city space.

Unlike previous mobile consoles like the Game Boy, the PSP can also be equipped with a GPS attachment. This attachment allows the PSP to make use of location-based services (LBS), meaning that virtual gamespaces and the real spaces surrounding users will blend together in the game console. In the long term, then, the PSP will become interesting when its functions can be appropriated by its users, making local actor updates available and subcultural networks and information platforms accessible to visitors unfamiliar with a given city location. Once that happens, the PSP will have become a device that makes new perceptions and uses of cities possible.

Project Description	Text	Project	Affiliation
	Mathias Fuchs	Mathias Fuchs, Steve Manthorp, Vera Schlusmans, Umran Ali, Kelvin Ward	School of Computing, Science and Engineering, University of Salford, UK, 2004

PLASTICITY
A Multiplayer Urban Planning Game

PlastiCity is a multiuser computer game based on the architectonic visions of British architect Will Alsop. Alsop's suggestion of replacing two of the most prominent buildings in the geographical center of Bradford with a lake was highly controversial. We used his urban planning provocation as a driving idea for designing the game.

PlastiCity enables residents of Bradford to experiment playfully with the city they live in. Based on a modification of the popular Unreal Engine, new tools and functions have been coded to provide players with special wands. These tools are point-and-shoot devices that encourage the players to instantly change the city. With them in hand, players can explore their urban environment, build or demolish buildings and modify existing buildings. In an intuitive way, the players can move and rotate buildings, shrink or expand them or apply new surfaces to their walls. In doing so, they have to come to terms with various planning strategies and problems. They also have to understand that they are not changing their city as individuals, but are rather partaking in a mutual exchange of suggestions and planning acts.

PlastiCity began with an investigation into the history of urban planning and research on cities of the future. Guided by Alsop's statement that "the absence of joy is the biggest threat to our society," we tried to emphasize the playful elements in urban planning and to question the technically more serious approaches.

PlastiCity is not concerned with construction costs, the diameter of water pipes or interest rates. Rather, it borrows Joseph Beuys' notion of plasticity as a universal term for thought and speech and introduces it into the arena of urban planning.

The first project phase of *PlastiCity* was conducted with the support of Lightwave Partnership, a Bradford-based organization. Phase One consisted of reseach into the "Master Plan." During this phase, we created a prototype with basic gameplay, 11 buildings implemented as realistic architectonic models and a set of functions for the modification and decoration of those buildings. The game has been tested in single- and multiplayer situations with different age groups. Whereas the first phase concentrated on existing historic buildings, the next phase will introduce specific "possible buildings" like the extension of a museum or a notorious mushroom building. The players of the game will be able to change the lake's water level and change Bradford into a Venice of the North, a subaquatic town or an island. Phase Two will also allow us to implement collaborative decision-making strategies for urban planning. We also intend to introduce ethnic-, age- and gender-specific gameplay elements.

Phase Two will intensify the dialogue between game designers and urban planners. We hope to receive suggestions for buildings and even building strategies from Alsop Architects. On a more practical level, the office could provide us with 3D models to be exported into Unreal. In return, we could provide Alsop's office with statistical data harvested from the game.

370

 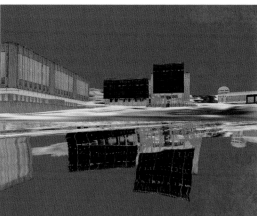

Kees Christiaanse (KC)
in conversation with Alexander Lehnerer (AL)

RULE-BASED URBAN PLANNING
The Wijnhaven Project, KCAP (Rotterdam)

AL
In the Wijnhaven area of Rotterdam today stand five high-rises founded on an urban design from KCAP. But there was never a plan for where and how these towers should be developed. The only things definitively specified were the slimness of the towers, the maximum base areas and the requirement that each have an unobstructed view of the Maas. Why no plan?

KC
Working with rules instead of a fixed plan was more or less an accident. At first, the rules were merely a form of service specifications or a catalog of requirements for how one could pack the at that time somewhat run-down Wijnhaven neighborhood with living space. From there, the idea grew: why not make these rules precise enough that they could serve not only as *our* guidelines, but as generally binding guidelines for any future investors and builders in the area?

AL
How does such a specification process work in relation to personal objectives?

KC
Naturally, these methodic tools are always meant to serve a vision. In this case, it was the vision of Manhattan; not the one of tall buildings, but of small ones – of SoHo or Greenwich Village, where smaller structures tower between Wilhelminian-style edifices and old industrial lofts. This vision was then mixed with the aforementioned catalog of requirements and, together with the consideration that in urban development one can hardly regulate everything, inspired not an exact definition of the building site, form, etc., but rather a limited number of interconnections in the form of rules.

AL
There are thousands of possible spatial articulations that obey these four to five rules. How can you be sure that among those articulations there won't also be some unintentional variation whose side effects aren't covered by your rule set?

KC
Many city neighborhoods function so well in terms of diversity and vitality precisely because their development is not determined by an excessive number of rules. But I must admit that we could not test every detail of the plan, and it contains an array of uncertainties that we must resolve or tinker with in further development.

AL
How does one communicate projects with such intrinsic uncertainty to the city or the public?

KC
I confess I am still surprised every time I see a new tower standing in Wijnhaven. A plan like this is not only hard to communicate because of

its unorthodox methodology, but also because it concerns tall buildings standing close together – something controversial in every European city. Maybe it was precisely the experimental character of our approach that contributed to the fact that I can now marvel at the fifth tower.

AL **On the one hand, your plan gives individuals more freedom to choose; but when there are numerous parties involved, this gives rise to an uncertainty of outcome. Can't this unpredictability also hinder the process?**

KC It is indeed a dilemma to afford individual freedoms and incentives and simultaneously intervene strongly enough that in the end the desired security of results is achieved. Especially in smaller areas, one quickly runs the risk of restricting oneself so much that only a quasi-fixed urban design remains. In this regard, we urban planners still have a lot to learn from good games.

AL **But even in Wijnhaven, the saying holds true: "the early bird catches the worm." The investor who wants to build a tower at a later date has limited leeway because he will often be blocking other towers' views or because potential building sites have already been allocated, etc.**

KC That's right, and it is a very large constraint upon the flexibility of a project. Moreover, cumulative constrictions produce an urban design normalcy: buildings emerge at the beginning and they, in turn, determine the conditions and context for further buildings. This coherence is indeed banal, but extremely important for the cautious development of an area.

AL **So you wouldn't call it unfair?**

KC No. It is a fully transparent approach and, no less important, it prods potential builders to invest as quickly as possible in order to secure the largest possible degree of freedom for their projects.

AL **A partial loss of authorship: rule-based urban design projects imply cooperation with others. The corollary to this polyphony is that the urban planner must concede a degree of control over the outcome. How can this willingness to compromise be used as an advantage?**

KC People who, like us, practice this type of city planning are always anxious to downsize. In other words, the less necessary we are – which, of course, will never be completely the case because we'll just create more refined rule sets – but the less we are needed and seen, the more successful our work and, ultimately, the project. The loss of authorship is a matter of psyche or vanity that is not important to us; being able to realize our design ideas is.

AL   **Whether in Wijnhaven or in the computer-aided *Kaisersrot* projects, your work is more about regulated spatial proceedings than about games. So why is it still worth it to reference the concept of a game?**

KC   I ask myself that as well. Once, architect Matthias Sauerbruch made a reference to our use of games in which he mentioned that there is actually no reason to play, but that a happy lifestyle always invites one to play. The game is surely not so much the goal of the discussion, but rather a recurring loop of undertakings that lead to inspiration for setting specific rules.

AL **Thomas Vinterberg once explained in an interview that rules are so important for him and his Dogma films precisely because they are capable of generating something like freedom. As a city planner, you use rules, amongst other things, for the very same reason. Why is freedom so important for urban design projects and those who participate in them?**

KC Freedom is important for all the players in the urban field, from landlords right up to tenants and the frequenters of public spaces. This obviously somewhat vague conception of freedom can thus actually be viewed as a basis for the functionality of a city, but not so much for the urban planning project per se. Nonetheless, when this freedom is allowed to develop individually, it engenders certain standards from which one can deduce important laws about urban planning. One learns from observing and adjusts accordingly.

AL **Rules in games and rules in urban planning are in this regard comparable?**

KC Definitely as far as their ability to create room for maneuver is concerned. The analogy to game rules is probably also useful for moving away from pure determinism to guidance through connections and mutual interdependencies.

AL **Do you have a favorite game?**

KC Regatta sailing.

AL **What about it intrigues you?**

KC The casting off of more abstract patterns in extreme physical conditions.

TIT FOR TAT AND URBAN RULES

Visible and Invisible Urban Hands

Economist Adam Smith's "invisible hand" describes a social mechanism by which each individual, while pursuing his own good, tends also to promote the good of his community. In contrast, the invisible hand of today's free market does not necessarily follow this altruistic conception. It relies on each individual's rational maxim and tendency to enlarge profit by the exploitation of his environment. It is very doubtful that these two invisible hands ever shake – unless maybe forced by a visible one. In Smith's time, before there were any explicit urban regulations, the common law of nuisance was still functioning. The latter offered latitude and was one of a very few guiding principles; it generally prohibited any person from using his land or property in a way that unreasonably interfered with the enjoyment and use of another person's property. But ever since the spawn of a new metropolitan reality at the beginning of the 19th century, both Smith's hand and the common law proved equally incapable of mediating between private and collective interests. New tools were needed that could anticipate developments, socialize the city, steer private development and simultaneously ensure its freedom. The City Beautiful movement – and the spectacular failure of Burnham's 1909 plan to reshape Chicago à la Haussmann – offered no plausible way out. Unlike Europe's autocratic examples, the North American endeavor failed because Chicago's private property successfully refused to be shaped by Burnham's much-too-visible hand. But by their actions, Burnham and his colleagues posed one of the most crucial questions within the discipline of urban design, made explicit by Jonathan Barnett 70 years later in his book *Urban Design as Public Policy*: "How can the city be designed, without designing its actual buildings?" (Barnett 1974)

The City's User Interface

Cities usually accomplish urban design goals in two ways. The first is through direct public investment in public property. Examples of this include the construction of parks, city buildings and infrastructure. The second method, which is the more intricate one, is the exercise of some form of control over private property when the public interest merits protection from an urban design standpoint. In other words, it is the attempt to relate certain private decisions to the form of the total environment. The latter method of urban design requires an additional procedural quality: the capability to adjust control, which means to establish a form of control via dependencies and relationships rather than prescriptions or limitations. But how can that be done? To find an answer, leave this essay for a moment and return to the games discussed in this book. Scrutinize the relationship of the single player towards the community of players and towards the game's guiding body. All these relationships could be roughly described as being established via more or less explicit rules within a certain field of action. But does the transfer of such rule- or game-based approaches to urban design help to solve Barnett's paradoxical question? Quite justly, you will remark that almost any city, given its limited interaction capacity, already heavily relies on rules in the guise of building codes, statutes and laws. Indeed, these urban rules somehow act as both the municipality's user interface and as the "rules of play" for private property. However, the mere existence of rules does not alone make a game. In fact, to pursue this goal would be overly ambitious and a little naïve anyway. The challenge of bringing a city's institutional regimes closer to a game's context instead lies in revising the rules of a city in terms of rigidity, scope and relational capabilities.

Good Rules, Bad Rules, the Rulers and the Ruled

Many of a city's rules lack potential to provide latitude or freedom for development and, as a result, limit the incentive for further individual engagement. This problem is clearly made evident by the very old but still pertinent example of the town of San Gimignano. In 1255, the height of the town hall tower was stipulated to be the maximum height for any further tower within the city limits. Thereafter, the booming physical development that had characterized the city came to an immediate end. The competition between striving aristocrats had triggered the building of higher and higher towers; each extra meter manifested the aristocrat's superior standing. But under the popular pretext of protecting public health and well-being, individual freedom was curtailed in order to keep the bold builders' loose stones from falling on the citizens' heads. However, setting the maximum building height to that of the town hall's was both arbitrary and very negligent: the threshold was too low! Any moderately wealthy aristocrat would have been easily able to construct a tower of that height and even higher had not the primary building incentive – namely, to top one's neighbors – been thwarted. Fun was over, the city coffers were drained by the plague and Florence's rise made San Gimignano politically irrelevant. Either excessive restriction, a shortage of means or missing motivation narrowed the scope of building possibilities for those who had long played a major role in shaping the city's identity.

Game Over!

Unlike San Gimignano's nobility, the classic New York developers of the last century were not easily intimidated by the city's institutional regimes. Invariably, they built and continue to build to the law's limits and into its loopholes. But the City of New York apparently likes to join in on the fun – as if the friction and contradiction between possibility and restriction were the necessary stimulus for a vital development of the city. Even though New York's regulatory body also relies on dimensional standards such as max. height and bulk, the possibility of blurring these thresholds by negotiation and special bargains is virtually built into New York's zoning ordinances.

Form Follows Rule

In the 1960s, New York's high-rises rapidly shed their formerly wedding-cakish appearance (just think of 5th Avenue) in favor of slender, elegant towers. Additionally, they started to hover above ground level, offer direct connections to the subway system and even provide benches to rest upon. Had their developers suddenly and unanimously become do-gooders or overly susceptible to the forces of style and fashion? Certainly not! The 1961 zoning revision had changed the rules: in addition to definite thresholds, the city introduced so-called incentives that allowed for developing greater amounts of floor space if public amenities were offered in return. Such tit-for-tat rules fit well into New York's cutthroat economy and produced over 500 privately owned public spaces such as plazas, atriums and passageways all supposedly open to the public, scattered across the city. Since the regulation's enactment, 82 acres of not always good quality public space created 16 million square feet of additional floor area (Kayden et al. 2000). Some of New York's best buildings reflect this development. Just think of the Citicorp tower's spectacular formal character: the impressive and costly floating of the main building mass – clearly motivated by the public space bonus system. By connecting usually separate realms – public space, floor area and height – the incentives also triggered a process of morphological differentiation, hard to trace but quite beneficial for the city. Buildings such as Metlife or One Penn Plaza manage to peer out over an otherwise generalized and uniform height limit. In this sense, what seems at first glance to go against the rules actually helps to loosen the usual uniformity that results from universal guidance.

Gentleman Trump's Loopholes

As an expert in challenging and playing with the city and its rule sets, Donald Trump managed to exceed the determined height limit for his Trump World Tower at United Nations Plaza almost as if there were no restrictions at all. On the purchased 20,083-square-foot lot, Trump was able to legally build a tower ten times the size of the plot's floor area – 200,830 square feet. But because the slender tower doesn't cover the whole plot, there is an empty space around the base of the building. In zoning terms, this space is considered a "plaza." As such, it earned Trump the aforementioned plaza bonus, which let him build 20% larger. He was thus legally able to add 40,166 square feet to his tower, whose very slenderness makes it seem even taller. But it didn't stop there. Trump also took a close look at the surrounding buildings and their plots. The plots are all covered by buildings, but not ones that extend to their full zoning-limit heights. After being offered considerable deals, the owners of seven of those plots willingly sold their virtual potential to build higher than they had. These air-rights were transferred to Mr. Trump and from then on belonged to him as development rights. Piled up on his own plot, these rights allowed him to exceed the original zoning another 526,105 square feet of floor area. Now, the resultant 767,101 square feet are stacked on top of each other. As the zoning resolution does not include any ceiling height limits, Trump further simply extended his ceiling 20% higher than average and thereby pushed the height of his tower even farther up (Chapman 2000). Starting with a potential building merely ten times the size of his lot, Trump now has a tower more than 38 times the size. At 856 feet tall, the tower clearly breaks the gentlemen's agreement of not building higher than the flanking UN Secretariat. And not just by a little, but by more than 300 feet!

Blackjack or Poker

Most of today's building codes are introduced to supersede direct contact with the owners of the building's immediate surroundings: as long as a new building adheres to the code, no controversy or negotiation with its neighbors' owners will ever have to evolve. This expedites processes but, on the other hand, also contributes to a segregating, generalized and universal guidance. Therefore, this context-free regulation will hardly be conducive to the creation of differentiated and diverse built environments.

The regulation creates a blackjack game of sorts, and playing continuously against the bank is more likely to become boring and monotonous than playing poker with a bunch of others around a green-covered table. Some city building codes indeed comprise rules that trigger object-oriented negotiations between neighboring entities and thereby offer differentiated guidance for differentiated contexts and users.

Once the urban designer acknowledges this potential and regards rules as instruments for design rather than mere restrictions of it, his predominant task will be to devise settings, operational rules and procedures that finally more closely resemble games than orthodox plans. Physical expressions such as buildings and infrastructure will quite naturally materialize through this game-like process, negotiated by its immediate stakeholders – vision-guided but not necessarily planned by a mediating institution.

◆ Barnett, J. (1974), *Urban Design as Public Policy; Practical Methods for Improving Cities*, Architectural Record/McGraw-Hill, New York NY. ◆ Chapman, P. (2000), "Built with a Merger here, a Bonus there," *Real Estate Weekly* no. 6 December. ◆ Kayden, J.S., The New York City Dept. of City Planning & the Municipal Art Society of New York (2000), *Privately Owned Public Space: The New York City Experience*, John Wiley, New York NY.

LIGHTLY AUGMENTING REALITY
Learning through Authentic Augmented Reality Games

Two teams with similar training and background are called in to handle environmental crises at different sites. The crises are quite similar, involving recently discovered contamination of the groundwater supply in high-profile locations. This means that the outcome is not only important for the health and well-being of area residents, but is also of concern for public relations.

The teams have the same tools at their disposal, and they set about their work taking samples to determine the extent of the contamination and interviewing experts and witnesses to uncover the underlying source of the contamination. After some time, the teams come to the same conclusion about the source and location of the contamination: it is from illegal dumping that dates quite some time back, and it is centered on a highly visible and valuable location on the site. They agree that there are no substantial health impacts caused by the presence of the toxin, since the local water supply does not come from the groundwater. They also agree that there are some legal and ethical concerns related to the problem, but those are less clearly defined and subject to interpretation.

But that is where the agreement ends. One team submits that the only proper way to handle the crisis is to follow the suggested protocol for handling the particular toxin – namely, by putting giant drill rigs in the middle of the site and pumping out the toxin over the next few years. The other team submits that given the absence of dangerous health impacts, they can be more discrete in what they do. Putting drill rigs in the center of the site will have a substantial negative impact on the location. Erecting a huge, noisy and ugly set of drill rigs will make the location look bad and worsen the contaminator's already tenuous relations with the community. The rigs will be what everyone driving by the site each day sees, and that could jeopardize future projects.

How did these two teams with such similar training, background and information come to two entirely different conclusions about the course of action that should be taken in this circumstance?

Degrees of Virtuality

In fact, these two teams did not have *exactly* the same information. When the team that advised following suggested protocol looked out at the community, they saw a 3D virtual representation of that community and saw themselves as avatars walking around in a Multi User Virtual Environment (MUVE). The second team, on the other hand, looked out and saw the actual community that it was studying, supplemented by a small amount of information available on handheld Personal Digital Assistants

380

(PDAs). In both cases, the toxic spill was (fortunately) simulated, and all of the sampling information came through virtual simulated instrumentation. Though the MUVE was an immersive and interactive environment, it did not capture all of the information of the real world. It did not, for example, contain the multitude of pedestrian and automotive traffic passing by the site or the details of individual buildings and people. Nor could it entirely capture the feel of physically moving about in the real world. Thus, when it came time to make decisions, the team that was actually out in the field was able to draw upon many of these intangible factors in suggesting a more nuanced solution to the problem, one which clearly incorporated personal experience in and observation of the given community.

The PDA-based version of this "game" (Klopfer & Squire 2005) was the first of what has become a series of Augmented Reality (AR) games created by the MIT Teacher Education Program. These are really what might be described as AR-lite (referred to as Pervasive or Ubiquitous Games by others). Participants in these games do not wear immersive helmets or don backpacks filled with equipment. Instead, they are equipped with location-aware PDAs (that use GPS outside and Wi-Fi positioning inside) that give them virtual information about their surroundings in the form of virtual data, interviews with game "characters," audio, video, images and text.

We are often asked why one should go through so much trouble creating games that require participants to trudge through the outdoors, sometimes across great distances, when it would be much easier to create 3D environments from which players sitting down at their computers could get the same information much faster. In fact, there are many advantages to a 3D world, such as being able to zip around from end to end in a matter of seconds, obtain multiple perspectives on the world and create visualizations in real time. However, these come as a tradeoff for forfeiting "feeling real" – that is, for forsaking some of the nuanced elements of the real world that foster a sense of realism and consequence difficult to create in entirely virtual environments, even highly immersive ones. I thus argue that in games in which decision-making is critical, the effort necessary to situate these games in the real world comes with great benefits – the realism of the real world for free.

In the world of "serious" or educational games, that sense of authenticity of experience and the associated actions of participants make the AR experience powerful and pertinent. In cases such as the one described above, in which the game is being used to train people to handle realistic situations, that sense of authenticity can be the difference between making flippant and informed decisions. People have acquired sophisticated skills for collecting information from their physical surroundings and using that information to make decisions. AR games capitalize on those innate skills to enable players to incorporate much more information than the game explicitly provides them. This makes AR particularly well-suited to helping people understand and come to complex realistic decisions that include a variety of social, political, scientific and practical considerations. Whether these be decisions made by professionals in training about recovering from an environmental disaster or decisions about the future of a neighborhood made by its residents, they are highly complex, and people need experience in order to make them.

Location Specificity

Of course, setting these games in the real world comes with real costs. One cannot simply play the same game at a new location. At a bare minimum, one must reposition a given game at a new location to make sure that players don't need to go out into the middle of a pond or enter an inaccessible building to obtain a critical piece of information. One option is to create games that can be played in generic playing spaces – a playing field, for example, or some other open space perhaps. This approach enables the game to be transported relatively easily, yet still has the advantage of preserving many of its real-world elements.

To really incorporate elements of the real world into an AR game though, one needs to connect the game to the physical place in a deeper and more meaningful way. When we were re-authoring (Squire & Klopfer 2007) the Environmental Detectives scenario for new locations, we worked with local facilitators to connect the games to particular elements of the actual location. At one location, this was achieved by making use of an interesting local topography and a history as a military base. At another location, it was done by connecting the game to a past record of actual illegal dumping on the site. These connections enhance AR games in two fundamental ways. First, they focus the game on the particular place where it is played, encouraging players to seek out and explore real information about that location and use whatever knowledge they possess about it. Secondly, they make creating an engaging game experience easier for designers: if a game's creators can connect players to the real world, the world itself will supply many interesting twists, turns and nuances that would be extremely hard to design into the game intentionally. The connection between the physical and virtual spaces furthers the sense of authenticity on the part of players, allowing them to see themselves as active participants in the game. They can influence the course of events and also be influenced by them, and thus feel as though their participation matters. Feeling a connection between the game and themselves enables players to develop much deeper understandings of the context in which the game is played.

Allowing designers to focus on connections with physical locations requires relieving the burden of location-based authoring. To that end, we have designed an AR editing tool that is currently in use at nearly 50 locations around the United Stated and will be publicly released shortly. This tool allows designers to import maps of their locations through Google Maps, automatically tag GPS coordinates and place virtual characters, data and media across their chosen locations. They can tailor information to individual roles within the game and create interactive spaces that change over time and respond to the actions of the players. In this case, the designers are schoolteachers who are creating or customizing games for their schools. Students can then use these games in their classes and, in some cases, become the designers of the games themselves.

Place-based Scenarios

Tapping into the realism of the real world not only requires deeply linking game content to game location, but also means choosing scenarios that can benefit from being situated in the physical world. The subject matter that we have chosen for games spans many topics, including environmental and health sciences, forensics, community development and even history. Many of these games are played by students (from the middle grades through university) learning about these topics, but they are also played by adult professionals seeking training in new areas and citizens seeking to understand complex issues.

There is another dimension of reality that we have so far eschewed in our games – real time. Most of the games that we have created compress time so that a week of events may happen in an hour. While this allows us to recreate certain events in the short timespan of a game, it does remove some of the sense of reality that we are trying to create. Our next iteration of AR game design is a game that can take place in real time across days or weeks instead of in compressed time in the span of a few hours. In this way, we hope to embed games within the lives of players, enabling them to check on whether simulated readings have changed when they happen to be in the vicinity of a particular location or to talk to a virtual character whom they happen to "bump into" when they are going about their daily routines. This means that the game no longer has tightly controlled physical or temporal boundaries and that players can think and strategize over long periods of time: in other words, it better approximates the way that players might really consider such problems and issues.

This is the future of AR-lite – games that can be casually played by regular players and engage those players with challenging and fun real-world problems. We have seen the rise of mobile devices (like cell phones and handheld platforms like the Nintendo DS, for example) as the platforms of choice for casual games designed for older players (over 18). AR games tightly linked to the real world and to relevant problems can tap into this trend and engage the emerging audience.

◆ Klopfer, E. (2006), "Blurring Lines with Mobile Learning Games," *Educational Technology Magazine*. [in press]. ◆ Klopfer, E. & Squire, K. (2005), "Environmental Detectives – The Development of an Augmented Reality Platform for Environmental Simulations," *Educational Technology Research and Development*. [in press]. ◆ Squire, K. & Klopfer, E. (2007), "Case Study Analysis of Augmented Reality Simulations on Handheld Computers," *The Journal of the Learning Sciences*. [in press].

SCENARIO GAMES
Vital Techniques for Interactive City Planning

In front of me, I have a poster for the *World Game 78*. Its introduction text reads as follows: "Energy, food, and resource shortages, environmental degradation, widespread poverty and political and economic instability reflect the ineffectiveness of existing policies and institutions to cope with global problems. Technologies, policies and specialized solutions, which do not take into account the complex and interdependent nature of society and the earth's biosphere, only intensify the crises. The World Game was introduced in the early 1960s by architect/designer/educator Buckminster Fuller. It is a procedure for enabling individuals to become participants rather than spectators in exploring new ways to service world-wide human needs in such areas as energy, food, shelter, communication and health care."

Buckminster Fuller's game was played at several workshops at the "Toward Tomorrow Fair" in Amherst, Massachusetts in 1978 and at several other occasions later on – for example, at the "Critical Paths to a Sustainable World" conference in the International House, Philadelphia in 1981. Its poster raises a few questions: "Does the world have enough resources for 100 percent of humanity? Can the basic needs of the world's 4.4 billion individuals be met [this is 1981!]? To what degree should values determine technology? Can needed technology be culturally and ecologically appropriate? Can the world make a peaceful transition to the resource-limited world of the future? What is our critical path?" And more. It then states: "The World Game, an innovative global planning tool, engaged in the development of strategies for making the world work for 100% humanity, will examine these questions and answers."

Fuller was far ahead of his times in his thinking about resources and energy and about the global nature of these issues. He also recognized early on that we would need interactive game structures to stimulate and sustain cooperation across disciplinary boundaries and political divides. His *World Game* remained at the workshop level only, but as I read these texts now, having never seen any results of the games, I get the uncanny feeling that we are now living in his future and are facing the crisis he was warning about. At that time, he did not yet know that the environmental crisis of global warming would, in fact, become the first big threat to humanity on a worldwide scale. His games – and I presume they were *scenario games* – were meant to identify globally relevant issues and analyze which technologies could be potentially helpful in dealing with them. He was an innovator: everything he made was a prototype, from his *Dymaxion map* to his *geodesic dome*. His dream was that these prototypes could be placed at the service of humanity through the vehicle of his games. Although in the late 70s *The New York Times* dedicated almost a whole page to him and his theories (imagine that today!), those theories were never seriously applied. But today, his "planetary planning" seems extremely relevant, as do his ideas for cooperative games in which participants become active actors.

Unaware of this, we started to do *scenario games* at the Architectural Association (AA) in London in the mid-90s. At that time, I had never really looked into Buckminster Fuller. We were working at the opposite end of the architectural spectrum: poetic form and material narratives, space as the vehicle for narrative meaning, the playfulness of John Hejduk's work with its use of simple and reduced-form language to deal with complex emotional states – these were our points of focus, although this started to change as we came into contact with people like Gordon Pask. We became interested in the dynamics of cities and their character; somehow narratives emerged in projects. "Traces of the city soul" was the title we used for an investigative project in Rotterdam. We tried to see how something evolved in the city and tried to simulate that. At the time, Pask, one of the fathers of cybernetics, was teaching with me in the AA unit. He talked about conversations and the learning process involved when actors conversed with each other. He also talked about the "underspecified," an aspect important in creating a narrative proposition for a project. The "underspecified" became an important component of narrative scenarios, since in *scenario games*, a reality is only gradually built up with fragments thrown in by participants. A reality is sketched out, while hard facts are only intermittently used when needed to create a precise moment or place a precise object or action. This is the act of dreaming up or imagining a strand of life through the city.

A *scenario game* is a simulation of reality, but of a limited reality composed of the ingredients a player puts into it. But *scenario games* are also aimed at testing a project, or better, a prototype. Prototypes are organizational forms given life in a scenario. The *scenario game* creates a context as an evolving narrative. The prototype, once inserted, evolves within the game – proliferates, adapts, mutates or dies. As several players insert prototypes, these coevolve and merge or cancel each other out.

Scenario games are planning methods to test the viability of prototypes before they are developed by the participants. A *scenario game* should be the community of a prototype; to sustain this community and its interactions through the game and the life of a prototype is the key to the success of a coevolving plan, a dynamic master plan.

Over the years, we developed game rules and started using the four basic processes we formulated after many attempts with role modeling and other characters failed: erasure, origination, transformation and migration as the drivers of the game. The four basic processes create the dynamic substance of the narrative while importing other key processes that form a reality through which a prototype can be tested. Participants are actors through these processes, but become authors once they insert prototypes. We have played *scenario games* in the AA, in Tokyo, in Taiwan, in the USA, in Austria, in France, in Switzerland, in the Netherlands, with universities, with the Ministry of Infrastructure in the Netherlands, with the light firm Zumtobel and recently in Edinburgh with the joint architecture faculties of the Edinburgh College of Art and the University of Edinburgh to develop fusion projects for their imminent joining of programs. Both at Buffalo University in New York and in Edinburgh, I introduced the world map as a second stage of the game after starting with maps of greater Buffalo and greater Edinburgh. The world map was an homage to Buckminster Fuller and an attempt to see where we could pick up from his *World Games* now that we are facing a truly global crisis and have to deal with carbon reduction and the use of renewable energy sources to try to stave off an environmental catastrophe along with social unrest and political turmoil.

In March 2007, we organized *scenario games* in Xiamen, China with three teams of students from different countries as well as local authorities and other invited decision-makers in order to address the issues of introducing carbon-trade-financed urban planning methods in China, where the explosive growth of cities will generate the latest addition to the environmental problem of global warming and possibly push it past the point of no return. *Scenario games* are becoming tools in the negotiation of much-needed prototypes that have to be inserted into master plans in order to be tested, but also to create a cultural and political mindshift in the populations of cities, soon more than 50% of the world's population. *Scenario games* will soon become vital techniques for interactive city planning that must be taught in the architectural curriculum.

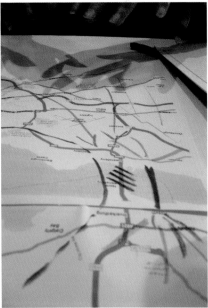

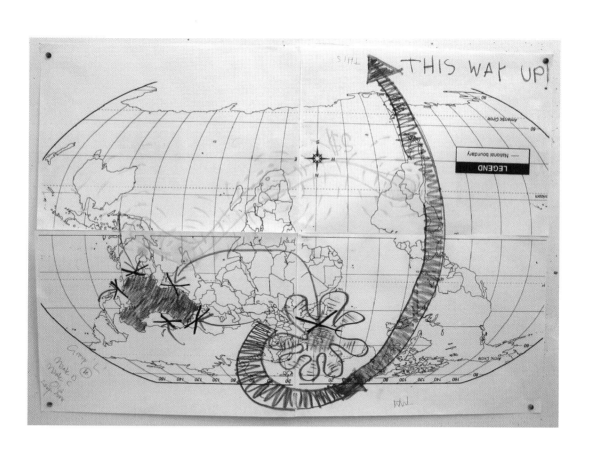

Project Description	Text	Project	Affiliation
	Tobias Løssing, Rune Nielsen, Andreas Lykke-Olesen, Thomas Fabian Delman	Tobias Løssing, Rune Nielsen, Andreas Lykke-Olesen, Thomas Fabian Delman	Project Havnen på Spil, Architecture Office Kollision, University of Aarhus, Aarhus School of Architecture, DK, 2003

THE HARBOUR GAME
A Mixed Reality Game for Urban Planning

The Harbour Game is an innovative, collaborative, game-based approach to urban planning. It was specifically designed for development of the harbor areas in Aarhus, Denmark, and it utilizes mixed and Augmented Reality techniques developed from an AR-Toolkit platform (www.hitl.washington.edu/artoolkit). The game development was completed in 2003. *The Harbour Game* is a debating game that employs a large game board, simple rules of play, visual tracking and pattern recognition to superimpose information – e.g. three-dimensional models, text and photos – on physical artifacts, thereby facilitating the understanding of complex relations in urban planning. The overall goal of the project is to challenge existing approaches to urban planning in which citizens typically are invited to join the process only after the plan has already been formulated, leaving no room for constructive and proactive participation, but only for reactive "yays" or "nays."

During the design and evaluation phases, we discovered that the single most important tool in serious game design is what we call "The Realism Scale." If you want to engage a wide variety of users, you cannot design a game based on very realistic simulations of real-life scenarios. To keep the game accessible to everyone, you must focus on simple rules and abstract issues. This, unfortunately, means that the final results will be similarly open-ended, especially in comparison to results from game simulations designed for experts with complex rules and highly detailed levels of information.

Through the game-based approach, we succeeded in actively engaging the citizens and making the debate concerning the future of the harbor areas in Aarhus an entertaining experience. We concluded that game-based citizen participation presents three benefits: it is fun, it is inclusive, and it facilitates basic learning. However, the results from the

game were too open-ended to be used meaningfully in an urban planning context. But *The Harbour Game* points to new possible uses for IT-supported games in planning processes.

www.havnespil.dk

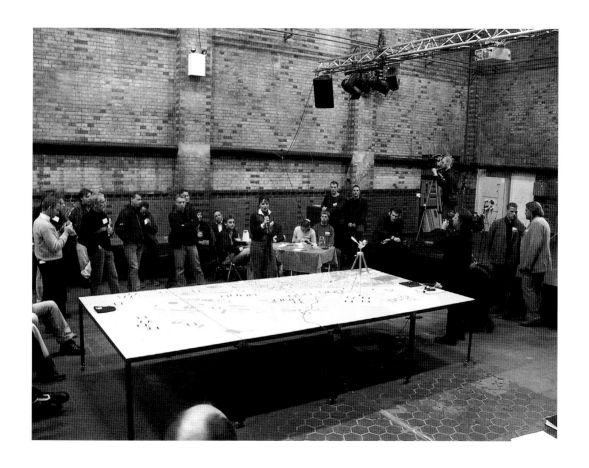

Project Description	Text	Project	Affiliation
	Frank Lantz	Nick Fortugno, Frank Lantz, Katie Salen with Janet Abrams, Mary de Laittre, Alex Terzich et al.	University of Minnesota Design Institute, Minneapolis, US, 2003

BIG URBAN GAME
A Playful Connection of the "Twin Cities"

In 2003, the University of Minnesota Design Institute commissioned game designers Katie Salen, Frank Lantz and Nick Fortugno to produce a city-wide game for the "Twin Cities" of Minneapolis and Saint Paul under the guidance of Institute director Janet Abrams. The goal of the project was to develop a tool that would change people's perspective on the urban space around them. In pursuit of this goal, the designers transformed the "Twin Cities" into the world's largest board game.

The *Big Urban Game (B.U.G.)* was a race between three teams, each of which was attempting to move a 25-foot-high inflatable game piece through a series of checkpoints over the course of five days. The game was played by residents of the Twin Cities. Players began participating by joining one of the three teams: Red, Yellow or Blue. Each day, local newspapers and the game's website showed the current locations of the three pieces along with two possible routes to each piece's next checkpoint. Players chose the route that they wanted their piece to take, submitting their votes online or through an 800 number. Each afternoon, a team of volunteer movers carried the pieces through the city, following the selected route. The time needed to travel the route was recorded and added to the respective team's total time.

During the days of the race, each piece stood as a kind of temporary monument at its given location, where it became a center for community activity. Players could visit the piece's location and roll a giant set of dice. The totals generated by each team's dice rolls were compared, and the team with the highest total got a head start in that day's run. On the last day of the game, all three pieces raced towards the final checkpoint. Each team's total time was calculated, and the team with the lowest cumulative time was declared the winner.

The alternate paths between each day's checkpoints were carefully chosen to present players with challenging decisions – one route might look shorter, but go uphill, while another one might take the piece down a street with heavy traffic or many low-hanging power lines. By drastically reframing the familiar territory of the players' urban environment, the game forced them to see that environment with fresh eyes.

B.U.G. was inspired both by the large-scale artworks of Claes Oldenburg and Christo and by the large-scale game dynamics of the New York Marathon and the Tour de France. The designers wanted the project to work both as a visual spectacle and as a participatory system complete with interesting choices for the players and the dramatic tension of a real competition.

http://design.umn.edu/go/project/TCDC03.2.BUG
www.decisionproblem.com/bug/bug2.html

Project Description	Text	Project	Affiliation
	Elizabeth Sikiaridi, Frans Vogelaar	Elizabeth Sikiaridi, Frans Vogelaar with Chloe Varelidi, Nina-Oanna Constantinescu, Katy van Overzee	hybrid space lab, Amsterdam, NL, 2004

SUBCITY
A Big Urban Game for the 2010 European Capital of Culture

The Ruhr region in Germany has long been defined by its underground, its subcity. In this mining area, the coal seams were the determining factors of historical development. Industrialization – and hence urbanization – were literally based in these subterranean layers. The heterarchical patterns of the above-ground phenomena mirror the submontane beds and follow the course of the mining galleries.

As an ex-mining area, the Ruhr Valley region is conscious that its sublayers represent the foundations of and driving force behind its development. Nevertheless, the way it views and approaches these sub-layers is somewhat ambiguous. The deeper layers are occupied by forgotten mining galleries, inaccessible tunnels and groundwater lakes. These underground areas reverberate with disasters from the past, the peril of the void and the threat of water.

The game SubCity focuses on these sublayers of the city. The game, played on mobile devices, reinterprets and recodes the communal urban substratum. In SubCity, inhabitants of and visitors to the Ruhr region can simulate and recreate the deep layers of the cityscape. They can dig virtual tunnels and mining galleries, develop and revitalize an urban underground and live there with their avatars and dreams. Together, they can recreate and transform the underground systems, weaving a solid tissue of hope under the city network.

-> roaming the urban network, searching for connections to the SubCity -> the keyholes to the SubCity are spread throughout the cityscape: you, the player, have to find them -> the moment you pass through a keyhole you become an actor in SubCity -> you communicate with your fellow actors and their dreams

-> using the SubCity tools, you exchange and interact -> while interacting, you create your avatar, the actor of your dreams -> you search for new keyholes -> the moment you repass through a keyhole you become a new actor -> you pass through the next keyhole -> in search of your docking elements -> in search of your home ->

The SubCity game can be played in a decentralized manner with mobile devices. It can also be played in groups or even in large communities.

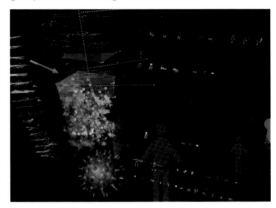

The virtual space of SubCity is only accessible in the City of Essen at the colliery of the Zollverein - a landmark of the Ruhr region, a UNESCO World Cultural Heritage site and the only working entry to the underground network. There, in a spatial interactive media simulation, you can enter this networked space of urban dreams and interact with the communal substratum of the cityscape.

SubCity is part of Neighbors Network City (NNC), a project proposed in 2004 by hybrid space lab (Amsterdam) for the Ruhr region and The City of Essen, which will be the European Capital of Culture in 2010.

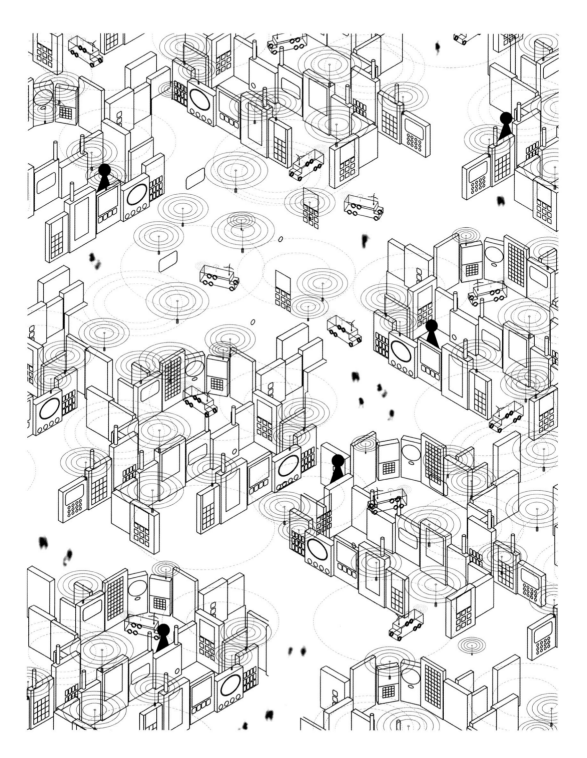

Project Description	Text	Project	Affiliation
	Troels Degn Johansson	Rasmus Nielsen, Jakob Fenger, Bjørnstjerne Christiansen with Rune Nielsen	Superflex, Copenhagen, DK, 1998

SUPERCITY
Visualizing Values in a Virtual World

The project *Supercity* grew out of *Karlskrona2*, a concept developed by art group Superflex along with architect Rune Nielsen in connection with an exhibition of relational art organized by the regional art society, Blekinge Museum in Sweden in 1998/99 (Gunér & Ernkvist 1999). Later on, the concept was adapted to the city of Wolfsburg, Germany as part of Superflex' first solo exhibition during winter 1999/2000. In later solo exhibitions and in its book, *Superflex Tools* (Steiner 2003), Superflex renamed the concept *Supercity* to stress its adaptability to other cities and its affiliation with Superflex' other projects ("*Supergas*," "*Superchannel*," etc.).

The concept consists of a virtual world based on a geographical 3D model and a large video screen to be raised in the host city's center. In its first inception, the idea was to facilitate a dialogue in the virtual world of *Karlskrona2* in which local citizens could model, negotiate and act out their visions for the future of the city. Karlskrona is a city of approximately 60,000 inhabitants in southern Sweden, which, during the time of the original exhibition, was undergoing change due to recessions in the navy's workforce and the introduction of a new local government initiative concentrated on the IT industry and higher education. Life in the parallel world of *Karlskrona2* was supposed to be displayed on a large, central video screen and thus form part of the public space of the city center. However, this part of the project was never realized, nor was the development of the actual game software. *Karlskrona2* thus only ever existed as a pilot version, a modification of the Active Worlds software running on this company's servers.

As a tool for urban planning, then, *Karlskrona2* is meant to function as a stage for the virtual representation of values and visions for the future (Johansson 2004), not for prognostic depictions of planned changes in the physical environment. The system indicates where users may "build" – i.e. make virtual models – and where not. In the case of *Karlskrona2*, the demarcations were established by locating Karlskrona's UNESCO-protected large square in the center of the virtual world, and letting users model their visions in the periphery. The physical and symbolic presence of the square thus represents both Karlskrona's historical Golden Age, when the city dominated the Baltic Sea, and the lack of possibilities following the reduction of the fleet and the preservation of a large part of the city space.

Although never fully realized, *Karlskrona2* is a testament to the interest taken in contemporary art by a city facing difficulties and change. *Karlskrona2* has been threefold canonized: by media scholars studying the development of virtual worlds and their references to places in the physical world; by planners interested in the application of new media to public participation in city planning; and, finally, by art critics following the strategies pursued by Superflex and other artists working in the field of relational and social art.

◆ Steiner, B. et al. (ed.) (2003), *Superflex Tools*, Walter König, Cologne. ◆ Gunér, T. & Ernkvist, P. (eds.) (1999), *Three Public Projects: Mike Bode, Superflex, Elin Wikström*, Blekinge Museum, Karlskrona. ◆ Johansson, T.D. (2004), "Staging Relations: Relational Art and Network Technologies in Superflex' Staging Strategies," in T. Mäkelä et al. (eds.), *Proceedings from the 12th International Symposium of the Inter-Society for the Electronic Arts*. Center for Media Culture in Finland, Helsinki.

www.superflex.net/tools/supercity

Project Description	Text	Project	Affiliation
	Rahel Willhardt	Björn Barnekow, Tobias Engel, Fiedel, Sven Neumann, Packet, Papillon, Tim Pritlove, Prom	Chaos Computer Club, Hamburg, DE, 2001

BLINKENLIGHTS
Look Who's Talking!

Small gifts sustain friendships; big ones can help make interactive media history – at least that is what the Chaos Computer Club did with the spectacular façade installation it gave itself as a 20th birthday present in 2001. Not only that, but the club also gave every halfway computer-savvy person the chance to participate in the creation of the project: whoever sent a symbol formation to the founder had a good chance of seeing it in colossal size, shining from the wall of the "House of Teachers" at Berlin's Alexanderplatz.

For five months, the building morphed into a computer-controlled playground, on whose illuminated façade silhouetted drawings, animations and love messages flashed about. Those passing Alexanderplatz in a playful mood could even use the classic example of GDR architecture as a gigantic screen on which to play the computer game *PONG* (Atari 1972): one cell phone call sufficed to enable players to drive a digital ball across the house by simply clicking the phone's keypad.

From a technical point of view, the *Blinkenlights* installation was based on an archaic prototype: 144 building emitters turned each of the windows in the building's top eight stories into a "pixel." So that the giant 8x18-pixel area always formed a coherent whole, relays, five kilometers of cable and three programmed control computers were used.

Last year, using similar technology, the Berlin agency realities:united bestowed Berlin's Potsdamer Platz with a gigantic display screen. The agency used 1,800 standard round lights situated in well-ordered relation behind the glass façade of the park colonnades.

Their coordinated alternations allowed gigantic digital art to shine upon a normally boring building wall. The project was an image-building measure for the real estate company HVB Immobilien AG, which was campaigning for new renters. In three-week cycles, there was a nonstop virtual coming and going in the "large capacity gallery." Amongst other things, the installation included a work from Rafael Lozano-Hemmer, which invited passersby to input important life questions into a terminal and then watch as they marched across the building in huge letters.

The Berlin SAP office at Rosenthaler Platz developed a similar artistic-dialogic, nocturnal life of its own, albeit a much more technologically complex one. For the company's 2004 inauguration, a deep blue spread itself across the building's stories at night. The "hidden world of noise and voice," developed by the New York based artists Golan Lewin and Zachary Lieberman, translated noises into forms and colors that then wandered through the house, so that the installation came alive through the voices and warm hands of pedestrians. The technical platform still remains and now hosts yearly changing art installations: sometimes night-owls can "ice up" the fixtures by laying their hands on them, sometimes "Magic Mirrors" trace human movement through colors or number clouds.

In the past years, artistic combinations of architecture, light and media have become common means for drawing attention to likeable art. It is less frequent that buildings are converted into stages for the minds and spirits of *flaneurs*, who can participate in images

www.blinkenlights.de

merely by passing them by; then, in the spirit of Bertolt Brecht's "Radio Theory" and its credo of dissolving the roles of sender and receiver, passive observer becomes active participant. But how wide does freedom extend? What happens when citizens of these newly created urban playrooms not only use art for art's sake, but also for expressing political claims or displeasures? Neither the media technologies used nor the action artists themselves preclude such uses. Ultimately, it is up to the users whether such installations will contribute to a pluralistic appropriation of the cityscape or devolve into decorative marketing gimmicks.

Antonino Saggio

THE NEW MENTAL LANDSCAPE
Why Games are Important for Architecture

I am naturally interested in the relationship between games and architecture.

I've long been an inconsistent and capricious player of computer games. I well remember *Dark Castle* (1986), which I played often with my son Raffaele when he was three and the Mac jumped to 512K of RAM from its original 128. In the year 2000, I had a rather profound relationship with *L'Amerzone,* designed by Benoît Sokal (1999). It belongs to the genre of adventure games, and I found it beautiful. For years, I would occasionally dream about some scene from *L'Amerzone*; I have mentioned Sokal's game in several public venues, and some of the game's screenshots have appeared in serious books. In 2001, I started to play *Myst III* (2001), certain of whose subterranean biological worlds I found beautiful, but which is overall a less emotionally involving game than *L'Amerzone*. So there you have it: my experience as an electronic player.

Now let's address what appears to me an interesting question: why are games important for architecture? There are architects like Lars Spuybroek, Marcos Novak and Kas Oosterhuis for whom the analogy between games and architecture is rather direct. Games are in several ways similar to the type of architecture they design. Games establish a set of rules that govern different forms of behavior. Architecture that employs this same rules-based approach can be just as mutable, changeable and interactive as electronic games.

But the question still remains: why should we be particularly interested in this?

To try to answer, we must introduce a key concept that can shed some light on the matter. I call it the "mental landscape" concept. In a word, "mental landscape" refers to the fact that architects of the new generation are working to make an architecture that draws upon certain aspects and characteristics of the virtual world. More specifically, architects "born with computers" are trying to spawn a new era of architecture that incorporates some of the mutable and interactive characteristics of electronic environments in general and electronic games in particular. For them, the importance of virtuality and information technology lies not in how they can help create newer, better *virtual* worlds, but in how they can *be returned to materiality and inspire a new type of architecture*!

Of particular interest to these architects is the generation of games that afford users the possibility to create their own environments. In such games, explains game designer Katie Salen,

> "You can see the relationship between the role of creation and imagination and... architecture development...Games on one side, and interactive and mutable architectures on the other, share methodology, share techniques, share possibilities to orient the practice of architecture towards understanding and shaping buildings as contexts for user interaction." (Salen 2006)

398

By allowing them to create their own space, games inspire players' imaginations and open their minds to the many possible configurations, spaces and behaviors that can ignite architectural thinking.

But imagining is a rather dramatic act, particularly when it is used for artistic purposes. In the minds of today's forward-thinking architects, imagination represents a means to negate the past industrial and mechanic paradigm in favor of an informational and interactive architecture. In this way of thinking, imagination is not just about creation, but also about negation and breaking rules. This, however, presents an interesting contradiction.

Imagine Marcel Duchamp, a key person in this discourse. "Why is he so important?" you may ask. For two reasons: For Duchamp, imagination is on the one hand all about breaking the rules (think only of his famous urinal!). But, on the other hand, Duchamp is the man who did nothing for several years but play chess, a game that is all about moving *within a set of rules*. Hence the contradiction: breaking the rules through active negation of artistic convention (e.g. the urinal) but then living almost as a virtual slave to rules (e.g. playing chess). It sounds incredible, but this is exactly the contradiction that we as architects *must face*. We must make use of imagination's ability to inspire new art and negate convention and at the same time accept a well-defined set of rules. Architects must operate like a pendulum swinging between these two opposites.

When considering the moment in which "games" became important for architecture, one must take into account a very serious crisis – namely, the moment when the modernist functionalist approach to architecture revealed itself as no longer useful for addressing contemporary artistic crises, and, as a result, the CIAM broke down both as a paradigm and an institution. It was at exactly that time – i.e. in the 1950s – that games assumed an increasingly important position in architecture! I am thinking of Dutch architect Aldo van Eyck, whose ideas originated from an anti-CIAM approach. The key to architecture for van Eyck, as well as for Alison and Peter Smithson and other members of Team X, was no longer a mechanic relationship between function and building. For these "new" architects of the 50s, architecture had to relate to anthropology. Their approach was a kind of new humanism to which the physical and psychological presence of man in space was integral. Games became an extremely interesting area of study for these architects.

Let us turn to another Dutch artist, Constant, and to the European Situationists generally. Naturally, the whole Situationist way of thinking focused on "how to break" certain rules of functionalistic and mechanistic cities and architectures – how to open the door to completely new visions. In the 60s, Constant and the rest of the Situationists ensured that the architectural discourse was confronted with the idea of creating a whole new set of rules within which new behaviors and new adaptable architecture could grow.

Given that games are unquestionably relevant to architecture and always have been, the above discussion hardly seems adequate (as you may have noticed, I didn't even touch on the most well-known syntactic approaches to game-architecture relations – namely, Wright's Froebel construction blocks and van Doesburg's neoplastic planes!). In other words, it is necessary to rethink the historical role of games in relation to architecture. More importantly, we must focus on the future intersections between the two. Naturally, there are environmental, user-community-related, modeling and constructive aspects of architecture that may benefit from games, but what I find most important is the *aesthetic* dimension. (And by aesthetics, I do not mean style, but a form of synthetic denotative knowledge.) Try for a second to imagine the modernity of functionalism and rationalism without their aesthetics. What would the modernist approach be without its aesthetic vision? Aesthetics was the blood that gave life and strength and direction. Coming back to the original question: why do we need to use and think about and elaborate upon games? Why are games important to contemporary architecture? I present my answer as five points:

Because games incorporate the recursive, changeable architecture of our electronic mental landscape.

Because games leave the construction of the environment to the users themselves.

Because through games, it is possible to address crises (*L'Amerzone* is all about addressing crises!) and move the imagination in new directions.

Because games share some performative aspects with music but are also task-oriented and based on algorithms.

Because games incorporate metaphors and interactivity, which represent the mainstays of the electronic esthetic of our times.

The list, of course, remains open and is sure to be lengthened in due course.

◆ *Dark Castle* (1986), developed and published by Silicon Beach Software. ◆ Salen, K. (2006), "They Must First Be Imagined," in K. Oosterhuis & L. Feireiss (eds.), *Game Set and Match II*, Episode Publishers, Rottderdam. ◆ *L'Amerzone* (1999), developed and published by Casterman/Microids. ◆ *Myst III* (2001), developed by Presto Studios, published by Ubisoft.

Jesse Schell (JS)
in conversation with the Editors of Space Time Play (STP)

"CAN I TELEPORT AROUND?"

STP **Over the years, you have been designing theme park rides, Massively Multi-player Games, browser games and handheld games. How would you compare the different spatial qualities of these designs?**

JS I think two of the most important qualities that define the nature of space are: Who is in it and who else is in it? Consider the *Pirates of the Caribbean: Battle for the Buccaneer Gold* virtual attraction, where you enter a little private room that has virtual space projected on all the walls, and you wear 3D glasses. But everyone in the room can see one another and speak one another and look at one another. You are entering that world together with them. But, by contrast, if you wear a head-mounted display, then the situation becomes very, very private. Console games happen in a living room, and we sit around together, and we talk, and we discuss. That is what differentiates these designs.

STP **Would you say that these qualities are a starting point for your design process?**

JS Game designer Rainer Knizia said that it is inadvisable to have multiple designs that have the same starting point because if we have the same starting point, usually we have the same ending point. Which you do not want. You always want a new ending point with the designs.

STP **So what are the particularities of designing a Disney space?**

JS The Walt Disney Company has a long history of creating wonderful spaces. Certainly, the spaces within the films are designed to be magical, evocative and special. But it is when you look to the theme parks that you really see this mastery of creating spaces, particularly in terms of spatial interaction. I believe Walt Disney Imagineering designer John Hench used to talk about the transitions between the different lands in the theme parks. When the designers thought about what they wanted these to be like, they didn't think about what they wanted them to *look* like, they thought about what the *experience* should be like. When you move from one part of Disneyland to another, they wanted it to be just like the experience of a transition in a movie from one place to another. They tried to make the music do the crossfade the same way it does in the corresponding film, they tried to make the visuals change in the same sorts of ways. Sometimes the transition is gradual, but sometimes they want something that is more of a cut, so that you turn the corner and suddenly you are confronted with a new thing or place. You know, with this, "Wow, what is this thing?!!" feeling.

When you are creating spaces for Disney the expectations are very high. Not just among the Disney designers; when people come visit a Disney space, they expect this magical quality. They expect: "I am going to enter into another world. And it is a world where I am going to feel safe and powerful, and I am going to have fun." Most importantly, Disney spaces try to make you feel like a child. Because one of the best ways to get people to play, particularly to get adults to play, is to make them feel like a child again.

STP **How does this approach apply, for example, to the web-based fairy creation application that your company, Schell Games, and Silvertree Media created for Disney?**

JS The architect Christopher Alexander states that an important quality of a living space is that it be free of inner contradictions. It is unacceptable if a place is designed to grant your wishes and then fails to do so. The only way to avoid this is through guest testing. You bring in people, and you watch them and hunt for those little moments of disappointment, find the root of that disappointment and change it. Because the feeling you want to inspire in people is: "I can do whatever I want!"

Now, of course, people never can do everything they want. In addition, you do not want things to occur to them that they would like to do but that the system cannot support, so you want to design a space such that it encourages them towards the things you can actually offer. I often say that the illusion of freedom is the only thing that matters. Basically, you just need to bend heaven and earth to make people able to do what they want and have their dreams come true. Then, you have to take it up a notch. You have to surprise them.

STP **You mentioned Alexander. How else does his work influence you as a game designer?**

JS I find Alexander to be tremendously inspiring – and I know I am not the only one. For example, it is said that Will Wright built *SimCity* (1989) after he read *A Pattern Language* (Alexander et al. 1977). He wanted a tool to play with patterns. In fact, I have heard several people say that if you use patterns from *A Pattern Language* when you design environments for your Sims, they are happier. Your Sims appreciate a light on two sides of a room or varying ceiling heights. I have not experimented with that myself, but it would not surprise me if it worked.

I find Alexander's first book, *The Timeless Way of Building* (Alexander 1979), tremendously helpful too, because in it, he encourages thoughtful iteration, which is central to game design. He also encourages a very human perspective, and I have often found that when a virtual place I have created does not feel right, when it is ugly or too hard or not enough fun, I flip through *A Pattern Language* to find inspiration. Do I have that? Do I not have that? What if I did have steps you could sit on? Would that change the way people interacted with this space? I didn't even think about making characters sit down, so…

In a world where there are no guidelines and no constraints, to be able to have something to cling to is important for designers creating virtual spaces. People creating real spaces have the luxury of constraints – constraints make designs so much easier. You know, we have got gravity; I cannot build a building a million feet tall. In virtual space, we bend these constraints so that we kind of like it there:

"Can I teleport around?"

"Yes you can."

"Can I have the building melt into puddles on the floor?"

"You can!"

I have been in many discussions with experienced game designers, and Alexander's books again and again and again come up as something valuable and something that can change and improve your perspective on creating virtual space.

◆ Alexander, C., Ishikawa, S. & Silverstein, M. (1977), *A Pattern Language: Towns, Buildings, Construction*, Oxford University Press, New York NY. ◆ Alexander, C. (1979), *The Timeless Way of Building*, Oxford University Press, New York NY. ◆ *SimCity* (1989), developed by Maxis, published by Maxis et al.

Bart Lootsma (BL)
in conversation with the Editors of Space Time Play (STP)

TOWARDS A GAME THEORY OF ARCHITECTURE

STP **At the moment, there is a big hype about the game** *Second Life* (2003), **which, at heart, is not a game at all, but a parallel world in which players can devise and shape their own social environments – a type of "Metaverse" like the one Neil Stephenson imagined in his book** *Snowcrash* **back in 1992.**

BL For me, the exciting thing about *Second Life* is that a sort of parallel economy is being built up in it. I can also easily imagine an architect operating there. As I see it, the primary importance lies in those implications for architecture that transcend the visual; in other words, the economics and dynamics of the development processes.

STP **Many things that happen in the "real" world can be pushed to the limits and simulated in this virtual world. At the same time, the constraints are different; gravity and weather don't exist. For architects, this opens up the possibility for a conception of space based on different parameters. Do you think that as a result, one can imagine wholly new types of architecture?**

BL I think that new media and especially new developments in the field of computer games have a very large influence on the way we currently experience cities and will in the future. One must differentiate between two things here: the effect on architecture and the effect on urban design. Just as in the 90s I thought that the new planning software could actually mean much more for city planning than for architecture, I now believe the same when it comes to the development of computer games into immersive parallel worlds. Thanks to its complexity, the large yardstick of the city as a whole is better suited to computer games than the yardstick of architecture. As far as architecture goes, I can imagine the development of a new school of design that understands the individual buildings as characters. This could give rise to a more sophisticated aesthetic, a multitude of diverse aesthetics in parallel. In any case, one should always separate the architectural and the urban design aspects.

STP **How do you envision changes in urban design?**

BL The use of interactive media in urban space – be it games, location-based services or GPS-based navigation systems – changes the way in which we move through space, the way we navigate. Simultaneously, the city – like a game – becomes programmable. This development did not begin with what we today call new or interactive media, but rather much earlier: in his time, Philip Marlowe's way of using the car and the telephone changed the sense of Los Angeles.

STP   **Ever more computer games are using real cities as their gamespace. With up-to-date mobile phones and other advanced handheld devices, the user gains access to new dimensions of urban space – an urban space superimposed with a layer of GPS-derived information.**

BL   These location-based services will fundamentally change cities. They enable ever smaller target groups to find one another and then meet up and organize anywhere in a city. This usage can be simulated and organized with games. And indeed, experimentation with games is important for further development because it will make ever more blurry the transition from game to reality, from game to the organization of a meet-up or even an official meeting. In principle, it doesn't make that big a difference whether one does something odd in a city, plays in a city or meets up with a group of people for any sort of discussion. What changes is the medium and the technology.

STP   **Does one still need the real meeting, then, or is it conceivable that in the long run, people will stay at home and meet one another in virtual public spaces?**

BL   So far, the actual meeting has been and is still very important. But I believe that the use of virtual public spaces will become more intensive in the future, mostly because the selection of people will become much more precise. Through the media, one can address much more specific target and niche groups. The actual meeting also remains important, but is one step further to being supplanted by the new media.

STP   **The thrill of pervasive gaming lies in the overlap between "real" and "virtual" space.**

BL   For us as architects and urban designers, most exciting is the way in which real and imagined space are layered. Wilfried Hou Je Bek wrote a program, *.walk*, which – totally without a computer – programs a Situationist Dérive for the user. The merging of media and urban spaces cannot only emanate from the media; inputting in the reverse direction is also very important.

STP   **Today, then, providing new interpretations of urban space is no longer just a project of the Situationists, but rather of city marketing above all else. Can one thus view a project that enables new perceptions of a city as a type of place-making tool?**

BL   Naturally. It is a new form of place-making accompanied by a new form of orientation in the city. We are far removed from the time when one simply went for a walk through a city and saw at first glance where the church steeple and town hall stood. We are equally far removed from the time of strolling; in suburbia, one can't stroll because one doesn't go on foot at all anymore. Precisely because of the great size and sprawled-out nature of suburbia, new media as orientation aids are becoming ever more important. GPS navigation will change city planning. When all of us are equipped with navigation systems in our cars and on our cell phones, we will speak very differently about city planning. We will then no longer be able to act on the assumption that a city is a place in which one must orient oneself. The task of orientation will be assumed by intelligent systems, exactly as will the programming of these wide-spread spaces.

STP **In the 70s, games were introduced to city planning as participatory instruments. Do you see the current introduction of games in urban spaces as a continuation of this tradition?**

BL Today's use of games is less political, less ideological. Instead, it obeys the neo-liberal market logic. Neoliberal strategies seek to seduce the user rather than shock him; games could be used as a tool in this process. I think it is important that we orient ourselves to the new control mechanisms in urban planning. These will be of a whole new form and will relinquish a large part of the development process to market influence, to a mass of individual decisions and initiatives that, as a whole, is rather uncontrollable and vague. Nonetheless, I believe that one can see specific developments and specific logics in these mechanisms. Playing games can help establish and test out new relationships. This may all be a necessity, a consequence of neoliberalism, but at the same time, one must keep on trying to uncover new possibilities. I believe that in urban planning and in architecture, there are always collective hazards to face, just as there are always collective desires and demands to satisfy. If this is done on a ludic level, it's enjoyable and also generates something new.

STP **You are now a professor of architectural theory in Innsbruck. There are several colleges that use games for architectural research. Are computer games also relevant to architectural theory – in the form, for example, of a city game theory for urban design?**

BL That is an important concern of mine. Here in Innsbruck, this is naturally an important question because we live in a landscape structured by the tourist leisure industry – a ludic landscape. Due to the prominence of leisure activities like hiking and back-country skiing, GPS devices are widely dispersed here; the overlay of real space with virtual dataspace is a constant. Location-based services, pervasive entertainment and the design of reality through changes in virtual space will also be important themes to explore.

◆ *Second Life* (2003), developed and published by Linden Lab. ◆ Stephenson, N. (1992), *Snowcrash*, Bantam/Spectra, New York NY.

William J. Mitchell (WM)
in conversation with the Editors of Space Time Play (STP)

ACTION IN THE HANDS OF THE USER

STP   **Have you ever played computer or video games, and what is your current perspective on games?**

WM   I'm not a big video game fan these days. They are for a younger generation. But I go back long enough to have played the first video games; I played *Spacewar!* (1962) when that was the only video game around and then games like *PONG* (1972) and *Pac-Man* (1980). Today's video games are much more spatial, often based on landscape and urban design models. As everybody knows, the interfaces have mostly been pretty miserable, joystick interfaces, which diminishes the spatial experience a great deal, though a couple of the recent video game consoles are much more sophisticated in this regard. Here, at the MIT Media Lab, we've just been working on a new interface. We developed a new kind of no-hands driving automobile seat in which you move your body around like you're using a surfboard or inline skates to control the driving. We played video games like *Grand Theft Auto* (1997-2006) with this interface, and it is incredible fun because it allows a kinesthetic and bodily engaging experience. I love that: it's like being on an exercise machine rather than just sitting in front of a video screen twiddling a joystick.

STP   **So for you, the spatial experience is not only inside, but also outside the game; the spatial experience is also the way the game is played.**

WM   Yes, I think the most exciting thing that's happening now is the shift towards bodily engagement. It goes all the way back to *Spacewar!*, in fact. Sitting in front of a computer and using some sort of screen interface device to control something on screen is the past; the future is to really create interfaces that are bodily engaging and sensual and therefore provide much more of a spatial experience. You can't have a real spatial experience without the kinesthetic experience, without the sense of motion and body speed and body moving through space.

STP   **In your books *City of Bits* (1995), *e-topia* (1999) and *Me++* (2003), you analyzed the relation between computerization and urban space. While *City of Bits* dealt with the digital city, *Me++* was more about the superimposition of a virtual layer of information over urban space. Today, we can see a comparable development in digital games. In the beginning, these featured interfaces that separated gamespace from everyday space, whereas today, we are confronted**

with ubiquitous, pervasive gaming in which everyday space and gamespace physically and psychologically merge.

WM   Yes, today we have the handheld device, and we can see an increasing prevalence of location-based technology. I think a lot of the uses of that are going to be spatial-game usages, though everybody thinks it's going to be all about advertising. I don't think it's going to be all about advertising. I think we'll see a lot of interesting spatial games. There is a long cultural tradition of spatial games – games like hide-and-seek and treasure hunt and that kind of thing, which, of course, go back centuries before the computer. I see an extension of that ludic tradition into a world essentially established by the overlay of location-sensitive devices onto physical spaces.

STP   **How greatly will these new technologies change the way we understand, read and experience cities?**

WM   These technologies create a new relationship between the city and its users. They create a new narrative of the city. And I tend to think that these narratives that unfold as you move through the city and the narratives that are mapped onto the city are very important for urban design. Narrative makes a city comprehensible. And of course the great novels like *Ulysses* (Joyce 1969), for example – that's all about narrative unfolding in the space of the city. Novels and plays basically provide experiences of situations and narratives and plots that in some sense are culturally engaging. And in many ways, computer and video games are the current form of fiction. And they are spatial fictions. So I think the relation between new game technologies and space is very important. In the future, location-based and pervasive games will create a new kind of narrative structure in urban space, and location-based devices will map the narrative down on the space of the city in very interesting new ways.

STP   **In addition to this invasion of the virtual world into the real world, we're also seeing the real world entering the game.**

WM   You're absolutely right: the blurring of the boundaries is operating in two directions. I'm kind of astonished at how literally a parallel world like *Second Life* (2003) fulfills what I have predicted in *City of Bits*. It took a while because the technology involves large-scale networking and parallel processing of rather massive environments, but I think that *Second Life* is incredibly impressive as a cultural phenomenon. The virtual world permeating the physical and the physical permeating the virtual leads to the development of ambiguous zones. And, of course, to me as a designer, the ambiguous zones are always the most interesting ones to operate with.

STP **Not too long ago, computer-aided design was something highly complicated even for professionals. And now, if we look at *Second Life*, computer-aided design is very easy; everybody is able to build a house in *Second Life*. Will that change users' attitudes towards real architecture?**

WM I think phenomena like *Second Life* that transform architecture into a popular art – like photography or gardening – have both a higher version that ends up in art galleries and an immense, popular manifestation. I think it's tremendously positive that people are actually getting their hands on visual and spatial composition and thinking about the organization of space and the organization of activity and so on. That can only be good for the discourse on architecture and urban design.

STP **Could this engagement and the knowledge it engenders be used for new forms of participation? Will using these kinds of games be an important part of urban planning?**

WM Yes, I think so. Over the course of my career, I have spent a lot of time in participatory design situations, and they've always been limited by the media that you could use. You could use rough, simple, physical models, or you could try to sketch very fast. Despite what we've tried to escape from, it was always the process of the professionals being very much dominant because they were the ones who could actually control the tools, who could actually draw properly and quickly. Something like *Second Life*, which empowers nonprofessionals to do pretty sophisticated things and therefore helps to engage them in the discourse, dialogue and design process, will bring participation to a much more effective level. I think it's extremely interesting and important, and we've only just begun to see the possibilities it will offer. It is, like an online configurator, a strategy for putting more of the action in the hands of the user.

◆ *Grand Theft Auto* (1997-2006), developed by Rockstar North et al., published by Rockstar Games et al. ◆ Joyce, J. (1969), *Ulysses*, Penguin, Harmondsworth UK. ◆ Mitchell, W. (1995), *City of Bits*, MIT Press, Cambridge MA. ◆ Mitchell, W. (1999), *e-topia*, MIT Press, Cambridge MA. ◆ Mitchell, W. (2003), *Me++*, MIT Press, Cambridge MA. ◆ *Pac-Man (*1980), developed by Namco, published by Midway. ◆ *PONG* (1972), developed and published by Atari. ◆ *Second Life* (2003), developed and published by Linden Lab. ◆ *Spacewar!* (1962), developed by Massachusetts Institute of Technology.

FAITES VOS JEUX

GAMES BETWEEN UTOPIA AND DYSTOPIA

OPS ROOM
I Like Instant Nirvana

In the interactive computer game *Ops Room* designed by Felix Stephan Huber, players are transported into a simulated historical location. They find themselves in a control room conceived in 1972 in Santiago, Chile by the cybernetics experts Stafford Beer and Fernando Flores and designed to deploy computer technology to assist President Salvador Allende in his efforts to steer the socialist economy. The room is represented in a painstakingly detailed reconstruction and is present in two possible realities between which players are able to switch. One version shows eight clones who are prompted by users to engage in discussion while background screens display documentary images of Allende's term in office and of the 1973 putsch against him, led by Augusto Pinochet. In a parallel room of identical appearance, the clones go wild while surfacing in the background are violent scenes from science fiction films of the 1970s that evoke the reign of terror of a totalitarian state.

In computer games, which are based on the idea of offering a number of options for action, the synchronous depiction of utopia and dystopia is made possible by a mere mouse click. By scenarizing Allende's control room as the location of a computer game, Huber sets the possibility of shaping history in the foreground while at the same time thematizing the failure of a utopian concept. The user is unable to intervene in the scenario, and interactivity – the essential trademark of any computer game – is reduced here by the artist to passive observation and critical reflection. To be sure, the observer triggers reactions (the discussion among the eight clones, the switching between the two parallel rooms), but he has no influence on the course of the discussion, which revolves around communicative structures and forms of technological regulation, and

whose fragments of dialogue are drawn from Beer's book *The Brain of the Firm* (1972). Statements such as, "Can we shape the things to come?" are addressed to efforts aimed at determining the future.

By simulating history in a computer game (especially given that in the entertainment industry, historical simulations generally take the form of war scenarios),

Huber is able to bring a historical locale to life. Of relevance to him, however, is not the repetition or replay of historical events, but instead reflections on the potential for action harbored in all scenarios. Huber reflects upon the beginnings of cybernetic thinking and on its sociopolitical potential under the altered conditions of contemporary network technologies and human–machine communication structures. His work is concerned with the increasing importance of computer-supported simulations, which no longer take the form of reproductions of reality, but instead of opportunities to actively shape it.

◆ Beer, S. (1972), *The Brain of the Firm*, Allen Lane, London.

http://fshuber.net/projects/ops-room/ops-room_01.html

Game Review	Text	Director	Production
	Rolf F. Nohr	John Badham	Metro-Goldwyn-Mayer, 1983

WARGAMES
More Than Serious Play

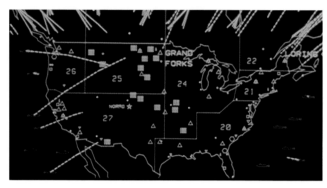

WarGames is a film about a young hacker who likes to play computer games. While attempting to crack the computer of a game manufacturer, he mistakenly accesses a military computer. There, he discovers a novel type of software that he takes to be a new computer game, which he immediately starts to play. But this is no game, it's a "real" simulation. This provides the basic conflict, then, that carries the film. At the start, the crew of a nuclear missile silo is suddenly confronted by the ultimate Cold War challenge: is the launch command genuine or merely a simulation? Are the turning of the key and pressing of the red button rehearsals with no real consequences (a game) or do they have very serious ones (life or death)? Considered as a game, *WarGames* has its longueurs. Its fast-paced opening fails to deliver what it promises, and what begins as a thrilling adventure that deals with the constructed nature of the game continues as part pubescent romance, part transfiguring hacker epic. The charm of the game emerges only in the boss fight: can the large-scale computer JOSHUA, which "runs amok," be persuaded, before the critical threshold has been reached, to recognize global thermonuclear war as an irresolvable zero-sum game? Here, the game becomes an enthralling strategic simulation with riddle-solving elements (attention: spoiler, it is winnable only by creating a game of tic-tac-toe based on a Neumannesque analogy of strategic simulation!). Formative for the heavy atmosphere of the finish level is certainly the design of the war room in the form of a spatial concept of the maps and computer screens filled with the parabolic curves approaching missiles and bombers. Only the claustrophobic and technocratic bunker setting invests this highly ambivalent serious play with the requisite seriousness.

The war room design of *WarGames* explicitly invokes Kubrick's *Dr. Strangelove* (Hawk Films 1964) and Ken Adam's seminal set design – just as today, it is impossible to conceive of visualizations of command centrals and control monitors that make no reference to this design. It was only to be expected that with *Defcon* (Introversion Software Ltd. 2006), a game would appear that would not only drive this (retro) aesthetic to new extremes, but also the cold decision-making logic of its (spatially) strategic warfighting. Even more decisive are the constantly repeated (and presumably perfectly accurate) anecdotes about the disappointment expressed by then incoming US president Ronald Reagan when confronted by the real-life war room, which failed to conform to his expectations, so conditioned by cinematic visions of commando centrals. As in *Tron* (Walt Disney Pictures 1982), we find here the stylistically formative, stereotypical design of immersive spaces. But in *WarGames* (as in *Defcon*), the degree to which these evocations of space are also spaces for inscribing nonmaterial knowledge becomes clear. As a result, these spaces, which are generated via narratives, also become places where information practices and knowledge of the world become concretized. The Cold War – as well as fears of its "heating up" – are consistently connoted by means of the growing parabolic curve of the approaching missiles. The style-generating stereotype of such visualizations, then, is also a spatial metaphor. It could also be asked what metaphors will be invented by games and films in order to concretize the "War of the 21st Century." Will *Black Hawk Down* (Revolution Studios 2001) or *Full Spectrum Warrior* (Pandemic Studios 2004) supply the necessary visual models? Or will we realize that both of these war narratives still scenarize war as a confrontation within (urban) space – and at a time when the "War Against Terror" has long since bid adieu to geopolitical or spatiopolitical scenarios?

WAR/GAMES AFTER 9/11

> "The enemy we're fighting is a bit different from the one we war-gamed against."
> *US General William Wallace* (Atkinson 2003)

> When asked what he meant when he said, "**The game is over,**" Iraq's UN ambassador
> Mohammed Al-Douri responded, "**The war.**"
> ("'Game is over,' says Iraq's UN envoy," Hareetz, 12 April 2003)

No war has been so enabled by the attributes, defined by the language and played by (and against) the rules of game than the war in Iraq. As the velocity of strategic movement was force-multiplied by the immediacy of the televisual moment; as the virtuality of high-technology warfare was enhanced by the reality of low battlefield casualties; as the military and the media as well as weapon-systems and sign-systems became mutually embedded; as the viewer became player: war and game melded in real time on prime time.

To speak of war as a game is always to invite attack, and in keeping with the spirit of the US national security strategy at the inception of the war, I would like to begin with a preemptive strike of my own. Let me be blunt: from the start, I considered the war with Iraq as the stupidest of games. I believed (and wrote) that it would prove to be a waste of lives, resources and the world standing of the United States. Indeed, it seems like a waste of time and intelligence even to speak of this war as rational activity, as a Clausewitzian continuation of politics by other means. Between the September 11 attack and the first shot of the second Gulf War, a mimetic war of fundamentalisms set a predestined course; in this regard, Bin Laden succeeded.

War-as-game, of course, is not the same as a war game. Yet the conflation and confusion of war with game would not be taking place were it not for the rapid development of war-gaming and its convergence with video gaming. Some history can illuminate this point. In 1889, Major William Livermore of the US Army Corp of Engineers joined William McCarty Little and Rear Admiral Alfred Thayer Mahan at the Naval War College in Newport, Rhode Island to establish the first modern system of war-gaming in the United States. Taking their cue from the Prussians, who successively used *Kriegsspiel* (war play) to defeat the Austrians in 1866 and the French in 1870, the early US war-gamers were proven justified in their efforts by the stunning Japanese victory over Russia in 1904 (plotted out beforehand with newly created war games) and later by the successful anticipation of just about every aspect of the Pacific campaign of World War II against Japan (aside from the use of kamikaze tactics). The Naval War College closed down its old tiled war-gaming room in 1958, replacing it with the computerized Navy Electronic Warfare System (NEWS) that cost more than 10 million US Dollars to build and that filled a three-story building. Today, a single desktop computer in the College's new state-of-the-art McCarty-Little Hall outperforms all of the NEWS technology. A quantum leap in verisimilitude has been made in war-gaming from the early spatial movement of toy soldiers and cardboard ships on contoured sand tables to the live, virtual and constructive simulations of fully immersive environments. Ironically, the better the simulation the higher the risk of confusing war with game.

With the future of the future at stake, "virtuous" war is leading the way in the hybridization of warring and gaming. Designed by the Pentagon, auditioned in the Balkans and dress-rehearsed in Afghanistan, virtuous war took center stage in the invasion of Iraq. Virtuous war projects a technological and ethical superiority in which computer simulation, media dissimulation, global surveillance and networked warfare combine to deter, discipline and, if need be, destroy the enemy. Ethically intentioned and virtually applied, virtuous war draws on the doctrines of just war when possible and holy war when necessary, always playing on its ambiguous status as a felicitous oxymoron. After September 11, as the United States chose coercion over diplomacy in its foreign policy and deployed a rhetoric of total victory over absolute evil, virtuous war became the ultimate means by which the United States intended to resecure its borders, assert its suzerainty and secure the holy trinity of international order – free markets, vassal states and preventive wars. It became the only game in town.

Obviously there is a difference between war and games. Unlike most games, war involves people dying. However, the technological properties and political imperatives of virtuous war skew the casualty rates both off and on the battlefield. From a superpower perspective, the trend is pronounced: 270 Americans died in the last Gulf War – over half by "friendly fire" or accidents; 18 Americans killed in the Mogadishu raid; an astonishing zero-casualty conflict for the NATO forces in Kosovo. In Afghanistan, by the end of the major hostilities in January, 20 American military personnel were killed overseas in the line of duty, the majority of whom died in accidents or by friendly fire. Only one soldier, Sgt. First Class Nathan Chapman, was actually killed by hostile fire. As was the case in the Kosovo conflict, more journalists covering the war were killed by hostile fire (ten by the end of major operations) than American soldiers fighting the war. And one of the most perverse aspects of virtuous war is that enemy and civilian casualties never receive a commensurate tallying.

The low risk, high yield strategy of virtuous war has a game logic of its own in which the human role is shrinking in numbers and significance in an increasingly robotic battlespace. To be sure, "boots on the ground" are still and will continue to be necessary in land warfare. But the pixels are already on the screen: at the macro-level of war-gaming, "OPLAN 1003 Victor" (the controversial war plan for the invasion of Iraq) called for three fewer divisions than had been recommended by Pentagon's traditionalists; and at the micro-level, virtuous war came of age when a Predator drone with Hellfire missiles was able to find an Al Qaeda "target of opportunity" in the Yemen desert and was ordered from 6,000 miles away to shoot to kill.

From the first to the second Gulf War, from Bosnia to Kosovo and from Afghanistan to Iraq, virtuous war also took on the properties of a video game, with high production values, mythic narratives, easy victories and few real bodies. From the decision to deploy troops to the daily order of battle, from the highest reaches of policy-making to the lowest levels of field tactics and logistics, war games, computer simulations and command post exercises made war into a game.

The White House and the Pentagon showed some sensitivity to the confusion of war as game. Before the war started, Deputy Defense Secretary Paul D. Wolfowitz visited the Council for Foreign Relations in New York City and said, repeatedly, "this is not a game":

> "Iraq has had 12 years now to disarm, as it agreed to do at the conclusion of the Gulf War. But so far it has treated disarmament like a game of hide and seek - or, as Secretary of State Powell has termed it, 'rope-a-dope in the desert.' But this is not a game."
> (Wolfowitz 2002)

In January 21, 2003, President Bush had a brief, unscripted exchange with the press:

> "This business about, you know, more time – you know, how much time do we need to see clearly that he's [Saddam Hussein] not disarming? This looks like a rerun of a bad movie and I'm not interested in watching it." (Bush 2003)

In other words, Iraq plays games, and the United States must make war. It all started to look, as great philosopher-baseball player Yogi Berra put it, "like déjà-vu all over again" (Berra 1998). But like the black cat twice seen by Neo in *The Matrix* (1999), déjà vu started to look like a symptom of something much worse: in this case, the glitch in the simulacrum revealed a war with no rational origin but the game itself. Déjà vu might produce great visions among shamans, but the only thing with which it provided our current leaders was the false security of an uncertain future tamed by global games.

Of course, the White House and the Pentagon had key allies in this campaign to preempt the future. When the future becomes a feedback loop of simulations (war games, training exercises, scenario planning and modeling) and dissimulations (propaganda, disinformation, deceit and lies), the vaunted firewall between the military and the media is about as formidable as an Iraqi border berm. As a result, the public faced a full-fledged infowar. Surfing the channels and scanning the pages of the US media exposed us to high doses of hi-tech exhibitionism and media voyeurism. Infowar, deployed after September 11 as the discontinuation of diplomacy by other means, became a force-multiplier in Iraq – a weapon of destruction as well as of persuasion and distraction.

There were new role-players in this high-stakes information game: the embedded journalists. After the protests by the press of being excluded from the US invasions of Grenada and Panama and from the first Gulf War, the Defense Department came up with the idea of selectively placing journalists in the various armed services, aboard ships at sea as well as on the frontlines of the battlefield. Lost in the hoopla over the stories and images streaming in from the desert was the fact that the military had also taken over the television studios. Retired generals and flag officers exercised full spectrum dominance on cable and network TV as well as on commercial and public radio. Fox News alone had enough ex-military personnel to stage its own Veteran's Day parade. A relationship that had always been intimate in times of crisis now appeared incestuous. Color commentary and shades of opinion were effectively reduced to the nightscope-green of videophone vérité in the desert and to red, white and blue in the studios.

However, new asymmetrical forms of power and a wider range of media emerged from this war-as-game. In many ways, the global war on terror can be interpreted as a last gasp or even as the denial of great powers to recognize a shifting configuration of power in world politics. Many scholars saw the end of the Cold War as an occasion to spin theories over the merits of multipolar over unipolar state-systems or to wax nostalgic over the stability of a bipolar order. The US may well be the dominant military and economic power; it is certainly difficult to identify any peer competitors on the horizon. However, post-Cold War *and* post-9/11, we witness the emergence of a new "heteropolarity" in which actors are radically different in identity and interests (state, corporate, group, individual) yet suddenly comparable in their ability to produce global effects. Deploying multimedia as they do, these new actors derive power as much from virtual networks as from territorial politics.

The question, then, is how long will this mimetic game of terror and counter-terror last? Bush, Bin Laden and Saddam Hussein all needed each other: it takes two to play. Magnified by the media, fought by advanced technologies of destruction and unchecked by the UN or US allies, this mimetic struggle developed a game logic of its own in which "assimilation or extermination" became credible policies. But historically, terrorist movements evolve into states or, without a mass base, weaken, rarely lasting longer than a decade. And empires, by overreach or defeat, inevitably fall.

In world politics, games with happy endings are hard to find. But what Edmund Burke called the "empire of circumstance" will surely – and let us hope not too belatedly – trump Bush's imperial game as well as Bin Laden's terrorist one. The temptation to solve the world's problems through preventive virtuous wars will remain. But we would all do best, when so tempted, to again heed the words of the great Yogi:

"If the world were perfect, it wouldn't be." (Berra 1998)

◆ Atkinson, R. (2003), "General: A Longer War Likely," *The Washington Post*, 28 March, p. A01.
◆ Berra, Y. (1998), *The Yogi Book: "I Really Didn't Say Everything I Said,"* Workman Publishing, New York NY. ◆ Bush, G. (2003), *Bush Says Iraq is Not Disarming as Required by the UN*. Retrieved June 15, 2007, from http://www.globalsecurity.org/wmd/library/news/iraq/2003/iraq-030121-usia02.htm
◆ *The Matrix* (Movie) (1999), produced and distributed by Warner Bros. Pictures et al. ◆ Wolfowitz, P.(2002), *Deputy Secretary Wolfowitz Speech on Iraq Disarmament*. Retrieved June 15, 2007, from http://www.globalsecurity.org/wmd/library/news/iraq/2003/iraq-030123-dod01.htm

WAR PLAY
Practicing Urban Annihilation

Making a Mess

Cities are destroyed, unmade and annihilated *discursively* and through symbolic violence, as well as through bombs, planes and terrorist acts. As various electronic media become ever more dominant in shaping the tenor of urban culture, so do their depictions of cities crucially affect collective notions of what cities actually are and of what they might actually become.

Increasingly, in these postmodern times, cities are depicted as sites of ruination, fear and decay, rather than development, order or progress. As early as the mid-1960s, for example, Susan Sontag observed that most sci-fi films are about the "aesthetic of destruction, the peculiar beauties to be found in wreaking havoc, making a mess" (Sontag 1966, pp. 203-218). Crucially, this means that very often the millennia-old "link between civilization and barbarism is reversed: City life turns into a state of nature characterized by the rule of terror, accompanied by omnipresent fear" (Diken & Laustsen 2002, pp. 290-307).

This shift taps into a century or more of apocalyptic, antiurban literature and films – from H. G. Wells' *War in the Air* (1908) to vast ranges of atomic-age and cyberpunk fiction. All such portrayals predict in their own way the final victory of weapons of annihilation over the very possibility of a conventional urban life (Franklin 1988). Continuing in this trend, a swathe of recent postapocalyptic films have so shaped the collective culture of urbanism that the stock response to the 9/11 catastrophe was that "it was just like a scene in a movie!" Whilst there was a brief pause in the production of such films after 9/11, they are now back in full throttle (Maher 2002).

Joystick War

Indeed, the complex links between virtual, filmic and televisual representations of city-killing and actual acts of urban war are becoming so blurred as to be almost indistinguishable. At least amongst US forces, the real targeting of cities is increasingly being remodeled as a "joystick war" – though only for those lucky enough to be geographically removed from the urban target. This operates through virtual simulations, computerized killing systems and a growing distanciation of the operator from the sites of the killing and the killed. In the process, the realities of urban war – at least for some – start to blur seamlessly with the wider cultures of sci-fi, film, video games and popular entertainment (Thussu & Freedman 2003).

As political violence is increasingly consumed by a voyeuristic public, so digital technologies bring the vicarious thrills of urban war directly to the homes of news-hungry consumers. Consumption of the Iraq war by people in the US, for

420

example, offered a wide range of satellite image-based maps of the enemy cities as little more than an array of targets to be destroyed from the air, in newspapers or on media websites.

In a perverse twist, corporate media and entertainment industries increasingly create both the consumer computer games and films that virtually simulate recent urban wars *and* the virtual and physical simulations of cities that US forces use to hone their warfare skills for fighting in Kabul, Baghdad and Freetown. Take, for example, the unmanned, low-altitude "Predator" aircraft that is already being used for extrajudicial assassinations of alleged terrorists (and whoever happens to be close by) in Yemen, Afghanistan and Iraq, whilst being "piloted" from a Nevada air base, just outside Las Vegas, 8,000 or 10,000 miles away. For the US military personnel doing the piloting, this "virtual" work is almost indistinguishable from a "shoot 'em-up" video game. Except in this case, the people who die are real. "At the end of the work day," one Predator operator recently boasted during Gulf War II, "you walk back into the rest of life in America" (Newman 2003). Predator controls for "pilots" have even been explicitly remodeled to resemble PlayStation controls. Michael Keaton, a Raytheon weapons designer, is unambiguous about the logic at play here: "There's no point in re-inventing the wheel. The current generation of pilots was raised on the [Sony] PlayStation, so we created an interface that they will immediately understand" (Richfield 2006).

"Geopolitics of Urban Decay and Cybernetic Play"

"In a world being torn apart by international conflict, one thing is on everyone's mind as they finish watching the nightly news: 'Man, this would make a great game!'" (Jenkins 2003)

Claire Sponster terms the particular obsession with decayed cityscapes within cyberpunk depictions on urban futures a "geopolitics of urban decay and cybernetic play" (Sponster 1992). Though cyberpunk stories have moved beyond the common Cold War, sci-fi obsession with postnuclear cities, their physical settings "look strikingly like the settling of any post-holocaust story: blighted, rubble-strewn, broken-down cityspaces; vast terrains of decay, bleakness, and the detritus of civilization; and the near complete absence of a benign and beautiful nature" (ibid., p. 253).

The wide array of virtual reality and simulation games in which players can be masters of urban annihilation further demonstrates the blurring of the actual and virtual killing of urban places (and their inhabitants). Three ranges of games are relevant here.

The first is simulated urban construction games – like the *SimCity* series (1989-2003). In these, participants endlessly construct and destroy cityscapes in repeated cycles of virtual urban cataclysm (Bleecker 1994, pp. 189-221). One *SimCity* introduction and guide available on the Web describes the fascination with virtual urban destruction amongst players as follows:

"My name is Dr Wright and I will be your guide and teacher as you set out to create bustling cities of sprawling urban wastelands. As Mayor, the choice is yours. Let's start off by destroying Tokyo! Studies show that nine out of ten mayors begin their careers with a frenzy of destruction ... Another curious fact about *SimCityTM* mayors is that one disaster is never enough. The reasoning goes something like this: 'gee, that monster was great, but there must be half a dozen buildings still standing. I wonder what it would take to destroy *EVERYTHING*!' … Simply point at the disaster(s) of your choice and push B to activate it."

Secondly, there are virtual combat games designed to allow (largely) western users to "fight" enemies in far-off cities. These provide omnipotent players with realistic – and often devastated – cities (usually in the Middle East) in which they can annihilate racialized and dehumanized enemies again and again. The rhetoric and marketing of such games, echoing George Bush's nationalistic discourse of "protecting freedom" and "ensuring democracy," imply that the task of the player is to infiltrate these cities in order to rid the world of terrorists and thereby fight for freedom.

The urban war of one's choice – *Black Hawk Down* (Mogadishu), *Gulf War I*, *Gulf War II*, the LA Riots, a myriad of urban antiterrorist operations – can thus be electronically simulated and consumed as entertainment. The comments of gamers are very telling: one *Delta Force: Black Hawk Down* (2003) player, for example, admits that "those graphics are so sweet you can almost feel the bullets whizz past your head and ricochet off walls around you. The scenery is good although if you are spending time admiring it then you're already dead!"

The construction of Arab cities as targets for US military firepower now sustains a large industry of computer gaming and simulation. Video games such as *America's Army* (2002) and the US Marines' equivalent, *Full Spectrum Warrior* (2003), have been developed by their respective armed forces, with help from the corporate entertainment industries, as training aids, recruitment aids and powerful public relations tools. Both games – which were amongst the world's most popular video game franchises in 2005 – center overwhelmingly on the military challenges allegedly involved in occupying and pacifying stylized, orientalized, Arab cities. Their immersive simulations "propel the player into the world of the gaming industry's latest fetish: modern urban warfare" (DelPiano 2004). Andrew Deck argues that the proliferation of urban warfare games based on actual, ongoing US military interventions in Arab cities works to "call forth a cult of ultra-patriotic xenophobes whose greatest joy is to destroy, regardless of how racist, imperialistic, and flimsy the rationale" for the simulated battle (Deck 2004).

Such games work powerfully to further reinforce imaginary geographies equating Arab cities with terrorism, as well as the need for "pacification" or "cleansing" via US military invasion and colonial occupation in the name of "freedom." More than further blurring the already fuzzy boundaries separating war from entertainment, they demonstrate that the US entertainment industry "has assumed a posture of co-operation towards a culture of permanent war" (ibid.). Within such games, as in the satellite images and maps discussed above, it is striking that Arab cities are represented merely as "collections of objects not congeries of people" (Gregory 2004, p. 201). When people *are* represented, they are rendered almost without exception as shadowy, subhuman, racialized Arabs, as absolutely alien "terrorists" – figures to be repeatedly annihilated, as bare life (*homines sacri*), in sanitized actions for the purpose of entertainment, military training or both. *America's Army*, for example, simulates counterterror warfare in densely packed Arab cities in the fictional country Zekistan. "The mission" of the game, writes Steve O'Hagan, "is to slaughter evildoers, with something about 'liberty' ... going on in the background... These games may be ultra-realistic down to the caliber of the weapons, but when bullets hit flesh people just crumple serenely into a heap. No blood. No exit wounds. No screams" (O'Hagan 2004, pp. 12-13).

Here, then, the only imagined role for the everyday sites and spaces of Arab cities is as environments for military engagement. The militarization of the everyday sites, artifacts and spaces of the simulated city is total. "Cars are used as bombs, bystanders become victims [although they die without spilling blood], houses become headquarters, apartments become lookout points, and anything to be strewn in the street becomes suitable cover" (DelPiano 2004). Indeed, there is some evidence that the actual physical geographies of Arab cities are being digitized to provide the three-dimensional "battle space" for these games. Forterra Systems Inc., a games developer that also develops training games for the US military, openly boasts that "we've [digitally] built a portion of the downtown area of a large Middle Eastern capital city where we have a significant presence today" (Callaham 2004).

In essentializing Arab cities as intrinsically devious labyrinths that require high-tech US military assaults to "cleanse" them of their supposed terrorists, these urban warfare video games obviously resonate strongly with the popular geopolitical pronouncements of military urban warfare specialists discussed above. Importantly, however, they also merge with increasing seamlessness into news reports about the actual war in Iraq. Kuma Reality Games, for example, which has sponsored Fox News' coverage of the "war on terror" in the US, uses this link to promote urban combat games based on actual military engagements in occupied cities. According to the company itself, one of these games centers on US Marines fighting "militant followers of radical Shiite cleric Muqtada al-Sadr in the filthy urban slum that is Sadr City" (Deck 2004).

A final range of games brings urban war to the "homeland." In these, the challenge is to destroy terrorists who are in the process of unleashing instant and unknown catastrophes on western cities. One user of the urban warfare game *Tom Clancy's Rainbow Six: Rogue Spear Platinum* (2001) describes its challenges: "Urban Operations really add to the gameplay," he says, "with missions in *live* public areas (London underground, open top markets, etc.). You can even shoot out the lights! [The spaces are] full of public people. And if a stray shot should kill any member of the public ... Game Over!" (Amazon.co.uk Review n.d.).

◆ Amazon.co.uk Review (n.d.), Retrieved from http://www.amazon.co.uk/ ◆ *America's Army* (2002), developed by MOVES Institute, published by US Army. ◆ Bleecker, J. (1994), "Urban crisis: Past, present and virtual," *Socialist Review*, no. 24, pp. 189-221. ◆ Callaham, J. (2004), *Army Massively Multiplayer Project Interview*. Retrieved from http://www.temple.edu/ispr/examples/ex04_03_08.html

◆ Deck, A. (2004), *Demilitarizing the playground. No Quarter*. Retrieved February 2006 from http://artcontext.net/crit/essays/noQuarter/ ◆ DelPiano, S. (2004), "Review of Full Spectrum Warrior," *Games First*. Retrieved February 2006 from http://www.gamesfirst.com/reviews/07.10.04/FullSpectrumRev/fullspectrumreview.htm. ◆ *Delta Force: Black Hawk Down* (2003), developed and published by NovaLogic. ◆ Diken, B. & Laustsen, C. (2002), "Security, terror, and bare life," *Space and Culture*, vol. 5, no. 3. ◆ Franklin, H. (1988), *War Stars: The Superweapon and the American Imagination*, Oxford University Press, New York NY. ◆ *Full Spectrum Warrior* (2003), originally developed by Pandemic Studios, Sony Imageworks and the Institute for Creative Technologies at USC (ICT) for STRICOM / (2004), commercial version published by THQ. ◆ Gregory, D. (2004), *The Colonial Present*, Blackwell, Oxford UK. ◆ Jenkins, H. (2003), "A war of words over Iraqi video games," *The Guardian*, 13 November, p. 18. ◆ Maher, K. (2002), "Back with a bang," *The Observer*, 30 June. ◆ Newman, R. (2003), "The joystick war," *U.S. News*, 19 May. ◆ O'Hagan, S. (2004), "Recruitment hard drive," *Guardian Guide*, 19-25 June. ◆ Richfield, P. (2006), "New 'cockpit' for Predator?," *C4ISR Journal*, 31 October. Retrieved from http://www.c4isrjournal.com/story.php?F=2323780 ◆ *SimCity* series (1989-2003), developed by Maxis, published by various. ◆ Sontag, S. (1966), "The imagination of disaster," in S. Sontag (ed.), *Against Interpretation*, Dell, New York NY. ◆ Sponster, C. (1992), "Beyond the ruins: The geopolitics of urban decay and cybernetic play," *Science Fiction Studies*, vol. 20, no. 2, pp. 251-265. ◆ Thussu, D. & Freedman, D. (eds.) (2003), *War and the Media*, Sage, London. ◆ *Tom Clancy's Rainbow Six: Rogue Spear Platinum* (2001), developed by Red Storm Entertainment, published by Ubisoft. ◆ Wells, H.G. (1908), *War in the Air, and particularly how Mr. Bert Smallways fared while it lasted*, The Macmillan Company, New York NY.

ENDER'S GAME
Towards a Synthetic View of the World

STP   **You were the Creative Director of the Institute for Creative Technologies (ICT) at the University of Southern California in Los Angeles from its foundation in 1999 up until early 2007. What were the reasons for founding the ICT, and what sort of work did the ICT do?**

JK   When the Institute for Creative Technologies was founded in 1999, there was a simple goal. The Department of Defense (DoD) wanted to leverage "Hollywood." In 1997, the National Science Foundation conducted a study that looked at the possible value of a connection between the DoD and the US entertainment industry. The results of the study suggested that the DoD would benefit from working with the entertainment software industry and Hollywood generally. More specifically, the DoD recognized that the computational simulation and virtual training products they were using were generally very high-fidelity simulations, but weren't necessarily altogether compelling, particularly for the generation of young people entering military service, many of whom were experienced "gamers." In short, the DoD was interested in Hollywood's ability to create immersive and enthralling fictional worlds: to spin a good yarn and hold people's attention.

STP   **Michael Macedonia, former Chief Technology Officer for the US Army Program Executive Office for Simulation, Training, and Instrumentation (PEO STRI, formerly know as STRICOM), once mentioned that Orson Scott Card's novel *Ender's Game* (1985) was an initial inspiration for the cooperation between the army and the entertainment industry. What can you tell us about that?**

JK   *Ender's Game* and *Ender's Shadow* (1999), the sequel that followed many years later, as well as the motion picture *The Last Starfighter* (1984) all shared a similar premise: namely, that in the future, warfare would become much more like a video game. For that reason, the authorities of the societies depicted in these stories recruited the best video game players and trained them in the art of warfare. *Ender's Game*, *Ender's Shadow* and *The Last Starfighter* were really useful as metaphors for the challenges that the Department of Defense faced at the time that it set up the ICT.

     The US Army had realized that most of the kids joining the military grew up as gamers. Ninety percent of them were at least casual gamers, and about 30% or more were serious gamers. What the army liked about these kids was that as gamers, they had the ability to teach themselves:

in the process of becoming gamers, they had learned how to learn. What you'll discover when you talk to most young gamers is that the first thing they do *not* do is to read the manual that comes with the game. Instead, the first thing they'll do is load the game up and start playing it. They figure the game out through the process of using it. This ability to work on fairly consistent interfaces and to learn from the application itself is very appealing to the military.

STP **To what degree are today's design concepts changing as a result of this type of game experience and these gaming abilities? Will any of the technical interfaces of complex military equipment be redesigned according to the interfaces of computer games – i.e. designed so that they are easier to control?**

JK The US Army's Future Combat Systems (FCS) is a good example of that. Future Combat Systems is a very extensive program essentially meant to modernize virtually all of the equipment that the army uses – all of the tanks and armored personnel carriers, the medical vehicles, etc. I built an FCS simulator that models three Common Crew Stations: the "cockpit" of all FCS manned platforms. What we did in this simulator was to create a warrior machine interface from scratch. We made it quite game-like, so it has a game interface as opposed to an engineering interface. For that reason, it's much more intuitive, it's much easier to figure out how to use, and the speed with which the user can make decisions and get information is faster. That's a very important shift; we're gravitating towards a very interesting concept not only for training but also for operations. The military is increasingly guided by a gaming sensibility in its design concepts.

STP **There are many commercial games that advertise with the assertion that a different version of the game is used by the military. Are those mostly hyped-up advertising claims or mostly based on fact?**

JK I can speak about a couple of examples that are genuine. *Full Spectrum Warrior* (2003), which was first developed for the Xbox and ultimately ported to the PC, was developed initially as a training application for the military. It was later transformed into an entertainment product, with a great many additions to make it look less like a trainer.

Another interesting product is *America's Army* (2002), a game that was developed as a recruiting tool for the US Army Accessions Command.

426

Future Force Company Commander (2006), or *F2C2*, was developed to get people familiar with command and control in the Future Combat Systems environment. *F2C2* is supposed to simulate a future system, but does not have any training purpose. Then there is the *Microsoft Flight Simulator* (2006) that is used in the Air Force to varying extent to get people used to the idea and concept of flying an airplane.

STP **In the future, there will probably be more of these games. Is there a danger that gamers might no longer be able to discern between game and reality, just as the children in *Ender's Game* are not sure when they are actually fulfilling missions or playing a game?**

JK We haven't yet come to the point where we're asking children to fight our wars. In *Ender's Game*, Ender was about ten years old and he had a child's perception and a child's sense of the world. He had to take on a great and awesome responsibility by essentially fighting his country's battles. All of that relies on warfare that is prosecuted entirely through a synthesized view of the world. The US expeditionary military experience in Iraq is the exact opposite of *Ender's Game*. As an upstart insurgent group, it is very difficult to win a fight against a technologically highly developed enemy like the US or any NATO member – if, that is, you try to meet the enemy "symmetrically," going head-to-head with a regular uniformed force. The best way to fight in such a situation is shown in the film *The Battle for Algiers* (1967), which centers on the French colonial experience in Algeria. The people of Algiers did exactly the same things that the insurgents in Iraq have been doing to the coalition forces. These insurgents don't come out, they don't wear a uniform and they don't meet their enemies on a field of battle. Instead, they're blending with the population, doing suicide bombing, using roadside improvised explosive devices and snipers to shoot people when they're on their way somewhere. You can't fight an *Ender's Game* kind of war with people who fight you either as transnationals or insurgents. You're engaging people ten or 15 meters away with direct fire. There's nothing video-game-like about it. You have to be out there, kicking doors down, looking for the enemy; and the enemy is everywhere. What you end up doing is engaging the enemy at a very close range, and that is not like a video game.

STP   **To what extent can virtual environments like *There* (2003) or *Second Life* (2003) be used to train for this one-to-one interaction?**

JK   There were a couple of advanced technology demonstrations developed by the army's Office for Simulation, Training and Instrumentation (PEO STRI) in Orlando. One relied on a technology developed initially in the multiplayer online game *There*. Ultimately, this technology became known as *Forterra*. *Forterra* essentially is a persistent online multiplayer environment. Usually, these technologies are used for social networking. But in *Forterra*, you have some people playing the enemy and some people playing coalition forces. I saw a demonstration where they had a checkpoint or they were searching a house for an insurgent.

You also can try to create a training environment using *There* or *Second Life*. But if you want to do a training exercise with a squad of soldiers, you also have to have a lot of people playing the enemy because there's a very limited capability for nonplayer characters in that technology. If you have subject-matter experts who really know how insurgents behave and how the people in Iraq behave, then you have a "good" enemy. The quality of the simulation depends on the "natural" intelligence (i.e. the human beings) that's engaged.

STP   **In pervasive technologies, a virtual environment is placed on top of the real world as a second layer of information. To what extent is this superimposition used by the military and to what extent does it change the way we perceive reality?**

JK   As any look at Future Combat Systems (FCS) makes clear, the US Military's vision of the future involves a network-centric type of warfare. The real hero of the future is the warfighter who has a complete situational awareness. This is a very significant paradigm shift. Traditional warfare is conducted entirely on line of sight, on everything you can see when you're holding up your binoculars. Future warfare is based on what you are aware of because you have a synthetic view of the world that you can work from. This synthetic view of the world is informed by a broad range of sensors, unmanned aerial vehicles like "Global Hawks" and "Predators" and unattended ground sensors, technologies that give you either seismic signatures, electro-optical views or infrared views of the world that's around you. This information can tell you that the enemy is located at a particular set of coordinates, which allows you to build up what is

428

referred to as a Common Operational Picture (COP). This COP becomes available to warfighters in a variety of ways and through a variety of interfaces and displays. One system that is common in the US Military today is called Force XXI Battle Command Brigade and Below (FBCB2). It was conceived in the 1980s and was used more or less successfully during the last decade. It gives you the ability to see how a brigade – which is about 3,000 soldiers and support people – is arrayed and where the enemy is. When you look at it, it looks like a game. It's basically a map with icons on it, and you have the option of choosing different viewpoints to see where those icons are. Using this kind of synthetic view of the world, people really get used to the idea of looking at the world as if it were a video game.

Institute for Creative Technologies: www.ict.usc.edu
US Army Future Combat Systems: www.army.mil/fcs
US Army Program Executive Office for Simulation, Training, Instrumentation: www.peostri.army.mil

◆ *America's Army* (2002), developed by MOVES Institute, published by US Army. ◆ *The Battle for Algiers* (Movie) (1967), produced by Casbah Film & Igor Film, distributed by Rizzoli et al. ◆ Card, O.S. (1985), *Ender's Game*, Tor Books, New York NY. ◆ Card, O.S. (1999), *Ender's Shadow*, Tor Books, New York NY. ◆ *Full Spectrum Warrior* (2003), originally developed by Pandemic Studios, Sony Imageworks and the Institute for Creative Technologies at USC (ICT) for STRICOM / (2004), commercial version published by THQ. ◆ *Future Force Company Commander* (2006), developed by Zombie, produced by Science Applications International Corporation (SAIC). ◆ *The Last Starfighter* (Movie) (1984), produced by Lorimar Film Entertainment & Universal Pictures, distributed by Universal Pictures et al. ◆ *Microsoft Flight Simulator* (2006), developed by Microsoft Game Studios, published by Microsoft. ◆ *Second Life* (2003), developed and published by Linden Lab. ◆ *There* (2003), developed and published by Makena Technologies.

Eyal Danon,
Galit Eilat

FORBIDDEN GAMES

The first computer games were developed for research purposes – to prove scientific ideas, not to provide pleasure. In 1947, the first computer game was created in the United States. In it, several knobs were used to adjust the speed and direction of a missile represented by a dot as it flew toward a target. Five years later, in 1952, a Ph.D. student at Cambridge University developed the tic-tac-toe (noughts and crosses) game *OXO* to illustrate his thesis about human–computer interaction. This situation continued for over a decade: scientists created games for super computers in research labs. In the 1970s, progress was made in miniaturization of computer chips and the development of personal computers, which enabled the creation of games on platforms accessible to the public. The two routes down which the market went afterwards were that of the home consoles connected to television sets and that of the arcades where people went to play games.

Now the video game industry is one of the leading entertainment industries in the world. This is made manifest by its growing exposure to larger audiences, which, in turn, yields substantial financial increases; the industry's revenues for 2003 reached 31 billion US Dollars, second only to the Hollywood film industry's, whose income in that year stood at some 44 billion US Dollars. In other words, video games are a highly significant factor in the western entertainment industry.

The industry produces Alternative Reality Games, community games and strategy games, of which the most predominant subcategory is the war games genre. The realistic war game, which has always been popular, has gained momentum in recent years concurrent with the media's increased use of terms such as "the axis of evil" and "the war on terror." The global war against terrorism has led to an intensification of nationalistic and patriotic feelings among gamers, and gaming companies have identified the potential and hurried to issue ideological fighting settings. Western gaming companies develop countless realistic war games with a clear-cut division between "good" and "evil." The American/European/Israeli hero will usually belong to some security force sent to thwart the sinister missions of the forces of evil threatening the free world.

In his 2005 Nobel Prize acceptance lecture, playwright Harold Pinter included a short, mock speech for George W. Bush, encapsulating the dichotomous worldview held by the US today: "God is good. God is great. God is good. My God is good. Bin Laden's God is bad. His is a bad God. Saddam's God was bad, except he didn't have one. He was a barbarian. We are not barbarians. We don't chop people's heads off. We believe in freedom. So does God. I am not a barbarian. I am the democratically elected leader of a freedom-loving democracy. We are a compassionate society.

430

We give compassionate electrocution and compassionate lethal injection. We are a great nation. I am not a dictator. He is. I am not a barbarian. He is. And he is. They all are. I possess moral authority. You see this fist? This is my moral authority. And don't you forget it" (Pinter 2005).

The worldview promoted by "the war on terror," simplistically crafted by President Bush after 9/11 in his "You are either with us or with the terrorists" formulation, sweepingly divides the world into good and evil without middle tones. The map of the world is divided into "friend" areas, which should be strengthened, and "enemy" zones, which should be conquered. The rules are clear and so is the mission, just as in war games. At times, it seems as though the excessive use of digital simulators for training and various war games has totally distorted our ability to read and analyze reality. Objectors to the current US policy strive to reveal the oversimplicity of the dichotomous view and the blindness it spawns, thereby exposing it as bankrupt and unfit to confront global terror. The continuous failures in Afghanistan, Iraq and, as of the writing of these lines, Lebanon only reinforce the feeling that there is room for a different way of thinking and a more intricate worldview.

In the "Forbidden Games" exhibition, we try to provoke discussions and debates amongst our visitors about harsh Middle Eastern geopolitical issues. Unlike at standard game exhibitions, visitors will not find the most advanced products in the field. Many of the games scattered among the rooms are activists' productions created with modest resources by avid players and independent programmers. The common thread is a connection to war and the contemporary political situation in the Middle East, from Syria to Lebanon and Israel.

Forbidden Games features more than 22 video games written and distributed independently of the entertainment industry by activist media, academies, ideological groups and companies as tools for addressing political and social issues. The alternative gaming they introduce is embodied in their political and ideological content, but also in their implicit suggestion of a reconsideration of the potentials inherent in the game medium, the language used therein and the open code. In each case, the final result is a single package that combines its creator's values with hours of pleasure and suspense. The games, which all present narratives antithetical to those presented today in the western media, are divided in the exhibition space according to how they do so: some are Web games centered on swift "gut responses" to topical issues such as the Lebanon war, the Gulf war, etc., others are games by activists criticizing the ideology currently dominating global politics, and yet others are performance games that require participation of the gamer's entire body. Media identities and images designed to foster the "war on terror" and the polar worldview it creates are part and parcel of the "war" itself. When you live in the Middle East, you cannot avoid the image ascribed to you by western media. The conceivers of video and computer games in Arab countries try to reinstate themselves with the responsibility of creating their own image, which, to their mind, has been distorted by the western media. They strive to recount the story behind the conflict with Israel and guide the youth playing computer games in constituting their knowledge of the world. A good example of this is the game *UnderSiege* (2005) developed by the Syrian company, Afkar Media. The game is based on the modern history of Palestine. It focuses on the life of a Palestinian family between 1999 and 2002, during the Second Intifada. It contains graphic violence and shooting at soldiers, but not at civilians. Its action is inspired by real stories of Palestinian society as documented by the United Nations (1978-2004). According to the UN, the West Bank and Gaza Strip constitute occupied land, and thus military actions there performed by local fighters against occupying forces are considered legitimate.

Another game that tries to deal with regional history is *Global Conflicts* (2007). The gamer plays a young journalist who has just arrived in Israel, where he tries to shape the region's future through peaceful means. The player must complete his assignment at all costs, navigating between Palestinian and Israeli sources of information to complete his article. Will the player be able to remain objective and gain the trust of both sides as the conflict escalates? What happens when people around him become more than mere sources? The game enables the player to learn about the Israeli–Palestinian conflict. It is informed by real personal stories that present the conflict from different perspectives.

At the opposite end of the spectrum is the game *Special Force* (2003), created by Hezbollah supporters in 2003. *Special Force* does not leave players much time to think about the point of view of the "other": the moment a mission starts, the player must find the Israeli snipers shooting at him and neutralize them with hand grenades. The game, which looks like a regular action game, was built on the *Genesis 3D* (1998) open source platform. Its introduction sequence shows the explosion of an Israeli tank. While the computer loads a series of drills – among them, shooting at Ariel Sharon's forehead, an action that grants the player ten points – a flurry around the burning of the Israeli flag is presented.

There are two games in the exhibition that try to deal with the First and Second Intifadas, each developed for a different end. *Intifada* (1989) – one of the few reality games produced in Israel – was created during the First Intifada in 1989 by Mike Medved. It attempts to simulate the relationship between the behavior of a single Israeli soldier faced with Palestinian demonstrators and the government's policies. The goal of the game is to scatter the demonstrators while killing and injuring as few of them as possible; this is achieved by using wooden clubs, rubber bullets, tear gas and other scattering devices. The political picture evolves throughout the course of the game: the Israeli Minister of Defense is replaced, and the government policy towards the demonstrations changes – as does the soldier's ability to react. The soldier in this game is a reflection of a given Israeli worldview; he is portrayed as a single soldier facing a charging crowd, a human and moral individual attempting to avoid unnecessary carnage, while his enemies are portrayed as bloodthirsty terrorists. The Israelis, according to this worldview, are always the few fighting the many, David facing Goliath.

The second game dealing with the Intifada is *Stone Throwers* (2003), developed by Syrian Mohammad Hamza as a manifestation of support for the Palestinian people. This game was created after the outbreak of the al-Aqsa Intifada. Nevertheless, it underscores the Palestinian perception of the resistance to the Israeli occupation, according to which the Intifada remains a popular uprising based on stone throwing, rather than a form of armed resistance. This game is centered upon a single

Palestinian who must throw stones at the Israeli policemen approaching him on both sides in order to protect the al-Aqsa mosque. Like the Israeli *Intifada* game, this game was designed to strengthen the perception of resistance as predicated upon the heroic struggle of an individual faced with numerous policemen. The individual portrayed here is waging a "pure" battle with no live ammunition, and he will win independence and honor through self-sacrifice.

The game *September 12* (2003), developed by newsgaming.com, focuses on the wider conflict between East and West and presents the wounding of innocent people in "the war on terror" as a dangerous consequence of fighting: air raids kill civilians and destroy houses, which leads to radicalization and thus an increase in the number of terrorists. Players must try to send "sophisticated bombs" and strike terrorists walking amidst civilians. But the bombs inevitably strike civilians as well, and other civilians consequently gather to mourn the innocent victims; some of them, in turn, then become terrorists. In other words, the player of *September 12* can never win. A localized success ensures the failure of the entire mission. The war against terror generates terror. After several bombings, the player inevitably starts to examine notions that have become highly prevalent in the media and the military discourse, such as "targeted killing," "surgical operation," "target bank," "sterile area," etc.

◆ *Genesis 3D* (1998), real-time 3D engine developed by Eclipse Entertainment. ◆ *Global Conflicts* (2007), developed and published by Serious Games Interactive. ◆ Pinter, H. (2005), *Nobel Lecture – Art, Truth & Politics*, Retrieved from http://nobelprize.org/nobel_prizes/literature/laureates/2005/pinter-lecture-e.html ◆ *September 12* (2003), developed by newsgaming.com. ◆ *Special Force* (2003), developed and published by Islamic Organization Hezbollah. ◆ *Stone Throwers* (2003), developed by Mohammad Hamza. ◆ *UnderSiege* (2005), developed by Afkar Media, published by Dar al-Fikr.

Global Conflicts: Palestine: http://www.seriousgames.dk/gc.html
September 12: http://www.newsgaming.com/games/index12.htm
Special Force: http://download.specialforce.net/english/indexeng.htm
The Stone Throwers: http://www.damascus-online.com/stonethrowers/
UnderSiege: www.afkarmedia.com
Gulf War 2: http://www.idleworm.com/nws/2002/11/iraq2.shtml
Intifada: http://www.old-games.org/game.php?game=intifada
Kuma/War: http://www.kumawar.com/
The Night Bush Was Captured: http://hotair.com/archives/2006/09/15/video-game-night-of-bush-capturing/contains
Suicide Bomber Game: http://newgrounds.com/portal/view/50323
Several "Nasrallah games": http://www.planetnana.co.il/atarsh//flashoo/nasral.html
http://www.amirlotan.com/nassralla/nasralla.html
http://www.tapuz.co.il/North/Game.asp
Terror: http://www.servus.at/cubic/(t)error.htm
Utz-Rutz and Tzirim: http://www.sketchbooksamurai.com/dmaot/?page_id=41
War in the North: http://img62.imageshack.us/img62/4782/battlesinthenorthxj5.swf
The War on Terror: http://war-against-terror.info
Wild West Bank: http://www.brand.co.il/unik/westbank

Game Review	Text	Developer	Publisher
	Stefan Werning	Kuma Reality Games	Kuma Reality Games, 2003

KUMA\WAR
Playing With Template Topographies

Kuma\War (KW), produced by Kuma Reality Games and released in 2003, is an ad-supported episodic third-person shooter that recreates (mostly) topical news events as playable missions only weeks after they occur. First and foremost, *KW* is as much a technological platform as it is a game in the traditional sense. Assets libraries – that is, tagged archives of reusable props and textures – as well as a flexible game engine – in the case of *KW2* (2006), the Source engine originally developed for the game *Half-Life 2* (Valve 2004) – are instrumental to the game's topicality.

These technological features imply a focus on preproducible spatial templates, or "prefabs" in game design lingo, which constitutes an important yet usually overlooked convergence with current developments in military simulation technology. For instance, the Evans & Sutherland Environment Processor (EP) allows for almost real-time updating of a "whole earth" environment database used in strategic military simulations; every actual military operation in new terrain automatically yields new data to populate the database. "Blank spots" are interpolated with "template data" intended to be asymmetrically refined. Through overlaps with commercial enterprises like *KW*, this practice is naturalized even though it results in imprecise information being used for planning actual operations.

The spatial experience of *KW* is essentially shaped by the (projected) patterns of its usage, which parallel the culturally constitutive practice of watching a daily news broadcast. This playing context results in a conceptual "hard-wiring" of *KW* imagery and "documentary" TV formats, stabilized by the use of photo-textures and satellite imagery. The consequence of this congruent form of spatial representation is to mutually reinforce the consumer's – both game player's and TV-watcher's – perception of the information as authentic. The Source engine's usability and its focus on character animation and physical realism are even supported by being used for a research project aimed at automating the generation of news formats (cf. http://infolab.northwestern.edu/project.asp?id=40).

Another important aspect of *KW* is its apparent de-purposing of the cityscape. *KW* frequently references urban iconography, virtually eliminating its functionality in the process; for instance, hardly any door in the game can be opened, meaning that the essential inside/outside hierarchization implied in a cityscape is not present. Furthermore, the game effectively demystifies iconic topography such as Tora Bora (Mission 31) or Abu Ghraib (Mission 43), commodifying the recreated terrain by functionally embedding it into gameplay. The singularity of the actual occurrences is furthermore compromised through "variations on a theme" missions, which are reworkings of previous missions with altered topography and starting constellations. Thus, the respective environments are read according to gameplay algorithms, not hermeneutic reasoning.

AMERICA'S ARMY
Shaping the Public Agenda through Spatial "Ideal Types"

America's Army (AA) is a tactical first-person shooter with a multiplayer focus that utilizes the commercial Unreal game engine (Epic Mega-Games 1998). Developed by the MOVES Institute at the Naval Postgraduate School in Monterey, CA and released in July 2002, the game is essentially a recruiting tool for the US Army, but also fulfills a number of different functions, through which it implants military themes in mainstream culture.

Popular recent topics in the academic discussion of *AA* are its viability as a "public sphere," its advertising potential, emotional aspects and actual training performance; the aspect of spatiality has not yet been a focal point.

In terms of spatial organization, *AA* does not radically depart from genre conventions. A key spatial property of *AA*'s multiplayer game modes is the symmetrical layout of most maps, which ensures balanced gameplay (e.g. by providing equal access to strategic positions). The example map, "Urban Assault," is characterized by a point-symmetrical distribution of starting points and objectives juxtaposed with an axis-symmetrical street grid. *AA* offers a number of ideal-type topographies designed for two-party multiplayer confrontations such as "urban assault," a desert "border village," an Afghan "insurgent camp" and a "hospital" with surrounding buildings. Clearly, many game scenarios bear (topographical) reference to recent news events like, for example, the extraction of Jessica Lynch and, since they are iteratively replayed, mark the topography as representative of "generic" types of war events. According to the game forums, many players are actual soldiers deployed in Iraq, likely to use ingame spatial experiences as cognitive filters.

Thus by virtue of the contingencies of adding new mission environments to every new version of the game, *AA* has an implicit but tangible "agenda setting" effect read against the chronology of the War on Terror. Formerly, people and events were the main elements on the public agenda. Yet structuring data according to quasi-*spatial* principles and broadening the understanding of *spatiality* were driving forces behind digital game technologies. As a result, digital games lead a shift towards Location as a primary means of agenda setting; this then carried over into other media (e.g. TV coverage of Abu Ghraib, Guantanamo, Hussein's Palace, etc.).

The level editor recently introduced to *AA* is a modification of the *UnrealEd* tool pertaining to the engine itself. More than other editors, it imposes the use of given assets and does not allow for importing own textures and geometry in order to prevent external content from undermining the game's objectives; default objects like staircases are even implemented as "brushes" shaping the expectable products by defining standardized work routines. As can be inferred from the game forum, only the increased workload caused by the imminent engine update "necessitated" opening the game for user-generated content in the first place.

While *AA* draws considerable attention away from other, less visible phenomena, it should be noted that, for example, non-western militaries like the Singapore Armed Forces are resorting to similar digital game technologies. Because, as noted above, spatial experience in these games depends on a number of external variables, a culturally comparative perspective might be needed.

Statement · Text

Wayne Piekarski,
Bruce H. Thomas

OUTDOOR AUGMENTED REALITY
Technology and the Military

The military has long been interested in the development of head-mounted display technology for use both in aircrafts and on the ground. As a result, most research involving Augmented or Virtual Reality has been supported by the military at some point in time. And indeed, our work at the University of South Australia was initially sponsored by the Defence Science and Technology Organisation (DSTO), an agency of Australia's Department of Defence, which provided us with our first wearable computer with which to perform user input studies (Thomas, Tyerman & Grimmer 1997). Later on, DSTO supported us in a project to develop a system that could provide navigation information to a head-mounted display. This eventually evolved into the *Tinmith* project.

One of the benefits of head-mounted displays, we quickly realized, is that they are useful in supporting collaboration between multiple users located outdoors as well as those who are managing them indoors. We extended the *Tinmith* system to support the Distributed Interactive Simulation (DIS) protocol – a worldwide standard of real-time war-gaming across multiple computers – so that it could communicate with other military simulation systems (Piekarski, Gunther & Thomas 1999). The ModSAF (Modular Semi-Automated Forces) system is one such system; it is a set of software modules normally used to generate the virtual entities that participate in military simulation scenarios. The *Tinmith* system is able to "see" these ModSAF entities outdoors by providing an overlay at their locations. Other visual simulation software such as MetaVR is able to use DIS packets from ModSAF as well as those generated by *Tinmith*, meaning that MetaVR users can see the real *Tinmith* user interacting with the virtual ModSAF entities. Now that 3D graphics hardware in mobile computers is so evolved, it is possible to render complete 3D models with intricate detail instead of the simple text and icon overlays used in the 1999 *Tinmith* system.

The public GPL release of id Software's *Quake* (1996) source code, a high-quality game engine that contains many of the components of the more complex and expensive ModSAF/MetaVR software, meant that anyone could modify the code. We adjusted the *Quake* source to support AR overlays and changed the control mechanism: instead of using a keyboard and mouse to control the game, position and orientation sensors in our *Tinmith* backpack are used to detect what action the user is taking. Our system, which we named *ARQuake*, allows users to run around outdoors and play against animated monsters. Since the system does not know the locations of real buildings in the physical world, we modeled parts of the university campus as transparent buildings. This forces the monsters to walk around physical buildings and prevents them from being rendered until they are visible. Most of the features of the original *Quake* are preserved in our modification, though there are some changes in the lighting so that objects are not as dark and thus more closely match the sunlit outdoor world.

Over time, our *Tinmith* system (Piekarski 2006) has evolved into a powerful piece of software that is capable of performing a wide range of tasks. The initial 1998 prototype supported simple navigation and rendering of 2D and 3D wire-frame models. Later on, in 1999, DIS support was integrated, and in 2000, *ARQuake* was developed. At that time, 3D accelerator hardware was starting to appear in laptops, revolutionizing outdoor Augmented Reality by allowing very realistic graphics to be generated with minimal effort. *Tinmith* was then further developed to support 3D modeling applications. Instead of simply supporting the viewing of models, we wanted the system to allow users to edit existing content and to create new content from scratch. To control the computer, gloves that could track a user's finger and hand movements were used.

The *Tinmith* system now has many powerful new applications, so we have begun to again explore other possibilities. The most obvious is to extend our work with *ARQuake* to build simulation systems that are more realistic and complex. Using the *Tinmith* software, it is possible to easily import large models of towns in VRML or 3DS format and allow the user to walk around them. This could be useful for situational awareness training, during which special forces need to be able to memorize the path they have to follow to enter a building. By using our existing DIS interface, complex 3D models can be overlaid onto entities that are generated in simulation systems such as ModSAF. This is useful because it means that the military can further capitalize on its existing investment in indoor simulation software by using it in real outdoor training as well.

But while the above scenario is the most obvious, our military partners are also particularly interested in supporting civilian tasks such as search and rescue applications. When a disaster such as a building collapse occurs, the outdoor environment can be filled with dust, which results in poor visibility. This means that existing infrastructure may not look as it did before the disaster, which can be very disorienting. But if some rescue workers are outfitted with AR systems, they will be able to "see" buildings as they were before they were destroyed and identify those areas where people might have been located; as a result, the optimal rescue efforts can be organized.

However, the real benefits of this type of system are gained when many users collaborate together. A big problem in disaster environments is that there are many people who need to be effectively coordinated. If the sensor data for each user is transmitted across a network, users will be able to know one another's locations. More importantly, indoor commanders who are coordinating the situation will also be able to see where their resources are being deployed and ensure that they are being used most effectively. In the past, these scenarios have relied on radio communications using verbal instructions. Now, using wearable computers, users can "see" each other and also use more advanced communications such as pointing and other hand gestures. For example, an outdoor user could draw an annotation onto the surface of a building to mark out a wall that has collapsed, and this information could then be sent immediately to headquarters for analysis. These types of applications are certainly of interest to military professionals, but to many others as well, such as architects, town planners, mining engineers, farmers and landscape architects.

In conclusion, the military has played a significant role in the development of Augmented Reality applications. It has sponsored a wide range of research at a number of different institutions to further improve the technology and its applications. However, the research that is being performed has a wide range of useful civilian applications as well. As with most military technology – such as jet aircrafts, computers and the Global Positioning System – the civilian applications of indoor/outdoor AR outnumber those initially envisaged by its military creators.

◆ Piekarski, W., Gunther, B. & Thomas, B. (1999), "Integrating Virtual and Augmented Realities in an Outdoor Application," *2nd International Workshop on Augmented Reality*, October 1999, San Francisco CA, pp. 45-54. ◆ Piekarski, W. (2006), "3D Modelling with the *Tinmith* Mobile Outdoor Augmented Reality System," *IEEE Computer Graphics and Applications*, vol. 26, no. 1, pp. 14-17. ◆ *Quake* (1996), developed and published by id Software. ◆ Thomas, B., Tyerman, S. & Grimmer, K. (1997), "Evaluation of Three Input Machanisms for Wearable Computers," *1st International Symposium on Wearable Computers*, Cambridge MA, pp. 2-9.

AFTER NET ART, WE MAKE MONEY
Artists and Locative Media

On March 31, 2004, *The New York Times* announced that three years after the collapse of the dot-com boom, the net art boom had also come to an end (Sisario 2004). In response, media artist Patrick Litchy observed, "this is not to say that net art is dead per se, but at least in institutional discourse it has been chiseled into art history and so has been drained of its dynamism," and urged Net Art to "morph into hybrid forms, or even to rebel against curatorial formalism in regards to their expectations" (Litchy 2004).

During the last several years, a new set of practices – which Turbulence.org director Jo-Anne Green collectively refers to as "Networked Performance" – has come to displace the hegemony of net art within media art circles (Networked Performance Blog n.d.). Art establishment venues such as ArtForum (Vanderbilt 2007) and Leonardo (Locative Media Special, Leonardo Electronic Almanac 2006) have used the term *locative media* to describe the emergent media art practices that, in response to the decorporealized, screen-based experience of net art, have laid claim to the world beyond either gallery or computer screen. For the purposes of this publication, we might thus think of locative media as a term for a subset of ubiquitous computing and pervasive gaming that is currently in favor in the networked art discourse.

Broadly speaking, locative media projects can be categorized under one of two types of mapping: either annotative – virtually tagging the world – or phenomenological – tracing the action of the subject in the world. Annotative projects generally seek to change the world by adding data to it. The paradigmatic annotative work is the *Urban Tapestries* project by Proboscis (http://urbantapestries.net). In a series of trials in 2003 and 2004, participants used mobile phones and handheld PDAs to annotate areas of London, thereby embedding social knowledge in the landscape of the city for others to retrieve later (Urban Tapestries n.d.). In their project *34n118w* (http://34n118w.net), Jeffrey Knowlton, Naomi Spellman and Jeremy Hight had users take Tablet PCs with Global Positioning Devices and headphones to a vacant lot in downtown Los Angeles adjacent to an old railroad depot now used as an architecture school (34n118w n.d.). As participants walked around the site, they would hear fictional statements through their headphones purporting to recount the history of the place. The result, Hight claims, "create[d] a sense that every space [was] agitated (alive with unseen history, stories, layers)."

Tracing-based locative media, for their part, suggest that we can reembody ourselves in the world. For an example of this type of work, we might look to Christian Nold's 2002 *Crowd Compiler* (Crowd Compiler 2002). Here, the artist generated time-lapse images of crowds in public space in order to understand the movement of all the individuals in one place over time simultaneously. Where annotative projects seek to demystify, tracing-based projects typically seek to use advanced technology to stimulate dying everyday practices such as walking or occupying public space, thereby escaping the prevailing sense that our experience of place is disappearing in late capitalist society. In this spirit, the *Open Street Map* project marks the paths of participants in the street via downloads from their GPS units, thereby locating participants in the world while also producing copyright-free maps of London (Open Street Map Wiki n.d.). Roughly, these two types of locative media – annotative and tracing – correspond to two archetypal poles winding their way through late 20th century art: critical art and phenomenology, perhaps otherwise figured as the twin Situationist practices of Détournement and the Dérive.

The current generation of artists sees art's purview as transdisciplinary and eagerly pursues projects that could be classified as research. In the case of locative media, this means that artists adopt the model of research and development wholesale, looking for corporate sponsorship or even venture capital. Proboscis, for example, received sponsorship from Orange, a 3G cellular network, and from computer hardware manufacturer Hewlett-Packard, as well as receiving a proprietary geodata donated by the Ordnance Survey for their *Urban Tapestries* project. Blast Theory, a locative media group composed of several London-based avant-garde theater artists, has gained renown for projects such as *Can You See Me Now?* (2001), *Uncle Roy All Around You* (2003) and *I Like Frank* (2004), in which it used location-aware mobile mapping devices to coordinate interactions between audience and performers in both real and virtual space (Blast Theory n.d.). Blast Theory's performances and installations have been supported through corporate sponsorship, public arts funding and through a six-year collaboration with the Mixed Reality Laboratory at the University of Nottingham (Mixed Reality Laboratory at the University of Nottingham n.d.). Hopefully, the relative commercial and critical success of these locative projects is representative of the melding of commercial and critical approaches that will characterize future pervasive games.

Of course, it almost goes without saying that video game developers have traditionally had a close relationship with capital. Indeed, even the aforementioned corporate-subsidized locative media projects seem extremely artsy and obscure in comparison to video games. As ubiquitous location-aware mobility becomes a reality, digital media producers are beginning to consider the streets as their canvas. With the booming gaming industry funding this push, pervasive game developers will soon be entering the space of architects and urban planners. In doing so, it would benefit them to engage in "conversation" with the locative media discourse.

The reluctance of many locative media practitioners to position their work as political has led some theorists such as Andreas Broekmann (director of the Transmediale Festival in Berlin) to accuse locative media of being the "avant-garde of the 'society of control,'" referring to Gilles Deleuze's description of the contemporary regime of power (1992, pp. 3-7). If some net art projects, such as *Carnivore* by Alex Galloway (Carnivore n.d), claimed autonomy through oppositionality and resistance by developing a radical political stance against the libertarian-entrepreneurial

"California Ideology" that, spread eagerly by *Wired* magazine, so dominated the discourse on the Internet in the 90s, it appears that for the moment, a fair number of locative media producers seems content to collaborate with industry and government. Where net art sought to maintain its autonomy from the dot-com boom in order to claim art status, locative media has been far less interested in such claims. It is thus no coincidence that one of the most important locative-media-related blogs goes by the name, "We Make Money Not Art" (deBatty n.d.).

The above article was derived from a lengthier piece entitled, "Beyond Locative Media," written in collaboration with Kazys Varnelis for *Leonardo*, vol. 39, no. 4 (2006), published by MIT Press, Cambridge MA.

◆ *34n118w* n.d. Retrieved March 8, 2007, from http://34n118w.net/34N ◆ *Blast Theory* n.d. Retrieved March 8, 2007, from http://www.blasttheory.co.uk/ ◆ *Carnivore* n.d. Retrieved March 8, 2007, from http://r-s-g.org/carnivore/ ◆ *Crowd Compiler* (2002) Retrieved March 8, 2007, from http://www.softhook.com/crowd.htm ◆ deBatty, R., n.d. *We Make Money Not Art*. Retrieved, March 8, 2007, from http://www.we-make-money-not-art.com/ ◆ Deleuze, G. (1992) "Postscript on the Societies of Control," *OCTOBER* Vol.59, Winter 1992, pp. 3-7, MIT Press, Cambridge MA. ◆ Litchy, P. (2004), *On the Death of Net Art*. Retrieved March 8, 2007, from http://www.voyd.com/voyd/lichtydeathofnetart.pdf ◆ Locative Media Special (2006), *Leonardo Electronic Almanac*. Retrieved March 8, 2007, from http://leoalmanac.org/journal/Vol_14/lea_v14_n03-04/intro.asp ◆ *Mixed Reality Laboratory at the University of Nottingham* n.d. Retrieved March 8, 2007, from http://www.mrl.nott.ac.uk/ ◆ *Networked Performance Blog* n.d. Retrieved March 8, 2007, from http://www.turbulence.org/blog/ ◆ *Open Street Map Wiki* n.d. Retrieved March 8, 2007, from http://wiki.openstreetmap.org/index.php/Main_Page ◆ Sisario B. (2004), "Internet Art Survives, but the Boom Is Over," *New York Times*. Retrieved March 8, 2007, from http://www.nytimes.com/2004/03/31/arts/artsspecial/31SISA.html ◆ *Urban Tapestries* n.d. Retrieved March 8, 2007, from http://urbantapestries.net/ ◆ Vanderbilt, T. (2007) "Circuit City," *ArtForum*. Retrieved March 8, 2007, from http://www.coldbacon.com/art/artforum/circuitcity.htm

"EASTERN EUROPE, 2008"
Maps and Geopolitics in Video Games

Representation of Space

With the introduction of 3D-graphics space, a fundamental change in video game aesthetics and performativity took place: virtual space is now predominantly generated as presented space or spatial presence (Poole 2000/McMahan 2003). However, spatial formations in video games confusingly are still referred to as "representational space" (Wolf 1997) in general, even though the pictorial appearance of the game is not always a literal representation. Rather, representations in video games have specific functions that define their role in the interactive play just like any particular form of spatiality does (Aarseth 2001/Fernández-Vara et al. 2005/Taylor 2005). The function of representations in games can sufficiently be described by Henri Lefebvre's (1991) trialectic of spatial processes, according to which the individual's perception of spacetime and the spatiotemporal structures of the social – "representational spaces" in Lefebvre's words – are reciprocally mediated by representations of space – namely, maps. Space in Lefebvre's understanding is thus threefold: a combination of perceived (*perçu*), conceived (*conçu*) and lived (*vécu*). Video games today are mostly a presentation of perceptual space in the way Lefebvre addresses the individual experience of space or what he also calls the "spatial practice." In contrast, representations of space differ from this phenomenal experience of space: as they are in real-life contexts, video game maps are essential for orientation, especially in games played from the first-person perspective, for in those games, one not only needs to see what one is aiming at, but also where one is located within the entire setting of the game. For this reason, maps in video games are either fully displayed and function as representations of the whole "playground" (which gamers usually call the "map"), or they are reduced to a visual element within the display, most frequently a radar that allows for orientation within the periphery of the position of the avatar or the ego in play. As in *Delta Force: Black Hawk Down* (2003), the radar is often integrated within the virtual Head-Up Display (HUD). It is not only

because of its first-person perspective, but also because of exactly this display element that Atari's *Battlezone* (1980) is the forerunner of the first-person shooter genre.

Maps: Symbols, Icons, Diagrams

From a historical perspective, maps have functioned as media ever since (Barber 2005); they have always mediated between a contingent standpoint and its larger context. But they have also always varied in their fundamental style of representation and, along with it, their type of orientation. There are at least two types or major styles of map: a map can be symbolic and make use of iconic inserts, or it can be rational and avoid any figurative representation. Any map lies within the realm of these two possibilities. Historically speaking, this is the result of a fundamental switch within the design of maps. Medieval maps offered a transcendent type of orientation and made use of symbols as well as of iconic presentations. On the contrary, modern maps are rational in that they are immanent in respect to orientation and make use of data gained through measurement.

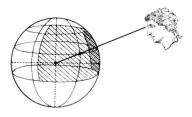

Edgerton 1975.

Kohlstock, P. (2004), Kartographie, Ferdinand Schöningh Verlag, Paderborn Germany.

The main principle that governs modern cartography was envisaged back in antiquity by Ptolemy and then rediscovered during the Italian Renaissance (Edgerton 1975): the idea of projection, which also underlines linear perspective construction and is rooted in the idea of an external beholder looking upon the world from a defined point of view outside it. But in contrast to perspective painting, a cartographical representation does not have one distinguished point of view, but an infinite number of viewpoints parallel to each spot on the map. The model of the external viewer is nonetheless important to imagine the function of projection as the plane in which the data of the survey are inscribed. After all, 18th-century cartography, mostly in the person of Carl Friedrich Gauss, effected the significant innovation of defining the status of the projection plane by treating the earth's surface as a physical body in itself, as a curved plane that has no thickness, but is nevertheless a 3D entity. Thus while to the external viewer the surface is nothing but projection plane, the geodesist can assign any data that is gained by trigonometric operations to the plane from within the plane. Because of this, maps – modern maps in particular – should be conceived not as pictures (even though they might still contain pictorial elements), but as diagrams. For what a modern map in most cases does is visualize a relation of two (or more) numeric values; this is especially true of topographical maps that indicate altitude at every given place, which, in turn, is identified by its degrees of longitude and latitude. Just like magnetic resonance imaging in the clinical context, topographical representations do not consist of pictorial presentations, but images that are gained from data and that do not resemble the appearance of any object. Maps, therefore, are visualizations that display certain knowledge about the world.

Preceding the Territory

Because modern maps are able to represent without resembling, they are also able to offer possible representations of things that do not (yet) exist in space purely

Schneider, u. (2004):
Die Macht der Karten.
Eine Geschichte
der Kartographie
vom Mittelalter
bis heute, Primus
Verlag, Darmstadt.

by naming their location. Jean Baudrillard (1988) thus determined that whereas in the premodern, the territory preceded the cartographic representation, in the modern, the map precedes the territory; what rational maps offer is the possibility to designate a position within space before that position is experienced individually or before anyone has ever even been there. Maps, then, do not only constitute territory

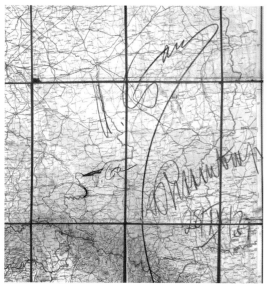

in the mathematical sense, but also in the practical sense: an intervention in the map can change the setting of the territory. This "active mapping" transcends geography and extends into the realm of geopolitics; whereas in everyday life maps provide orientation and thereby reify the structures of the life-world, geopolitical action can directly affect the medium by changing its spatial representation. A famous example of this is the 1939 "extinction" of Poland brought about by Joseph Stalin and the German Foreign Minister Joachim von Ribbentrop when they drew a new borderline between Germany and the Soviet Union on a map. By signing the map, they made use of it not only in the literal sense – map as charta (from the Latin for "document") – but in an active, political power-playing sense as well.

Playing the Map: Interactive Representations

Handling a map in a video game is not always an apparent geopolitical act, but in many cases, the handling of maps in games and in geopolitics rely on the same potentiality – namely, the potential to act through the map. This applies first of all to strategy games, in which interaction takes place only within the map. In these cases, the map is the game itself. The representation of space becomes the primary space for the player, and the virtual world is reduced to the map. Nevertheless, the character of the map in such contexts is fundamentally changed: it no longer functions as a source of orientation for an acting subject in space, but rather visualizes transformations that are imposed onto a developing world. In first-person shooter games, on the contrary, the map retains its function as a tool of orientation, but nevertheless serves as a geopolitical mechanism for transforming space: the map is used not only

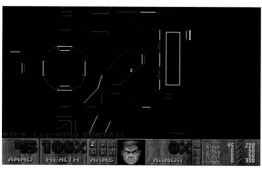

as a tool for orientation, but also for direct strategic maneuvers within the game's space.

The first time maps were used in first-person shooter games was in 1993 in the game *Doom*. In it, the map – commonly termed the "automap" – offered a feature that has become essential to the computer game: interactivity. One made use of the *Doom* map by switching between the perceptual and conceptual modes of space by simply pressing the tab button. This is interaction in a very basic sense, to be sure. But nevertheless, by switching between the two maps, a "third space" – as Edward Soja (1996) renamed Lefebvre's "lived space" – is constituted. It does not exist separately or outside the first-sight presentation and conceptual representation of space, but rather in between the two. The map transfers a contingent location in gamespace into a defined position in gamespace. In other words, the

Schneider, u. (2004): Die Macht der Karten. Eine Geschichte der Kartographie vom Mittelalter bis heute, Primus Verlag, Darmstadt.

map in *Doom* is not a picture of the gamespace, but a representation of what is known about the gamespace. This knowledge is of a dynamic character because the map in *Doom* is also interactive in another respect: when the player moves his ego-avatar in space, the map is extended room by room. Every time the player's ego in virtual space enters a new place or even looks through a window onto a backyard, the newly discovered area is added to the map. It seems as though the process of mapping, which used to be the reserve of the cartographer, has been passed to the player. True, any possible player discovery is anticipated by the design of the gamespace, but within the act of playing, that space is revealed to the user of the game and on his game maps for the first time. The *Doom* map is also interactive in a third respect, namely in that one can steer one's ego simply by navigating its representation on the map through the gamespace represented on the map. If there were no enemies (which are not represented on the

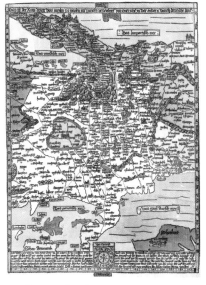

map), this type of navigation or "interactive mapping" would be sufficient for the spatial discovery of the game. But that type of playing would be fully conceptual, and, as a result, the shooter game would turn into a strategy game.

Orientation and Cartographic Design

In his famous text on *The Practice of Everyday Life*, Michel de Certeau (1984) deplored the loss of symbolism within maps caused by the processes of modernity. To Certeau, premodern maps preserved certain aspects of experience, which, until the early modern period, had always been the premise for drawing a map. Like Erhard Etzlaub's famous "Rom-Weg" map from 1500, premodern maps contained icons that resembled, for example, the monasteries and churches located on the way to Rome, those designated points for a stopover during a pilgrimage. Far from being maps in the modern sense, those maps did not offer a visualization of pure rational facts. Rather, medieval maps displayed systems of possible passages and relevant places along the way to the desired goal. According to Certeau, this practical aspect of a map has today all but vanished; it can now be found only in something like a tourist map designed for orientation purposes. However, Certeau didn't anticipate the extensive technical developments that would follow his writing. Today, for example, many cars are equipped with a GPS. The GPS maps are highly subordinated to the purpose of the user – namely, reaching a certain destination and identifying locations and stopovers on the way. The GPS can also mix first-space presentations with topographical representations in the 3D-mode available as a projection on the windscreen of the car. The empirical aspect of "mapping" in the literal sense has thus reemerged in car GPSs. But unlike the possibilities offered by computer games, which constitute their own spaces of experience, those offered by car navigation systems belong under the heading "Augmented Reality," in which Virtual Reality and actual reality are interwoven. This differs from interacting with a map in a computer game in that the first-space experience is something that is already a pictorial presentation, not perception of actual space. Therefore, in the case of computer simulations, it would be more precise to speak of an "Augmented Virtuality."

Geopolitics: Strategy and Alternative History

One of the most outstanding examples of map usage in a computer game can be found in the shooter game *Tom Clancy's Ghost Recon* from 2001. As in *Doom*, the map in *Ghost Recon* is interactive in at least two respects: firstly, the gamer can switch between the spatial presentation and the cartographical representation, and secondly, the gamer can steer his or her ego through the gamespace only by using the map. Unlike in *Doom*, however, in *Ghost Recon* there are not different rooms that have to be discovered; instead, the whole plan is viewed at once. What nevertheless *are* left for the player to discover are the locations of his or her hidden enemies. Whereas in *Doom* this could only be achieved by using a first-space presentation, in *Ghost Recon*, some areas of the gamespace are best discovered by *not* choosing to have a first-person experience. Rather, one must make use of the possibility of commanding different teams. In the multiplayer mode, separate players navigate different mem-

bers of a team; in the single-player mode, one player directs the egos of all team members. *Ghost Recon* is thus one of the few games in which the user can be a multiplayer *by himself* because he can switch between the various egos and make use of different standpoints and armaments. Even more remarkably, when played in the single mode, the game turns the player into the chief leader. That which has always been separated in military acting comes together in this game: the soldier is commander not only of someone else, but also of himself or herself. It is because of this that *Ghost Recon* is far more "strategic" than common strategy games. In tricky situations, it is advisable to use only the cartographic representation instead of the first-person perspective. If one does so, the first-person acting is then taken over by the game's AI. In turn, the gamer then interacts directly with the spatial setting. He or she directs and redirects any action of the mission by pointing at spots to which a specific team should go next, which detour it should take or to where it should retreat. On a very basic level, this constitutes geopolitical acting on the map: the setting in space – "where one is" – is changed by simply pointing at the map with the computer's pointing device. The map thus precedes the territory: strategic planning is done in the realm of the map and instantly has an effect on the virtual space of experience. This performance aspect is the nucleus of geopolitics in *Ghost Recon*, and through it, political decisions are directly applied onto the territory.

But geopolitics is approached in a far more obvious way in the game's introduction. *Ghost Recon* introduces the conflict map by referring to a hypothetical political incident in the near future. The game description reads as follows:

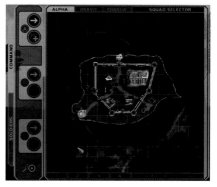

> "Eastern Europe, 2008. The world teeters on the brink of war. Radical ultranationalists have seized power in Moscow – their goal, the reestablishment of the old Soviet empire. Ukraine, Belarus and Kazakhstan – one by one the nearby independent republics slip back into the Russian orbit. Russian tanks sit in the Caucasus Mountains and the Baltic forests, poised to strike to the south and east."

The narrative framing of the game is thus based not only on stereotypes of communistic revanchism, but also on a scenario that is much more likely than that on which the *Doom* series is based – a future colonization of the planet Mars or one of its moons set in the 22nd century. *Ghost Recon* makes use of a type of fiction that is known as "alternative history" (Hellekson 2001): even though 2008 is still in the future and was in the future when the game was designed, the political decisions and martial interventions that would lead to the development described in the game's introduction must have already taken place in order to become real in 2008. And even though there have been heavy conflicts in the former member states of the Soviet Union since its collapse, between now and 2008 is too short a time span for a development like the one envisioned in the game to occur. Nevertheless, it could happen in the near future if an unexpected coup d'état occurs. And it is exactly this fact that the introduction is getting at; games like *Ghost Recon* are not realistic because they make use of polygonal rendering in the pictorial presentation of first-space, but because they take place within a plausible constellation – i.e. within a possible world.

◆ Aarseth, E. (2001), "Allegories of Space. The Question of Spatiality in Computer Games," in M. Eskelinen & R. Koskimaa (eds.), *Cybertext Yearbook 2000*, University of Jyväskylä, Jyväskylä Finland, pp. 152-161. ◆ Barber, P. (2005), *The Map Book*, Weidenfeld & Nicholson, London UK. ◆ *Battlezone* (Arcade) (1980), developed and published by Atari. ◆ Baudrillard, J. (1988), "Simulacra and Simulations," in M. Poster (ed.), *Selected Writings*, Stanford University Press, Stanford CA, pp. 166-184. ◆ de Certeau, M. (1984), *The Practice of Everyday Life*, University of California Press, Berkeley CA. ◆ *Delta Force: Black Hawk Down* (PC) (2003), developed and published by NovaLogic. ◆ *Doom* (PC) (1993), developed and published by id Software. ◆ Edgerton, S. (1975), *The Renaissance Rediscovery of Linear Perspective*, Basic Books, New York NY. ◆ Fernández-Vara, C., Zagal, J. P. & Mateas, M. (2005), "Evolution of Spatial Configurations In Videogames," Proceedings of *DiGRA 2005 Conference: Changing Views: Worlds in Play*. Retrieved December 3, 2006, from http://www.gamesconference. org/digra2005/papers/d0f28517012721ec75728a62b9038477.doc. ◆ Lefebvre, H. (1991), *The Production of Space*, Blackwell Publishers, Oxford UK et al. ◆ Hellekson, K. (2001), *The Alternate History. Refiguring Historical Time*, Kent State University Press, Kent OH. ◆ McMahan, A. (2003), "Immersion, Engagement, and Presence. A Method for Analyzing 3-D Video Games," in M. Wolf & B. Perron (eds.), *The Video Game Theory Reader*, Routledge, New York NY/London UK, pp. 67-86. ◆ Poole, S. (2000), *Trigger Happy. The Inner Life of Videogames*, Fourth Estate, London UK, pp. 125-148. ◆ Soja, E. (1996), *Thirdspace. Journeys to Los Angeles and Other Real-and-Imagined Places*, Blackwell Publishers, Cambridge MA et al. ◆ Taylor, L. (2005), *Toward a Spatial Practice in Video Games*. Retrieved December 3, 2006, from http://www.gameology.org/node/809. ◆ *Tom Clancy's Ghost Recon* (PC) (2001), developed by Red Storm Entertainment, published by Ubisoft. ◆ Wolf, M. (1997), "Inventing Space. Towards a Taxonomy of On- and Off-Screen Space in Video Games," *Film Quarterly*, vol.51, pp. 11-23.

Gerhard M. Buurman (GMB)
in conversation with the Editors of Space Time Play (STP)

THE GAME OF INTERACTION

STP **How are games relevant to your work as an interaction designer as well as to your teachings and your research?**

GMB Grappling with technology always has its ludic aspects. Why do we struggle with bad systems and programs again and again? Because we cannot accept losing to a machine. It is this feeling of defeat, of capitulation that causes us, when we can't manage to discover the secret of a machine, to enforce our will upon it. This is a typical ludic approach. And everything new begins as playfully as possible. Our whole technological history is probably the history of ludic challenges.

STP **What role does space play in this scenario, in this evolution?**

GMB It is exactly there that I see room for possibility, or even experience. I broaden myself and my abilities when I learn to handle technology, when I conquer ludic intricacies, but also when I am only facing a practical, everyday technology. As I conquer it – that is, learn to operate it – I expand my realm of possibilities. And on this topic, an academic debate is important and desirable. In discussing the topic "Games," we can learn how to generate "fun with technology." When we speak today of man–machine interactions that should be self-explanatory and enable "joy of use," then it is probably the ludic character in particular that should be consciously encouraged. This will be accomplished only once we've found out what makes a good game.

STP **Against the backdrop of our technologized society, how do you read the following, well-known Schiller quotation: "Man only plays when he is in the fullest sense of the word a man, and he is only fully a man when he plays?"**

GMB We should not displace our gamespace with technological systems so that there is no longer any way out of the game. I mean this absolutely existentially. Such a situation would have dramatic consequences because then the game would develop into an inescapable reality. In order to be a game, every game also needs a second layer, a setting – that which is nongame. But should technology advance so far that it leads us, in a clever and ludic manner, into a state of increasing bondage, so far that there are no more ways out, no more areas of freedom outside the technological life? We must act with caution, remain vigilant and always be clear when it comes to answering the following question: where does the game begin and where does it end? Maybe it ends beyond my consciously

450

accepted role as a consumer, beyond my consciously played role as a citizen, and begins at that point where I must be a human being, which, to close with Schiller's long-time friend, Goethe, is a truly new game.

STP **What you just said stands in antithesis to the artistic posture of the "This Is Not a Game" design movement, whose credo is to leave potential gamers in the dark, at least at first, as to whether or not an object – a website or sensor-equipped artifact, for example – belongs to a game. Jane McGonigal speaks here of a desired "secretiveness" of the technological object, which, if cloaked in such secrecy, charges the world with magic – a reference to the "enchanted village" vision of ubiquitous computing pioneer Rich Gold. It would interest us to hear what you have to say about that.**

GMB Again and again, one gets involved in certain games, in private or more open, charming, ludic or even very serious interventions, which are characterized by the fact that they have a beginning and an end, and one experiences them more or less consciously. Like life itself, these game-tragedies are not to be forgotten. But to build subversive strategies out of that goes against everything that technology has always meant for me: to better reveal the possible ways I can exist in the world.

STP **You spoke earlier of realms of freedom and experience. What potency, then, can an experience rife with ludic interactions provide?**

GMB What I have learned about games is that the player sees, amongst other things, an essential and defining quality in exchanging the role that life has assigned him with a different one. This playing with identities and roles, with aesthetics, gender and sexuality and with social status is im-portant and surely constitutes one part of the fascination. For me, it is magical to experience the emergent awareness that that which I produce ludically – the role, the character, the people, the identity that I adopt...

STP **...or the perspectives or the activities...**

GMB ...or the perspectives or the activities that I take up in the game, are not things located outside myself, but rather within me – that is, they are a part of my own reality. In this respect, the magic moment is achieved when I realize that I am thrown into the game as myself, that despite everything, I am totally with myself.

ATOPIA (ON VICE CITY)

01.   It's like paradise here. Everything seems pastel-hued as you drive by with the radio on. The car is stolen, but so long as the police didn't see you, it won't matter. *Vice City* is a nice place (Grand Theft Auto: Vice City 2002). It is not quite utopia. And nor is it some dark dystopia. There's no storyline here where paradise turns nasty, in which the telling early detail turns out to be a clue to the nightmare beneath the surface, the severed ear of *Blue Velvet* (1986). Without the possibility of dystopia, there's no utopia either. In *Vice City* there is no "beyond." As one would expect in a high-end land of vice, its offer is *all-inclusive*.

02.   In gamespace, the very possibility of utopia is foreclosed. No space is sacred; no space is separate. Not even the space of the page. The gamelike extends its lines everywhere and nowhere. And yet, a pure digital game like *Vice City* might still perform some curious, critical function. Why do so many choose to escape from their everyday gamespace into – yet more games?

03.   Utopia was a place to hide, where a topic could develop of its own accord, safe within the bounds of the book. Utopias do their best to expel violence. In a utopian text, there is always a barrier in space – distant and difficult terrain – or a barrier in time. The real barrier is rather that troublesome line that divides what is on the page from what is outside it. Utopia was a place on a page where violence was pushed to the margins by the power of sheer description.

04.   Utopia restricted itself to a particular topic, the topic of the page, and a particular line, the line of writing. The book is a line: a trajectory, a connection through time and space with certain qualities. Among its qualities is the way it partitions off the smooth space of the page from the rough-and-tumble world without. It rules off from the world that special tempo where text plays its subtle games against its reader.

05.   When the lines of telesthesia – telegraph, telephone, telecommunications – connect topics into a topographic space, extensively mapped and storied, utopia is recruited from the page and comes out to play. Rather than a retreat from the world – showing in its positive creation of a new world what the actual one beyond its lines lacks – utopia becomes something else. The book becomes an alibi for more worldly lines of communication, some with the power of an order: diagrams, memos, reports, telegrams. Utopia becomes part of something instrumental, but thereby loses its power. Topographic lines are now there to make the world over by the book, but in the process, they make the book over as well, reducing it to just another line. The smooth plane of the blank page is the greenfields site for delineating a pure topography of the line.

06.   Topography learned to live without its utopias and settled into a mundane resignation to the here and now. It assuaged its boredom in special times, special places, where different rules applied. Postwar play theorist Roger Caillois' answer to the Nazis was to build a postwar society with ample margins for games of what he calls "agon" (competition) mixed with games of what he calls "alea" (chance). Each would have its proper place and time alongside but not above everyday life. This would be the antidote to the Nazi's toxic mix of two other kinds of play – intoxication and spectacle (Caillois 2001). Games of agon would take place outside of the uncertainties of mundane time and space in special zones where consistent rules apply. Such spaces are "heterotopias." Michel Foucault: "Their role is to create a space that is other, another real space, as perfect, as meticulous, as well arranged as ours is messy, ill-constructed and jumbled" (Foucault 1967). Heterotopias are at some remove from the dull repetition of meaningless labors with incalculable purpose in workaday life.

07.   Heterotopian spaces are very varied. Each has its own particular rules and seasons. There are heterotopias of bare necessity: prisons, hospitals, schools. These need not concern gamer theory much. More interesting are the heterotopias of useless luxury: galleries, arenas, sports domes. These, in turn, subdivide into heterotopias of aesthetic play and of the calculated game. One is a space of pure qualities; the other, pure quantities. In one, the ideal is that play is free; in the other, that the game is fair. In both heterotopias, these values have their limits. Outside the heterotopia that makes their autonomy possible, they amount to nothing.

08.   Heterotopias of luxury contain subdivisions of play and game, each existing within allotted times and spaces, which are subdivided in turn. The space of play contains separate worlds of literature, art, theater, cinema, even spaces for sexual play. These are now just "special topics," ruled off from any larger ambitions for remaking the world. Aesthetic play tried again and again to break out of its heterotopia, to take the derangement of the senses into the streets. Guy Debord: "For Dadaism sought to abolish art without realizing it, and Surrealism sought to realize art without abolishing it. The critical position since worked out by the Situationists demonstrates that the abolition and the realization of art are inseparable aspects of a single transcendence of art" (Debord 1994). It was not to be. The heterotopian space of the art world instead abolished Debord's Situationists by realizing Situationism entirely within the confines of the playpen of art history.

09.   Art tried again and again to break out of its heterotopia. Not only was it no match for the game, it ended up playing a subordinate role within the expansion of the game beyond a mere heterotopia. Art provides the images and stories for mediating between the gamer and gamespace. Rather than actual games played in actual arenas, art expands the reach of the game to imaginary games played in a purely digital realm, anywhere and everywhere, an *atopia* of gamespace.

10.   Heterotopias of the game have never been of much interest to theory, whose practitioners have tended to view them as the places of the mob. But to gamer theory, which doesn't hold such prejudices, heterotopias of the game may be a key precursor to gamespace. Among them are separate worlds pitting different attributes of body and mind into contests of skill or luck, from badminton to backgammon.

Every way of measuring what one body does against another – each finds its own special heterotopia.

11.　　　For a gamer theory, the genealogy of gamespace might pass through these heterotopias of the game more than those of play, and those of play more than those of necessity. Theory has been looking for the keys to contemporary life in all the wrong places. The playtime aesthetics of the avant-garde of art yield to the "ludology" of gamespace. It was the genius of Caillois, the lapsed Surrealist, to grasp this. In topography, his alea and agon become the dominant modes; intoxicating vertigo and dissimulating spectacle (what he calls ilinx and mimesis) become the minor modes. The obsessions of the Situationists – passive spectacle and active insurrection against it – form an obsolete couple, each drawing support in decline from the other.

12.　　　No utopia pulls at the topological world, calling it away from itself. Even dystopian texts become marginal, confined to the playground of literary gamesmanship. The once discrete heterotopian spaces no longer coexist with everyday life as compensation. Rather, gamespace seeps into everyday life, moving through its pores, transforming it in its own image, turning up everywhere from cellphone *Tetris* to your quarterly pension fund statement. Rather than a timeless utopian ideal in which history ends, rather than the allotted hour of the heterotopian, everyday life now pulses constantly with moments of unrealized *atopian* promise. Everywhere, all the time, the gamer confronts the rival impulses of chance and competition, intoxication and spectacle, as homeopathic antidotes to a boredom that challenges his being from within. In *Vice City*, all of Caillois' four kinds of play – chance and competition, intoxication and spectacle – come together. The destruction of the spectacle becomes the spectacle of destruction; the derangement of the senses becomes the arrangement of drug deals. In *Vice City*, you chance your arm in an agon of all against all.

13.　　　No work of art can aspire to transcend this gamespace, which has realized art by suppressing its ambitions. Yet perhaps a game like *Vice City* can function as the negative of gamespace, its *atopian* shadow, parallel to the way that the very positivity of a utopia acts as a negation of the world outside its bounds. Not the least of the charms of *Vice City* is that while it appears to be about a life of crime, it is thoroughly law-abiding. It is a game about transgression in which it is not possible to break the rules. This is the *atopian* dream of gamespace, where the lines are so dense, the digital so omnipresent, that any and every object and subject is in play, and all of space is a gamespace. The game imagines topology perfected.

14.　　　*Atopia* has one quality in common with utopia: its aversion to ambiguity. *Vice City* may take place in a dark world of guns and drugs, but every mission produces an exact and tangible reward. If utopia thrives as an architecture of qualitative description and brackets off quantitative relations, *atopia* renders all descriptions arbitrary. All that matters is the quantitative relations. By excluding relations, utopia excludes violence; by privileging relations, *atopia* appears as nothing but violence, but only because it instead excludes any commitment to stable description. The relentless working out of the algorithm leaves behind a carnage of signs, immolated in the transformation of one value into another.

15.   The rules of *Vice City* call for a vast accumulation of cash, cars and cronies, of weapons and real estate. Most of these activities are outside the law, but law is just part of a larger algorithm. In any case, the story and the art are arbitrary, mere decoration. If in utopia everything is subordinated to a rigorous description, a marking of space with signs, in *atopia*, nothing matters but the transitive relations between variables. The artful surfaces of the game are just a way for the gamers to intuit their way through the steps of the algorithm. Hence the paradox of *Vice City*. Its criminal world is meant to be shocking to the literary or cinematic imagination in which there is still a dividing line between right and wrong and in which description is meant to actually describe something. But to a gamer, it's just a means to discover an algorithm.

16.   In *Vice City*, the world exists already made-over as a complete gamespace, an *atopia*. It is not "nowhere" (utopia) or "elsewhere" (heterotopia), but "everywhere" (*atopia*). The various spaces already have the required properties of a certain kind of play. The space itself, rather than the gamer who crosses it, is already *atopian*. This space is perfect, seamless – and bounded like Thomas More's *Utopia*. And just as the utopia points to what is lacking beyond the page, so too, *atopia* points to what is lacking beyond the game. *Atopian* space is a real enclave within imaginary social space. The possibility of *atopian* space is a result of the impossibility of adequate and effective spatial and social quantification and calculation.

17.   In games as in gamespace, some calculations happen quicker than others. Sometimes there is a moment to think it over, negotiate. Sometimes not. When there is no time for calculation, the gamer must act on the basis of a calculation made in advance. There's always a backstory, providing some dividing line along which to weigh one's interests. The *atopia* of the game is a safe haven in which to enact the problem of being as it appears in gamespace, but without the oppressive stakes of one's own life on the line.

18.   Out of the heterotopian games of chance and competition arise the *atopias* of gamespace, via which topology makes itself known to us as an ever more intricate matrix of the digital line. Both the prisoner's dilemma of game theory and Foucault's theory of disciplinary power begin and end in dystopian dungeons. They offer no account of the new forms of power and being that arise out of the transformation of the line from the topographic to the topological. Too much dungeon, not enough *Dungeons & Dragons*. The power of theory falters on the theory of power. It's not that theory, even a gamer theory, can achieve all that much when confronted with the digital indifference of gamespace; but it might aspire merely to describe what being now is.

This text is a condensed version of the "Atopia" chapter in McKenzie Wark's book *Gamer Theory*.

◆ *Blue Velvet* (Movie) (1986), produced and distributed by De Laurentiis Entertainment et al. ◆ Caillois, R. (2001), *Man, Play and Games*, University of Illinois Press, Urbana IL. ◆ Debord, G. (1994), *The Society of the Spectacle*, Zone Books, New York NY, p. 191. ◆ Foucault, M. (1967), *Of Other Spaces*. Retrieved from http://foucault.info/documents/heteroTopia/foucault.heteroTopia.en.html ◆ *Grand Theft Auto: Vice City* (2002), developed by Rockstar Games, published by Take-Two Interactive.

PLAYING WITH ART

STP   **The Merz collage artist and writer Kurt Schwitters once wrote: "A game with serious problems: that is art." Are games and playing potentially the basis of design and art?**

HPS   The notion that art can be a game burst strongly forth as early as the Romantic era. The Schwitters quote alludes to the fact that a work of art exists precisely because it is contingent – that is, it doesn't come into existence according to predetermined rules, nor does it boil down to a specific goal, deducible through hermeneutic operations. It is this fact alone that is essential to discuss because it stands in conscious opposition to the teleological game. On the one hand, the game is rarely geared towards a specific, useful purpose; but on the other hand, what Schwitters meant with the phrase "serious problems" was that the themes of artworks tend to be existential problems.

STP   **Let's talk about the target-oriented – i.e. teleological – computer game. It is founded upon the rehearsing, or practicing, of certain activities; one could argue that as cultural practices, computer games don't provide spaces of freedom, but rather commercialized consumer worlds.**

HPS   Without fail, computer games feature this potential for indoctrination, which one can see as a negative or positive thing. On the one hand, this potential can obviously lead to manipulation. But then again, the specific medial competencies that are necessary in our contemporary world and will be even more necessary in the future – above all, for our children and youth – can be practiced via computer games. The question remains: when does practice become alteration – that is, when does someone become so manipulated that he can only react to something in a very specific manner? I think it is important to concern oneself with these games and the theory behind them in order to find this boundary.

STP   **Is finding this boundary one of the responsibilities of reflecting on and designing games in an art and design college?**

HPS   I consider it the central challenge because it concerns not only the computer game, but rather every poster, every other visually communicated statement that strongly entails the potential to manipulate. At art colleges, it has always been important to glean the exact location of the line between pure manipulation and a statement that provides its recipient with the leeway he needs to grapple with it on his own and thereby become more competent in the given medium. It's the same with certain advertising concepts that have been around for much longer, since before the time of computers. But only someone very competent at an art college can develop this critical potential. At an art college, practical competence exists alongside the ability to reflect critically. This has long consitituted the essence of the artistic approach to a medial concept.

STP   **In games, competitive situations are often reproduced; they are about survival and death, winning and losing. At the same time, the secondary world of the game is also always linked to escape. In your opinion, what potential does escapism hold in the field of art and design?**

HPS   Art places the tangible world alongside a parallel word. I don't, however, consider this a form of escapism. This parallel world can sometimes be idyllic, as in its romantic conception, or it can be hard, as in certain realistic models. This creation of parallel worlds is definitely a classic method of artistic pursuit, at least since the advent of the Modern. It is important that this escapism has not come so far that one can completely shut oneself off from one's own reality and live only in these artistic realities – which, if possible, would lead to cultural autism. There was a time, about 15 years ago, when people were always talking about this "Virtual Reality." One got the idea of giving oneself over completely to this subversive system. I find the notion "Expanded Reality" very exciting – this vision independent of hypostasization, this notion that enables exactly these intersections between virtual and real. The notion of "interfaces" is also well suited for delineation. To formulate these interfaces in such a way that they become consciously perceptible to the player is in my opinion one of the challenges we face with computer games. The interactive artists of the 90s were also concerned with making exactly such consciousness perceptible, with immersing viewers in a Virtual Reality but also bringing them back out of it, and with using the tension between these two experiences of reality as artistic and aesthetic motivation for their art.

S.T.A.L.K.E.R.: SHADOW OF CHERNOBYL
Ludic Space as Memorial

For some years, researchers in the field of architecture have demonstrated a growing interest in interactive virtual spaces. An architect may design a virtual space that depicts a fictitious place or one that depicts a real, but inaccessible place. Virtual spaces may be found in computerized works of art and in educational exhibits of various sorts. The virtual Mayan ruins presented at the Science Museum in Ueno, Japan between 18 March and 18 May 2003 serve as a useful example of the latter.

I have argued that video games use virtual spaces in a manner analogous to film sets. The primary function of a film set is to support the narrative of the film. Similarly, the primary function of a ludic space is to support the gameplay of the game. However, a ludic space also has a secondary function, which is to *entertain in its own right* by a variety of means. These include offering novelty (spaces the player has never seen before and would enjoy seeing) and creating an atmosphere that complements

458

the gameplay: grim spaces for grim activities, amusing spaces for humorous activities and so on. However, there is another possible function of ludic space, hitherto largely unexplored: namely, memorialization.

S.T.A.L.K.E.R.: Shadow of Chernobyl is a video game developed by the Ukrainian company GSC Game World and released by publisher THQ in March 2007. The game is set in The Zone of Alienation, a 30km exclusion region around the Chernobyl nuclear power plant. This area is so contaminated by radiation that it had to be abandoned following the Chernobyl disaster and may not be inhabitable again for centuries. All the vehicles and buildings in The Zone are too toxic even for salvage.

S.T.A.L.K.E.R. is a first-person shooter, and much of its gameplay is conventional, but its use of ludic space is nearly unique among video games. Rather than create a fictitious landscape, GSC Game World has chosen to render The Zone of Alienation as it exists today, with a high degree of accuracy (although some modifications have been made to meet the demands of gameplay). Using maps and satellite photos, the developers have reconstructed the decaying city of Pripyat in detail, as well as the abandoned vehicles that litter the surrounding landscape. The game also correctly depicts many other features of the landscape, particularly the rolling hills and the native flora.

It is not unusual for a game to depict a real place or a place as it once was or might have been. What sets *S.T.A.L.K.E.R.* apart is its depiction of a place that *still exists*, but that cannot be inhabited, rather only remembered.

The real-life Zone of Alienation continues to change, as trees grow up through the Pripyat football field and wild animals flourish in the absence of man. In time, the buildings will fall and be buried like Mayan ruins. We will have photographs and documentary films to memorialize the place as it once was. But to that archive we may now add something new: a ludic space that people may experience in three dimensions. A video game will keep alive the memory of a poisoned town.

SHADOW OF THE COLOSSUS
Player versus Terrain

Gameworlds too often provide a virtual landscape no different than a playing field, a carefully demarcated surface that functions simply as a set of topographical rules. *Shadow of the Colossus* stirred both popular and critical interest by defying convention and producing one of the more meditative and complex gamespaces to date.

While the conventions of the action adventure genre demand a series of levels, increasingly challenging and concluding with an end-of-level battle against a "boss," *Shadow* artfully twists this formula. The game's central feature is that it uniquely presents the game level itself as the level boss. To progress, the game's hero must assess, navigate and ultimately destroy each of the colossi scattered across an otherwise desolate landscape.

The story begins with and the conflict revolves around a central cathedral inhabited by ghosts and a disembodied voice promising to raise the player's true love from the dead in return for the destruction of the colossi. Riding across sweeping plains and rugged mountains, the player moves through a spatial void surrounding this central cathedral, seeking active terrain where the colossi live.

If the connection between the colossi and the landscape appears too tenuous at first glance, the game reiterates their bond at the moment of defeat: once a colossus has fallen to the hero's sword, the massive corpse tumbles into a natural tableau with the surrounding land. What was once a visage turns into a craggy stone face, a torso into a mounded earthen mass with arm-like hillocks running off its sides.

Because the environment itself remains inert – only a scampering lizard or circling bird animates the sterile and empty places – the question arises: who is threatened by the colossi? The conclusion, whether apprehended directly or left uncovered in the subtext of the game's narrative, is simple: the hero combats the environment itself. It's a question of man versus nature, the player versus the environment as represented by the colossi.

The timeless story of the human environment as a transformation of the natural environment echoes throughout the game. Maneuvering the hero up a colossus like a skilled rock climber scaling a peak, the gamer plays out man's domination over nature. Even though a geyser of blood exploding as the killing blow is struck replaces the traditional flag placed at the mountain summit, the parallels remain obvious and powerful.

By so brashly presenting the land in humanoid, or at least anthropomorphized form, the game creates a human-scale conflict without featuring very many humans. Ultimately, the game's rendering of our efforts to mindlessly destroy and transform nature, to terraform the land's creatures, the colossi, provides a unique look at how people mark, control and contest terrains, how blood and soil intertwine. And it provides a platform for discussing and experiencing the constant turmoil of a landscape racked by ghostly motivations and demands of the human heart.

CHINESE GOLD FARMERS
Immigrant Workers in the Game Land

Virtual goods in MMORPGs (Massively Multiplayer Online Role Playing Games), from ingame currency to epic weapons to top-level avatars, are often traded against real-world currencies in a process dubbed RMT (real-money trading). A myth has been circulating in the gamer community for the past several years: namely, that a large portion of the virtual goods in the RMT market are mass produced by gaming sweatshops in China that hire people to play online games day and night. During field research in China, I've found that this myth actually comes quite close to the truth.

The gamer community uses the term "gold farmer" to refer to a person who plays MMORPGs solely for the purpose of accumulating virtual goods and selling them for real-world currencies. Sociologist T.L. Taylor (2006, p. 320) observed, "Although it is certainly not only Chinese workers participating in the growing economy of RMT practices in MMOGs, as a tag the conflation of *Chinese* with *gold farmer* has seemed to come all too easy and now transcends any particular game." This overextended stereotype – gold farmers are Chinese and vice versa – stems from gamers' frequent encounters with gold farmers from China in many MMORPGs. Gold farming has indeed developed into a significant industry in China, and according to the insiders I interviewed, there are hundreds of thousands of gaming workers in China who are taking all kinds of jobs in almost every gameworld that has a virtual economy – killing monsters, mining gems, blacksmithing, tailoring and power leveling ("leveling up" a customer's character to his desired level) in the virtual lands (regional game servers) of America, Europe, Korea, etc.

Most factory-style gold farms in China emerged in late 2003 with the release of global game hits like *Lineage II* (2004) and *World of Warcraft III* (2004). The large-scale Chinese gold farms have hundreds of computers and employees. I believe that China has become the world factory of virtual goods mainly for the following reasons. First, China has a strong gaming culture and a big population of youth who love playing online games. Second, China is poor, and people's wages there are low, but the country has invested heavily in Internet infrastructure over the past years, so high-speed Internet and good computers are accessible in most cities. Third, the culture of entrepreneurship is strong in China. Many gaming workers started their own gold farms after they learned the trade working on others' gold farms, so the industry has expanded quickly. Fourth, though no policy has been designed yet to regulate this new industry, the government has thus far been tolerant of it. Because gold farming reduces the mass of unemployed youth on the street, most local officials simply let it exist. Furthermore, RMT is usually considered legitimate under Chinese law; there have been court cases in which gamers won virtual property disputes with game developers.

Typically, the factory-style gold farms provide meals and dorms so that "farmers" can live on the farm and work 12-hour shifts with short breaks. There are usually twice as many farmers as computers, so that the given game is running 24/7. The salary for gaming workers ranges from 40 US Dollars to 200 US Dollars per month. I even found some farms whose gaming workers are willing to work unpaid as long as they have a place to live and can play games for free.

The Chinese gold farms are sometimes referred to as "gaming sweatshops." This term does, in fact, capture some characteristics of the farms, which reflect China's current role in the global economy: a source of cheap labor. Staring at a computer, clicking a mouse and killing imaginary monsters for 10-12 hours a day is certainly an exhausting job, but not more exhausting than most factory work in China. Furthermore, the term "gaming sweatshop" is an oversimplification that obscures the complexity of the phenomenon. Many of the gaming workers were already game fans before they went "professional." What's more, the gameworld can be a space of empowerment and compensation for them. In contrast to their impoverished real lives, their virtual lives give them access to power, status and wealth that they can hardly imagine in real life. It is precisely for this reason that many of them are addicted to their jobs.

All the gaming workers I met are male, primarily in their early 20s. Most of them do not have better alternatives; they were either unemployed or had worse jobs before they found this one. Many said that it was a fun job at the beginning, but gradually became very exhausting and boring because unlike regular gamers, the workers often have to stay at the same spots in the game and perform the same tasks again and again. There are other sources of frustration that come with the job as well. For example, gaming workers cannot socialize freely. This is partly because of language and cultural barriers, but also because they are afraid of being reported to the game companies, which might ban their accounts. If they are power-leveling for a customer, for example, it's usually part of their contract that they will not interfere in the social life of the customer and that they will keep it a secret that the character has been power-leveled. Also, these workers are very uncertain about their futures; the skills they have honed for their jobs on the gold farms can hardly be transferred to other jobs, but at the same time, the gold farm industry is still highly controversial, and no one knows if it will last. What's more, though the workers wish that people would recognize their job as a normal and serious one, most people in China don't understand it, much less respect the professional skills it requires.

The gold farming industry turns one man's play into another's work, but most gaming workers see a clear difference between work and play. At work, they are often deprived of the socializing and venturing aspects of games. Some workers get so bored and frustrated that they go to Internet cafes after work to play the same games for themselves, but on Chinese servers, just to relax and have some fun. This demonstrates that the right to play is a privilege, only available to those who can afford to spend a significant amount of their time and effort on activities with no material rewards attached.

The Chinese gold farm is often seen as a new form of outsourcing. However, there is a difference between the two: when a shoe factory is moved from America to China, the shoe making workers and consumers in America do not meet the Chinese shoe making workers in person. But RMT in gameworlds puts Chinese gold farmers and American gamers in the same virtual space where they *have to* interact with each other, be it through competition, collaboration or trade. In this sense, Chinese gold farmers are more like virtual immigrants that the "native" gamers must face. As such, the anxiety they inspire in many gamers is very similar to the anxiety inspired by real-life immigrants. The following excerpt of an email from one of my interviewees serves as a telling example:

> "Do you ever try to explain to the Chinese Gold Farmers that they ruin the gaming experience for millions of people? These people take a simple game made for entertainment and exploit it, costing the real gamers artificial inflation, time, and in some respects, money. My opinion (and millions of others) of these people is beyond low. Coming from a society of honor, tradition and respect these people clearly have none. I can understand making money as an incentive to do this, but really they need to get the fuck out of our games and try making a respectable dollar. Please pass on this message to any RMT (real-money trader) that they are a complete waste of life, and if given the opportunity, I would break their faces with a baseball bat without thinking twice."

The artificial inflation this gamer points to is really the devaluation of his time in the game land, the result of the fact that he has to compete with people whose time has lower economic value than his. And when he emphasizes that the games are "our games," he clearly indicates a belief that game lands have national borders that should not be crossed. Although he will not have a chance to attack Chinese gold farmers in real life, he can participate in the virtual "war on farmers" not uncommon in games like *World of Warcraft* and *Lineage*.

Chinese gaming workers have diverse views on the impact of their work on regular gamers. Some of those to whom I spoke said they just mind their own business and don't mess with regular gamers at all. But others said they know that the huge number of Chinese gaming workers does change the environment of gameworlds. They have many stories of conflicts with regular gamers, but they also have stories of collaboration and friendship. Lao Liu, a five-year veteran gaming worker, said the following:

> "It's true that we influence regular gamers' experience. We have an assignment from the boss to get a certain amount of gold everyday. So we pick certain good spots, stay there, and keep killing the same mobs and looting gold. If some other gamers come, then we have to fight with them to drive them away, because we have pressure from our boss … But the main problem is communication. I think with sufficient communication even a policeman and a thief can become friends … I wish I knew how to say 'Let's play together' in English."

Though much of the controversy over Chinese gold farmers results from intensified competition for ingame resources that can lead to xenophobia, many gamers put the blame on the very existence of RMT, rather than on Chinese gold farmers personally. Robert Holt (2005), a game reviewer for NPR, says that "in the game, unlike in the real world, all users start on a level playing field. I like that. There should be no advantage to you in the game if you're rich in real life." (He seems to neglect that real-life advantages other than wealth, such as leisure time, a good computer and a fast Internet connection, can be translated into ingame advantages. Is the game really a level playing field?) Edward Castronova (2006, p. 6) also argues that RMT erodes the pleasure of total immersion in a game: "This loss of fun, more broadly, can be seen as an externally imposed disturbance of the game, a perturbation away from the gameplay as intended by the designers... In this, RMT is like a pollution of a service that the designers are attempting to provide to their customers." This thread of argument assumes that the gameworld is supposedly more fair, pure and fun than the real world and should remain so.

If our concern is whether or not the cultural consumers get the "escape" they need or whether or not the game companies can sell their games well, then the above argument against RMT is sufficient. But if we are concerned about the deep-er cultural implications of the game-world, then some different lessons can be learned. What does the existence of Chinese gold farmers tell us about our Internet-driven global village? First, that the world is not flat and that economic inequality in the real world tends to be reproduced in the virtual world. Sec-ond, that the underlying value system of most MMORPGs like *World of Warcraft* centers on the endless pursuit of virtual status, power and wealth. If a cultural consumer is willing to pay for subscrip-tion – the access to such a pursuit – why wouldn't he be tempted to pay for what is actually pursued? As far as the answer to this question is "he would," RMT does not pollute the gameworld because the gameworld has never been more inno-cent than the real world. And last, the existence of gold farming tells us that the Internet-driven global village gives labor a border-crossing mobility (the border can be that between the virtual and the real as well as that between na-tions). Consequently, gaming workers

can be disembodied and turned into virtual immigrants, teleported to foreign game lands, reembodied as mythical hunters, warriors or rogues and complete game tasks that others find too boring or time-consuming.

◆ Castronova, E. (2006), *Synthetic Worlds: The Business and Culture of Online Games*, University of Chicago Press, Chicago IL. ◆ Castronova, E. (2006), "A Cost-Benefit Analysis of Real-Money Trade in the Products of Synthetic Economies," *Info*, vol. 8, no. 6. ◆ Holt, R. (2005), "All Things Considered – Paying Real Money to Win Games," Radio Program, *NPR*, Washington D.C., 30 November. ◆ *Lineage II* (2004), developed and published by Ncsoft. ◆ Taylor, T.L. (2006), *Play Between Worlds - Exploring Online Game Culture*, MIT Press, Cambridge MA. ◆ Taylor, T.L. (2006), "Does *WoW* Change Every-thing? How a PvP Server, Multinational Player Base, and Surveillance Mod Scene Caused Me Pause," *Games and Culture*, vol. 1, no.4, pp. 318-328. ◆ *World of Warcraft III* (2004), developed by Blizzard Entertainment, published by Vivendi.

ADVERTISEMENT IN VIDEO GAMES
"Sell My Tears," Says the Game Publisher

Advertising is spreading into the world of video games. It will no doubt change the way the virtual environment looks. But will it also change reality?

In physical reality, advertising has degenerated into normalcy. The advertising industry occupies everything, at every time – magazines, television programs, movies, billboards, private cars, shopping bags, chocolate bars. A person wakes up in the morning. The radio alarm clock plays the first advertising jingle. The bombardment of advertisements has begun. Only in the late evening will it quiet down after the last advertising segments of the evening program on cable have aired. To escape this bombardment has become virtually impossible. Maybe in conversations with good friends from time to time, but even then, the targeted penetration PR messages from opinion leaders give rise to an intentional word-of-mouth propaganda. Yet more advertising.

Until a few years ago, most video and computer games were places of calm for those harassed by constant advertising. Combats with aliens uninterrupted by soft drink manufacturers, an ad-free training circuit on the Nürburgring, an unsponsored skate run on Tony Hawk's half-pipe: that's how it was back then. Games on consoles and computers became – and continue to become – more and more popular, which is the best way for anything to become its own discipline within the field of mass media communications… and to advance itself into a focal position. Because where a large number of potential contacts to normally hard-to-reach, increasingly segmented target groups exists, greediness quickly awakes in all those looking to advertise their products or services. The advertising industry is getting ready to change the architecture of the virtual world – and it may have some consequences for the real cityscape. Because as people stroll through virtual worlds more and more, advertisement from reality must follow them to virtuality.

So what does the virtual life of, for example, the German gamer really look like nowadays? Based on available media budgets, investments in entertainment software have doubled since 1995 across all age groups. In Germany alone, a fourth of the entire population plays video and computer games at least occasionally. In the first half of 2006, this translated into 19.7 million Germans sitting at consoles and PCs, 75 percent of them men. Forty-three percent of them were 15 years old or younger, 27 percent were 29 years old or younger and the astonishing remainder was older than 30. Traditionally, the majority of gamers in Germany plays on the computer; but consoles comprise somewhat more than 40 percent of the entire market – and are growing more and more important by the day.

The data thus indicate a distinct mass market. It is the qualitative analyses that raise the big question marks. Advertising in video and computer games: how can its value be measured at all? Is it the next big thing? More important than Web 2.0? Will it forever change games and players? And if so, how and to what end?

As a systematic and integral extension of traditional marketing in the "real world," the development of paid advertising campaigns in the virtual world of video and computer games is still in its infancy. Precisely for this reason, there is as yet no uniform definition for such campaigns. Sometimes the advertisements in video games are simply called ingame advertising, sometimes the shortened IGA,

sometimes branded entertainment, sometimes advergaming. In each case, the general idea is the same: companies embark upon advertising initiatives in video games so that they can reach their advertising goals.

For many years, ingame advertising has been just an accidental side effect. Due to an increasing determination to simulate reality, designers of racing games created the market for ingame advertising in the early 1980s. The desire for more realism in games inspired the placement of the first billboards along game routes. For the most part, they contained self-marketing, or the programmers simply plastered them with their favorite logos of real products. Problems soon ensued. In 1989, the US tobacco company Philip Morris caused an uproar when it sued Namco (for *Final Lap* (1987)) and Sega (for *Super Monaco GP* (1990)) for using illegal trademarks in their video games. In both cases, billboards containing advertisements for Marlboro cigarettes line the sides of the route. In 1997, the collaboration between Sony Computer Entertainment and the Austrian soft drink manufacturer Red Bull ushered in a new era. At the beginning, it was "just" a classic reciprocal business deal with no payment involved, according to the following exchange: trading billboard placement for event marketing. Since then, a paradigm shift has taken place: the producers of video and computer games, led by market leader Electronic Arts, increasingly see themselves as being in a position to make demands, thanks to the fact that their hit games can boast circulations in the millions. Brands that want to jump on the video and computer game train are no longer desperately begged to grant brand usage rights, but rather politely asked to the cash register. At the same time, the market environment got more professional. There are already, for example, agencies whose sole concentration is video and computer game advertising commerce.

Today, ingame advertising already exists in many forms with many nuances. The most common are virtual billboards and perimeter advertisements – sensorial, passive advertising forms that are seen, but not used in the gameplay context. The billboards are either flexibly allocable (DIGA, dynamic-ingame-advertising) or are concretely integrated during programming (SIGA, static-ingame-advertising). Significantly more interesting – especially from the perspective of the advertiser – are products and brand advertising that support game realism. Two forms of the latter are widespread: the on-set placement, which encompasses any far-reaching, usually incidental product or brand placement in the gameworld, or the creative placement, the purposeful ingame placement of a product – roughly based on its applicability – as a positively connoted object meant to propel the narrative flow.

Ideally, the presence of real brands or products in video and computer games serves to bolster realistic-as-possible representation and authentic playability. For that reason, the existence of perimeter advertising in soccer simulations is not a breach of the game experience; the expectation – acquired in reality – that there will be perimeter advertisements on the sidelines of a soccer field has been seamlessly transferred to virtuality. In ten years, this learning process may have reversed itself to some degree for today's youth. It is quite probable that future forms of advertisement will be conceived for use in virtual worlds and then make their way back to reality. But first billboards will disappear from cities and be replaced by virtual billboards. Banners in virtual worlds acquire relevance because they can be specifically targeted in accordance with analyses of the buying behavior of largely transparent consumers. You just bought the obligatory case of Sprite in the supermarket, a stick of Axe deodorant and a jar of peanut butter. Everything was paid for with the credit card. Your monthly fees for online games are charged on that very same card. The game publisher buys the bonus evaluation data from the supermarket operator, compares the enclosed credit card numbers with its data-bank and sends gamers advertisements from the appropriate product categories via billboards erected in their current favorite games. Technologically speaking, this is absolutely possible. Which means that one of these days, this idea will be converted into reality. The purchasing data of passersby will be automatically read from their credit card RFID chips as they walk by a certain location, and a few seconds later, the appropriate advertisement will appear on the digital, changeable, real billboard 100 meters further down the road. For now, this is still a fictional scenario, no more, no less.

At present, it is still largely unclear how the effectiveness of advertising in virtual gameworlds can be measured. The few serious studies on the topic hardly provide conclusive findings on or insights into how (or better, how effectively) ingame advertising influences its audience. A plausible conjecture supported by, for example, findings related to product placement in films, could be that ingame advertising leads to brand prominence, association of a brand with a game's plot and, through multisensory transmissions, to increased remembrance of the brand or product on the part of the gamer. Then again, one could just as persuasively argue that, for example, the presumed transfer of positive emotions activated by a pleasurable experience (like, for example, playing) does not have a positive effect, but rather no effect or even an altogether negative effect on brands advertised through product placements. Or even that video gamers simply don't have time to register the advertisements in games because they are too preoccupied with the steering of their racing cars or killing of their foes.

Altogether, there is much to support the contention that advertisement will increasingly vanish from the real cityscape into the virtual one. The interactive and immersive character of video and computer games makes possible a high degree of involvedness: the player is not the passive recipient of experiences, but rather an active operator. It is still unclear whether or not there will ever be a virtual equivalent of, for example, the Chrysler Building that over decades will become a visual symbol as widely recognized as the car manufacturer's skyscraper. But the dangerous Naxxramas dungeon in *World of Warcraft* (2004) is already a fixed notion in the minds of over 7.5 million players worldwide. It is thus only a matter of time before the big companies make use of this potential communications power.

◆ *Final Lap* (1987), developed and published by Namco. ◆ *Super Monaco GP* (1990), developed and published by SEGA. ◆ *World of Warcraft* (2004), developed by Blizzard Entertainment, published by Vivendi.

Game Review	Text	Director	Production
	Rolf F. Nohr	Peter Weir	Paramount Pictures, 1998

THE TRUMAN SHOW
Simulating Life

The Truman Show is hardly a film you would automatically speak about as a game. At first glance, it is tempting to interpret the story of Truman Burbank – his perpetual subjection to the artificial (tele-visual) world of Seahaven and its gargantuan reality TV project, his eventual escape from the "OmniCam Ecosphere" building and the paternalistic surveillance of director Christof – as the stuff of classic cinema, as a classical coming-of-age tale in the form of an ironic dystopia and a media critique. If, however, we understand the figure of Truman as a (remote control) avatar and the strictly delimited setting of Seahaven as a playing field, then the game analogy becomes telling. In that case, *The Truman Show* becomes a game from the genre of real-life simulations. Design your own avatar. Watch him growing up in a normal Rockwellesque American aesthetic, winning the game by internalizing its normality. See yourself as well, to the extent that you are just like everyone else. Scenarize yourself on the stage that is your own life. Purchase the products that will allow you to become rich and successful. Never leave the protected community of the total Sims.

The Truman Show anticipates the computer game *The Sims* (Maxis Software 2000) and thematizes the closed and fully controlled space of life-simulation on the basis of a normative canon of values and consumerist strategies for success. Like *The Sims, The Truman Show* represents the declension of a neoliberal urbanistic space.

To be effective, the media develops a concept of narrative technique based on stereotypes. If *Tron* (Walt Disney 1982) or *WarGames* (MGM 1983) founded urban or architectural metaphors, *The Truman Show* instead founds a spatio-social stereotype. These stereotypes (in the sense of visual and thematic conventionalizations) become independent cultural signs. Their character, however, must be regarded as ambivalent in nature. On the one hand, they are deficient, since as perpetual citations, they take the form of immobilized and static statements. In the best cases, they construct references and citations; in the worst cases, they are simply plagiaristic. But they are also – and this must be emphasized – functional. And spatiodesign stereotypes are functional to the extent that as forms of communication, they guarantee instant comprehensibility. The "familiar, normal, and dependable" is only a problem in cases of nonconformity with that which is intended – as in the case of the Truman simulation. But when this conventionalization of the narrative serves the immersive and the playful, when the spaces we enter in the cinema are not only familiar, but also present in the preconscious and invested with meaning, then immersion can emerge in all of its effectiveness. Then the space of simulation of *The Truman Show* (as with *The Sims*) reflects a space of action that, in fact, guarantees us security: the familiar, normal and dependable quality of a regimented world, one in which identity is not least the sum of all attributes, commodities and symbols associated with it.

Text	Developer	Publisher
Marie Huber, Achim Nelke	Elisabeth Magie	Parker Brothers, 1935

MONOPOLY
The Multiple Career of a Concept

In 1904, inspired by the ideas of American social philosopher and political economist Henry George, Elisabeth Magie laid out a model city on a game board. With her *Landlord's Game*, she wanted to illuminate the nexus connecting land laws, property rights and social injustice. The Georgists demanded the introduction of a land tax, which would be the sole tax, and which was conceived as an exit from the dilemma of progress and poverty. Correspondingly, the message of this board game is a hostility toward speculative activity. The rectangular playing field, whose sequence of squares allows continuous playing, was the first board game in modern history to have no goal point located at the conclusion of a sequence of squares. Players move by turns, buying up the city – already subdivided into parcels – piece by piece. Once all the parcels have been sold, they are then traded in five rounds. The player with the greatest amount of money wins.

Monopoly is a subsequent development of *The Landlord's Game* that emerged from private circles, one in which the original ideological intention was turned on its head: a *Monopoly* game is not limited in time by rounds, and the individual parcels have been developed and filled in with buildings. Now, moreover, the winner is the ultimate owner of the city. Beginning in 1935, *Monopoly* was commercially marketed by Parker Brothers and quickly became a best-seller. Today, it is the most frequently played and successful board game in the "western" world (*Monopoly* was banned east of the Iron Curtain as the symbol of the historical world of individualistic capitalism). Whether it's the *Here & Now* edition, which includes tokens for McDonald's French fries and credit card readers, the *Reykjavik* edition, or the ironically intended *Ghettopoly*, *Ökolopoly* (known in English as *Ecopolicy*), invented during the board game craze of the 1980s, or even the worldwide record time-breaking *Monopoly* game played in a tree house, the core message of *Monopoly* catches on everywhere without difficulty, undergoing a multitude of culturally specific appropriations and transformations.

The fulcrum and linchpin of the game is always a reduced and abstracted plan of Atlantic City (USA). Within this external framework, players find inner freedom: by becoming fused with the players' imaginations, the preestablished game board allows the actual space of place to emerge, so that playing the game becomes a highly personal experience. But why did *Monopoly* experience its worldwide triumph just when the capitalist market economy was plunging into the abyss of the Great Depression? Perhaps because it offered an escapist refuge from the daily realities of capitalism. From dishwasher to millionaire in a couple of hours: the game enacts the attainment of the capitalist dream, even for the majority who remain forever cut off from the possibility of experiencing its fulfillment.

Project Description   Text   Project

Stephan Trüby,   Stephan Trüby,   2006
Stephan Henrich,   Stephan Henrich,
Iassen Markov   Iassen Markov

CHANGING THE GUARD
Through Surveillance to "Sousveillance"

When it comes to surveillance, no country tops the United Kingdom, and when it comes to surveillance in the UK, no place has more CCTV cameras per square mile than London where, as Andy Warhol might have said, everybody can be famous, every 15 meters. Nowhere does this hold more true than in Shoreditch. Since 2005, residents of this trendy East London neighborhood have been able to receive *Asbo TV* - television beamed live to their homes from CCTV cameras on the surrounding streets. This electronic neighborhood watch is offered by the Shoreditch Trust ("Fight crime from your sofa!") as part of its Shoreditch Digital Bridge (SDB) project, which aims to build a broadband digital network covering 20,000 residents on housing estates in the Shoreditch area. As part of the £12 million scheme funded by the Office of the Deputy Prime Minister, residents of Shoreditch are also able to compare characters they see behaving suspiciously with an on-screen "rogues' gallery" of local recipients of antisocial behavior orders (*Asbos* for short). Viewers are able to use an anonymous email tip-off system to report to the police anyone they see breaching an *Asbo* or committing a crime. The area was picked because it is among the country's poorest.

There's only one problem: *Asbo TV* has become the most boring TV channel in the world precisely because

it is too successful. Nothing happens on the streets anymore. The game *Changing the Guard*, currently under development, is a response to this phenomenon: it forces players to watch the Shoreditch CCTV footage more carefully because the films are necessary for a game dramaturgy about stealing TV sets from neighbors in order to construct private panoptic "war rooms." The title alludes to *Changing the Guard* at Buckingham Palace, one of Britain's main tourist attractions. Accordingly, the famous soldiers in full-dress uniform

of red tunic and bearskin hat turn into camera robots during the game and try to disturb the players as they attempt to install a higher degree of "sousveillance" within an emerging regime of surveillance.

474

Project Description	Text	Project	Affiliation
	Sheldon Brown	Sheldon Brown, Alex Dragulescu, Mike Caloud, Joey Hammer, Erik Hill, Carl Burton, Daniel Tracy	Experimental Game Lab, Center for Research in Computing and the Arts, UCSD, US, 2006

THE SCALABLE CITY
Zones, Conflicts and Aesthetics

Cities are becoming inputs and outputs of algorithms. The real world becomes an expression of algorithmic desire, adapting itself to computational consumption. *The Scalable City* extrapolates this situation into an interactive artwork that is similar to a computer game. The play involves constructing this virtual city by interacting with a data visualization pipeline. Satellite data and ground photogrammetry

are transformed through a series of exaggerated algorithmic gestures. The forms of this synthetic world are clearly related to the original, but the process of their algorithmic digestion and re-manifestation has loaded them with artifacts. This tension between original and outcome is emblematic of a number of underlying conflicts present in the work. An aesthetic of conflict is used to reconnect to the real-world tensions that are the project's ultimate concerns.

Currently, *The Scalable City* utilizes data from Southern California for its particular engagement with the generative collisions between nature/culture, First World/Third World and self/society. By subjecting these elements to the interactive algorithms of the work, we expose their underlying tensions. The means for this revelation are aesthetic in nature. First, algorithms are misapplied (algorithms developed to modulate data from a specific domain are now applied to an entirely different type of data). The landscape is formed by treating a 3D form as a 2D image with cut, copy and paste routines. Computer vision techniques analyze the resultant form for viable areas, which are occupied by a road system consisting of Archimedes spirals growing via an L-system. Architectural fragments imbued with rudimentary functional knowledge are scattered throughout the landscape. Players of *The Scalable City* are embodied by a particle system of photogrammetrically derived automobiles. The player moves the particle system through the landscape. As this vortex of vehicles flies through the environment, it stirs up the architectural detritus. As the pieces land, they attempt to assemble themselves into collaged houses. The houses have the structures of migrant worker shanties rebuilt with formal elements drawn from suburban McMansions (though only the perturbed optical skins of these objects of desire remain).

The gameplay of the work serves two primary functions. First, it extends the viewer's gaze into the complex realm of the work's data, algorithmic and social interactions. Only by interacting with this situation can one hope to make sense of it. Second, these interactions are implicated as the operative crux in the ongoing dilemmas of the social and cultural milieu. The game becomes a visceral engagement with these abstractions of the lived situation. Through its extensions and limitations of game transformations, the gameplay creates an enacted connection to the social roles we inadvertently perform in this matrix rather then the more empathetic role viewers typically assume in cultural inquiries taking different forms.

Project Description	Text	Project	Affiliation
	Jane McGonigal	Jane McGonigal, Kiyash Monsef, George Porter, Monica Slufft	The Ministry of Reshelving, US, 2005

THE MINISTRY OF RESHELVING
Political, Pervasive Game Design

Some preliminary observations about public space and gameplay: 1. "The public" is less and less to be found in so-called public spaces. To engage the public, we must look to commercial and privatized sites that now serve as the most-trafficked social sphere. One such space is the large retail bookstore. 2. Social phenomena that emerge in online spaces may have interesting applications offline. Analog gaming structures designed for real-world spaces can test this potential. One phenomenon worth testing is the bottom-up tagging and sorting process known as folksonomy. 3. Classification has social and political consequences. The twin categories of fiction and nonfiction are an excellent place to start challenging the usually tacit tyranny of traditional taxonomies. 4. Game structures are excellent mobilization tools. Massively scalable micro-play is a powerful frame for social action, especially for those unlikely to act under more serious frames. *The Ministry of Reshelving* is a pervasive and political game.

This distributed gameplay project represents game development stripped to its fundamentals: the rules of interaction. Our rule set was intended for viral digital distribution, designed to spread and thrive via the existing network of social media. It was conceived as an experiment in creating a digital gaming community through ludic content rather than software. On August 24, 2005, we invited the public to visit local bookstores to relocate copies of George Orwell's *1984*. The following is an excerpt from the original announcement: "Unless *The Ministry* has already visited the bookstore, *1984* is probably incorrectly classified as Fiction or Literature. Discreetly move all copies of *1984* to a more suitable section, such as Current Events, Politics, US History or True

Crime. Insert a *Ministry of Reshelving* bookmark into each copy of any book you have moved. Leave a notecard in the empty space the books once occupied so that booksellers and buyers can find your reshelved texts." We made PDF files of the bookmarks and notecards available for downloading and requested that agents submit tallies and photographic evidence of successful missions. The gameplay was designed to be massively collaborative, with a single win condition for the entire player base; success or failure would be a collective experience. As the announcement put it, "Our goal is to relocate 1,984 copies and to complete successful reshelving of *1984* in all 50 United States."

The original goal of reshelving 1,984 copies of Orwell's books was met within 71 days. Reports were received by *The Ministry* from 39 of the 50 United States. Additional reports were filed internationally from Canada, the UK, Australia, France and Singapore. Over 40,000 web entries were created about *The Ministry of Reshelving* in the first month. The American Librarian Association, the American Booksellers Association, the National Writers Union and over 100 other local book, library and writers' groups weighed in on the project. Media outlets such as NPR, CNET and Slate also covered the reshelving efforts. Records indicate that agents frequently widened their efforts to include other titles; several reports were filed on the relocation of evolution textbooks to Science Fiction, for example. Participants preferred to submit evidence of their missions via email rather than contribute to a central public pool by a ratio of 23:1. Booksellers, librarians and writers were more supportive of the project than bookstore and library patrons by a factor of roughly ten.

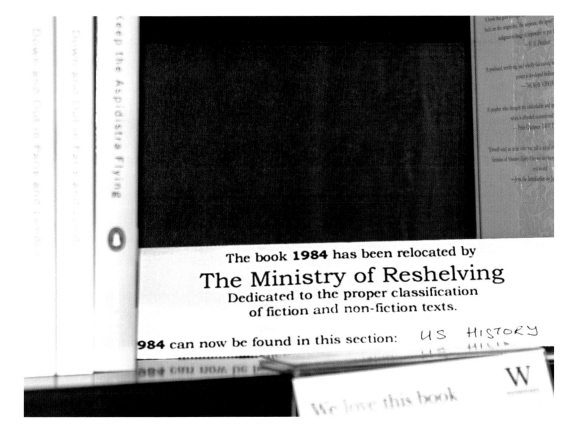

The book **1984** has been relocated by

The Ministry of Reshelving

Dedicated to the proper classification
of fiction and non-fiction texts.

984 can now be found in this section: US HISTORY

We love this book

RE-PUBLIC PLAYSCAPE
A Concrete Urban Utopia

"Depending on what you are after, choose an area, a more or less populous city, a more or less lively street. Build a house. Furnish it. Make the most of its decoration and surroundings. Choose the season and the time. Gather together the right people, the best records and drinks. Lighting and conversation must, of course, be appropriate, along with the weather and your memories. If your calculations are correct, you should find the outcome satisfying. (Please inform the editors of the results.)" (Psychogeographical Game of the Week 1954)

These few lines from *Potlatch* #1, published in 1954 as the first of a series of information bulletins by the Lettrist International (a predecessor of the Situationist movement), are the synthesis of our utopia, the horizon to move towards, the (im)possible game of an architecture that prefigures the possibility of constructing its own environment and tunes every single element to its own wishes and moods, restores to man the *means to produce space,* eliminating the *alienation* of the space itself – that is, of its being *alien* because thought up and produced not by the people living in it but by someone else.

But besides the huge though harmless spaces of online video games, what real space must exist in order to build up such games? Where to start?

The incidents in the *playscape* that will follow help us to concretely measure this freedom, revealing the political dimension of the game, today often forgotten, which seems to overbearingly reemerge when, as in this playful architecture, we begin to reconsider decision processes and inspection forms outside the range of the harmless installation or of the artistic practice, in public space and in the architecture itself.

It all started three years ago, when, for the Europan VII competition, in the announcement of competition, which is a sort of catalog of European urban conditions that (a bit like the initial screen of a video game, where you need to choose the setting and the level of difficulty of the game, trying to imagine difficulties and obstacles that we would need to overcome) we chose to challenge ourselves with the theme "revitalizing the over-planned housing development" and to work on a working-class neighborhood (in France they are called HLM, Habitation à Loyer Modéré) built in the 60s by a well-known French architect, Macel Lods[1] in Drancy, on the outskirts of Paris, one of the municipalities that was formerly part of the so-called "red belt" and home to the working class of the French capital.

This, like other similar 20th-century neighborhoods, is the furthest-away starting point to reach our horizon, and for us keen players represents the biggest challenge: here, the opposite game translates into architecture, where the project defines a way of living; here, microorganisms are created, enabling us to study

On http://housingproto-types.org/project?File_No=FRA017, you will find one of his most famous projects, the Cité de la Muette, also carried out at Drancy.

1 >

the dream, the pseudoscientific thinking or that propaganda that every kind of architecture carries as a justification that becomes reality through the shape and the structure of space. These neighborhoods provide a unique occasion to try to solve the complex relationships between a construction project and lived life that determine the success or failure of a part of a city. They are, in other words, proper playgrounds where architecture tried, with disastrous results, to impose a social game through its own internal project regulations, depriving people of the possibility to make changes, to adapt them over time and make them their own.

In short, the announcement of competition underlines two major problems for which a solution has to be found. The problems are quite common in such neighborhoods: the first is the adaptability of private space to the changing of inhabitants' needs, asking planners, as often happens nowadays in housing competitions, to propose highly flexible apartments and a diversification of structure and typology. The second problem, persistent in contemporary cities and particularly in their outskirts, relates to public spaces that are full of shadows and consequently become dangerous places. They are not used often or regularly. Partial demolition of buildings is allowed only if a convincing enough argument is provided as well as a proposal for a built replacement.

We interpret the instructions of the competitions as a request for greater flexibility in the use of private space and greater use of public space generally.

The project thus suggests that we work in these two areas – public space and private space – identifying two different *playgrounds*, each one with its own logic and own rules appropriate to the technologies and the people working on it.

Increasing the flexibility and malleability of private space is very easy, requiring just a two-meter extension of the surface of the apartment, doubling both façades, just as in the surrounding little *pavillonaire* houses, every inhabitant has an open space at his disposal, a little land that can be used as a garden or simply to expand the flat in order to allow a reconfiguration of internal spaces.

The rules of the game, since the architect is always required to produce some, and no game comes without rules, consist of an abacus for the frames – all the possible frames by opening typology – to be chosen in accordance with the interior space.

In time, the result should be a mosaic of different openings/closings, an external projection of a multifaceted and multicolored landscape, something very similar to what illegally happens with many terraces and balconies.

For the public space, we offer an economic playground, able to marry *opening*, *continuity* and *intensity* of use through a few simple attributes:

1. Affirmation of *priority* given to pedestrians, creating underground car parks.

2. Emphasis on *continuity* of space produced by demolishing the commercial building at the tip of the lot and encouraging the movement of commercial activities located at the base of the building, an area that has been made available due to the moving of the lodgings to the top floor.

3. Inducement of an intense use of public open space by designating it for multiple uses and/or periodically for weekly markets and playgrounds for so-called "urban sports."[2]

Activities that can colonize public space without privatizing it. One example is skateboarding, which has spread numerous forms of appropriation in contemporary cities.

< 2

The material that we choose is asphalt: cheap, flexible, easy to paint, shaped, occupied and easily reshaped, just like the blackboard on which we write a project report the night before the deadline with a few key concepts, sketches and quantitative data.

To be sure, the result is a bit strong, and this empty space of asphalt that stands in front of us should be filled up with an infinity of activities in order to communicate its potential, but it is late at night while we are working on it, and this emptiness looks as if it declares its openness to something that cannot be foreseen but will be constructed later in time, in the reality, tracing in the space lines and regulations of multiple playgrounds.

However, even here, the more or less radical the image that comes out from the computer, the model is like that of any other Paris boulevard with its *marchés hebdomadaires* and the kids who ride their skateboards.

In reality, we discover that the strong image and emptiness of our project has been a delight and pleasure for us all.

When, in February 2004 we anxiously leave for the awards at the French forum, the one where we finally meet the management in order to see whether there is the possibility of carrying out the *playscape* at Drancy, we already understand from the very first meeting with the Europan France organizers that we have won. But something does not go the right way.

The meeting with two representatives of Drancy municipality – the mayor was not there – finally enlightens us.

The local administrators – we invite the reader to determine their political orientation – who are already irritated, after giving their negative opinion regarding our project, tell us that they would carry out any other project but ours because:

The space does not belong to the *public* but to the *republic*, therefore it is the *republic* that decides what to do with it.

The only thing that the *republic* can consider convenient is the *privatization* of the space, as the only possible way to make surveillance of it possible.

Because there is no convenience in having a public space, especially given the arrival of new immigrants with whom current residents share neither culture nor religion (at least, these officials say, the Italian immigrants believed in their same God).

And most important is that profit is not possible given the existence of so many street basketball players (because, funnily enough, in every image there is a basketball player with a suspicious skin color, which, in the French suburbs, is apparently synonymous with dealing drugs).

And also because the court is a space that street gangs can easily control: they can hide their illicit traffic, and, with a lookout at every entrance, it is easy to warn of police arrival.

Is the message clear? The public ground is no longer *res publica* (common ground), a space for playing together, but has to be privatized and cleaned up so that it can be controlled. They are prepared to demolish entire buildings because, and this is new to us, the "court" is a playground that encourages criminality.

When we leave our meeting, we are absolutely astonished, like when you expect a kiss and instead receive a slap. But slowly – slowly – we become *proud of* ourselves for pulling out, modifying the relationship between project, control and decision, this burning issue of architectural politics, of being *polis*.

The circle now closes, we've found issues that we thought were left behind years ago, we test first-hand the political value of a ludic architecture, we recognize our opposition to an idea of a city with *private* spaces for the public. We can now better read through those images of urban party a more concrete utopia made of much freedom and few rules, with the simplest means and an indispensable good dose of optimism.

◆ "Psychogeographical Game of the Week" (1954), *Potlatch #1*. Retrieved from: http://www.cddc.vt.edu/sionline/presitu/potlatch1.html

GAMESPACE

"Are you sure you want to exit the game?" the machine asks in disbelief. Surely you must have made a mistake when hitting the "ESCAPE" key, accidentally finding a way out, a door that the machine warns you not to open. Are you sure that you can handle the real world? Why would you ever stop playing? Couldn't you at least save yourself by saving the game? In an inexplicable act of bravery, you ignore the signs and start leaving. The computer gets even more worried for you and asks again if you know what you are doing. But two or three clicks later, you are out, abruptly back in your room. Like taking a side exit from a cinema and suddenly finding yourself in the street. For a moment, maybe even some seconds, the physical space around you seems to be part of the fantasy, a hyper-real twist in the game. But the new space is at once too intense and too quiet. All your sensors are reading the wrong signals in the environment. It cannot be processed and the body's settings soon revert to the defaults. Normality snaps back. You have left the game.

This is not like putting a book down or turning off the TV. A computer game is not one more channel added to all those other media that we constantly monitor. It is a rival package of channels, an alternative reality that demands total attention, a space that compresses the logic of all other spaces into itself. Its extraordinary sense of realism is not produced by the precision of the latest visual or acoustic effects, the real-time physics of complexly interacting objects on the screen, the uncanny plausibility of the artificial intelligence or the presence of other players hooked up to the broadband feed. The realism comes from taking hold of all the senses at the same time in a symphonic assault. To preserve even the smallest awareness of the everyday environment is to stop playing. The sound of a telephone ringing, someone outside or the throb of an aching wrist are but distant signals from another world, muffled voices vainly calling for your return from utopia.

A computer game player has no need for food, friends or buildings. Or, more precisely, the game dissolves the building you are in so that all the other buildings in the world can be absorbed into the game, obsessively consumed. Architecture is turned into food.

Game makers sell space. The array of available games is like an encyclopedia of spatial systems, a detailed catalog of architectural types. To choose a game is to choose an architecture, to pull it out of the world and perfect it by turning it into your whole world – a calculated escape from everyday life, a dense, ever-evolving, uncontrollable collage of competing spatial systems. To be in a physical space, whether a house, street, office, plane or beach, is simultaneously to be in a cluster of rival social, legal and information spaces. The mobile phone sings, and suddenly

484

you straddle two different architectural worlds. Electronics act as a new kind of joint between diverse spatial systems that demands a new kind of infrastructural detailing – a seam. In the seamless electronic space of computer games, there is no such friction between heterogeneous spaces, no difference between physical and electronic. The electronic experience is so intense that it is experienced physically. Paradoxically, electronic games offer a form of sanctuary from electronic space, a refuge. Gamespace is the only space that mobiles and email don't reach. There are no messages from another world because there is no other world. The only messages come from other players. The only news comes from the inside. The inside *is* the only news.

Digital Equipment Corporation PDP-1 mini-computer, 1961.

To play is to be completely enveloped in the space of the game, a precisely designed interior, a total work of art like that dreamed of by 19th-century artists and architects: an immense immersive space of endless liquid flows in which the player bathes in a kind of prenatal innocence even when devoted to the annihilation of some kind of rival force, the solution of a puzzle, the perfectly simulated swing of a golf club or the construction of yet another empire. This is an interior within which the only real risk, as before birth, is to exit. We game players are not yet children.

This all-absorbing monastic interior is constantly expanding. The amount of detail wrapping the player, the number of players and the amount of time they play keeps increasing. The first interactive computer game was designed in 1962 on the PDP-1, one of the first transistorized mini-computer systems, and was soon included with each installed machine. Not by chance, the game was called *Spacewar!* (1962) and used the dark surface of the cathode ray tube to create a circular image of the infinity of outer space in which two rival vehicles could battle against an accurately modeled night sky of stars featuring familiar constellations. Space itself was absorbed into the machine. Three years later, Gordon Moore published his famous prediction that the quantity of transistors would double every two years, and the game designer's capacity to swallow space has increased exponentially ever since.

There are now more computer games sold in the United States each year than the total population of the country, and the growing support for the 100-US-Dollar-computer for developing nations will undoubtedly spread the gaming logic to the whole planet. As the type of software demanding the most processing power, games drive the computer hardware industry in a relentless cycle. Yet the increase in human processing power is even more remarkable, compelling the designers to add more and more simultaneous channels to keep the players precisely at the limits of their senses. Gamespace exponentially increases as the time required to process information exponentially decreases. The space of escape is getting bigger than the space being escaped from. The alternative worlds assembled inside the machine now dwarf the exterior world. To look into a monitor is to look into a landscape vastly bigger than that outside any window. The openings in the outside walls of our houses have become but vestigial traces of an outmoded worldview, and there is no longer a difference between window and door. As the computer itself shrinks into just a keyboard attached to a mobile image, the game player carries a portable exit able to perforate any physical space.

The ever-expanding space of this parallel world is not simply that of the idealized architectures depicted on the screen, but the space defined by the complete occupation of one's senses. The real key to the architecture of gamespace, like any other architecture, is the entrance and exit. While the abruptness of exiting

a game suddenly reveals how deeply one has been immersed, the entrance is carefully engineered to avoid even this momentary perception. It is softer and slower in order to stealthily remove the sense that there is an outside to the game. As in cinema, a sequence of overlapping thresholds gently lowers the player into the dreamscape. Atmospheric music, imagery and animations ease in the action. The would-be player is kept busy adjusting the settings, and somewhere in between all of the clicking, enters the game. Or, more precisely, leaves the physical room without knowing it, dissolving the everyday environment, conquering it by putting it on hold.

Spacewar! game on PDP-1, 1962.

Architectural fantasies of control in an uncontrollable world? Easy to say. But harder to really know what it means when so many millions spend so much time traversing vast electronic designer interiors. Games don't begin by asking, "Are you sure you want to exit your environment?" We are sure.

◆ *Spacewar!* (PDP-1) (1962), developed by Massachusetts Institute of Technology.

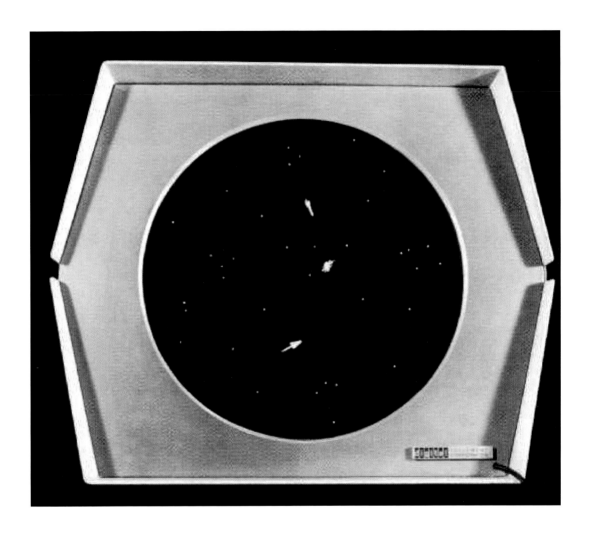

AUTHOR BIOGRAPHIES

IMAGE COPYRIGHTS

A

Espen Aarseth
(*1965 in Bergen, Norway) Associate professor and principal researcher at the Center for Computer Games Research at IT University of Copenhagen and Professor II, University of Oslo, Department of Media and Communication. Editor-in-Chief of Gamestudies.org.

Thiéry Adam
(*1981 in Ville-Marie QC, Canada) Lead designer, game and level designer currently working at Ubisoft Montreal and teaching Level Design at Matane College. Lives in Laval QC, Canada.

Ernest W. Adams
(* in the USA) Game design consultant, writer and teacher currently working at International Hobo and living in Normandy, Surrey, UK.

Neil Alphonso
(*1977 in Mississauga ON, Canada) Interactive designer for video games currently working as lead level designer at Guerrilla Games on Killzone PS3 and living in Amsterdam, Netherlands.

Gillian "Gus" Andrews
(* in Portland ME, USA) Doctoral student and researcher on virtual worlds, networks and media studies currently working as a researcher for Second Life and living in San Francisco CA, USA.

Wayne Ashley
(* in Los Angeles CA, USA) Producer, curator and program director in the fields of performance, media and technology currently working on the transformation of 2D drawings into 3D sculptures. Lives in New York, USA.

Olivier Azémar
(*1976 in Montereau-Fault-Yonne, France) Architect and "game city" lead designer currently working at Ubisoft and living in Annecy, France.

B

Rafael "Tico" Ballagas
(*1977 in Atlanta GA, USA) Ph.D. candidate and Research Associate in Computer Science at RWTH Aachen University working on human-computer interaction, ubiquitous computing, mobile interactions and pervasive games. Lives in Aachen, Germany.

Aram Bartholl
(*1972 in Bremen, Germany) Architect, media artist, freelance concept creator and designer for MVRDV, DMC, Fraunhofer Institut Fokus, Institute for Electronic Business, City & Bits and others.

Richard A. Bartle
(*1960 in Ripon, UK) Computer scientist and co-author of the first Multi-User Dungeon (MUD). Currently Visiting Professor at Essex University and living near Colchester, UK.

René Bauer
(*1972 in Sassenloh, Switzerland) Game developer, software engineer and co-founder of the art group AND-OR. Currently working as a lecturer on Game and Interaction Design at HGKZ Zurich and living in Zurich, Switzerland.

Steve Benford
(*1964 in Cambridge, UK) Professor of Collaborative Computing at the Mixed Reality Lab at the University of Nottingham working on new technologies to support social interaction across computer networks. Lives in Nottingham, UK.

Staffan Björk
(*1973 in Göteborg, Sweden) Senior lecturer at Göteborg University and senior researcher at the Interactive Institute working in the fields of interaction design and gameplay design. Currently researching pervasive games within the IPerG project.

Matthias Böttger
(*1974) Architect, co-founder of the architectural firm raumtaktik – specializing in spatial reconnaissance and intervention – and Research Associate at the Institut für öffentliche Bauten und Entwerfen, Stuttgart University. Lives in Berlin, Germany.

Ian Bogost
(*1976 in New Mexico, USA) Assistant Professor at the School of Literature, Communication, and Culture at the Georgia Institute of Technology - Affiliated Faculty, Graphics Visualization and Usability Center (GVU). Co-founder of Persuasive Games, an independent game studio based in Atlanta GA, USA.

Iain Borden
(*1962 in Oxford, UK) Architectural Historian and Urban Commentator currently Head of the Bartlett School of Architecture at University College London and Professor of Architecture and Urban Culture. Lives in London, UK.

Friedrich von Borries
(*1974) Architect, co-founder of the architectural firm raumtaktik – specializing in spatial reconnaissance and intervention – and Research Fellow at ETH Zurich. Lives in Berlin, Germany.

Dariusz Jacob Boron
(*1980 in Krakow, Poland) Architect currently working as an Assistant Architect at Foster+Partners and living in London, UK.

Stephen Boyd Davis
(*1953 in Boston, UK) Head of Lansdown Centre for Electronic Arts at Middlesex University. Academic interests include advanced interaction, spatiality, depiction and visualization. Lives in London, UK.

Gregor Broll
(*1979 in Munich, Germany) Research Assistant at Ludwig-Maximilians-Universität (LMU) Munich working on mobile computing, mobile interaction and pervasive gaming. Lives in Neubiberg, Germany.

Sheldon Brown
(*1962 in Colorado, USA) Director of the Experimental Game Lab and of the Center for Research in Computing and the Arts at the University of California, San Diego. Currently working on the project The Scalable City. Lives in Encinitas CA, USA.

Martin Budzinski
(*1979 in Tübingen, Germany) Architect and urban planner currently working at the architectural firm Kauffmann Theilig & Partner and living in Stuttgart, Germany.

Raoul Bunschoten
(*1955 in Deventer, Netherlands) Architect and founding director of CHORA Architecture and Urbanism.

Gerhard M. Buurman
(*1961 in Hamburg, Germany) Product and Interactive Media Designer. Professor of Interaction Design and head of the Interaction and Game Design program at the Zurich University for the Arts. Lives in Konstanz, Germany and Zurich, Switzerland.

Ed Byrne
(*1975 in New York, USA) Game designer and illustrator currently working as lead designer for Zipper Interactive and living near Seattle WA, USA.

C

Diane Carr
Research Fellow in Media and Education at the Institute of Education, University of London. Currently working on the project "Learning from Online Worlds; Teaching in Second Life."

Edward Castronova
(*1962 in Cleveland OH, USA) Director of Graduate Studies in the Department of Telecommunications at Indiana University Bloomington. Academic interests include synthetic worlds and their economies. Currently conducting research on the MMORPG Arden: The World of William Shakespeare.

Dean Chan
(*1969 in Malaysia) Lecturer at the School of Communications and Contemporary Arts at Edith Cowan University in Perth, Australia. Currently researching Asian digital game cultures and Asian-Australian cultural production.

Kees Christiaanse
(*1953 in Amsterdam, Netherlands) Architect and urban designer currently professor at the ETH Zurich and partner at the firm KCAP Architects & Planners in Rotterdam. Lives in Zurich, Switzerland.

James J. Cummings
(* in Syracuse NY, USA) Graduate student at Indiana University's Department of Telecommunications and Lead Writer for the MMORPG *Arden: The World of William Shakespeare.*

Patrick Curry
Game designer and writer currently working on *John Woo Presents Stranglehold,* developed and published by Midway Games. Lives in Chicago IL, USA.

D

Eyal Danon
(*1972 in Tel Aviv, Israel) Curator currently working at The Israeli Center for Digital Art. Lives in Tel Aviv, Israel.

Drew Davidson
(*1970 in Chapel Hill NC, USA) Professor, producer and player of interactive media. Director of the Entertainment Technology Center at Carnegie Mellon University Pittsburgh and editor of the ETC Press, living in Pittsburgh PA, USA.

Frank Degris
Research Assistant at the Chair for German Language and Literature Studies, Department of German Philology, University of Mannheim.

Thomas Fabian Delman
(*1973 in Denmark) Architect and urban planner currently working at Aarhus School of Architecture, University of Aarhus and at the architectural firm Kollision. Lives in Aarhus, Denmark.

Christy Dena
Cross-Media Entertainment Researcher, Consultant and Designer. Ph.D. candidate at the School of Letters, Art and Media, University of Sydney and business owner of Universe Creation 101. Lives in Sydney, Australia.

James Der Derian
Research Professor of International Relations at the Watson Institute for International Studies at Brown University, Providence RI, USA. Director of the Global Security Program and the Information Technology, War, and Peace Project.

Andreas Dieckmann
(*1974 in Lüneburg, Germany) Architect. Currently Assistant Teacher and Researcher at the Chair for CAAD at RWTH Aachen University and co-founder of the architectural firm IP arch. Lives in Düsseldorf, Germany.

Zhao Chen Ding
(*1967 in Taipei, Taiwan) Architect and game theorist currently teaching Game Design at the Academy of Arts and Design at Tsinghua University Beijing. Associate Professor and head of the Game Program at Beijing Institute of Clothing Technology. Lives in Beijing, China.

E

Galit Eilat
(*1965 in Haifa, Israel) Writer and curator. Currently Director of The Israeli Center for Digital Art. Lives in Tel Aviv, Israel.

Will Emigh
Student in the Masters in Immersive Mediated Environments program at Indiana University Bloomington in the USA and co-founder of Studio Cypher, a company that creates games in real spaces.

James Everett
(*1982 in Comox BC, Canada) Game designer currently working at Artificial Mind and Movement on an unannounced PS2/GameCube action title and living in Montreal QC, Canada.

F

Noah Falstein
(*1957 in Chicago IL, USA) Game designer, producer and writer currently heading The Inspiracy, working on an adventure game and on a serious game title. Lives in Greenbrae CA, USA.

Michael Fatten
(*1976 in Bloomington IL, USA) Computer programmer and systems analyst. Currently the Lead Designer for *Arden: The World of William Shakespeare* and a graduate student at Indiana University's Department of Telecommunications.

Lukas Feireiss
(*1977 in Berlin, Germany) Teacher, writer and curator for various international projects. Deeply involved in the discussion and mediation of architecture, art and media beyond its disciplinary boundaries. Lives in Berlin, Germany.

Clara Fernández-Vara
(*1977 in Barcelona, Spain) Ph.D. candidate in Digital Media at Georgia Institute of Technology. Currently a researcher for the Singapore-MIT GAMBIT Game Lab at the Massachusetts Institute of Technology. Lives near Boston MA, USA.

Wolfgang Fiel
(*1973 in Alberschwende, Austria) Architect, artist and Ph.D. candidate currently doing research on "Dissipative Urbanism." Member of the group "tat ort." Lives in Vienna, Austria.

Phil Fish
(*1984 in Montreal QC, Canada) Game designer and co-founder of Kokoromi, an experimental video game design collective. Currently working for a large Montreal Studio. Lives in Montreal QC, Canada.

Mary Flanagan
(*1973 in Milwaukee WI, USA) Computational media artist, book editor and activist game designer at the TiltFactor lab. Teaches in the Integrated Media Arts program at Hunter College. Lives in New York NY, USA.

Winnie Forster
(*1969 in Starnberg, Germany) Journalist, media and game analyst. Editor of the "Encyclopedia of Game.Machines" published by his company Gameplan, currently working on an "Encyclopedia of Game.Makers." Lives in Utting/Ammersee, Germany.

Mathias Fuchs
(*1956 in Erlangen, Germany) Game artist and musician. Currently Program Leader of MSc Creative Games at the School of Art & Design, Salford University, UK. Lives in Manchester, UK.

G

Christian Gaca
(*1975 in Dortmund, Germany) Video game journalist and ingame advertising consultant. Currently studying Business Communication Management at FHTW Berlin and living in Berlin, Germany.

Chaim Gingold
(*1980 in Haifa, Israel) Game designer currently working at Maxis/Electronic Arts on Will Wright's latest project *Spore* and living in Berkeley CA, USA.

Fabien Girardin
(*1974 in Switzerland) Research Scientist focusing on human-computer interaction. Currently working at Barcelona's Pompeu Fabra University in the Department of Technologies and living in Barcelona, Spain.

Ulrich Götz
(*1971 in Erlangen, Germany) Architect and game designer. Currently Head of the Game Design Program and Head of the Game Research Lab at the University of Applied Sciences and Arts Zurich. Lives in Zurich, Switzerland and Berlin, Germany.

Stephen Graham
(*1965 in Tynemouth, UK) Professor of Human Geography and Deputy Director of the Center for the Study of Cities and Regions (CSCR) at Durham University, UK.

Stephan Günzel
(*1971 in Coburg, Germany) Research Associate in Media Theory at Friedrich-Schiller-University Jena. Currently researching the role and use of space in video games. Lives in Berlin, Germany.

H

Jochen Hamma
(*1966 in Spaichingen, Germany) Producer, game and interface designer for over 30 PC and mobile games. Teacher of Game and Interface Design at various universities. Lives in Böttingen, Germany.

Stephan Henrich
(*1978) Architecture student

at University of Stuttgart's IGMA. Worked with Schneider+Schuhmacher in Frankfurt and with R&Sie in Paris as an expert in robotics.

Sabine Himmelsbach
(*1966) Art historian. Currently Director of the Edith-Ruß-Haus for media art in Oldenburg, Germany.

Jussi Holopainen
Head of the Game Design Group at Nokia Research Center, Finland. Founding member and current member of the executive board of the Digital Games Research Association (DiGRA).

Jochen Hoog
(*1973 in Heidelberg, Germany) Architect. Currently a Lecturer at the Vienna University of Technology's Institute of Architecture and Design and member of the firm Prozess.architektur. Lives in Vienna, Austria.

Wilfried Hou Je Bek
(*1975) Left school at 16 to become an artist, writer and squatter. Under the moniker of socialfiction.org, he as organized countless psychogeographic walks around the world.

Ludger Hovestadt
(*1960 in Gelsenkirchen, Germany) Professor for Computer Aided Architectural Design at the ETH Zurich, conducting an interdisciplinary research group looking for new forms, structures and processes applicable for current architectural practice. Founder of several companies, living in Zurich, Switzerland.

Marie Huber
(*1982 near Munich, Germany) Student of New and Medieval History and Sociology at the Technical University Berlin. Academic interests include issues of spatially- and economically-driven urban processes. Lives in Berlin, Germany.

I

Alberto Iacovoni
(*1966 in Rome, Italy) Architect, co-founder of the architectural firm ma0/emmeazero in Rome, curator of a "playgrounds" section on interactive architecture

for the webzine www.architettura.it.

Henrik Isermann
(*1977 in Saarbrücken, Germany) Architect, urban planner and audio engineer currently working as a freelancer for several architectural and design agencies. Lives in Berlin, Germany.

J

Rachel Jacobs
(*1972 in London, UK) Artist and project manager. Co-founder and partner of Active Ingredient, working on 'Ere be Dragons. Lives in Nottingham, UK.

Stephen Jacobs
(*1961 in Washington, D.C., USA) Technology writer and Associate Professor of Game Design and Development at B. Thomas Golisano College of Information and Computer Sciences, Rochester Institute of Technology. Lives in Rochester NY, USA.

Aki Järvinen
(*1971 in Tampere, Finland) Ph.D. candidate in Game Studies at the University of Tampere, Finland. Currently developing electronic games for the Finnish National Lottery. Lives in Helsinki, Finland.

Margarete Jahrmann
(*1968 in Vienna, Austria) Artist, performer and neo-patphysist writer. Currently Professor of Ludology at the Game Design Department of The School of Arts and Design Zurich and co-founder of the Ludic Society. Lives in Zurich, Switzerland.

Mikael Jakobsson
(*1969 in Boden, Sweden) Associate Professor of Interaction Design at the School of Arts & Communication at Malmö University. Lives in Malmö, Sweden.

Tomasz Jaskiewicz
(*1980 in Gdynia, Poland) Architectural Ph.D. student conducting research on a complex systems-based approach to the creation of interactive architecture at the Knowledge Centre Hyperbody TU Delft. Lives in Rotterdam, Netherlands.

Henry Jenkins
(*1958 in Atlanta GA, USA) Professor of Literature; currently the Peter de Florez Professor of Humanities and Co-Director of the Comparative Media Studies Program at the Massachusetts Institute of Technology in Cambridge MA, USA.

Ge Jin
(*1976 in Shanghai, China) Ph.D. candidate working on communication research and new media in China at the Department of Communication, University of California, San Diego. Lives in San Diego CA, USA.

Benjamin Joffe
(*1977 in Paris, France) Mobile technologies and Internet business consultant. Currently the CEO of +8* | Plus Eight Star Ltd. and co-founder and organizer of the "Mobile Monday Beijing." Lives in Beijing, China.

Troels Degn Johansson
(*1967 on Zealand, Denmark) Associate Professor at the Centre for Design Research at the Danish Design School in Copenhagen. Lives in Copenhagen, Denmark.

KP Ludwig John
Professor of Design of Interactive Media at the University of Applied Sciences Augsburg and co-founder of XINOBER, a firm that works on mobile experience projects. Lives in Augsburg, Germany.

Alex de Jong
Architect and urban planner currently working for the Office for Metropolitan Architecture (OMA) and running Studio Popcorn together with Marc Schuilenburg.

Staffan Jonsson
(*1982 in Stockholm, Sweden) Game researcher currently working at The Interactive Institute and on IPerG (Integrated Project on Pervasive Gaming). Lives in Stockholm, Sweden.

Jesper Juul
(*1970 in Århus, Denmark) Game theorist, designer and developer, and book author. Founder of Soup Games. Currently Assistant Professor at IT University of

Copenhagen. Lives in Copenhagen, Denmark.

K

Heather Kelley
(*1969 in Connecticut, USA) Game designer and researcher, currently working at Artificial Mind & Movement. Co-founder of Kokoromi, an experimental video game design collective. Advisor of the "Women in Game Development" group of the International Game Developers Association (IGDA).

Peter Kiefer
(*1980 in Nuremberg, Germany) Research Assistant and Ph.D. candidate in Applied Computer Sciences at the University of Bamberg. Currently working on the Geogames project. Lives in Bamberg, Germany.

Sungah Kim
(*1965 in Busan, South Korea) Architect, designer and Associate Professor of Architecture at Sunkyunkwan University South Korea, teaching digital media and design. Lives in Seoul, South Korea.

Eric Klopfer
(*1970 in New York, USA) Associate Professor at the MIT Teacher Education Program, focusing on Games and Simulations in Education. Currently working on location-based and mobile simulations for learning. Lives in Winchester MA, USA.

Ragna Körby
(*1982 in Hamburg, Germany) Studies Urban Planning at the Technical University of Berlin and works for Berlin-based firm raumtaktik. Lives in Berlin, Germany.

James H. Korris
(*1950 in New York, USA) President and founder of Creative Technologies Inc., a firm that works on creative Visualization and Immersive Simulation for the defense industry, e.g. Future Combat Systems Mobile Demonstrator. Lives in Los Angeles CA, USA.

Julian Kücklich
(*1974 in Munich, Germany) Ph.D. candidate at the Centre

for Media Research, University of Ulster, Coleraine, currently working on the politics of play in digital games production. Lives in Berlin, Germany.

Dörte Küttler
(*1974 in Elmshorn, Germany) Architect and media manager currently running the consulting agency "enter the metaverse" and teaching Architecture in Computer Games at University of Technology, Business and Design Wismar. Lives in Rendsburg, Germany.

Tobias Kurtz
(*1982 in Neuhaus/Rwg., Germany) Studies Urban Planning at the Technical University Berlin and lives in Berlin, Germany.

L

Andreas Lange
(*1967 in West Germany) Curator, author and consultant for interactive digital entertainment culture. Currently Director of the Computer Game Museum in Berlin and CEO of DiGA e.V. - The Digital Game Archive. Lives in Berlin, Germany.

Frank Lantz
(*1963 in Kansas City MO, USA) Game designer. Cofounder and Creative Director of area/code in New York, which creates large-scale, real-world games using mobile and location-aware technology. Lives in Hoboken NJ, USA.

Neil Leach
(*1963 in the UK) Architect and theorist. Research Professor at the University of Brighton and author of 15 books. Has taught in several of the world's leading schools of architecture.

Alexander Lehnerer
(*1974 in Erlangen, Germany) Architect and urban designer. Currently Lecturer and Researcher at the Institute of Urban Design, ETH Zurich and Partner of ALSO-Architects. Lives in Zurich, Switzerland.

Tor Lindstrand
(*1968 in Helsingborg, Sweden) Architect and artist currently working for the International Festival, an ongoing project

encompassing both architecture and performance at The Theatre for Steirischer Herbst in Graz. Lives in Stockholm, Sweden.

Irma Lindt
(*1977 in Limbazi, Latvia) Computer scientist. Currently working as Research Associate in the Department of Collaborative Virtual and Augmented Environments at Fraunhofer FIT and managing the IPerG project (Integrated Project on Pervasive Gaming). Lives in Bonn, Germany.

Peter Ljungstrand
Lecturer, researcher and Ph.D. candidate in Computing Science at Chalmers and Göteborg University and PLAY research studio at the Interactive Institute in Sweden.

Daniel G. Lobo
(*1974 in Madrid, Spain) Urbanist, researcher and artist currently working for The American Institute of Architects' Center for Communities by Design. Lives in Washington, D.C., USA.

Bart Lootsma
(*1957 in Amsterdam, Netherlands) Historian, critic and curator of architecture, design and the visual arts. Currently Professor for Architectural Theory at the Leopold-Franzens University in Innsbruck. Lives in Innsbruck, Austria.

Tobias Løssing
(*1972 in Denmark) Architect and urban planner currently working at Aarhus School of Architecture, University of Aarhus and at the architectural firm Kollision. Lives in Aarhus, Denmark.

Peter Ludlow
(*1957) Professor of Philosophy and Linguistics at the University of Michigan, Ann Arbor. Research interests include the emergence of laws and governance structures in and for virtual communities. Lives in Ann Arbor MI, USA.

Andreas Lykke-Olesen
(*1975 in Denmark) Architect and urban planner currently working at Aarhus School of Architecture, University of Aarhus and at the architectural firm Kollision. Lives in Aarhus, Denmark.

M

Winy Maas
(*1959 in Schijndel, Netherlands) Architect, urban planner and partner of the Rotterdam-based architectural firm MVRDV. Lives in Rotterdam, Netherlands.

Carsten Magerkurth
Psychologist and computer scientist, formerly head of the "AMBIENTE - Smart Environments of the Future" division of the Fraunhofer Institute IPSI and now senior researcher at SAP Research CEC St. Gallen, Switzerland. Founder of the annual PerGames symposia on pervasive gaming.

Lev Manovich
(* in Moscow, Russia) Artist, architect and computer scientist. Currently professor of Visual Arts at the University of California, San Diego in the USA, where he teaches New Media Art and Theory. Director of The Lab for Cultural Analysis, part of the California Institute for Information and Telecommunication.

Iassen Markov
(*1980) Studied Ecology, Art and Architecture. Currently teaches at the University of Stuttgart's IGMA and a member of Igmade.

Sebastian Matyas
(*1979 in Backnang, Germany) Research Assistant and Ph.D. candidate in Applied Computer Sciences at the University of Bamberg. Currently working on the *Geogames* project and living in Bamberg, Germany.

Marc Maurer
(*1969 in Eindhoven, Netherlands) Architect, designer, artist and co-founder of the Maastricht-based architectural practice Maurer United Architects [MUA].

Nicole Maurer-Lemmens
(*1969 in Slenaken, Netherlands) Architect, designer, artist and co-founder of the Maastricht-based architectural practice Maurer United Architects [MUA].

Jane McGonigal
Game designer and researcher. Founder of the experimental design project Avant Game

and currently resident game designer at the Institute for the Future, working on massively collaborative play.

Nathan Mishler
Student at the Masters in Immersive Mediated Environments program at Indiana University Bloomington in the USA and co-founder of Studio Cypher, a company that creates games in real spaces.

William J. Mitchell
(*1944 in Australia) Architect and urban designer. Currently Professor of Architecture and Media Arts and Sciences and Director of the Design Laboratory at the Massachusetts Institute of Technology. Lives in Cambridge MA, USA.

Magnus Moar
(*1959 in the UK) University Lecturer in Digital Design currently teaching Design for Interactive Media, Electronic Arts, Game Design and Interactive Arts at Middlesex University. Lives in London, UK.

Nick Montfort
(*1972 in the USA) Author and theorist of interactive fiction. Currently Assistant Professor of Digital Media at the Massachusetts Institute of Technology (MIT) in Cambridge MA, USA.

Markus Montola
(*1978 in Helsinki, Finland) Researcher in the fields of pervasive games and role-playing games at the University of Tampere. Currently involved in the IPerG project. Lives in Helsinki, Finland.

Gregory More
(*1973) Architect and designer. Currently a lecturer in Architecture and Design at RMIT University in Melbourne. Research Fellow of SIAL (Spatial Information Architecture Laboratory) and Director of The Agency of Architecture. Lives in Melbourne, Australia.

Florian "Floyd" Müller
(*1973 in Freiburg, Germany) Interface Inventor and Interaction Researcher. Worked at the Xerox Palo Alto Research Center in the USA and at the Media Lab Europe in Dublin, Ireland.

Achim Nelke

(*1979 in Frankfurt/Main, Germany) Studies Urban Planning at the Technical University Berlin, focusing on the design of urban space and its sociocultural framework. Lives in Berlin, Germany.

Martin Nerurkar

(*1981 in Nürtingen, Germany) Architect working on game and graphic design as well as on digital and analog architecture. Lives in Stuttgart, Germany.

Thé Chinh Ngo

(*1971 in Saigon, Vietnam) Architect currently working as Art Director at Ubisoft's Montreal studio on the development of *Conviction*, the fifth installment of the *Splinter Cell* series.

Rune Nielsen

(*1972 in Denmark) Architect and urban planner currently working at Aarhus School of Architecture, University of Aarhus and at the architectural firm Kollision. Lives in Aarhus, Denmark.

Michael Nitsche

(*1968 in Braunschweig, Germany) Assistant Professor of Digital Media at the Georgia Institute of Technology's School of Literature, Communication, and Culture. Lives in Atlanta GA, USA.

Rolf F. Nohr

(*1968 in Stuttgart, Germany) Junior Professor of Media Culture at the HBK Braunschweig in Germany and Director of the AG Games at the Society for Media Sciences. Lives in Bochum, Germany.

Nicolas Nova

(*1977 in France) Research scientist currently working on human-computer interaction in the Media and Design Lab at the EPF Lausanne, Switzerland. Lives in Geneva, Switzerland.

Kas Oosterhuis

(*1951) Architect currently working at the Knowledge Centre Hyperbody TU Delft, iWEB Protospace Laboratory TU Delft and running the architectural firm ONL in Rotterdam. Lives in Hoek van Holland, Netherlands.

Celia Pearce

(*1961 in Burbank CA, USA) Designer, writer and creative director. Currently Assistant Professor at the Georgia Institute of Technology and Director of the Experimental Game Lab in the School of Literature, Communication and Culture. Lives in Atlanta GA, USA.

Johan Peitz

(*1977 in Växjö, Sweden) Runs Free Lunch Design, an independent game developer whose *Icy Tower* is one of the world's most downloaded and played games. Lives in Göteborg, Sweden.

Jack W. Peters

(*1965 in Portland OR, USA) Outdoor author adventurer and shipwreck archeologist working as a facilitator for corporate team-building programs inspired by *Geocaching*, which are commonly referred to as *Geoteaming*.

Steve Peters

(*1961 in Van Nuys CA, USA) Game designer, producer, writer and composer. Currently lead designer for 42 Entertainment and founder of the Alternate Reality Gaming Network (argn.com). Lives in Granada Hills CA, USA.

Claus Pias

(*1967 in Cologne, Germany) Professor of Epistemology and Philosophy of Digital Media at the Institute for Philosophy at the University of Vienna. Currently researching the History and Philosophy of Computer Simulation and the Archaeology of Media Theory. Lives in Vienna, Austria.

Wayne Piekarski

(*1978 in Adelaide, Australia) Senior Lecturer and Researcher currently working on Augmented Reality and 3D computer graphics at the Wearable Computer Lab at the University of South Australia. Lives in Adelaide, Australia.

Cindy Poremba

(*1975 in Toronto ON, Canada) Digital media theorist, producer and curator currently researching documentary and video games through Concordia University's Humanities Doctoral program in Montreal, Canada.

Howard Rheingold

(*1947 in Tucson AZ, USA) Critic and writer. Non-Resident Fellow at the Annenberg Center for Communication, Visiting Professor at De Montfort University and founding editor of HotWired, the first commercial web magazine. Lives in Mill Valley CA, USA.

Travis Ross

(*1980 in Columbus OH, USA) Information scientist currently working as community manager for *Arden: The World of William Shakespeare* and living in Bloomington IN, USA.

Paolo Ruffino

(*1984 in Rome, Italy) Studies Semiotics and Game Design Theory at the University of Bologna. Currently working in *Second Life* and on subvertising campaigns. Lives in Bologna, Italy.

Peter Russell

(*1963 in Ottawa, Canada) Architect. Currently Professor of Computer Aided Architectural Design at RWTH Aachen University and co-founder of the architectural firm IP arch. Lives in Plombières, Belgium.

Will Ryan

Doctoral student in the field of Human-Computer Interaction at Indiana University's School of Informatics. Lives in Bloomington IN, USA.

Antonino Saggio

(*1955 in Rome, Italy) Author of architecture, founder of the research group Nitrosaggio and currently Associate Professor in the Department of Architecture at La Sapienza University Rome. Lives in Rome, Italy.

Katie Salen

(*1969 in Denver CO, US) Associate Professor of Game Design at the Gamelab Institute of Play and Director at Parsons New School for Design. Currently working as lead designer for Gamestar Mechanic. Lives in Brooklyn NY, USA.

Jürgen Scheible

(*1970 in Karlsruhe, Germany) Media artist and researcher. Ph.D. candidate at the University of Art and Design, Helsinki, doing research on designing interactive systems – mobile phones and urban screens.

Jesse Schell

Game designer, programmer and manager. CEO of Schell Games Currently and on the faculty of the Entertainment Technology Center at Carnegy Mellon University.

Andreas Schiffler

(*1968 in Saarbrücken, Germany) Expert in computing and software programming currently working as senior software architect at IC-Agency in Bathurst, Canada and doing research for his Ph.D. on the "Possibilities of Physics in Computer games."

Christoph Schlieder

(*1960 in Brussels, Belgium) Professor of Computer Science at the University of Bamberg, where he is also head of the research group on Computing in the Cultural Sciences. Lives in Bamberg, Germany.

Florian Schmidt

(*1979 in Berlin, Germany) Graphic designer and author currently studying and working as a freelancer. Lives in Berlin, Germany.

Karen Schrier

(*1977 in New York, USA) Media producer, writer, designer and educator. Currently a doctoral student at Columbia University researching Games and Learning and working as a producer at Nickelodeon. Lives in New York, USA.

Hans-Peter Schwarz

(*1945 in Bielefeld, Germany) Designer and art historian. Currently president of the Zurich University for the Arts. Lives in Zurich, Switzerland.

Elizabeth Sikiaridi
(* in London, UK) Architect and urban designer currently working as a professor at the University of Duisburg-Essen in Germany.

Adriana de Souza e Silva
(*1975 in Rio de Janeiro, Brazil) Director of the Mobile Gaming Research Lab and Assistant Professor of Communication, Technology and Gaming at the Department of Communication at North Carolina State University. Lives in Raleigh NC, USA.

Kurt Squire
(*1972 in Valparaiso IN, USA) Game designer and developer currently working as Assistant Professor at the Academic ADL Co-Lab, University of Wisconsin-Madison. Lives in Madison WI, USA.

Sean Stewart
(*1965 in Lubbock TX, USA) Novelist and pioneer in interactive and multimedia fiction. Currently working as lead writer for 42 Entertainment and living in Davis CA, USA.

Axel Stockburger
(*1974 in Munich, Germany) Artist and theorist. Research Assistant in the Department for Visual Arts and Digital Media at the Academy of Fine Arts Vienna. Lives in Vienna, Austria.

Mirjam Struppek
(*1973 in Gelsenkirchen, Germany) Urbanist, researcher and consultant. Founded Urban Screens Conferences and is currently working on implementing outdoor screens for a sustainable urban society. Lives in Berlin, Germany.

Beat Suter
(*1962 in Baden, Switzerland) Artist, writer and publisher. Currently Lecturer for Game Design and Interaction Design at the Zurich University for the Arts and member of the art group AND-OR. Lives in Zurich, Switzerland.

Dave Szulborski
(*1957 in McAllen TX, USA) Alternate Reality Game designer, immersive marketing consultant and author. Currently working on projects for various companies

and on an ARG-based training program for the US military. Lives in Macungie PA, USA.

T

Bruce H. Thomas
(*1957 in Washington DC, USA) Professor of Computer Science at the School of Computer and Information Science at the University of South Australia. Currently focusing on wearable computers, Augmented Reality and graphical user interfaces. Lives in Adelaide, Australia.

David Thomas
(*1965) Game journalist, Ph.D. candidate and planning and design instructor at the University of Colorado's College of Architecture and Planning. Lives in Denver CO, USA.

Stephan Trüby
(*1970) Architect. Currently Assistant Professor of Architectural Theory and Design at Stuttgart University's Institut Grundlagen moderner Architektur und Entwerfen (IGMA). Member of Igmade and founder of the architecture, design and consultancy firm Exit Ltd.

Marc Tuters
(*1975 in London, UK) Artist and interactive media researcher. Currently working at the Interactive Media Division of the University of Southern California on direct manipulation of 3D avatars. Lives in Los Angeles CA, USA.

Ville Tuulos
(*1981 in Oulu, Finland) Researcher in the Department of Computer Science at the University of Helsinki, where he focuses on statistical information retrieval and extends it into new dimensions.

V

Frans Vogelaar
(* in the Netherlands) Industrial designer, architect and urban designer. Professor at the Academy of Media Arts in Cologne, Germany, where he heads the Department of Hybrid Space (i.e. combined analog-digital space).

Georg Vrachliotis
Architect, philosopher and science historian. Currently Teacher and Research Associate at the Chair of CAAD of the Federal Institute of Technology Zurich and Guest Teacher at the Department of Architectural Theory at the Technical University Vienna. Lives in Zurich, Switzerland.

Ronald Vuillemin
(*1970 in Friedrichshafen, Germany) Co-founder and president of Toradex AG, Luzern. Past president at Ageia-NovodeX AG, Switzerland. Lives in Zofingen, Switzerland.

W

Michael Wagner
(*1967 in St. Pölten, Austria) Professor of Technology, Enhanced Learning and Multimedia at the Department for Interactive Media and Educational Technology at the Danube University Krems. Lives in St. Pölten, Austria.

Bo Kampmann Walther
(*1967 in Odense, Denmark) Associate Professor at the Center for Media Studies, University of Southern Denmark. Current areas of research and academic interest include modern soccer, computer games and new media. Lives in Odense, Denmark.

Steffen P. Walz
(*1973 in Böblingen, Germany) Game designer and research associate at the ETH Zurich's Chair for CAAD. Founder of the entertainment consultancy playbe and the music label playbe records. Lectures and workshops at universities in Europe, the USA and Asia. Lives in Zurich, Switzerland and Stuttgart, Germany.

McKenzie Wark
(*1961 in Newcastle, Australia) Associate Professor of Media and Cultural Studies at The New School for Social Research in New York. Lives in New York, USA.

Matt Wattkins
(*1971 in Billericay, Essex, UK) Artist and designer. Co-founder and partner of Active Ingredient. Currently working on *Love City*, a pervasive game

played between three cities. Lives in Nottingham, UK.

Stefan Werning
(*1978 in Münster/Westf., Germany) Ph.D. candidate at the University of Bonn conducting research on the technological convergences of programmable media in civilian and military contexts. Also a product analyst at Nintendo and an affiliate scholar of the Convergence Culture Consortium. Lives in Aschaffenburg, Germany.

Troy Whitlock
(*1970 in the USA) Game designer and lecturer. Creative director at EA's casual games division, Pogo.com. Lives in San Mateo CA, USA.

Mark Wigley
(*1956 in New Zealand) Architect and author. Currently Professor at and Dean of the Columbia University Graduate School of Architecture, Planning and Preservation in New York. Lives in New York NY, USA.

Rahel Willhardt
(*1967 in Kassel, Germany) Journalist writing on the interfaces between real estate, architecture, marketing and design for various professional magazines and newspapers. Lives in Aachen, Germany.

Katharine S. Willis
(*1972 in London, UK) Researcher, architect and artist currently working on the MEDIACITY Project at the Bauhaus University Weimar. Lives in Weimar, Germany.

Image copyrights

p. 20 *Dance Dance Revolution* © Konami Digital Entertainment, **p. 24** *Wii Sports* © NINTENDO, **p. 32** *PONG* © Atari Corporation, **p. 34** *Asteroids* © Atari Corporation, **p. 36** *Battlezone* © Atari Corporation, **p. 38** *Defender* © Williams Electronics Games Inc., **p. 40** *Wolfenstein 3D* © ID Software, **p. 42** *Counter-Strike* © Valve Corporation, **p. 48** *Myst* © Cyan Worlds Inc./Ubisoft Entertainment, **p. 50** *Super Mario Bros.* © NINTENDO, **p. 52** *Tetris* © The Tetris Company LLC., **p. 54** *Ico* © Sony Computer Entertainment Europe, **p. 64** *Zork* © Activision, **p. 66** *Lemmings* © Sony Computer Entertainment Europe, **p. 68** *Worms* © Team17 Software Limited, **p. 70** *Max Payne* © Rockstar Games Inc., **p. 78** *Pac-Man* ®&© NAMCO BANDAI Games Inc., **p. 80** *Diablo* © Blizzard Entertainment, **p. 82** *Silent Hill 2* © Konami Digital Entertainment, **p. 84** *Splinter Cell* © Ubisoft Entertainment, **p. 86** *Sam & Max hit the Road* © Lucasfilm Entertainment Company Ltd., **p. 94** *Kirby: Canvas Curse* © HAL LABORATORY INC./NINTENDO, **p. 96** *Katamari Damacy*, ™ & © NAMCO BANDAI Games Inc., **p. 98** *EyeToy Play* © Sony Computer Entertainment Europe, **p. 101** *Space Invaders* © Taito Corporation, **p. 102** *Ms. Pac-Man* © Bally Midway Games/Atari/NAMCO, *Pengo* © SEGA Corporation, **p. 103** *Super Bomberman* © Hudson Soft, **p. 104** *Elite* © Acornsoft/Firebird, **p. 106** *Prince of Persia* © Ubisoft, **p. 108** *Super Mario 64* © NINTENDO, **p. 114** *Rez* © SEGA Corporation/United Game Artists, **p. 116** *Descent* © Parallax Software/Interplay Productions, **p. 121** *Call of Duty* © Activision, *Counter-Strike* © Valve Corporation, *Deus Ex* © Eidos Interactive Ltd., **p. 122** *Super Monkey Ball* © SEGA Corporation, **p. 124** *Tony Hawk's American Wasteland* © Activision, **p. 126** *Legacy of Kain: Soul Reaver* © Crystal Dynamics Inc./Eidos Interactive Ltd., **p. 128** *Rescue on Fractalus* © Lucasfilm Games/Atari Corporation, **p. 130** *Quake* © ID Software, **p. 140** *Tron* © Walt Disney Pictures, **p. 142** *Neuromancer* © James Warhola, **p. 144** *Snow Crash* © Bruce Jensen, **p. 150** *The Sims* © Electronic Arts Inc., **p. 152** *There* © Makena Technologies Inc., **p. 154** *Entropia Universe* © MindArk PE AB, **p. 156** *Second Life* © Linden Research Inc., **p. 165** *Alphaworld* © Activeworlds Inc., **p. 168** *Lineage* © Ncsoft Corporation, **p. 170** *Kingdom Hearts* © Disney Interactive, **p. 172** *World of Warcraft* © Blizzard Entertainment, **p. 178** *Sid Meier's Civilization* © Firaxis Games Inc./MicroProse, **p. 180** *Animal Crossing* © NINTENDO, **p. 183** *Competing in Metagame Gamespace* © Deutscher eSport Verband/Frank Sliwka, **p. 190** *Dark Chronicle* © Sony Computer Entertainment Europe, **p. 192** *The Getaway* © Sony Computer Entertainment Europe, **p. 194** *Grand Theft Auto: San Andreas* © Rockstar Games Inc., **p. 196** *Grim Fandango* © Lucasfilm Entertainment Company Ltd., **p. 198** *Psychonauts* © Double Fine Productions/Majestico, **pp. 206-210** *SimCity* © Electronic Arts Inc./Maxis Software, **p. 212** *Majestic* © Electronic Arts Inc., **p. 229** *The Beast* © 42 Entertainment LLC., **pp. 230-231** *Barcode Battler* © Epoch Co. Ltd., **pp. 234-237** *Tombstone Hold 'Em* © 42 Entertainment LLC., **p. 239** *Perplex City* © Mind Candy, **p. 242** *I love bees* © 42 Entertainment LLC., **p. 244** *Perplex City* © Mind Candy, **p. 247** *The Art of the Heist* © Campfire Media/Audiworld, **p. 281** *Urban Free Flow* © Karsten Uhlmann, **p. 289** *Demor* © Rob Voss, **p. 314** *eXistenZ* © Alliance Atlantis Communications Inc., **p. 397** *Blinkenlights* © Harald & Erhard Fotografie, **pp. 412-413** *OPS Room* © Felix Stephan Huber, **p. 414** *Wargames* © Metro-Goldwyn-Mayer Studios Inc., **p. 434** *Kuma\War* © Kuma LLC., **p. 436** *America's Army* © America's Army, **p. 463** *Tom Clancy's Ghost Recon: Advanced Warfighter* © Ubisoft Entertainment, *Burnout Revenge* © Electronic Arts Inc., **p. 458** *S.t.a.l.k.e.r.: Shadow of Chernobyl* © THQ, **p. 460** *Shadow of the Colossus* © Sony Computer Entertainment Europe, **p. 470** *The Truman Show* © Paramount Pictures, **p. 472** *Monopoly* © Hasbro

LET'S PLAY!